LIBRARY OF HEBREW BIBLE/
OLD TESTAMENT STUDIES

593

Formerly Journal for the Study of the Old Testament Supplement Series

LESHON LIMMUDIM

Essays on the Language and Literature of the Hebrew Bible in Honour of A. A. Macintosh

Edited by

David A. Baer and Robert P. Gordon

B L O O M S B U R Y

LONDON · NEW DELHI · NEW YORK · SYDNEY

Bloomsbury T&T Clark

An imprint of Bloomsbury Publishing Plc

50 Bedford Square	1385 Broadway
London	New York
WC1B 3DP	NY 10018
UK	USA

www.bloomsbury.com

Bloomsbury is a registered trade mark of Bloomsbury Publishing Plc

First published 2013

British Library Cataloguing-in-Publication Data
A catalogue record for this book is available from the British Library.

ISBN:	HB:	978-0-56711-866-0
	ePDF:	978-0-56730-823-8

Library of Congress Cataloging-in-Publication Data
Leshon Limmudim / David A. Baer and Robert P. Gordon p.cm
Includes bibliographic references and index.
ISBN 978-0-5671-1866-0 (hardcover)

Typeset by Forthcoming Publications Ltd (www.forthpub.com)
Printed and bound in Great Britain

A. A. Macintosh

CONTENTS

Part I
THE LANGUAGE AND LITERATURE OF THE PENTATEUCH

Part II
THE LANGUAGE AND LITERATURE OF THE HISTORICAL BOOKS

PREFACE

It has been a pleasure for us to collaborate on a volume that we trust will honour our friend and colleague Andrew Macintosh. The enthusiasm with which the invited contributors responded to our summons, together with the testimony of several that they had taken their first steps in Hebrew under Andrew's tutelage, was one of the project's heart-warming features. We trust that the honorand will be pleased with the volume that our little band now offers to him.

It is specially gratifying that the volume contains an essay by the late Edward (Ed) Ball, for many years a teacher of Old Testament at Nottingham University and a highly respected member of the British Old Testament community. He is warmly remembered by Andrew for his academic ability and exemplariness as a pupil. Ed in his turn won golden opinions among his pupils as a caring and inspirational teacher whose meticulous research and editorial pen undergirded his classroom contributions.

Special thanks are due to Cindy Pastrick, DAB's capable administrative assistant, for her willingness to deal with certain technical aspects of production that exceeded the skill and the work capacity of the volume editors. We also wish to thank the LHBOTS editorial board for accepting *Leshon Limmudim* into their series, and Andrew Mein in particular for his guidance and forbearance as "the project" progressed.

David A. Baer
Robert P. Gordon
March 2013

ABBREVIATIONS

AB	Anchor Bible
ABD	*Anchor Bible Dictionary*. Edited by D. N. Freedman. 6 vols. New York, 1992
AHw	*Akkadisches Handwörterbuch*. Edited by W. von Soden. 3 vols. Wiesbaden, 1965–81
AJSL	*American Journal of Semitic Languages and Literature*
AnBib	Analecta Biblica
ANET	*Ancient Near Eastern Texts Relating to the Old Testament*. Edited by J. B. Pritchard. 3d ed. Princeton, 1969
AOAT	Alter Orient und Altes Testament
ARM	Archives royales de Mari
ASOR	American Schools of Oriental Research
ATD	Das Alte Testament Deutsch
ATLA	American Theological Library Association
ATM	Altes Testament und Moderne
AV	Authorized Version
BBB	Bonner Biblische Beiträge
BCP	*Book of Common Prayer*
BDB	*A Hebrew and English Lexicon of the Old Testament*. Edited by F. Brown, S. R. Driver and C. A. Briggs. Oxford, 1907
BETL	Bibliotheca ephemeridum theologicarum lovaniensium
BHK	*Biblia Hebraica*. Edited by R. Kittel. Stuttgart, 1905–1906, 1925, 1937, 1951, 1973
BHQ	*Biblia Hebraica Quinta*. Edited by A. Schenker et al. Stuttgart, 2007–
BHS	*Biblia Hebraica Stuttgartensia*. Edited by K. Elliger and W. Rudolph. Stuttgart, 1983
BibInt	Biblical Interpretation
BJS	Brown Judaic Studies
BKAT	Biblischer Kommentar, Altes Testament
BL	H. Bauer and P. Leander, *Historische Grammatik der hebräischen Sprache des Alten Testamentes*. Halle, 1922
BN	*Biblische Notizen*
BRev	*Bible Review*
BSac	*Bibliotheca Sacra*
BTB	*Biblical Theology Bulletin*
BThZ	*Berliner theologische Zeitschrift*
BZAW	Beihefte zur Zeitschrift für die alttestamentliche Wissenschaft
CAD	*The Assyrian Dictionary of the Oriental Institute of the University of Chicago*. 21 vols. Chicago, 1956–2010
CAT	Commentaire de l'Ancien Testament
CBC	Cambridge Bible Commentary
CBQ	*Catholic Biblical Quarterly*
CBQMS	Catholic Biblical Quarterly Monograph Series

CCSL	Corpus Christianorum, Series Latina
CDCH	*The Concise Dictionary of Classical Hebrew.* Edited by D. J. A. Clines. Sheffield, 2009
CHANE	Culture and History of the Ancient Near East
ConBOT	Coniectanea Biblica: Old Testament Series
CSEL	Corpus Scriptorum Ecclesiasticorum Latinorum
DB	*Dictionnaire de la Bible.* Edited by F. Vigouroux. 5 vols. Paris, 1895–1912
DCH	*Dictionary of Classical Hebrew.* Edited by D. J. A. Clines. 8 vols. Sheffield, 1993–2011
DJD	Discoveries in the Judaean Desert
EB	Études bibliques
ESV	English Standard Version
ESHM	European Seminar in Historical Methodology
ET	English Translation
EThL	*Ephemerides Theologicae Lovanienses*
EvQ	*Evangelical Quarterly*
ExT	*Expository Times*
FAT	Forschungen zum Alten Testament
FOTL	Forms of the Old Testament Literature
FRLANT	Forschungen zur Religion und Literatur des Alten und Neuen Testaments
GCS	Die griechischen christlichen Schriftsteller der ersten [drei] Jahrhunderte
GK	*Gesenius' Hebrew Grammar.* Edited by E. Kautzsch. Translated by A. E. Cowley. 2d ed. Oxford, 1910
HALAT	L. Koehler, W. Baumgartner and J. J. Stamm, *Hebräisches und aramäisches Lexikon zum Alten Testament.* 6 vols. Leiden, 1967–96
HALOT	L. Koehler, W. Baumgartner and J. J. Stamm, *The Hebrew and Aramaic Lexicon of the Old Testament.* Translated and edited under the supervision of M. E. J. Richardson. 5 vols. Leiden, 1994–2000
HAT	Handbuch zum Alten Testament
HCOT	Historical Critical Commentary on the Old Testament
HeyM	Heythrop Monographs
HKAT	Handkommentar zum Alten Testament
HTKAT	Herders theologischer Kommentar zum Alten Testament
HTR	*Harvard Theological Review*
HUBP	Hebrew University Bible Project
ICC	The International Critical Commentary
IJST	*International Journal of Systematic Theology*
Int	*Interpretation*
JBL	*Journal of Biblical Literature*
JCS	*Journal of Cuneiform Studies*
JETS	*Journal of the Evangelical Theological Society*
JHS	*Journal of Hebrew Scriptures*
JNES	*Journal of Near Eastern Studies*
JNWSL	*Journal of Northwest Semitic Languages*
JPSTC	The Jewish Publication Society Torah Commentary
JSJ	*Journal for the Study of Judaism*
JSJSup	Journal for the Study of Judaism: Supplement Series
JSOT	*Journal for the Study of the Old Testament*

JSOTSup	Journal for the Study of the Old Testament: Supplement Series
JSPSup	Journal for the Study of the Pseudepigrapha: Supplement Series
JSS	*Journal of Semitic Studies*
JSSSup	Journal of Semitic Studies: Supplement Series
JTS	*Journal of Theological Studies*
KAT	Kommentar zum Alten Testament
KeHAT	Kurzgefasstes exegetisches Handbuch zum Alten Testament
KHCAT	Kurzer Hand-Commentar zum Alten Testament
KJV	King James Version of the Bible
KTU	*Die keilalphabetischen Texte aus Ugarit.* Edited by M. Dietrich, O. Loretz and J. Sanmartín. Neukirchen–Vluyn, 1976
LCL	Loeb Classical Library
LHBOTS	Library of Hebrew Bible/Old Testament Studies
LXX	The Septuagint
MPI	Monographs of the Peshiṭta Institute, Leiden
MT	The Masoretic Text
NAU	New American Standard Bible, Updated ed.
NCB	New Century Bible
NEB	New English Bible
NIBC	New International Bible Commentary
NICOT	New International Commentary on the Old Testament
NIDOTTE	*New International Dictionary of Old Testament Theology and Exegesis.* Edited by W. A. VanGemeren. 5 vols. Grand Rapids, 1997
NJPS	The New Jewish Publication Society translation
NRSV	New Revised Standard Version
NTT	*Nederlands Theologisch Tijdschrift*
OBO	Orbis biblicus et orientalis
OLA	Orientalia lovaniensia analecta
OTL	Old Testament Library
OTM	Oxford Theological Monographs
OTS	*Oudtestamentische Studiën*
PEQ	*Palestine Exploration Quarterly*
PG	*Patrologia Graeca*
PL	*Patrologia Latina*
PMHRA	Publications of the Modern Humanities Research Association
PRSt	*Perspectives in Religious Studies*
PTA	Papyrologische Texte und Abhandlungen
QD	Quaestiones Disputatae
RB	*Revue biblique*
REB	Revised English Bible
RHPR	*Revue d'histoire et de philosophie religieuses*
RIMAP	The Royal Inscriptions of Mesopotamia. Assyrian Periods
RTP	*Revue de théologie et de philosophie*
SB	Sources bibliques
SBLABib	Society of Biblical Literature Academia Biblica
SBLABS	Society of Biblical Literature Archaeology and Biblical Studies
SBLDS	Society of Biblical Literature Dissertation Series
SBLMS	Society of Biblical Literature Monograph Series
SBOT	The Sacred Books of the Old Testament
SBS	Stuttgarter Bibelstudien
SBTS	Sources for Biblical and Theological Study

SJLA   Studies in Judaism in Late Antiquity
SJOT   *Scandinavian Journal of the Old Testament*
SPB   Studia Post-Biblica
SSB   Semitica et Semitohamitica Berolinensia
STDJ   Studies on the Texts of the Desert of Judah
TDOT   *Theological Dictionary of the Old Testament.* English translation of
              ThWAT. Translated by J. T. Willis, G. W. Bromiley and D. E. Green.
              15 vols. Grand Rapids, 1974–2006
ThWAT   *Theologisches Wörterbuch zum Alten Testament.* Edited by G. J.
              Botterweck, H. Ringgren and H.-J. Fabry. 10 vols. Stuttgart, 1973–
              2000
TLOT   *Theological Lexicon of the Old Testament.* Edited by E. Jenni and
              C. Westermann. Translated by M. E. Biddle. 3 vols. Peabody, 1997
TOTC   Tyndale Old Testament Commentary
TRE   *Theologische Realenzyklopädie.* Edited by G. Müller and G. Krause.
              Berlin, 1977–2004
TTZ   *Trierer Theologische Zeitschrift*
TU   *Texte und Untersuchungen zur Geschichte der altchristlichen Literatur*
TUMSR   Trinity University Monograph Series in Religion
UCOP   University of Cambridge Oriental Publications
UF   *Ugarit-Forschungen*
UUÅ   Uppsala Universitets Årsskrift
VT   *Vetus Testamentum*
VTSup   Supplements to Vetus Testamentum/Vetus Testamentum Supplements
WBC   Word Biblical Commentary
WMANT   Wissenschaftliche Monographien zum Alten und Neuen Testament
WUNT   Wissenschaftliche Untersuchungen zum Neuen Testament
ZAW   *Zeitschrift für die alttestamentliche Wissenschaft*
ZDMG   *Zeitschrift der deutschen morgenländischen Gesellschaft*
ZTK   *Zeitschrift für Theologie und Kirche*

ANDREW ALEXANDER MACINTOSH:
APPRECIATION

Andrew Macintosh's earliest memories are of the sounds and fear of war. Eastbourne, Sussex, lay just twenty-two miles from occupied France. As German bombers in 1940 passed over Eastbourne on their grim errand to London and then back again, they dropped excess bombs on Eastbourne.

The windows of the Macintosh family's Sussex home were blown out no fewer than ten times. Shrapnel embedded itself in ceilings. Several of Andrew's childhood friends were carried off by the devastation. Andrew cowered in the "table shelters," wondering "When will it end?"

He also watched his father, a priest in the Church of England, speed off on his motorcycle while bombs still fell, in order to minister to the injured and dying. "That made me want to be ordained. It made sense," Andrew reports. This conviction would mature and become firm in the coming years, but its origins can be traced to those nights in Eastbourne. An appreciation of Andrew's career must take into account the central fact that he is an ordained minister of the Church of England.

Andrew went to preparatory school at the age of seven, and by the time he was twelve he had discovered the pleasure of learning Latin, French and Greek. He remembers brilliant teachers, pedagogues who exercised their craft "magnificently," both inside the classroom and without.

At fourteen, he was enrolled in a public (which in the English context means "private") school where the emphasis lay more upon military-style discipline than upon inspiration and learning. The contrast was telling. When he had the opportunity to return as a volunteer to his preparatory school, he found he "loved"—the word spills out repeatedly as he describes the joy he has experienced in the classroom—teaching maths, Latin and Greek to eight-year-old pupils.

Andrew went up to Cambridge in 1956 to read for the Theological Tripos. Upon arriving at St. John's College, he found himself in the care of several teachers worthy of emulation. His college tutor was J. S. Bezzant, a priest and Dean of St. John's College. Bezzant was best known as the former chaplain of HMS Repulse, the Renown-class battle cruiser that had been sunk by Japanese aircraft in 1941.

Bezzant's mind and tutoring style were "broad-sweeping." He was particularly strong in the philosophy of religion. Andrew remembers that Bezzant would address

> all the big questions. I would sit there for hours listening to him and admiring his photographic memory… He was a great person, his teaching was broad-brush, cosmic, and sweeping. Can you imagine the young person of nineteen or twenty, exposed to that kind of wisdom, that kind of חכמה if you please! He had that kind of *reality* about him… He would say things like, "What you do *not* do when someone is suffering is talk about the philosophy of religion. What you *do* do when someone is suffering is hold his hand."

He describes Bezzant's teaching as a "huge" influence upon his life. "If you are kind enough to say that I could teach…it was a combination of my prep-school experience and this kind of stuff [at Cambridge]."

Having achieved first class marks in Hebrew in both parts of the Theological Tripos, Andrew was accepted by David Winton Thomas, the Regius Professor of Hebrew at Cambridge, to read for the postgraduate Part III of the same Tripos. The set texts were formidable, embracing Isaiah in its entirety, Hosea,[1] chs. 10–20 of Proverbs, and Book IV of the Psalms. In addition to Thomas, he had been taught by Peter R. Ackroyd, who later held the Samuel Davidson chair in Old Testament at King's College, London.

Following his studies at Cambridge, Andrew was awarded a scholarship by the Anglo-Israel Association in 1960 and spent some six months in Jerusalem studying at the Hebrew University, during which time he took an intensive Modern Hebrew course at an Ulpan. As well as Hebrew, Winton Thomas had a fascination with the Arabic language that had greatly impressed Andrew. And so, "billeted with an Arab Israeli in Musrara under the city walls…I resolved to teach myself that language." That marked the beginning of a lifelong association with Jerusalem and the region. Andrew lectured at St. George's College, Jerusalem, for three of their courses in the early 1980s. For about 20 years he was also a guest lecturer on the St. George's yearly trips to Sinai, beginning in the late 1980s.

On his return from Jerusalem, Andrew undertook theological study at Ridley Hall, Cambridge, in order to "learn which end of a baby to baptize." Nurtured in the Catholic wing of the Church of England, he was now exposed to the perspectives of "liberal Evangelicalism." It was

---

1. One wonders whether it is mere coincidence that two of the first texts Andrew studied have provided the basis for his two major monographs.

a time for deepened appreciation of a "different tradition of Christianity," as also for the establishing of deep friendships with fellow Ridley students.

Andrew was ordained deacon in Lincoln Cathedral in 1961 and priest in 1962. Following his marriage to Mary Joan Browning in 1962, he took up pastoral ministry in "a deeply rural parish" in Lincolnshire. It was during this two-year term of "serving my title" that Mary—a trained nurse—began taking in foster children with troubled family backgrounds and/or disabilities. Their home would over several decades become home as well for nearly one hundred such children, in addition to their own three "home-made" children. In 1992, Mary was decorated with the award of the British Empire Medal (B.E.M.) for her service, a recognition that perhaps ranks second to the gratitude of so many of the children who passed through the Macintosh home. Andrew and Mary are the parents of Rachel, Alexander and Thomas, who have distinguished themselves in education, the armed forces (The Queen's Household Division) and business.

In 1967, Andrew's old college became his parish when the Master of St. John's invited him to become the college's Chaplain. In 1979, he was appointed Dean of Chapel. He has carried out his pastoral duties at the college with extraordinary energy. "I wanted to be where the problems were," Andrew says in describing the bonds he established with undergraduates. Having been a rower himself in earlier days, he "coached a boat," in part because of his passion for the sport and in part because of his conviction that students learn as much on the water as in the tutorial. His 1980 monograph, *Isaiah XXI: A Palimpsest*, is dedicated "To my wife and to all others who have cheered on the tow-path."

The role of the English tradition of church music is a related thread that began early and continued through Andrew's service as Chaplain and Dean of the renowned St. John's College Chapel. He found himself fascinated by church music at an early stage. "I pestered my parents to give me organ lessons," he remembers. "I was accompanying simple services in my school chapel at the age of eleven." Those who have known him in the context of college or home will understand the near-ubiquity of music and his intimate familiarity with his preferred musical tradition.

When Andrew came to St. John's as its Chaplain, he asked whether he might be allowed some time for academic research in addition to his "main job, which was the care of undergraduates." Permission was forthcoming, on condition that "you must do your job first." He was well prepared by his previous study at Cambridge for the rigours of academic

research. His publication list follows upon this "Appreciation." Of particular note are the aforementioned work on Isa 21 and his volume on
Hosea in the *International Critical Commentary* series.[2] This almost
lyrically written commentary describes a work that was more or less
complete by the time it arrived in Judah following the fall of the northern
kingdom of Israel in 722 B.C.E. and in which traces of its northern
provenance have survived the standardizing impulses of southern editors.
Far more than most works of its kind, it draws upon the rich interpretive
and philological traditions that are to be found in the Jewish mediaeval
exegetes and in the resources of the Arabic lexicon, both of which have
contributed much to Andrew's study of the Hebrew Bible.

On the strength of his publications, Andrew was awarded the Bachelor
of Divinity degree in 1980. (At Cambridge the B.D. is a postgraduate
degree and its award recognizes "a significant contribution to the
knowledge" of some aspect of Christian theology.) Again on the basis of
his published work, he was admitted in 1997 to the degree of Doctor of
Divinity—the oldest, and therefore most senior, of the university's
higher degrees, as he likes to point out.

If Andrew has earned both appreciation and affection as a priest and
scholar, he is by his own assessment most often remembered for "the
rumour that I have been a teacher." For some forty years he taught
introductory Hebrew in the Cambridge Faculty of Divinity and became
"an institution." He applied insights that he had gathered in his early
school years when he had experienced inspiring teaching and its opposite, and he soon became known as a superb, and profoundly humorous,
classroom teacher of Biblical Hebrew. Using stories, puns and his trusted
mnemonics—a penchant picked up at school while studying Classics—
he engaged, amused and instructed his students, sometimes with unexpected results. In one class he remarked that it was very clever to name
the national Israeli airline from a verse in an eighth-century prophet (see
Hos 11:7). A Jewish student present announced that it was her uncle who
had chosen the name!

Undergraduates may be heard lauding Andrew's teaching of Hebrew
as "passionate."[3] Several of the contributors to this volume received their
first Hebrew tuition from him. One former pupil, now an accomplished
academic in her own right, describes the disorientation of her first year

---

2.   A. A. Macintosh, *Hosea* (ICC; Edinburgh: T. & T. Clark, 1997).
3.   DAB has memories of his own from the time when, during his doctoral studies
in Cambridge, he assisted Andrew with his Hebrew class. When he did not produce
the expected "American" response to a rhetorical question, Andrew pungently
decried his "pure colonial obstreperousness!"

as an undergraduate in the university's Faculty of Divinity: "It was Andrew who kept me at Cambridge. It was Hebrew class with him. He *cared* for us."

In thinking about his legacy as a teacher, centred on the teaching of Biblical Hebrew, Andrew muses, "I have the feeling that I am a bit like my apostolic namesake, in that he and I have been privileged to make some very important *introductions*. I have *loved* introducing people to Hebrew and seeing some of them come to love it."

From 1967 to the present time, the setting of Andrew's work as priest, scholar and teacher has been St. John's College, Cambridge. In recognition of his long and distinguished service to St. John's, he was elected President in 1995. Upon his retirement in 2002, he was made a Life Fellow of the college.

The title of this volume—*Leshon Limmudim*—plays upon a phrase in the book of Isaiah. Andrew will know it well, at least since the days when he read "the whole of Isaiah" for Part III of the Cambridge Theological Tripos.

> The Lord GOD has given me *the tongue of a teacher*, that I may know how to sustain the weary with a word. Morning by morning he wakens— wakens my ear to listen as those who are taught. (Isa 50:4, NRSV)

Placed by common understanding upon the lips of the "servant of the LORD," the enigmatic expression *leshon limmudim* is the kind that Andrew enjoys pondering: challenging for the grammarian, opaque for the exegete, evocative for the theologian.

Is the servant endowed with "the tongue of a teacher" (NRSV)? Or is his "the tongue of the learned" (KJV)? Does his bearing display the self-possession of one who, when he speaks, employs "the tongue of those who are taught" (ESV)? Or has he, perhaps, "a skilled tongue" (JPS)?

It could be said of Andrew Macintosh that each of these interpretations could feature in an account of the qualities that have so much endeared him to his students and his colleagues.

PUBLICATIONS OF A. A. MACINTOSH

1969	A Consideration of Hebrew נער. *VT* 29: 471–79.
1969	Review of Peter R. Ackroyd and Barnabas Lindars, eds., *Words and Meanings: Essays Presented to David Winton Thomas on his Retirement from the Regius Professorship of Hebrew in the University of Cambridge, 1968*, *The Franciscan* 11: 160.
1970	A Note on Proverbs xxv 27. *VT* 20: 112–14.
1970	(with D. L. Frost) Review of A. Neame, ed., *The Jerusalem Bible: The Psalms for Reading and Recitation*, *Theology* 73: 33–36.
1971	Exodus viii 19, Distinct Redemption and the Hebrew Roots פדה and פרד. *VT* 21: 548–55.
1971	(with D. L. Frost and G. Stanton) The New English Bible Reviewed. *Theology* 74: 154–66.
1972	From the Ancient Languages to the New English Bible. Pages 132–66 in *The Making of the Old Testament*. Edited by E. I. Mellor. CBC. Cambridge: Cambridge University Press.
1972	The Spider in the Septuagint Version of Psalm xc 9. *JTS* NS 23: 113–17.
1973	Psalm xci 4 and the Root סחר. *VT* 23: 56–62.
1974	A Third Root עדה in Biblical Hebrew? *VT* 24: 454–73.
1975	Review of Hans Walter Wolff, *Anthropology of the Old Testament*, *Theology* 78: 558–59.
1976	A Consideration of the Problems Presented by Psalm ii 11 and 12. *JTS* NS 27: 1–14.
1976	Review of J. L. McKenzie, *A Theology of the Old Testament*, *JTS* NS 27: 434–35.
1977	*The Psalms: A New Translation for Worship*. London: William Collins. Adopted by the Church of England as the Psalter of *The Alternative Service Book* (1980). AAM was the Secretary of the translation panel under the chairmanship of J. A. Emerton. Online: http://www.iocs.cam.ac.uk/resources/texts/Liturgical_Psalter_and_Notes.pdf .
1977	*Psalms: A New Translation for Worship. Notes on the Text*. London: Church Information Office.
1980	*Isaiah XXI: A Palimpsest*. Cambridge: Cambridge University Press.
1982	A Consideration of Psalm vii 12f. *JTS* NS 33: 481–90.
1985	The Meaning of מכלים in Judges xviii 7. *VT* 35: 68–77.
1991	Hosea: Revelation and Retrospect. *The Tel Aviv Review* 3 (1991): 180–89.
1995	Hosea and the Wisdom Tradition: Dependence and Independence. Pages 124–32 in *Wisdom in Ancient Israel: Essays in Honour of J. A. Emerton*. Edited by John Day, Robert P. Gordon and H. G. M. Williamson. Cambridge: Cambridge University Press.
1997	*Hosea*. ICC. Edinburgh: T. & T. Clark.

1998	Review of Jorg Jeremias, *Hosea und Amos: Studien zu den Anfängen des Dodekapropheton*, *JTS* NS 49: 183–87.
1999	(with J. A. Emerton and D. L. Frost) *A Daft Text: The Psalter, 1998: A Critique of the New Psalter*. Cambridge: Aquila.
2001	Review of H. Pfeiffer, *Das Heiligtum von Bethel im Spiegel des Hoseabuches*, *JTS* NS 52: 167–70.
2002	Hosea: The Rabbinic Commentators and the Ancient Versions. Pages 77–81 in *Biblical Hebrew, Biblical Texts: Essays in Memory of Michael P. Weitzman*. Edited by Ada Rapoport-Albert and Gillian Greenberg. JSOTSup 333. Edinburgh: T. & T. Clark.
2003	English language editor of Zipora Talshir, *The Alternative Story of the Division of the Kingdom: 3 Kingdoms 12:24a–z*. Jerusalem Biblical Studies 6. Jerusalem: Simor.
2005	Review of E. J. Pentiuc, *Long-Suffering Love: A Commentary on Hosea with Patristic Annotations*, *JTS* NS 56: 507–9.
2006	Review of Carmel McCarthy and John F. Healey, eds., *Biblical and Near Eastern Essays: Studies in Honour of Kevin J. Cathcart*, *JTS* NS 57: 599–606.
2008	Review of Brad E. Kelle, *Hosea 2: Metaphor and Rhetoric in Historical Perspective*, *JSS* 53: 342–45.
2008	Review of Ehud Ben Zvi, *Hosea*, *JSS* 53: 341–42.
2009	English language editor of A. Rofé, *Introduction to the Literature of the Hebrew Bible*. Winona Lake: Eisenbrauns. Heb. ed. מבוא לספרות המקרא. Jerusalem: Simor, 2006.
2011	Light on ליץ. Pages 477–92 in *On Stone and Scroll: Essays in Honour of G. I. Davies*. Edited by J. K. Aitken, K. J. Dell and B. A. Mastin. Berlin: de Gruyter.
2011	Review of Roman Vielhauer, *Das Werden des Buches Hosea: Eine redaktionsgeschichtliche Untersuchung*, *JSS* 56: 412–14.
2012	Proverbs 30:32 and the Root נבל. Pages 77–93 in *Let us Go Up to Zion: Essays in Honour of H. G. M. Williamson on the Occasion of His Sixty-fifth Birthday*. Edited by Iain Provan and Mark J. Boda. VTSup 153. Leiden: Brill.
2012	RPG. Pages 1–5 in *Studies on the Text and Versions of the Hebrew Bible in Honour of Robert Gordon*. Edited by Geoffrey Khan and Diana Lipton. VTSup 149. Leiden: Brill.

LIST OF CONTRIBUTORS

David A. Baer, President, Overseas Council, Indianapolis, Indiana, U.S.A.

*Edward Ball, Formerly Lecturer in Old Testament and Hebrew, University of Nottingham

William D. Barker, Senior Minister, LifePoint Church, Quincy, Illinois, U.S.A.

Ronald E. Clements, Emeritus Samuel Davidson Professor of Old Testament Studies, King's College, University of London

Graham Davies, Emeritus Professor of Old Testament Studies, University of Cambridge

John Day, Professor of Old Testament Studies, University of Oxford

Katharine J. Dell, Senior Lecturer in Old Testament Studies, University of Cambridge

Gönke Eberhardt, The Lutheran Parish of Detmold, Germany

Charles L. Echols, Visiting Professor of Biblical Studies, Union Biblical Seminary, Pune, India

Cynthia L. Engle, The Diocese of Texas, Houston, Texas, U.S.A.

David F. Ford, Regius Professor of Divinity, University of Cambridge

Robert P. Gordon, Emeritus Regius Professor of Hebrew, University of Cambridge

Judith M. Hadley, Associate Professor of Theology and Religious Studies, Villanova University

William Horbury, Emeritus Professor of Jewish and Early Christian Studies, University of Cambridge

Erica C. D. Hunter, Lecturer in Eastern Christianity, School of Oriental and African Studies (SOAS), University of London

Rachel M. Lentin, Independent Scholar

Diana Lipton, Visiting Lecturer, Department of Hebrew Culture Studies, Tel Aviv University; formerly Reader in Hebrew Bible and Jewish Studies, King's College, University of London

Nathan MacDonald, Lecturer in Hebrew Bible, University of Cambridge

Hilary Marlow, Course Director at The Faraday Institute for Science and Religion, St Edmund's College, Cambridge

B. A. Mastin, Emeritus Senior Lecturer in Hebrew, University of Wales, Bangor

Stefan C. Reif, Emeritus Professor of Medieval Hebrew Studies, University of Cambridge

Alexander Rofé, Emeritus Professor in Jewish Studies, the Hebrew University of Jerusalem

H. G. M. Williamson, Regius Professor of Hebrew, University of Oxford

Part I

THE LANGUAGE AND LITERATURE OF THE PENTATEUCH

A TEXT IN SEARCH OF CONTEXT:
THE *IMAGO DEI* IN THE FIRST CHAPTERS OF GENESIS

Nathan MacDonald

1. *In Search of Context*

Genesis 1:26 is a text in search of context. Context covers many inter-related things. Context means disciplinary location. Here a large breach exists between biblical scholars and systematic theologians in their discussion of the image.[1] The former have typically sought to know what might have been the intent of the original writer of Gen 1, probing especially behind the text; the latter have typically also worked with the verse's *Wirkungsgeschichte*, not least the *imago*'s reappearance in the New Testament and its relevance for Christology and theological anthropology.[2]

Context also means the historical location of scholars. As Jónsson demonstrated in his monograph on the *imago* in biblical scholarship, the understanding of the *imago dei* has shifted markedly as the academic context has changed over the last hundred or so years. In the late nineteenth and early twentieth centuries scholarly proposals emerged under the influence of historical criticism, the history of religions and Darwinian evolution. Biblical scholars saw the image in the intellectual or moral abilities that distinguished humans from animals or as a physical similarity between God and humans. Under the influence of dialectical theology and Barth, the image was understood as an I–Thou relationship that existed between God and man. Since the 1950s biblical scholars

---

1. For attempts to bridge that breach, see J. R. Middleton, *The Liberating Image: The Imago Dei in Genesis 1* (Grand Rapids: Brazos, 2005); N. MacDonald, "The *Imago Dei* and Election: Reading Genesis 1:26–28 and Old Testament Scholarship with Karl Barth," *IJST* 10 (2008): 303–27.

2. See, e.g., the account in P. A. Bird, "'Male and Female He Created Them': Gen 1:27b in the Context of the Priestly Account of Creation," *HTR* 74 (1981): 129–59.

have reacted strongly against Barth's proposal, contextualizing the language of image and likeness in the world of ancient Near Eastern kingship and, finally, insisting that the proper context for understanding the image language was within the priestly writing. These two contexts are often seen as mutually supportive of a functional interpretation of the *imago dei*, which Jónsson could describe in 1988 as "the predominant view" in Old Testament scholarship. Since the publication of Jónsson's account of research there has, of course, been no diminishment in the attempts to understand the *imago dei*. In many respects, though, his assessment that the functional view is the predominant view among Old Testament scholars remains valid. According to this view, the image of God consists in human dominion. Human beings represent the deity and act as his vicegerent on earth.[3] Contemporary theological significance is often given to this view by observing that compared to the ancient Near Eastern concept of the divine image, which was restricted to the king, the priestly vision offers an important "democratization" of the concept.[4]

Context also means textual location, as we have already begun to see. Should we understand the language of image and likeness in primarily an ancient Near Eastern context, in the context of the priestly writer, in a wider biblical context, or something else? Within biblical studies the emphasis has been on the ancient Near East or P, or both together, as the proper textual context for understanding the *imago dei*. This view was forged in resistance to Barth's relational interpretation. Barr, Bird and Groß each take Barth and theologians influenced by him to task for failing to respect the *original* historical context.[5] Thus, Bird insists on attention to "the ancient writer's thought and intention."[6] The ancient Near East and the rest of the priestly document provide controls on what might conceivably have been in the priestly writer's mind as he wrote.

The insistence on the priestly writer as the context for understanding the *imago* has become an essential presupposition of Old Testament discourse about the *imago dei* in the Anglo-American world. This is

---

3. G. A. Jónsson, *The Image of God: Genesis 1:26–28 in a Century of Old Testament Research* (ConBOT 26; Stockholm: Almqvist & Wiksell, 1988).

4. See, e.g., Middleton, *The Liberating Image*; B. Janowski, "Die lebendige Statue Gottes: Zur Anthropologie der priesterlichen Urgeschichte," in *Gott und Mensch im Dialog* (ed. M. Witte; BZAW 345/I; Berlin: de Gruyter, 2004), 183–214.

5. Bird, "Male and Female"; J. Barr, *Biblical Faith and Natural Theology: Gifford Lectures for 1991* (Oxford: Clarendon, 1994); W. Groß, *Studien zur Priesterschrift und zu alttestamentlichen Gottesbildern* (SBA 30; Stuttgart: Katholisches Bibelwerk, 1999).

6. Bird, "Male and Female," 132. For Bird's failure to understand Barth's hermeneutics, see MacDonald, "The *Imago Dei*."

apparent if we examine some of the more recent proposals about the *imago* that seek to replace or nuance the accepted consensus. In an extensive grammatical and linguistic investigation, Garr discerns the demise of the pantheon with humanity taking their place.[7] Recently, Crouch has argued that the *imago dei* affirms the divine parentage of humanity.[8] Both of these proposals assume that an investigation of the *imago dei* must be restricted to an analysis of Gen 1:26–28; 5:1–3; 9:6, understood as part of a self-contained priestly document. This is also arguably true of F. Watson, who in seeking to relate Old and New Testament accounts of the *imago*, wants to establish his view that humans physically resemble God in the priestly account of Genesis, according to the norms of current Old Testament scholarship.[9]

2. Recent Scholarship on the Compositional History of Genesis 1–3

If we shift our gaze to a European context, the familiar assumptions of Anglo-American scholarship begin to be called into question. To see how this is the case we need to examine recent redaction-critical treatments of the early chapters of Genesis. By doing so it will become clear that the restriction of any discussion of the *imago dei* to the priestly writer can no longer be maintained, at least not without justification. P is not the only context in which we can, or even should, consider the *imago*.

The Anglo-American consensus about the *imago dei* takes its starting point from the traditional critical consensus that Gen 1:1–2:4a belonged to an independent priestly document that was subsequently redacted with the earlier Pentateuchal sources. The redactional contribution was relatively minor. In the case of Gen 1–3 the redactor appended the Yahwist creation story to the priestly creation story, perhaps smoothing the transition with 2:4a or 2:4b.[10] In a variety of ways recent work on

---

7. W. R. Garr, *In His Own Image and Likeness: Humanity, Divinity, and Monotheism* (CHANE 15; Leiden: Brill, 2003).

8. C. L. Crouch, "Genesis 1:26–7 as a Statement of Humanity's Divine Parentage," *JTS* NS 61 (2010): 1–15.

9. F. Watson, *Text and Truth: Redefining Biblical Theology* (Grand Rapids: Eerdmans, 1997), 277–304. Watson does not speak of P, but his analysis shows clear evidence of being influenced by the scholarly consensus.

10. R. Smend, *Die Entstehung des Alten Testaments* (4th ed.; Stuttgart: Kohlhammer, 1984), 40; B. S. Childs, *Introduction to the Old Testament as Scripture* (Philadelphia: Fortress, 1979), 149.

Pentateuchal criticism challenges this understanding of the compositional history of Gen 1–3. First, the question of whether P is an independent source, a redaction or, even, a compositional layer has been a matter of considerable discussion. Although recent work shows a strong tendency towards accepting P as an independent source, this can no longer be taken as an *a priori*.[11] Second, there has been a tendency to attribute a much greater role to the redactor (R) of the Pentateuchal sources. Thus, Witte attributes not only the relocation of 2:4a and the divine name יהוה אלהים to the redactor, but also 2:7b, 9b–15, 17aα, 19aγ, b, 20aα; 3:14aα*, 18b, 22, 24.[12] Third, the idea that non-priestly material is almost always pre-priestly can no longer be assumed. Each case must be considered on its own merits. Thus, in the case of Gen 1–3, it needs to be argued that the second creation account had a prior and independent history to the first creation account. The possibility that Gen 2:4b–3:24 was the result of *Fortschreibung* cannot be excluded.

The compositional history of Gen 1–3 is hardly a settled matter, but each of these factors can be seen to influence recent redaction critics as they wrestle with the text. The most secure element in recent assessments of these chapters is undoubtedly the attribution of 1:1–2:4a to P and a belief in its literary integrity. Steck's rejection of Schmidt's attempt to discern two accounts, a *Tatbericht* and a *Wortbericht*, has been decisive for most interpreters.[13] In contrast, the literary assessment of 2:4b–3:24 is still a matter of considerable disagreement. Levin has argued that we have a story of the creation of the human couple which is found in ch. 2 and continues with 3:20. Levin argues that the "Schlüssel zur Trennung von Quelle und Redaktion findet sich in 3,20–21."[14] The

11. Note especially the work of L. Schmidt in arguing the case for P as an independent source (see, e.g., L. Schmidt, *Gesammelte Aufsätze zum Pentateuch* [BZAW 263; Berlin: de Gruyter, 1998]).

12. M. Witte, *Die biblische Urgeschichte: Redaktions- und theologiegeschichtliche Beobachtungen zu Genesis 1,1–11,26* (BZAW 265; Berlin: de Gruyter, 1998).

13. O. H. Steck, *Der Schöpfungsbericht der Priesterschrift: Studien zur literarkritischen und überlieferungsgeschichtlichen Problematik von Genesis 1,1–2,4a* (2d ed.; FRLANT 115; Göttingen: Vandenhoeck & Ruprecht, 1981); W. H. Schmidt, *Die Schöpfungsgeschichte der Priesterschrift* (WMANT 17; Neukirchen–Vluyn: Neukirchener, 1964). For exceptions see C. Levin, "Tatbericht und Wortbericht in der priesterschriftlichen Schöpfungserzählung," *ZTK* 91 (1994): 115–33, and J. Hutzli, "Tradition and Interpretation in Gen 1:1–2:4a," *JHS* 10 (2010). Online: <http://www.arts.ualberta.ca/JHS/Articles/article_140.pdf>.

14. C. Levin, *Der Jahwist* (FRLANT 157; Göttingen: Vandenhoeck & Ruprecht, 1993), 83. For a rehearsal of the arguments see idem, "Genesis 2–3: A Case of Inner Biblical Interpretation," in *Genesis and Christian Theology* (ed. N. MacDonald, M. W. Elliott and G. Macaskill; Grand Rapids: Eerdmans, 2012), 85–100.

crucial observation is that Adam's naming his wife Eve because she was the mother of all living does not easily follow the curse in 3:17–19. This creation story was subsequently expanded with the story of the garden and the disobedience of the human couple. This entailed the introduction of much of ch. 3 as well as the garden and trees of ch. 2 which are essential for the story of disobedience. Levin attributed the early story to the pre-Yahwist source, and the subsequent expansion to the Yahwist.[15] At the same time as Levin published his study of the Yahwist, Carr published a remarkably similar account in the *Journal of Biblical Literature*.[16] The essential elements of this critical analysis have been accepted by Witte, Kratz, Rottzoll and Spieckermann.[17] Whilst Witte and Kratz see the story of the garden as a pre-P composition, Spieckermann argues that the story of the fall presupposes the priestly creation story. On the other hand, a number of interpreters, including Blum, Otto, Pfeiffer, Schmid and Gertz, have insisted that the stories of the creation of humanity and the garden belong together literarily.[18] For Blum, the story is a concise literary unity that can be interpreted without reference to any place in a larger literary whole. Gertz views the matter similarly, though he insists on the unity of Gen 2:4–4:26, with some additional material resulting from the redaction with the priestly creation story. Otto, on the

15. Levin, *Der Jahwist*, 82–92.

16. D. Carr, "The Politics of Textual Subversion: A Diachronic Perspective on the Garden of Eden Story," *JBL* 112 (1993): 577–95.

17. Witte, *Die biblische Urgeschichte*, 151–65; R. G. Kratz, *The Composition of the Narrative Books of the Old Testament* (London: T. & T. Clark, 2000), 252–54; D. Rottzoll, "Die Schöpfungs- und Fallerzählung in Gen 2f.," *ZAW* 109 (1998): 481–99, and 110 (1998): 1–15; H. Spieckermann, "Ambivalenzen: Ermöglichte und verwirklichte Schöpfung in Genesis 2f.," in *Verbindungslinien: Festschrift für Werner H. Schmidt zum 65. Geburtstag* (ed. A. Graupner et al.; Neukirchen–Vluyn: Neukirchener, 2000), 363–76.

18. E. Blum, "Von Gottesunmittelbarkeit zu Gottähnlichkeit: Überlegungen zur theologischen Anthropologie der Paradieserzählung," in *Gottes Nähe im Alten Testament* (ed. G. Eberhardt and K. Liess; SBS 105; Stuttgart: Katholisches Bibelwerk, 2004), 16–30; E. Otto, "Die Paradieserzählung Genesis 2–3: Eine nach-priesterschriftliche Lehrerzählung in ihrem religionshistorischen Kontext," in *"Jedes Ding hat seine Zeit…": Studien zur israelitischen und altorientalischen Weisheit* (ed. A. A. Diesel et al.; BZAW 241; Berlin: de Gruyter, 1996), 167–92; H. Pfeiffer, "Der Baum in der Mitte des Gartens: Zum überlieferungsgeschichtlichen Ursprung des Paradieserzählung (Gen 2:4b–3:24)," *ZAW* 112 (2000): 487–500, and 113 (2000): 2–16; K. Schmid, "Die Unteilbarkeit der Weisheit: Überlegungen zur sogenannten Paradieserzählung Gen 2f. und ihrer theologischen Tendenz," *ZAW* 114 (2002): 21–39; J. C. Gertz, "Von Adam zu Enosch: Überlegungen zur Entstehungs-geschichte von Genesis 2–4," in Witte, ed., *Gott und Mensch*, 237–58.

other hand, argues that Gen 2–3 is a post-priestly redaction. In particular, Gen 2–3 provides an explanation for the appearance of evil that the original priestly document lacked.[19]

The likelihood of some form of compositional relationship between Gen 1 and Gen 2–3 finds further confirmation when we compare the detailed account of human creation in Gen 2–3 and the priestly creation story of Gen 1. In Gen 2 the man has similarities to the animals created on the sixth day of the priestly account. He is a living creature (נפש חיה, 2:7; cf. 1:24) and made from the ground (מן־האדמה, 2:7; cf. תוצא הארץ, 1:24). In both accounts he is given the fruit of trees for his food (מכל עץ־הגן אכל תאכל, 2:16; cf. ואת־כל־העץ...נתתי לכם, 1:29), and has dominion over the animals (2:19–20; cf. 1:26, 28).[20] In addition, the male–female distinction and human fruitfulness are integral to both accounts. Much more significant for our purposes are the similarities between the account of the *imago dei* in 1:26–28 and the references to likeness to God in 3:5 and 3:22. Despite some differences in phraseology we have the remarkable conjunction of God referred to in the plural and the question of likeness to God:

נעשה אדם בצלמנו כדמותנו

"Let us make man in our image according to our likeness." (1:26)

והייתם כאלהים

"you will be like God" or "you will be like gods."[21] (3:5)

הן האדם היה כאחד ממנו

"Behold, the man has become like one of us." (3:22)

In the light of these similarities a few scholars have begun to analyse Gen 1:26 within the context of Gen 3.

---

19. See now W. Houston, "Sex or Violence? Thinking Again with Genesis about Fall and Original Sin," in MacDonald, Elliott and Macaskill, eds., *Genesis and Christian Theology*, 140–51.

20. Note how close the descriptions of the animals in Gen 1 and Gen 2 are: כל־חית השדה (2:18, 19), cf. ולכל־חית הארץ (1:25, 28, 30; cf. 1:24) (שדה is the preferred description of the environment of the first people in Gen 2–4 [cf. 2:5; 3:18; 4:8]); כל־עוף השמים (2:18), cf. ובעוף השמים (1:28); נפש חיה (2:18), cf. נפש חיה (1:20, 24, 30) (נפש חיה is a rare lexical combination in the Hebrew Bible); כל־הבהמה (2:19), cf. ואת־הבהמה (1:25).

21. See already LXX's ὡς θεοί.

3. Imago Dei *and Being Like God*

In 1992 Sawyer argued that the story of Gen 2–3 be read as "an expansion of the 'image of God' story in ch. 1." Sawyer does not dispute the source-critical assignment of the chapters to P and J, but suggests that "we are nevertheless intended—and have been since the text began—to read Gen 1–3 as a continuous narrative."[22] Although Sawyer evades the question of agency in a manner that is not entirely satisfactory, he does open a question that had long remained closed due to source-critical arguments. In Sawyer's view, Gen 1 tells of the creation of humans and how they resembled the divine, while Gen 2–3 tells the same story in more detail explaining exactly how this resemblance took place. The story of the garden explains that the divine likeness consists in knowledge of good and evil, which Sawyer understands as the full range of human experience. The subduing of nature in 1:28 is explained through the almost violent struggle with the serpent and the ground that is the result of the curses in 3:14–19. The curses suggest that being like God also entails tasting pain and grief (cf. Gen 6:6–7), and being able to imagine a better world without death. Although Sawyer does not do so, these two sides of human existence could well be parsed as the good and evil that the human couple now know.

Sawyer views the relationship between the image of God in Gen 2–3 and Gen 1 as neutral. The story of the garden provides a narrative exposition of the compact and opaque divine statement about the human couple in 1:26–28. Schüle, however, believes that Gen 2–3 offers an interpretation and critique of the *imago dei*. The priestly *imago* is vague, but Gen 1:26–28 suggests that the concept touches upon a number of relationships. The human couple corresponds to God's being and represents him to the world. All humans resemble God and this is connected in some way to the differentiation of the sexes. According to Schüle, P meant "to give full account of what it means to be a human being," but Gen 2–3 challenges this and asserts that there are "aspects to human life that are not contained by the concept of the image."[23] The story of the garden includes a focus on the differentiation of Adam from his wife. Schüle argues that the description of the woman as כנגדו "as opposite

22. J. F. A. Sawyer, "The Image of God, the Wisdom of Serpents and the Knowledge of Good and Evil," in *A Walk in the Garden: Biblical, Iconographical and Literary Images of Eden* (ed. P. Morris and D. Sawyer; JSOTSup 136; Sheffield: JSOT, 1992), 64–73 (64).

23. A. Schüle, "Made in the 'Image of God': The Concepts of Divine Images in Gen 1–3," *ZAW* 117 (2005): 1–20 (11).

him" (2:18) is a critique of כדמותנו "as our likeness" (1:26). There is a human need for companionship that God cannot meet. There is also the need for human creativity, and thus wisdom. The human aspiration to be like God in knowing good and evil is also essential to the fuller account of human life in Gen 2–3. Finally, the story narrates another aspect of human nature: the freedom of human beings to resist God's commandment.

Spieckermann profitably marks a different way that could be seen to mediate between the neutral approach of Sawyer and the critical approach of Schüle. The garden narrative does offer an interpretation of the priestly concept of the *imago dei*, but it does so from the perspective of the ambivalence of human existence. Spieckermann agrees with Otto in finding evidence of later wisdom concepts in Gen 2–3, but sees these as evidenced in the temptation narrative of Gen 3 and the expansions of Gen 2 that accompanied it.[24] The story of the fall has concerns that are characteristic of other Near Eastern stories and that are represented by the two trees: the human desires for wisdom and immortality. To possess both is to be like God. The story of human disobedience in the garden is the story of the ambivalence of human existence. Human beings are like God, yet not like God. They have a knowledge of good and evil, but are mortal. The story of the fall is an aetiology of human existence, but also a tantalizing glimpse at a different possibility that was once within the grasp of humans.[25]

Whether one accepts Spieckermann's reconstruction of an independent creation narrative and a later post-R fall narrative or follows Otto in attributing most of Gen 2:4b–3:24 to a post-redactional author, it seems to me that Spieckermann's interpretation is a more insightful way of understanding the relationship between Gen 1 and Gen 2–3, and especially the presentation of human nature in each account, than that offered by Sawyer and Schüle. Developing Spieckermann's observations, we can say that Gen 2–3 is the earliest interpretation of the *imago dei* that invites the reader to reflect on the meaning of human likeness to God. What does it consist of? How desirable is it? The narrative provides no definitive answer to the first question, but plays with (at least) two possibilities that seem to be mutually exclusive for human beings. To the second question the answer seems to be that being the divine image is a double-edged sword.

24. Cf. Witte, *Die biblische Urgeschichte*.
25. Spieckermann, "Ambivalenzen."

4. *The Image in the Garden*

This interpretation of the *imago* in Gen 2–3 moves in significantly different directions from that found in an originally independent Priestly document. For P the *imago dei* appears to be an inalienable endowment, as continued references to it in Gen 5 and 9 suggest. In Gen 2–3 the man is created from dust that is animated by the divine breath. The likeness to God emerges only in the temptation of the couple. Only when the man and his wife are disobedient and take of the fruit of the tree of the knowledge of good and evil do they become as God or gods (3:5, 22). They possess divine knowledge, but not divine immortality. Despite running in different directions, both stories can clearly be seen as aetiologies of human existence.

Since the man begins the second creation story as nothing more than animated dust and ends it with knowledge of good and evil, recent scholarship has often questioned the established Christian interpretation of the narrative as a universal fall into sin. If the endowment of the *imago* is related to the likeness that is wrested from God, how are we to judge the actions of the human couple? The difficulties are further compounded when it is recognized that knowing good and evil is not a negative human achievement elsewhere in the Old Testament. Rather, to know good and evil is a sign of maturity; only children lack this capacity.[26] As a result many scholars have proposed that Gen 2–3 be recognized as originally a story of human maturation, a "fall upwards."[27] Such a reading, with its emphasis on individuation, is not merely a reflection of twentieth-century Jungian psychology, but is also evidenced as early as the Gnostics.

The desirability of wisdom to the human couple, and in the Old Testament more broadly, together with the apparent necessity of expulsion from the garden before human culture can develop (Gen 4) clearly speak for this interpretation. Yet despite its popularity with some Old Testament interpreters, it is not without its difficulties, especially when the story is contextualized, as it is, within the Primary History. First, the maturity of the human couple is reached only as a result of disobedience to something that God commanded (צוה, 2:16; 3:11, 17). It is difficult to see how an act of disobedience to a divine commandment can be read positively within Torah. Barr sought to ameliorate this difficulty by

---

26. Cf. Deut 1:39; 2 Sam 14:17; 1 Kgs 3:9; Isa 7:15–16.

27. E.g. L. M. Bechtel, "Genesis 2:4b–3:24: A Myth about Human Maturation," *JSOT* 67 (1995): 3–26.

appealing to the common complaint "What a fuss about a mere apple!"
According to Barr, we have here "a God who is not insisting upon any
very central ethical principle." Later he says of God that "he has made an
ethically arbitrary prohibition."[28] In the light of the Old Testament's
dietary laws, however, we must judge this to be no more than an unreflec-
tive prejudice on Barr's part that sheds no light on Gen 3. In addition, if
there are good grounds for thinking that Eden was represented as a
sanctuary, it is not surprising that at its heart there are objects that are
forbidden to the human couple.[29] In other biblical narratives when *sancta*
are violated the transgressors are struck down. The threat of death is,
thus, entirely in keeping with the offence. Eve's extension of the commandment so that it is not touched would be a logical and necessary
corollary of understanding the fruit as a *sanctum*. Second, there exist a
number of parallels between the story in Gen 3 and the story of Cain and
Abel in Gen 4. As Westermann observes, "the parallels between Gen 4
and 3 are so striking and thorough so as to make the intention…unmis-
takable, namely to construct in ch. 4 a narrative of crime and punishment
corresponding to that in ch. 3."[30] Westermann's comment points particularly to the similarity in form. A crime is committed which leads to an
investigation by YHWH and punishment of the transgressor. The divine
response is similar in both cases: questions "Where?" and "What have
you done?" (3:9, 13; 4:9, 10), followed by a curse which involves driving
the perpetrator eastwards from the land (3:14–19, 23; 4:11–12). There
are also a number of verbal parallels, most especially between the curse
on Eve and God's warning to Cain: ואל־אישך תשוקתך והוא ימשל־בך (3:16)
and ואליך תשוקתו ואתה תמשל־בו (4:7).[31] Recent critical analyses have
attributed most of the Cain and Abel story to the same hand as the

28. J. Barr, *The Garden of Eden and the Hope of Immortality: The Read-Tuckwell Lectures for 1990* (London: SCM, 1992), 11–12.

29. The presentation of the world as a sanctuary in Gen 1:1–2:4a is well known. Wenham has made a good case that a similar logic underlies the presentation of the garden of Eden. Both the Temple and Eden open to the east, cherubim guard the way, and the menorah is often understood as a stylized tree of life (G. J. Wenham, "Sanctuary Symbolism in the Garden of Eden Story," *Proceedings of the World Congress of Jewish Studies* 9 [1986]: 19–25).

30. C. Westermann, *Genesis 1–11: A Commentary* (Minneapolis: Augsburg, 1984), 285.

31. For discussion of the similarities between the stories, see A. J. Hauser, "Linguistic and Thematic Links between Genesis 4:1–16 and Genesis 2–3," *JETS* (1980): 297–305; D. Rudman, "A Little Knowledge is a Dangerous Thing: Crossing Forbidden Boundaries in Gen 3–4," in *Studies in the Book of Genesis: Literature, Redaction and History* (ed. A. Wénin; BETL 155; Leuven: Peeters, 2001), 461–66.

temptation narrative,[32] and it is doubtful that there was an earlier story or tradition in the background.[33] Taking the language of commandment and the parallels between Gen 3 and 4 together we have good grounds for regarding the actions in the Garden of Eden as inauspicious.

The appeal of both a "fall downwards" and a "fall upwards" in the history of the interpretation of Gen 2–3 underlines the interpretative potential of these chapters. They provide further evidence that one of the purposes of the chapters is to promote reflection, perhaps more than to prescribe a single view about humanity and the creation. Whether or not human likeness to God is a benefit to human beings, and in what ways, are deeply complicated questions it seems. The formulation of Gen 1:26–28 is far from simple, but the subsequent chapters add many more dimensions of complication. The textual context of Gen 1–3(4) offers an unexpectedly rich interpretation of the *imago* provided we see beyond the quest for *the* original reading, as valuable and instructive as that exercise has been.

5. *Irenaeus and the* Imago Dei

In this essay I have sought to show that attempts to restrict the "meaning" of the *imago dei* to a few occurrences in P fail to grapple with the problem of context and the complicated history of reception already present within the biblical text. In her study of the Garden of Eden story Susan Gillingham protests against "the unreasonableness of commentators when they select one supposedly 'right' reading…and then propose that it has a monopoly over any others."[34] The same charge could be brought against many recent interpretations of the *imago dei*.

---

32. It has long been observed that the story of Cain and Abel is an expansion of the Cainite genealogy (4:1, 17–24). There is some disagreement, however, about how much of the story was already part of the original genealogy, and how much was added by the author of the Garden of Eden story. Kratz thinks the original story of the creation of humankind (2:4b–22*; 3:20–21) continued with the birth of Cain and the development of human society (4:1*, 17–22) (Kratz, *Composition*, 252–54). Levin thinks that the occupations of the brothers and the murder of Cain were already part of the Yahwist's source material. It was only with the Yahwist, however, that the material was developed into a narrative with parallels to Gen 3 (Levin, *Der Jahwist*, 82–102). Witte goes further than either and attributes vv. 3–5 to his proto-Yahwist (Witte, *Die biblische Urgeschichte*, 166–71).

33. J. Van Seters, *Prologue to History: The Yahwist as Historian in Genesis* (Louisville: Westminster John Knox, 1992), 143.

34. S. E. Gillingham, *The Image, the Depths and the Surface: Multivalent Approaches to Biblical Study* (JSOTSup 354; Sheffield: Sheffield Academic, 2002), 13.

One of the consequences of contextualizing the *imago dei* exclusively within a history of ancient Near Eastern thought or the theology of P has been an unfortunate detachment from the history of interpretation. Prior understandings of the *imago* become no more than negative foils for the "right" reading, illustrations of methodological failures now corrected. Despite its detractors, Childs's canonical approach had as one of its virtues the desire to make sense of both the history of composition and the history of interpretation.[35] Attention to the canonical form of the text is not made at the expense of a literary-critical analysis, but on the basis of it. In this way the interpreter is able to understand how the text functions in its "final" form, but is also well aware of the many aporias, tensions and disjunctions that the text presents to readers, how these probably came about, and how, if at all, the "final" text adjudicates these problems. It is only with attention to both approaches that the interpreter can make sense of the history of interpretation. Wrestling with the before and after of the canonical text is no easy task—as Childs's different Exodus and Isaiah commentaries reveal—but a necessary one for the canonical interpreter.

When the history of interpretation of the *imago dei* is rehearsed, Irenaeus has usually had the unhappy position at the head of the procession. He is not only the earliest interpreter of the *imago* that can be discussed in any detail, but is also a parable for false exegesis. Irenaeus' contribution to the discussion of the *imago* is often presented as no more than the introduction of a tendentious distinction between *imago* and *similitudo*, a natural and supernatural likeness to God. Thus, Irenaeus is seen to take the first false step in the interpretation of the *imago dei*, and one with significant consequences for the understanding of the *imago* for the modern age.[36] For Old Testament interpreters he is a good example of the failures of ancient exegesis, which modern exegesis is now able to correct with hard-won philological insights. While Irenaeus' philological deficiencies are rightly criticized, Irenaeus' detractors have failed to recognize the extent to which he did do some justice to the immediate textual context of the *imago*, about which recent continental scholarship has begun to remind us. Although I shall not be able to present a comprehensive picture of Irenaeus' complex deployment of the *imago dei* in his writings, I shall hope in my concluding remarks to commend some aspects of Irenaeus' account of the *imago*.

35. For a critique of many common misrepresentations of Childs, most especially by J. Barton and J. Barr, see now D. R. Driver, *Brevard Childs, Biblical Theologian: For the Church's One Bible* (FAT 2/46; Tübingen: Mohr Siebeck, 2010).

36. See Westermann, *Genesis 1–11*, 148; G. J. Wenham, *Genesis 1–15* (WBC 1; Waco: Word, 1987), 29.

We might first begin by observing that, despite Westermann's attribution of the distinction between *imago* and *similitudo* to Irenaeus, interpreters of Irenaeus are agreed that only the germs of the later understanding are present. For Irenaeus the matter is more complex. Indeed, there is no little disagreement about whether Irenaeus' understanding of the *imago dei* is consistent or self-contradictory.[37] Certainly, Lawson is correct to observe that "the terms 'image' and 'likeness' are somewhat fluid...Irenaeus can use them of Adam both before and after the Fall."[38] On occasions Irenaeus does distinguish between the two. *Similitudo* can mean the freedom and intelligence that humans share with God, but also the becoming like God through obedience. *Imago* is the accordance between human beings and the Son of God.[39]

Central to Irenaeus' understanding of the *imago* is the relationship between protology and eschatology. The incarnate Son both restores to humanity what was lost at the beginning and leads humanity to their destiny. In this way Irenaeus seeks to do justice to the two sides of the Garden of Eden story that we have already observed. For Irenaeus Gen 3 is, indeed, a fall, but also a step on the way to full maturity in Christ. What is it that is lost in the fall? Holsinger-Friesen summarizes as follows: "Losing the image and likeness of God entails a loss of *life* and a loss of *fruitfulness*."[40] Irenaeus appears to be sensitive to the relationship of immortality to divine likeness in Gen 2–3. He understands there to have been a loss of immortality, which he equates with the sentence of death passed on Adam and Eve for disobedience.[41] On the other hand, Irenaeus judges that the man and his wife were like children in Eden.[42] Paradise was designed for the perfecting of the human couple, but in their naivety they were deceived by the serpent. They were not able to acquire knowledge properly in their immaturity, but knowledge of good and evil is the destiny of humans. "For it was necessary, at first, that nature should be exhibited; then, after that, that what was mortal

37. D. Minns, *Irenaeus* (Outstanding Christian Thinkers; London: G. Chapman, 1994), 60.

38. J. Lawson, *The Biblical Theology of Saint Irenaeus* (London: Epworth, 1948), 200.

39. E. F. Osborn, *Irenaeus of Lyons* (Cambridge: Cambridge University Press, 2001), 214–16.

40. T. Holsinger-Friesen, *Irenaeus and Genesis: A Study of Competition in Early Christian Hermeneutics* (Journal of Theological Interpretation Supplements 1; Winona Lake: Eisenbrauns, 2009), 127 (italics original).

41. See *Adv. Haer.* III.18.3; V.23.1.

42. *Epid.* 12.

should be conquered and swallowed up by immortality, and the corrupti-
ble by incorruptibility, and that man should be made after the image and
likeness of God, having received the knowledge of good and evil."[43] In
the divine providence humanity progresses towards the divine image by
way of the fall. As Ian Hislop notes, "the basic idea that St. Irenaeus is
trying to express seems to be that man is created an innocent child, who
is destined, under Providence, to discover himself and reach a greater
appreciation of God's nature by passing through the corruption of sin."[44]

Irenaeus' understanding of the *imago* is thoroughly Christological and
forged in the fires of controversy with various forms of second-century
Gnosticism. Thus, the context within which he understands the *imago* is
much broader than the immediate textual context of Gen 1–3(4), for
which I have pressed. Despite this we can see in Irenaeus a close
attention to the complexities of Gen 1–3. The ambivalence of human
existence that Spieckermann discerns in Gen 2–3 is appreciated by
Irenaeus. Irenaeus also recognizes a relationship between this and the
imago dei of ch. 1. In this way Irenaeus develops his understanding of
human existence that ultimately sees humanity possessing the fruit of
both trees of the garden through conformity to the divine image in Christ.

---

43. *Adv. Haer.* IV.38.4.
44. I. Hislop, "The Image of God in Man According to St. Irenaeus," *New Blackfriars* 27 (1946): 69–75 (73).

EVENSONG IN EDEN:
AS IT PROBABLY WAS *NOT* IN THE BEGINNING

Robert P. Gordon

In a companion study to the present one it was suggested that Gen 4:26b is so phrased, using the unique passive "it was begun (to call upon the name of the Lord)," in order to avoid a form of words that would be ambiguous within the larger context and that could be misinterpreted as a statement about Adam and his first experience of what we might call "divine worship."[1] The ancient writer's apparent eschewal of ambiguity draws attention to the fact that nothing is said in either Genesis creation narrative about the first humans in relation to worship, and prompts the question, In what sense (if any) were Adam and Eve worshipful creatures in Eden? It is only in later tradition that Adam is associated with altar-worship, and this relates to life after his expulsion from Eden. For example, *Targum Pseudo-Jonathan* to Gen 8:20 informs that the altar used by Cain and Abel was that "which Adam built in the time when he was expelled from the Garden of Eden, and upon which he had offered oblation."[2] Adam's altar is also said to have been used by Noah, which is why *Pseudo-Jonathan* mentions it at Gen 8:20; it had been destroyed in the flood, but Noah rebuilt it (MT "Then Noah built an altar to the Lord").[3] Genesis itself describes an Eden without cult, and indeed without even the "unmediated worship" which is sometimes assumed for it.[4]

---

1. See R. P. Gordon, "Who 'Began to Call on the Name of the LORD' in Genesis 4:26b? The MT and the Versions," in *Let us Go up to Zion: Essays in Honour of H. G. M. Williamson on the Occasion of his Sixty-Fifth Birthday* (ed. I. Provan and M. J. Boda; VTSup, 153; Leiden: Brill, 2012), 57–68.

2. M. Ginsburger, *Pseudo-Jonathan (Thargum Jonathan ben Usiel zum Penta-teuch)* (Berlin: S. Calvary, 1903; repr., Georg Olms, Hildesheim, 1971), 15.

3. For other references to Adam's altar in rabbinic writings, see C. T. R. Hayward, *Saint Jerome's Hebrew Questions on Genesis, Translated with Introduction and Commentary* (Oxford Early Christian Studies; Oxford: Clarendon, 1995), 120.

4. E.g. M. O'Connor, "The Biblical Notion of the City," in *Constructions of Space II: The Biblical City and Other Imagined Spaces* (ed. J. L. Berquist and C. V.

Eden and Sanctuary

If there are no direct statements about worship in Eden, an oblique angle on the subject is offered by the suggestion that the description of the Eden garden introduces sanctuary features whose significance is borne out by other biblical (as well as post-biblical) texts that make a more straightforward connection between Eden and tabernacle/temple. A similar case has been made for the first Genesis creation narrative, where the account of the making of the "cosmos" is often said to incorporate sanctuary and, more broadly, priestly elements. The sanctuary view has been pursued most recently by John H. Walton,[5] for whom "creation" in Gen 1 functions as a cosmic temple, and the more generally priestly approach by Mark S. Smith, who exploits the "priestly" associations of Gen 1 in a maximal kind of way.[6] As for Gen 2–3, a whole series of features in the Eden narrative are explained by their connection with the Pentateuchal depiction of the tabernacle or with the temple accounts in 1 Kings and Ezekiel, with the result that Eden itself is described as a kind of sanctuary.[7] A list of salient features would include the following: the

Camp; LHBOTS 490; New York: T&T Clark International, 2008), 18–39 (20). O'Connor observes that Genesis and Revelation are similar in depicting both primordial and eschatological worship as "unmediated." The New Testament apocalypticist seems to make the point when he reports that he "saw no temple" in the new Jerusalem (Rev 21:22).

5. J. H. Walton, *The Lost World of Genesis One: Ancient Cosmology and the Origins Debate* (Downers Grove: InterVarsity, 2009).

6. M. S. Smith, *The Priestly Vision of Genesis 1* (Minneapolis: Fortress, 2010), 14–17, 27–32, 75–76, 107–8, 124, 178–79.

7. See J. D. Levenson, *Sinai and Zion: An Entry into the Jewish Bible* (New Voices in Biblical Studies; Minneapolis: Winston, 1985), 128–33; 142–45; G. J. Wenham, "Sanctuary Symbolism in the Garden of Eden Story," in *Proceedings of the Ninth World Congress of Jewish Studies, Division A: The Period of the Bible* (Jerusalem: World Union of Jewish Studies, 1986), 19–25; idem, *Genesis 1–15* (WBC; Nashville: Thomas Nelson, 1987), 65, 67; E. E. Elnes, "Creation and Tabernacle: The Priestly Writer's 'Environmentalism'," *Horizons in Biblical Theology* 16 (1994): 144–55 (147–53); G. K. Beale, *The Temple and the Church's Mission: A Biblical Theology of the Dwelling Place of God* (New Studies in Biblical Theology 17; Leicester: Apollos, 2004), 66–80. For a study of the Eden section of the book of *Jubilees* from a temple perspective, see J. T. A. G. M. van Ruiten, "Eden and the Temple: The Rewriting of Genesis 2:4–3:24 in *The Book of Jubilees*," in *Paradise Interpreted: Representations of Biblical Paradise in Judaism and Christianity* (ed. G. P. Luttikhuizen; Themes in Biblical Narrative 2; Leiden: Brill, 1999), 63–81.

garden is planted in the east (2:8),[8] which is the cardinal point associated with temple access (Ezek 40:6; 43:4); the description of Adam's responsibility in terms of "working" and "keeping" uses terms with liturgical possibilities (2:15; cf. Num 3:7–8; 8:26; 18:5–6); the tree of life in the middle of the garden (2:9) mirrors the stylized tree in the outer compartment of the tabernacle (Exod 25:31–40; Lev 24:1–4); the onyx stone of 2:12 recalls the high priest's ephod and breastpiece (Exod 25:7; 28:9; 35:27; 39:6, 13); the "good" gold of 2:12 points to the extensive use of gold in the furnishing of the tabernacle and temple; God "walks about" in the garden (3:8) just as, through his presence in the tabernacle, he "walks among" his people (Lev 26:11–12); God clothes Adam and Eve when their nakedness is exposed (3:21), just as his priests are specially "clothed" in order to carry out their duties in the tabernacle (e.g. Exod 28:41; 29:8–9); and, finally, there is a small cluster of tabernacle features in 3:24, describing the expulsion and its sequel, when God "stations" (*škn*) cherubim (cf. Exod 25:18–22; 26:31; 1 Kgs 6:23–29) on the east side of Eden in order to guard the way to the tree of life.

Taken cumulatively, this list looks impressive, but it is of variable quality. Sometimes the "fit" is not sufficiently exact to be convincing: most obviously, the onyx stone and the gold are in the land of Havilah, which is outside and away from Eden (2:11–12). The description of Adam and Eve "unfallen" as naked (2:25) may also bear on the question of Eden's sanctuary status. At the least, no such cultic concern as dictated Exod 20:26 ("Do not go up to my altar on steps, lest your nakedness be exposed on it") or Exod 28:42–43 ("Make linen undergarments… reaching from the waist to the thigh…so that they will not incur guilt and die") colours the description. Moreover, when God provides clothing for Adam and Eve it is made from animal skins (3:21), this admittedly in relation to what should be regarded as their "post-priestly" existence after their expulsion. For all that, being clothed or unclothed seems to have little or nothing to do with quasi-priestly status in the garden.

To Work and to Keep

In the wider discussion, the statement in 2:15 that the man is put in the garden "in order to work it and to keep it" has been required to bear a particularly heavy weight. Because the verbs "work" (*ʿbd*) and "keep"

---

8. T. Stordalen, *Echoes of Eden: Genesis 2–3 and Symbolism of the Eden Garden in Biblical Hebrew Literature* (Contributions to Biblical Exegesis and Theology 25; Leuven: Peeters, 2000), 261–70, makes a case for a temporal rather than geographical sense for *mqdm* in Gen 2:8.

(*šmr*) can denote religious service, whether to God in an absolute sense or in relation to the cult or to observance of divine commands, Adam's role was being explained in cultic terms already in antiquity. This is the explanation given in *Gen. Rab.* 16:5:

> "To work it and to keep it": These are the sacrifices. As it is said, "You shall serve [*ʿbd*] God," and [as] it is written, "You shall be careful [*šmr*] to make offering to me at its appointed time."[9]

In the MT of Gen 2:15 both "work" and "keep" carry a third person feminine singular suffix, which raises a question about antecedence, for *gan* ("garden") is otherwise a masculine noun in the Old Testament. This led Cassuto to repoint both verbs, with the omission of the *mappîq*, as infinitives construct with the so-called feminine ending.[10] Thus relieved of an object, the referentiality of the verbs becomes less earth-bound: the text is then freed to say that Adam was put in the garden to do as *Genesis Rabbah* suggests. And if the Eden–sanctuary parallel is invoked, Adam may be compared to a Levite serving (*ʿbd*) the tent of meeting, as in Num 8:15. This is, however, to overwork two common or garden verbs which, whatever additional senses they may have in defined contexts, ordinarily mean "work" and "keep, protect." Cassuto's translation "to serve and to guard" is elliptical and allusive, whereas the activity in question is stated very concretely in an earlier verse: "but there was no one to work (*ʿbd*) the ground" (v. 5). We might even surmise that the feminine singular suffixes in v. 15 have the earlier reference to the ground in mind.[11] The association of *ʿbd*, in the sense of work, with "ground" in early Genesis supports this interpretation; see also 3:23; 4:2, 12.[12]

The tendency to overload "work" and "keep" in 2:15 is partly fed by ecological concerns, in order to bring out the full potential of texts that may have something timely to say about human stewardship of the earth, or that at the least may help towards a more accurate and less incriminating representation of what the Old Testament says or implies on the subject. So it has been argued that the "working" and "keeping" in this verse indicate the promotion of the interests of the earth, and its protection from harm. This finds strong expression in Mark Brett's *Genesis:*

9. *Bereshit Rabbah*, I (ed. E. E. Halevi; Tel-Aviv: Machbaroth Lesifrut, 1956), 117.

10. U. Cassuto, *A Commentary on the Book of Genesis*. Part I. *From Adam to Noah. Genesis I–VI 8* (trans. I. Abrahams; Jerusalem: Magnes, 1961), 122–23.

11. *Pace* ibid., 122. Cassuto notes the occurrence of "ground" in v. 9, but still disallows the possibility of influence from an earlier verse.

12. For other occurrences of "work the ground," see 2 Sam 9:10; Isa 30:24; Jer 27:11; Zech 13:5; Prov 12:11; 28:19.

Procreation and the Politics of Identity, in which he suggests that the second creation narrative may have been put in its present position in order to counter the anthropocentric emphasis of Gen 1.[13] Brett thinks that the statement "there was no human to work the ground" in 2:5 seems to "place the needs of the land before those of the human," and perhaps even, in keeping with a connotation of Biblical Hebrew *ʿbd* already noted, requires to be rendered "there was no human to *serve* (= work for) the land." Viewed from this perspective, "serve" and "keep" in 2:15 effectively reverse the mandate to rule and subdue the earth in 1:26–28.[14] For Ellen Davis there is "meaningful ambiguity" in the verbs "work" and "keep," since the former can have the connotation of "working *for*" and the latter may, in addition to the basic sense of "keep," imply the *observing* of the earth in order to learn and respect the limits relating to its use.[15] Davis's amplification tentatively stretches a little further: "serve" may include the connotation of worship ("cautiously applied"), in keeping with usage in some other biblical contexts, and "keep" may resonate with biblical texts where the same verb describes Torah observance. Thus a paraphrase of 2:15b might run: "[and he placed him in the garden of Eden] to work and serve it, to preserve and observe it."[16]

On the basis of the foregoing, we may conclude that the parallels claimed for the Garden of Eden and the tabernacle/temple are of variable strength and relevance for our question about Eden and worship. A fuller discussion would also have to accommodate Stordalen's conclusion that ancient Near Eastern deities lived in houses, "gardens being hardly more than peripheral setting for the heavenly palace."[17] However, to sharpen the issue, we shall look at two strongly contrasting views, both from long after the biblical period, on the religious experience of Adam and Eve in the garden.

13. M. G. Brett, *Genesis: Procreation and the Politics of Identity* (London: Routledge, 2000), 30.

14. This is also noted by, for example, T. Hiebert, *The Yahwist's Landscape: Nature and Religion in Early Israel* (New York: Oxford University Press, 1996), 158; cf. H. Marlow, *Biblical Prophets and Contemporary Environmental Ethics: Re-Reading Amos, Hosea, and First Isaiah* (Oxford: Oxford University Press, 2009), 76. Marlow's footnoted comment (n. 126) about the semantic range of *ʿbd* not being limited to service to a superior is quite to the point.

15. E. F. Davis, *Scripture, Culture, and Agriculture: An Agrarian Reading of the Bible* (Cambridge: Cambridge University Press, 2009), 29–30.

16. Ibid., 30; cf. p. 104.

17. Stordalen, *Echoes of Eden*, 160.

Paradise Lost

In Book IV of *Paradise Lost* John Milton, as is well known, has something to say on devotions in the garden. He describes how Adam and Eve, on arriving back at their "shady lodge" at the end of the working day, worship God *al fresco* (ll. 720–35). They honour God as creator of their "delicious place," which is too large for them now that his abundance "wants / Partakers, and uncropped falls to the ground." They cherish the promise of "a race / To fill the earth"—descendants who, like Adam and Eve, will hold devotions morning and evening. Milton noticeably limits their expressions of worship to the praise of the lips:

> This said unanimous, and other rites
> Observing none, but adoration pure
> Which God likes best… (ll. 736–38)

Perhaps it is Milton's Puritan sympathies that are most apparent at this point, though what he says is quite in accord with his Genesis text, which says nothing of worship—even of the kind that he envisages.

In Book V Milton has a longer account of morning devotions in Eden (ll. 136–208):

> Lowly they bowed adoring, and began
> Their orisons, each morning duly paid
> In various style… (ll. 144–46)

Their worship was not only "various" but *ex tempore* ("in fit strains pronounced or sung / Unmeditated," ll. 148–49). It was expressed "in prose or numerous verse" (l. 150) and was *a cappella* ("More tuneable than needed lute or harp / To add more sweetness…," ll. 151–52). A sample of their elevated praise is given in ll. 152–208, concluding with "So prayed they innocent, and to their thoughts / Firm peace recovered soon and wonted calm" (ll. 209–10). The early Methodist biblical commentator Adam Clarke identified this morning hymn with Ps 148:

> The beautiful morning hymn of Adam and Eve (Paradise Lost, book v., line 153, &c.),—"These are thy glorious works, Parent of good; Almighty, thine this universal frame," &c.—has been universally admired. How many have spoken loud in its praises, who have never attempted to express their feelings in a stanza of the *hundred and forty-eighth* psalm! But to the rapturous adorers of Milton's poetry what is the song of David, or this grand music of the spheres! Know this, O forgetful man, that *Milton's* morning hymn is a *paraphrase of this psalm*, and is indebted to it for every excellency it possesses. It is little else than the Psalmist speaking in English instead of Hebrew verse.[18]

18. A. Clarke, *The Holy Bible: The Old Testament*. Vol. 3, *Job to Solomon's Song* (London: Thomas Tegg, 1836), 2406–7. This is Clarke's concluding comment

Others before Clarke had associated Ps 148 with Adam. Isaac Watts's hymn based on the psalm begins, "Ye tribes of Adam, join / With heav'n, and earth, and seas," where the mention of Adam may reflect awareness of the tradition of Adamic authorship. Robert Lowth believed that the first humans had been endowed with poetic gift and he therefore had no problem in attributing the psalm to Adam.[19]

Karl Barth on Romans

A very different view of Eden is represented by Karl Barth in his commentary on Romans.[20] For Barth, there is no absolute or relative in Eden, "no 'Higher' and 'Lower', no 'There' and 'Here'." At first, humans were not conscious of their creatureliness. "The world was originally one with the Creator, and men were one with God." To illustrate, Barth calls on Michelangelo's "Creation of Adam," in which God and Adam look each other in the face, "their hands stretched out towards one another in a delicious freedom of intercourse." This represents the original and true state of things in Eden. By contrast, Michelangelo's "Creation of Eve" depicts her rising slowly, "posing herself in the fatal attitude of— worship." Barth observes the "warning arm and careworn, saddened eyes" of the Creator who sees Eve's gesture of adoration as implying consciousness of distinction such as she is not intended to have. Only the "Fall" brings that distinction properly into view. Barth describes Eve as the first "religious personality" who was "the first to set herself over against God, the first to worship Him." For Barth, humanity's troubles begin with "the emergence of religion." Since he is referring to Eve "unfallen," Barth is not basing himself on Genesis; rather, he is allowing his own interpretation of Michelangelo to inform his reading of the biblical text which itself makes no distinction between Adam and Eve in this or most respects. Some clue as to the inspiration for Barth's thinking

in his section "Notes on Psalm CXLVIII." He begins the notes by observing that the psalm is untitled, but is attributed by the Peshitta to Haggai and Zechariah "and the Septuagint and the Aethiopic follow it" (p. 2405). For an appreciation of Clarke's biblical scholarship, see S. B. Dawes, *Adam Clarke: Methodism's First Old Testament Scholar* (Cornish Methodist Historical Association Occasional Publication 26; Redruth: Cornish Methodist Historical Association, 1994); see pp. 6–12 for a discussion of Clarke's views on the authorship of the Psalms.

19. R. Lowth, *De sacra poesi hebraeorum: Praelectiones academicae oxonii habitae* (Oxford: Clarendon, 1753), 334 (*Praelectio* XXV).

20. K. Barth, *The Epistle to the Romans* (trans. of 6th German ed. by E. C. Hoskyns; pbk ed.; London: Oxford University Press, 1933; 1968), 247–49 (on Rom 7:8–9).

about Eve, other than Genesis or the history of art, is suggested by his including among the causes of opposition to God the excessive attention paid by humans to the serpent's theme of a direct relationship between humans and God, "especially by women, since they are more acutely disturbed than men are by the riddle of direct relationship."

Choosing between the Options

Milton and Barth represent opposite positions on the subject of worship in Eden. As we have already noted, the biblical text is silent. Neither Adam nor Eve says or does much at all in Gen 2–3. Adam combines poetry and etymology in a few lines beginning "This at last (or 'now') is bone of my bones" (2:23), apparently expressing satisfaction that God's animal experiment designed to provide him with a companion has been superseded (2:18–20). Otherwise, speech by the two is confined to Eve's reply to the serpent in 3:3 and to their mutual blame-casting when the Lord God comes inquiring after them (3:12–13). In his portrayal of Eden's devotions Milton has given sanctified imagination free rein, but Barth's exposition of the divine–human relationship as "an equality of friendship" is just as problematical when we try to map it on to the text. Matthew Boulton, in a fairly recent study that includes discussion of Barth on worship, notes a potential problem in "secrecy as a condition of intimacy"—the idea that God withholds knowledge within a relationship of ostensible equality—but offers some explanation and defence of it.[21] He argues that, since according to 2:17 the divine secret concerns "the possibility of sin, of separation and estrangement from God," it is an act of kindness to withhold this knowledge from Adam. Moreover, real life experience teaches that it is both necessary and beneficial for relationships intimate and equal to involve the withholding of information: "Genuine intimacy involves secrecy, not secrecy that covers up what should be uncovered, but secrecy that—out of love and wisdom— refrains from uncovering what should remain covered."[22] However, even if we concede these general points to Boulton, a bigger problem remains in the undoubted hierarchy that is reflected in the prohibition of 2:17. It is a hierarchy that must be as obvious to the Adam of the narrative as it is to the reader of the text: "on the day you eat you will die."

21. M. M. Boulton, *God Against Religion: Rethinking Christian Theology Through Worship* (Calvin Institute of Christian Worship Liturgical Studies; Grand Rapids: Eerdmans, 2008), 38–40.
22. Ibid., 39.

In his book on Genesis and narration, Hugh White is not at all concerned with Barth, yet the following could almost have been written as a response to Barth: "It is important to note at this juncture that the relationship established between the divine Voice and Adam in the utterance of the prohibition is a hierarchical relationship... The relationship is thus not one of mutuality between partners, but one involving the exercise of authority by a superior party over an inferior."[23] The hierarchical stance is maintained in the next verse where God declares to himself, or to his divine council, that it is not good for the man to be living alone; but Adam is neither addressed nor consulted. We need not assume, either, that the talk of death in 2:17 goes over Adam's head. Death has not featured in the narrative so far, but that does not mean that the warning of death accompanying the prohibition is merely a *vox nihili* where Adam is concerned. And if that is so, 2:17 already represents an encroachment upon that innocence of the imagination that Barth constructs for us, as when he says, "The behaviour of men must not be governed by knowledge of the contrast between the primal state and its contradiction."[24]

The Wider Context

The absence of the language of worship in Eden is all the more noticeable when Gen 2–3 is considered in relation to the flanking chapters. As we have noted, the "priestly" narrative of 1:1–2:4a does not talk about worship as such, yet its account of creation climaxes with the specially hallowed seventh day ("and God blessed the seventh day and hallowed it," 2:3). This is the only aspect of creation that is both "blessed" and "hallowed." It is true that the actual term "Shabbat/sabbath" is not used—perhaps surprisingly in a narrative that features several namings (1:5 [×2], 8, 10 [×2])—nevertheless there is no doubt that it is Shabbat/sabbath that is in view. This first creation narrative also notes that the (unnamed) sun and moon were appointed "for signs and for *mwʿdym*" (1:14), where *mwʿdym* should be translated "festivals" (cf. REB), rather than "seasons" as in NIV.[25] And if the heavenly bodies regulate festivals,

23. H. C. White, *Narration and Discourse in the Book of Genesis* (Cambridge: Cambridge University Press, 1991), 123.

24. Barth, *The Epistle to the Romans*, 247.

25. According to BDB, 417b, it is "most probable" that the reference is to "the sacred seasons as fixed by the moon's appearance"; Ps 104:19 ("he made the moon for *mwʿdym*") is cited in support. It is not certain that any occurrences of *mwʿd* denote "season" in a purely "seasonal" sense. The common and recognizable senses are "set time or place; meeting; assembly."

it is no doubt Israelite festivals that are intended.[26] Worship is also prominent in the chapter immediately following the Eden narrative: the first part of ch. 4 turns on altar worship, and on the acceptableness or otherwise of the offerings brought by Cain and Abel, while 4:26b makes a major statement about the beginnings of worship. Genesis 5, with its succession of obituary notices, is not going to provide similar material. Even so, in a manner still relevant to our worship theme, it is twice said of Enoch that he "walked about (*hthlk*) with God" (5:22, 24). Noticeably, the occurrence of *hthlk* in Gen 3:8 describes the walking of the Lord God in the garden in the cool of the day, and comes only after the act of disobedience; there is no such usage for Adam and Eve that would suggest an Enoch-type relationship with their creator.

After Eden, worship begins with Cain and Abel, but it falters. Without preliminary or explanation, they present their offerings to God. However, when Cain and his offering are rejected and Abel is murdered, there is not much prospect of worship until the birth of Seth.[27] In the time of Seth's son Enosh,[28] "people began to call on the name of the Lord" (4:26). Here MT *'z* is best translated "then," "at that time," referring to the generation of Seth/Enosh, as against Westermann's suggestion of a broader reference to "primeval times."[29] Joshua 8:30, again in a cultic context, provides a parallel: "At that time (*'z*) Joshua built an altar to the Lord the God of Israel." "Calling upon the name of the Lord" is not something expressly said of Cain and Abel; it is only with Abel's replacement that worship takes root among the early generations. Viewed in that light, the worship of Cain and Abel seems almost to represent a false start, if only because there is a hiatus until Seth comes as the "other seed" taking the place of the murdered Abel (4:25).

As Genesis proceeds, worship develops. After the flood, Noah builds an altar and sacrifices burnt offerings on it (8:20). Abraham likewise builds his altars and "calls on the name of the Lord" (12:8; cf. 13:18). The specific language of worship in the form of the verb *hšthwh* first appears in Gen 22:5: "Stay here with the donkey while the boy and I go over there. We shall worship and then we shall come back to you." This, of course, happens at the mountain of the Lord in "the land of Moriah": 2 Chr 3:1 appears to link the location of the Jerusalem temple with the

---

26. Cf. Smith, *The Priestly Vision*, 98.

27. The other sons and daughters attributed to Adam and Eve in 5:4 are born after Seth.

28. If "then" refers to the time of Seth, the sense is much the same.

29. C. Westermann, *Genesis*. Vol. 1, *Genesis 1–11* (BKAT 1/10; Neukirchen–Vluyn: Neukirchener, 1974), 463.

place where Abraham sacrificed the ram in place of his son Isaac.[30] The *religious* sense of *hšthwh*, which has already been used in 18:2 and 19:1 in its ordinary sense of "bow down" in greeting, seems almost to be reserved for the occasion and the place. This is the mountain where "God will provide," which meaning of "YHWH *yrʾh*" (Gen 22:14) is signalled in Abraham's own statement, "God will provide (*yrʾh*) himself with the lamb for a burnt offering" (v. 8). At the same time, the gloss on the name in v. 14 introduces an ambiguity—and in this of all places: "As it is said to this day, 'On the mount of the Lord *yērāʾeh*'," where *yērāʾeh* is variously translated "it shall be provided" (NRSV; cf. NIV) or "he shall be seen" (NRSV [footnote]). This latter sense applies in all other occurrences of Biblical Hebrew *rʾh* (niphal) in Genesis, from 12:7 onwards, describing God's appearances to Abraham, Isaac and Jacob (17:1; 18:1; 26:2, 24; cf. 35:1, 9; 48:3).[31]

Mundane Eden

Eden makes no contribution to this theme of worship, and we may judge that, in their different ways, both Milton and Barth are pitching too high, the former by imaginative reconstruction of daily devotions in the garden and the latter by sublimating the relationship between Adam and Eve and their creator to a level beyond that in which worship was appropriate. The reality appears to be more mundane, and some recent writing on the Pentateuch may have relevance for our discussion of this less idealized view of Eden. In the first place, scholars such as F. V. Winnett,[32] J. B. Van Seters,[33] H. H. Schmid,[34] and C. Levin[35] have argued that the Pentateuchal Yahwistic source is to be located much later than the conventional dating, and possibly as late as the Babylonian exile. The details

30. This identification of Moriah with the temple mountain is also implied in our text itself (v. 14b); cf. R. W. L. Moberly, *The Theology of the Book of Genesis* (Old Testament Theology; Cambridge: Cambridge University Press, 2009), 188.
    31. The pun "see"/"is (or, shall be) seen" is recognized by G. von Rad, *Das erste Buch Mose: Genesis Kapitel 12,10—25,18* (2d ed.; ATD 3; Göttingen: Vandenhoeck & Ruprecht, 1956), 207.
    32. F. V. Winnett, "Re-examining the Foundations," *JBL* 84 (1965): 1–19.
    33. J. B. Van Seters, "Confessional Reformulation in the Exilic Period," *VT* 22 (1972): 448–59 (454, 459), and *Prologue to History: The Yahwist as Historian in Genesis* (Louisville: Westminster John Knox, 1992).
    34. H. H. Schmid, *Der sogenannte Jahwist: Beobachtungen und Fragen zur Pentateuchforschung* (Zurich: Theologischer Verlag Zürich, 1976).
    35. C. Levin, *Der Jahwist* (FRLANT 157; Göttingen: Vandenhoeck & Ruprecht, 1993), 430–35.

of the discussion need not concern us here. In this kind of atmosphere it
was only a matter of time until the suggestion was made that the Yahwistic material postdates the Priestly elements identified in the Pentateuch,
and in Gen 1–11 in particular.[36] Thus in one of the more recent explora-
tions of this theme, in the volume *Abschied vom Jahwisten*, Joseph
Blenkinsopp sets out his view that the Yahwistic material in Gen 1–11
"comprises the residue of a self-contained lay source which has been
appended to the Priestly narrative (P) as a supplement and, to some
extent, a corrective supplement."[37] He also notes that, on his view, Gen
1–11 is *sui generis* and "cannot be subsumed under a documentary
theory embracing the entire Pentateuch, Tetrateuch or Hexateuch."[38]
Moreover, the features of the J source that were thought to tie it to the
(early) monarchical period—enthusiasm for kingship, state, cultus, etc.—
are not based on Gen 1–11, which is seldom taken into account in the
profiling of J.[39] This would mean, of course, that the Priestly narrative of
Gen 1:1–2:4a precedes in time the account of 2:4b–3:24, and the
function of the latter becomes that of explaining how evil insinuated
itself into the good creation. "The idea is that, in contrast with the
Mesopotamian mythic tradition, the emergence of evil is subsequent to
creation. Evil is not, so to speak, built into the cosmic order, as it is in
enuma elish."[40] Thus, according to Blenkinsopp, the second creation
narrative moves on from "the hieratic prose of P" and introduces "a more

---

36. See Wenham, *Genesis 1–15*, xxxvii–xlii; idem, "The Priority of P," *VT* 49
(1999): 240–58; E. Otto, "Die Paradieserzählung Genesis 2–3: Eine nachpriester-
schriftliche Lehrerzählung in ihrem religionshistorischen Kontext," in *"Jedes Ding
hat seine Zeit…": Studien zur israelitischen und altorientalischen Weisheit* (ed.
A. A. Diesel et al.; FS D. Michel; BZAW 241; Berlin: de Gruyter, 1996), 167–92;
K. Schmid, "Die Unteilbarkeit der Weisheit: Überlegungen zur sogenannten
Paradieserzählung Gen 2f. und ihrer theologischen Tendenz," *ZAW* 114 (2002): 21–
39 (23). At the same time, see the discussion in E. Blum, "Von Gottesunmittelbarkeit zu Gottähnlichkeit: Überlegungen zur theologischen Anthropologie
der Paradieserzählung," in *Gottes Nähe im Alten Testament* (ed. G. Eberhardt and
K. Liess; SBS 202; Stuttgart: Katholisches Bibelwerk, 2004), 9–29 (14–16).
37. J. Blenkinsopp, "A Post-exilic Lay Source in Genesis 1–11," in *Abschied
vom Jahwisten: die Komposition des Hexateuch in der jüngsten Diskussion* (ed. J. C.
Gertz, K. Schmid and M. Witte; BZAW 315; Berlin: de Gruyter, 2002), 49–61 (49).
See also Blenkinsopp's earlier essay, "P and J in Genesis 1:1–11:26: An Alternative
Hypothesis," in *Fortunate the Eyes that See: Essays in Honor of David Noel Freedman in Celebration of His Seventieth Birthday* (ed. A. B. Beck et al.; Grand Rapids:
Eerdmans, 1995), 1–15; cf. also Brett, *Genesis*, 29–30, already noted above.
38. Blenkinsopp, "A Post-exilic Lay Source," 49.
39. Ibid., 50.
40. Ibid., 54.

reflective and less optimistic assessment of the human condition."[41] And, in his concluding comments, Blenkinsopp returns to what he regards as the principal aim of the J "supplement": "to balance the optimism of P with a more sober and secular view of human existence as essentially problematic."[42]

The view that the second creation narrative is intended to counterbalance the first is also favoured by Jean-Louis Ska, in an essay published in 2008.[43] Ska suggests that Gen 2–3 is "more or less contemporaneous with Genesis 1,"[44] but he holds that the priestly account of creation was offset in chs. 2–3 by a vision of the world originating with the "people of the land" who remained in Judah during the exile: "To this account—an account which, in the end, justifies even for the most part the claims of the priests of Jerusalem who wanted to reorganize the people of Israel in the province of Yehud around the temple of Jerusalem—the 'people of the land' oppose a simpler account which demonstrates that the creator God established on the 'earth' a farmer, the ancestor of 'the people of the land'."[45]

This view of the relationship of the two Genesis creation narratives, in which the second responds to the first, suits well the emphasis within this essay on the restricted "paradisial" content, in the narrower utopian sense of "paradisial," of Gen 2–3. On this view, the account of Eden in ch. 2 can be more easily explained as transitional between the well-ordered universe of the first narrative and the "loss of Eden" as recounted in ch. 3. This, however, would be to attempt to underpin interpretation with an explanation of the relationship between the two narratives that has long been sidelined and has only more recently found advocacy among some Pentateuchal specialists. In fact, the scaled-down expectation of the Eden narrative in ch. 2 is evident even when it is read without reference to the sequel in ch. 3. It is not just in ch. 3 that disobedience supervenes and the negativities appear. The introduction of the tree of the knowledge of good and evil in 2:9 implies a dimension to the created world that is not suggested in ch. 1, while the prohibition and the warning of the

---

41. This, as Blenkinsopp notes (ibid., 59), is the opposite of the case argued by Martin Rose, viz., that P was written to offset J's pessimism about the human part in securing divine favour; see M. Rose, "La croissance du corpus historiographique de la bible – une proposition," *RTP* 118 (1986): 217–36 (232).

42. Blenkinsopp, "A Post-exilic Lay Source," 60.

43. J.-L. Ska, "Genesis 2–3: Some Fundamental Questions," in *Beyond Eden: The Biblical Story of Paradise (Genesis 2–3) and Its Reception History* (ed. K. Schmid and C. Riedweg; Tübingen: Mohr Siebeck, 2008), 1–27 (16–23).

44. Ibid., 20.

45. Ibid., 22.

penalty of death in 2:17 give some indication of what "evil" signifies in these contexts.[46] There are more positive features—the garden and its fruit, the river, the precious stones, the creation of the animals, Eve and the aetiology of marriage—but it is all quite restrained by comparison with later envisionings of paradise in Jewish and Christian writing. As we have noted, even the creator's walking in the garden in the cool of the day is mentioned only after the act of disobedience (3:8).

The absence of positive characterization of either Adam or Eve in Gen 2–3 is striking, and is perhaps most noticeable in ch. 3 where the couple, having been assured that their end is to return to the ground whence they had been taken, are denied access to the tree of life. Physical death may not be imminent, yet in Adam's sentence "to work the ground from which he was taken" (3:23) the echo of the earlier judgment-text is unmistakable: "until you return to the ground, for from it you were taken" (3:19). Nothing is said of life in any other dimension; there is no hint of a hope of "life with God" in the way of a number of Old Testament texts that take account of afterlife. And just as there is no hint of sublimity in the ending, so we are forced to acknowledge that there is little in what precedes that could be so described.

Commentators and other writers on the Old Testament have largely adjusted to this reality of the Genesis "Paradise," even though they may occasionally use the term in titles and headings for studies of Gen 2–3.[47] Sometimes they may be found comparing or contrasting the Eden of these chapters with the Eden references in the prophets, though these latter imply nothing beyond the luxuriance of the garden growth in Eden, whether in "the garden of the Lord" (Isa 51:3; cf. Gen 13:10) or "the garden of God" (Ezek 28:13; 31:9; cf. 36:35; Joel 2:3). The silence of Gen 2–3 on the subject of worship should, then, be interpreted in the light of this less-than-idealized recounting of "Paradise" in these chapters. They do not touch on worship, not even "unmediated worship."

It is a pleasure to pay tribute, by means of the foregoing essay and through the co-editing of this volume, to the very special contribution that Andrew Macintosh has made to the teaching of Hebrew in Cambridge and, in his publications, to the philological and exegetical study of the Judaeo-Christian Scriptures.

---

46. On the originality of both trees in the second creation narrative, see T. N. D. Mettinger, *The Eden Narrative: A Literary and Religio-historical Study of Genesis 2–3* (Winona Lake: Eisenbrauns, 2007), 124.

47. See the comments by Stordalen, *Echoes of Eden*, 250.

NOAH'S DRUNKENNESS, THE CURSE OF CANAAN, HAM'S CRIME, AND THE BLESSING OF SHEM AND JAPHETH (GENESIS 9:18–27)

John Day

Genesis 9:18–27, which tells of Noah's drunkenness, Ham's crime, the cursing of Canaan and the blessing of Shem and Japheth, is truly one of the strange stories of the Bible. Martin Luther called it "a silly and altogether unprofitable little story,"[1] and more recently John Gibson roundly declared: "The distasteful story of the curse of Canaan ought not to be in the Bible."[2] There was a time in the not so far distant history of the church when it was used by some as a biblical support for the oppression of the so-called Hamitic, black peoples of the world and against the abolition of slavery. The point has frequently been made, however, that the story does not in fact recount the cursing of Ham at all but rather of his son Canaan, thereby providing an aetiology of the subsequent subordination of the Canaanites to the Israelites. The process by which the cursing of Canaan got attached to Ham instead, and with such devastating effects, is a subject to which we shall return at the end of this study. Meanwhile, this short passage raises various other important questions of interpretation on which there is still no consensus. Thus, why is it that it is Canaan who is cursed by Noah when it is rather his father Ham who is allegedly guilty? What exactly is the nature of Ham's crime? What is the significance of the blessing of Japheth (alongside Shem) towards the end of the story? These are all questions which will be reconsidered here.

---

1. Martin Luther, *Luther's Works.* Vol. 2, *Lectures on Genesis Chapters 6–14* (ed. J. Pelikan; St. Louis: Concordia Publishing House, 1960), 166.
2. J. C. L. Gibson, *Genesis* (2 vols.; The Daily Study Bible; Edinburgh: The Saint Andrew Press; Philadelphia: Westminster, 1981), 1:201–2.

1. *What was Ham's Crime?*

On a surface reading Ham's crime was that he saw his drunken father
naked and, unlike his brothers, he merely talked about it and took no
action to rectify the situation. Because to a modern reader this sounds
more like a peccadillo than a major crime, a number of more serious
crimes have sometimes been suggested to account for Noah's curse. All
these alternative interpretations, however, involve reading into the text
what is simply not there. First there is the view that Ham's crime con-
sisted of castrating his father. This is attested in variant forms in a number
of rabbinic sources (*b. Sanh.* 70a; *Gen. Rab.* 36:7; implicit in *Targum
Pseudo-Jonathan* on Gen 9:24), though in modern times, so far as I can
see, it has been taken seriously only by Robert Graves and Raphael Patai,
who even speculated that the original castrating instrument was a
pruning-knife from Noah's vineyard![3] However, A. I. Baumgarten has
shown that the castration motif is not original but was developed to
explain certain features of the biblical text in the second century C.E.,
when it is first referred to by Theophilus of Antioch (*Ad Autolycum*
3.19), doubtless dependent on Jewish exegesis, with which he was much
familiar.[4] A different rabbinic view (*b. Sanh.* 70a) which has had rather
more support in modern times is that Ham sexually abused his father
Noah. Supporting this view are scholars such as A. Phillips, M. Nissinen
and R. A. J. Gagnon.[5] However, whereas Gagnon emphasizes the act as
one of homosexual rape, Nissinen sees it more as an expression of Ham's
hunger for power. An alternative view first put forward in modern times
is that Ham had heterosexual relations with Noah's wife. Those supporting the heterosexual understanding include F. W. Bassett, J. S. Bergsma
and S. W. Hahn.[6] Both the homosexual and heterosexual interpretations

---

3. R. Graves and R. Patai, *Hebrew Myths: The Book of Genesis* (London:
Cassell, 1963), 122–24. U. (M. D.) Cassuto, מנח עד אברהם (Jerusalem: Hebrew
University of Jerusalem, 1959), 102–4 (ET *A Commentary on the Book of Genesis*.
Vol. 2, *From Noah to Abraham* [trans. I. Abrahams; Jerusalem: Magnes, 1964],
150–53), rejects this view only after much hesitation.
4. A. I. Baumgarten, "Myth and Midrash: Genesis 9:20-29," in *Christianity,
Judaism and Other Greco-Roman Cults: Studies for Morton Smith at Sixty*. Vol. 3,
Judaism before 70 (ed. J. Neusner; SJLA 12; Leiden: Brill, 1975), 55–71.
5. A. Phillips, "Uncovering the Father's Skirt," *VT* 30 (1980): 38–43 (41);
M. Nissinen, *Homoeroticism in the Biblical World: A Historical Perspective* (trans.
K. Stjerna; Minneapolis: Fortress, 1998), 52–53; R. A. J. Gagnon, *The Bible and
Homosexual Practice: Texts and Hermeneutics* (Nashville: Abingdon, 2001), 63–71.
6. F. W. Bassett, "Noah's Nakedness and the Curse of Canaan: A Case of
Incest?," *VT* 21 (1971): 232–37; J. S. Bergsma and S. W. Hahn, "Noah's Nakedness
and the Curse on Canaan (Genesis 9:20-27)," *JBL* 124 (2005): 125–40.

are based on the assumption that the reference to seeing the nakedness of Noah is the same as that of uncovering Noah's nakedness, that is, having sexual intercourse. However, the two expressions are not identical and there is just one place in the Hebrew Bible where they appear to be identical in meaning, namely Lev 20:17. But this cannot be the case in Gen 9, since the fact that Shem and Japheth have to walk backwards so as not to see Noah's nakedness makes clear that it is a case of literal seeing. Faced with this problem, Bassett is forced to conclude that the passage about the brothers walking backwards must be a later gloss, but this serves only to highlight the weakness of his case. In fact, not only the heterosexual but also the homosexual and castration interpretations of Ham's deed run counter to the natural interpretation of the text, which clearly implies that Ham's seeing of Noah's nakedness must be a case of literal seeing, since Shem and Japheth are said to have walked backwards in order not to see their naked father. Also the further objection may be made that it was not in the nature of J to be overly coy in his descriptions of sexual relations. Finally, a curious view first put forward in modern times by H. Hirsch Cohen should be noted: this supposes that Ham saw Noah naked while the latter was having sexual intercourse with his wife and that Ham thereby acquired his potency.[7] Consequently, Noah was unable to curse him, so he cursed Canaan instead in order that his potency should not get transferred to him. However, this view, which seems far-fetched, has gained no following.

So we are left with the literal interpretation, which implies that Ham saw his father's nakedness but that this involved a serious lapse of filial obligation on Ham's part. This obligation is clearly spelled out in the Ugaritic Aqhat epic, where one of the duties of the son towards his father is specifically stated to be "to take his hand in drunkenness, to bear him up [when] full of wine" (*KTU* 1.17.I.30–31). Deutero-Isaiah also refers to this obligation when he says of Jerusalem, drunk with the wrath of God, "There is no one to guide her among all the sons she has borne; there is no one to take her by the hand among all the sons she has brought up" (Isa 51:18). So what the story in Genesis illustrates is not just a peccadillo but a serious failure of filial obligation on Ham's part.

2. *Why was Canaan Cursed rather than Ham?*

The first question that puzzles the attentive reader is why it should be Canaan who was cursed by Noah when it was rather his father, Ham,

---

7. H. Hirsch Cohen, *The Drunkenness of Noah* (Tuscaloosa: University of Alabama Press, 1974), 13–30.

who was guilty of seeing him naked, a problem already noted in antiquity, for example, by Philo of Alexandria, *Quaestiones in Genesim* 2.77. Some explanations are bound up with rabbinic and other interpretations of the story that we have already rejected above. Thus, the view that Ham had sexual intercourse with Noah's wife seeks to explain the cursing of Canaan on the basis that he was the offspring of that vile relationship. However, the text suggests that Canaan was already in existence at the time of the curse in the immediate aftermath of Noah's drunkenness (Gen 9:24–25). Again, the view that Ham castrated Noah sought to explain the cursing of Canaan on the basis that the latter was Ham's fourth son, and so this was fitting retribution for Noah himself having been made unable to beget a fourth son. Further, the notion found in some rabbinic sources that Canaan himself castrated Noah prior to Ham's seeing his nakedness (*Pirqe R. El.* 23) is likewise unfounded in the text. According to another ingenious rabbinic explanation attributed to Rabbi Judah in *Gen. Rab.* 36:7, Ham could not be cursed because God had previously blessed him (alongside his brothers and father) in Gen 9:1, and consequently his son Canaan was cursed instead. Interestingly, this interpretation is attested even earlier at Qumran in 4Q252 (4Q *Pesher Genesis*[a]) 1.2.6–7. However, this will not convince a modern critical scholar, since Gen 9:1 is from P and Gen 9:18–27 is from J.

Rather, the old critical arguments that various tensions in the text indicate that it was originally Canaan who was guilty of seeing his father naked, thereby meriting the curse, look extremely convincing.[8] First, there is the important point that in one of the poetic verses (Gen 9:25) it is Canaan rather than Ham who is declared to be the brother of Shem and Japheth. Secondly, in Gen 9:24 the one who sees Noah's nakedness is described as "his youngest son,"[9] which contradicts the impression we receive from the constant references to "Shem, Ham and Japheth" elsewhere, and suggests that Ham was the middle son. Thirdly, it is highly odd that Canaan alone should be cursed, and not Ham directly at all.

---

8. E.g. J. Wellhausen, "Die Composition des Hexateuchs," *Jahrbücher für Deutsche Theologie* 21 (1876): 392–450 (403), subsequently taken up in idem, *Die Composition des Hexateuchs und der historischen Bücher des Alten Testaments* (3d ed.; Berlin: G. Reimer, 1899), 12–13; J. Skinner, *A Critical and Exegetical Commentary on Genesis* (ICC; Edinburgh: T. & T. Clark, 1912), 182; G. von Rad, *Das erste Buch Mose: Genesis* (5th ed.; ATD 2.4; Göttingen: Vandenhoeck & Ruprecht, 1958), 112 (ET *Genesis* [trans. J. H. Marks; 2d ed.; OTL; London: SCM, 1963], 131–32).

9. It has occasionally been suggested that one could circumvent this problem by translating בנו הקטן as "his younger son," but this does not correspond with Hebrew usage.

Although one might try to explain away each of these points individually by saying that the word "brother" is used in a loose sense, that the names "Shem, Ham and Japheth" are not in strict order of age, and that Ham and his Canaanite descendants are closely identified, to explain away all three points simultaneously does seem highly forced. It seems far more natural to suppose that behind our current story there was an earlier tradition according to which the three sons were Shem, Japheth and Canaan, with Canaan being the youngest and the one who saw his father's nakedness. This alternative tradition has been imperfectly incorporated into a narrative in which Noah's three sons are now Shem, Ham and Japheth. We should therefore conclude that underlying our text was an earlier version that spoke about "Canaan" rather than "Ham, the father of Canaan" (cf. Gen 9:18, 22). However, in the final form of the text it is Ham who sees Noah's nakedness, not Canaan, so the redactor who put the text together as we now have it, admittedly not too cleverly, presumably had some view on the matter. Most probably, the final redactor simply envisaged Ham as being punished through his Canaanite descendants.

3. *The Blessing of Shem*

In Gen 9:26 we have Noah's blessing of Shem. It is generally accepted that Shem symbolizes Israel, which is supported by the fact that Shem is said to be the father of all the children of Eber (Gen 10:21), the eponymous ancestor of the Hebrews (עבר, Eber, being doubtless a back projection from עברי, "Hebrew"). It is further reinforced by the fact that this verse speaks of YHWH as Shem's God, in contrast to the next verse, where the deity is spoken of merely as Elohim in connection with Japheth.[10] As is widely agreed, the blessing of Shem, which speaks of Canaan's enslavement, clearly provides an aetiology of Israel's enslavement of the Canaanites in the wake of the settlement and rise of the United Monarchy (cf. Josh 9:27; Judg 1:28, 30, 33; 1 Kgs 9:20–21).

However, while there is general agreement as to the interpretation, there is some disagreement among scholars regarding the precise translation of the verse. As it stands Gen 9:26 does not directly speak of the blessing of Shem but reads, "Blessed be the Lord God of Shem; and let Canaan be his slave." This reading is universally followed in our Hebrew

---

10. This is comparable to the deliberate use of different divine names in the books of Jonah and Job. See J. Day, "Problems in the Interpretation of the Book of Jonah," in *In Quest of the Past: Studies on Israelite Religion, Literature and Prophetism* (ed. A. S. van der Woude; OTS 26; Leiden: Brill, 1990), 32–47 (43–44).

manuscripts as well as being presupposed in all the ancient versions. It is thus the traditional rendering (cf. AV, RV), and is still followed in a number of modern translations (NAB, NIV, JB, NJB), and defended by some modern scholars, for example, G. von Rad and W. Zimmerli.[11] However, at first sight there appears to be a problem here in that the context leads one to expect that it will be Shem who is to be blessed, not the God of Shem, in keeping with the parallel blessing of Japheth and curse of Canaan (vv. 25, 27). Initially the simplest way to get round this problem might be to make a slight emendation of the MT, reading אֱלֹהַי for אֱלֹהֵי, and rendering "Blessed by the Lord *my God* be Shem" (so RSV, NRSV). However, apart from this lacking any textual support in the ancient versions or Hebrew manuscripts, it needs to be noted that a perusal of other Old Testament passages involving "blessed" (ברוך) indicates that the name of the person being blessed regularly follows immediately after the word "blessed," while the one by whom one is blessed should be indicated by the preposition ל. These observations would similarly rule out emending to read "Blessed of the Lord be *the tents* (אהלי) of Shem..." (cf. the phrase "tents of Shem" in the next verse). The NEB and REB diverge further from the MT by additionally emending the first word ברוך to an imperative, "Bless (בָּרֵךְ), O Lord, the tents of Shem." But without any versional support this seems too speculative, and the very fact that the previous sentence started with the word "Cursed" makes it natural to retain "Blessed" here. These considerations tend to favour the retention of the Masoretic text. In support we may compare a frequently overlooked passage in one of the tribal blessings in the Blessing of Moses in Deut 33, where God is similarly blessed rather than the tribe directly. This is Deut 33:20, where we read "Blessed is the one who enlarges Gad!," that is, God.[12] This further strengthens the plausibility of accepting the Masoretic text in Gen 9:26, where the implication must surely be that if Shem's God YHWH is blessed, so too is Shem.[13]

11. Von Rad, *Das erste Buch Mose: Genesis*, 114 (ET *Genesis*, 133); W. Zimmerli, *1. Mose 1–11* (3d ed.; Zürcher Bibelkommentare; Zurich: Zwingli, 1967), 355–56.

12. Noted by J. H. Tigay, *Deuteronomy* (JPSTC; Philadelphia: Jewish Publication Society, 1996), 331. The NRSV translates "Blessed be the *enlargement* of Gad," and NEB and REB more paraphrastically render, "Blessed be Gad, *in his wide domain*," but these are not natural renderings of the hiphil participle מרחיב, lit. "the one who enlarges."

13. Many translators in earlier centuries rendered עבד למו as "their slave" rather than "his slave" both here and in v. 27; cf. RV margin. However, while the expression למו is capable of meaning both "to him" and "to them," the context here

4. *The Blessing of Japheth*

Following the curse of Canaan and blessing of Shem we find in Gen 9:27 Noah's blessing of Japheth, with its evident word-play: "May God make space (יַפְתְּ) for Japheth (יֶפֶת), and let him live in the tents of Shem; and let Canaan be his slave." The blessing of Shem is not surprising, since this figure was the ancestor of the Hebrews. There is, however, no unanimity on the subject of the blessing of Japheth. Some older views are now generally rejected since they lack adequate support, and are consequently only rarely discussed by recent commentators. Apart from the old rabbinic (e.g. *Targum Pseudo-Jonathan*) and patristic interpretation that it refers to the conversion of the gentiles,[14] these include the view that Japheth denotes the Phoenicians,[15] who are clearly inappropriate since they were Canaanites, Sidon being a son of Canaan in Gen 10:15, whereas Japheth is explicitly contrasted with Canaan; that it refers to the Hittites,[16] though they too are regarded in the Old Testament as being closely bound up with the Canaanite population, Heth being a son of Canaan in Gen 10:15; or that it signifies the Assyrians or Babylonians,[17] though they did not live in the area denoted by Japheth.

Some commentators nowadays find it too difficult to come to a conclusion about Japheth,[18] while a few do not even bother to discuss the matter.[19] Of views which are currently held, two minority ones may be noted. First, W. C. Kaiser and J. J. Scullion still maintain the view earlier

suggests the former, since Gen 9:25 states that Canaan will be a slave to each of his brothers, not to God as well.

14. Still accepted in part by S. R. Driver, *The Book of Genesis* (Westminster Commentaries; London: Methuen, 1904), 111.

15. K. Budde, *Die biblische Urgeschichte (Gen 1–12,5)* (Giessen: J. Ricker, 1883), 330–65.

16. H. Gunkel, *Genesis* (Göttinger Handkommentar zum Alten Testament 1.1; Göttingen: Vandenhoeck & Ruprecht, 1910), 83 (ET *Genesis* [trans. M. E. Biddle; Macon, GA: Mercer University Press, 1997], 84).

17. J. Hoftijzer, "Some Remarks on the Tale of Noah's Drunkenness," in B. Gemser et al., *Studies on the Book of Genesis* (OTS 12; Leiden: Brill, 1958), 22–27 (25–26 n. 7). Hoftijzer also concedes that the reference might be to the Philistines, but regards a reference to the Assyrians, or more likely the Babylonians, as most probable.

18. C. Westermann, *Genesis 1–11* (BKAT 1.1; Neukirchen–Vluyn: Neukirchener, 1974), 660 (ET *Genesis 1–11: A Commentary* [trans. J. J. Scullion; London: SPCK, 1984], 493); G. J. Wenham, *Genesis 1–15* (WBC 1; Waco: Word, 1987), 202–3.

19. N. M. Sarna, *Genesis* (JPSTC; Philadelphia: Jewish Publication Society, 1989), 67; B. T. Arnold, *Genesis* (New Cambridge Bible Commentary; New York: Cambridge University Press, 2009), 112–13.

attested in *Jub.* 8:18, Philo of Alexandria and certain rabbinic sources
(e.g. *Targum Neofiti 1* and *Targum Onqelos*; *Gen. Rab.* 36:8; *b. Yoma*
10a; Rashi; Ibn Ezra) that the one dwelling in the tents of Shem is not
Japheth at all but rather God.[20] This, however, does not seem a natural
interpretation, as it is difficult to understand how God's dwelling in the
tents of Shem would constitute a blessing on Japheth, and since a wish is
expressed for Japheth to expand, it makes sense that it is Japheth who is
to dwell in the tents of Shem. Secondly, Van Seters sees here a very late
Hellenistic textual expansion referring to the Greeks.[21] However, the
existence of such a late gloss in the Pentateuch would be surprising;
Num 24:24 (referring to ships from Kittim coming to afflict the Near
East), which Van Seters compares, more naturally refers to the Philistines than the Greeks, since Alexander the Great did not come by ship,
whereas the Philistines did, and the overall context of Num 24:17–24
concerns the conquests of the United Monarchy, so a reference to the
Philistines is only to be expected in the original text. (On this passage,
see more below.) Moreover, Gen 9:25–27 speaks of Canaan serving his
brothers, which most naturally implies joint rule over Canaan by Shem
and Japheth, whereas the Greeks did not share rule over Canaan with
Israel but rather conquered Israel.[22]

When a confident view is expressed nowadays it is usually that
Japheth represents the Philistines.[23] This makes sense, since Japheth

20. W. C. Kaiser, *Toward an Old Testament Theology* (Grand Rapids: Zonder-
van, 1978), 37–39, 81–82; J. J. Scullion, *Genesis: A Commentary for Students,
Teachers, and Preachers* (Old Testament Studies 6; Collegeville: Liturgical [A
Michael Glazier Book], 1992), 86.

21. J. Van Seters, *Prologue to History: The Yahwist as Historian in Genesis*
(Louisville: Westminster John Knox, 1992), 179, 186 n. 22. Further, Van Seters
speculatively thinks that Noah's words originally related only to Eber and Canaan,
who were subsequently replaced by Shem and Ham. A. Bertholet, *Die Stellung der
Israeliten und der Juden zu den Fremden* (Freiburg i.B.: J. C. B. Mohr [Paul
Siebeck], 1896), 76–77, 198, and J. Herrmann, "Zu Gen 9 18-27," *ZAW* 30 (1910):
127–31, similarly saw the blessing of Japheth as a later addition and maintained that
the story originally concerned only Shem and Canaan.

22. Presumably Van Seters would maintain that Canaan's serving of Japheth
followed on afterwards and replaced his serving of Shem, but this is not the most
obvious reading of the biblical text.

23. This view appears to go back to Wellhausen, "Die Composition des Hexateuchs," 403, subsequently taken up in *Die Composition des Hexateuchs*, 13;
E. Meyer, *Geschichte des Alterthums. Band 1* (1st ed.; Stuttgart: J. G. Cotta, 1884),
214 n. 1 (tentatively), and idem, *Die Israeliten und ihre Nachbarstämme* (Halle:
Max Niemeyer, 1906), 221 (more confidently). More recently, this view has been
followed by von Rad, *Das erste Buch Mose: Genesis*, 114–15 (ET *Genesis*, 134–35);

clearly denotes the Mediterranean, especially island, nations, in addition to certain parts of western Asia, and it is difficult to envisage any other people from this area apart from the Philistines (or associated Sea Peoples) who shared rule with the Israelites over the Canaanites, which is what Gen 9 appears to have in mind. Although not dependent on it, this view also coheres with the fact that the name Japheth, ancestor of the Mediterranean nations and islands, is plausibly related to that of the Greek mythological Titan called Iapetos,[24] who was the ancestor (great-grandfather) of Hellen, the father of the Hellenic peoples. Interestingly, Japheth was the son of the biblical flood hero, Noah, and Iapetos was the grandfather of the Greek flood hero, Deucalion. (The Greek flood story has clear Near Eastern roots.)

However, so far as I am aware, no one hitherto has succeeded in dealing with two objections to which the Philistine interpretation has sometimes been subject. First, there is the question why the Philistines should be represented as descended from Japheth, when Gen 10:14 attributes them (and Caphtor, their place of origin) to Ham. In response it may be noted that the reference to the Philistines coming from Caphtor in Gen 10:14 is a later gloss (as its current misplacing following Casluhim shows).[25] Moreover, in Num 24:24—which is similarly from

E. A. Speiser, *Genesis* (AB 1; New York: Doubleday, 1964), 62–63; Zimmerli, *1. Mose 1–11*, 359. Similarly, D. Neiman, "The Date and Circumstances of the Cursing of Canaan," in *Biblical Motifs: Origins and Transformations* (ed. A. Altmann; Cambridge, Mass.: Harvard University Press, 1966), 113–34, though he relates the text to the thirteenth or twelfth century B.C.E.; and A. P. Ross, "The Curse of Canaan," *BSac* 137 (1980): 223–40 (237), and V. P. Hamilton, *The Book of Genesis Chapters 1–17* (NICOT; Grand Rapids: Eerdmans, 1990), 325–27, two conservative scholars who see this as prophetic rather than aetiological.

24. This view is found already in writers from the Renaissance period, and has been quite frequently followed in modern times, by, e.g., D. Neiman, "The Two Genealogies of Japhet," in *Orient and Occident: Essays Presented to Cyrus H. Gordon on the Occasion of His Sixty-Fifth Birthday* (ed. H. A. Hoffner; AOAT 22; Kevelaer: Verlag Butzon & Bercker; Neukirchen–Vluyn: Neukirchener, 1973), 119–26 (123–25). However, M. L. West, *The East Face of Helicon: West Asiatic Elements in Greek Poetry and Myth* (Oxford: Clarendon, 1997), 289–90, feels somewhat sceptical, as he does not see much resemblance in role, in spite of the admitted similarity of name. However, since Iapetos was the ancestor of the Hellenic peoples, there is a similarity here to Japheth.

25. However, G. A. Rendsburg in "Gen 10:13-14: An Authentic Tradition concerning the Origin of the Philistines," *JNWSL* 13 (1987): 89–96, has argued that the MT's reference to the Philistines coming from Casluhim is authentic. He understands Casluhim to refer to Lower Egypt (with Naphtuhim referring to Memphites [Middle Egypt] and Pathrusim, as is generally agreed, alluding to Upper Egypt), and

the Yahwist,[26] and a part of the oracles of Balaam alluding to the defeat of Israel's enemies at the time of the United Monarchy—what appear to be the Philistines come in ships from Kittim (Cyprus) to afflict the Near East prior to their defeat.[27] Now according to Gen 10:4 Kittim was regarded as a son of Japheth. That J in Gen 9 should designate the Philistines by the name Japheth thus makes sense in the light of J's association of Kittim, a son of Japheth, with the Philistines in Num 24:24. There is, moreover, some archaeological evidence that the Philistines came to Canaan via Cyprus (Kittim).[28] For reasons already noted above, this is preferable to the view of H. Rouillard and J. Van Seters that the reference in Num 24:24 to ships coming from Kittim is a late Hellenistic gloss alluding to Alexander the Great.[29] Secondly, it has sometimes

claims that the Philistines originally came from there before moving on to Crete. However, all this seems very speculative. Moreover, it is noteworthy that when we delete the reference to the Philistines, Gen 10 has precisely 70 nations, which is what we should expect in view of the Jewish concept of 70 nations paralleling the 70 sons of God (Deut 32:8).

26. The traditional ascription of the Balaam oracles to the J source has much to be said for it. Note, for example, that both the Balaam oracles and the J source in Genesis have the common anticipation of Israel's becoming a great nation (Gen 12:1–3; Num 24:17–24), both refer to Seth (Sheth) and Cain (Kain) in close proximity (Gen 4:1–17, 24, 25–26; Num 24:17, 22), and it is only in Gen 3 and Num 22 that the Hebrew Bible refers to speaking animals (the Eden serpent and Balaam's ass).

27. In Num 24:24, prior to the demise of their power ("and he also shall perish for ever"), the ships coming from Kittim "shall afflict Asshur and Eber." Eber clearly has Israel in mind, but how can the Philistines be envisaged as afflicting Assyria? Here I would note that Rameses III states with regard to the invasion of the Sea Peoples that "No land could stand before their arms, from Hatti, Kode, Carchemish, Arzawa, and Alashiya on" (*ANET*, 262), some of which could be construed as falling within the Assyrian sphere of influence. Similarly, recently discovered texts from Tell Tayinat and Aleppo indicate that there was a powerful kingdom of "Palastin" with Aegean connections in northern Syria during the Early Iron Age. See J. D. Hawkins, "Cilicia, Amuq, and Aleppo: New Light on a Dark Age," *Near Eastern Archaeology* 72 (2009): 164–73; T. P. Harrison, "Neo-Hittites in the 'Land of Palastin': Renewed Investigations on the Plain of Antioch," *Near Eastern Archaeology* 72 (2009): 174–89.

28. Cf. A. Killebrew, *Biblical Peoples and Ethnicity: An Archaeological Study of Egyptians, Canaanites, Philistines, and Early Israel 1300–1100 B.C.E.* (SBLABS 9; Leiden: Brill, 2005), 197–245; A. Yasur-Landau, *The Philistines and Aegean Migrations at the End of the Late Bronze Age* (Cambridge: Cambridge University Press, 2010), 334, 339.

29. H. Rouillard, *La péricope de Balaam (Nombres 22–24): La prose et les oracles* (Etudes bibliques; Paris: Gabalda, 1985), 462–64; cf. p. 458; Van Seters, *Prologue to History*, 186 n. 22. Cf. P.-E. Dion, "Les *KTYM* de Tel Arad: Grecs ou

been regarded as unlikely that an Israelite writer would represent the Philistines as being the object of a divine blessing. However, what at first might seem a surprisingly positive view of the role of the Philistines is not unparalleled in the Hebrew Bible, for Amos 9:7 similarly presupposes the belief that God was responsible for bringing the Philistines to Canaan (Amos being from a rather similar date to J, in my view).[30] Moreover, as Zimmerli and von Rad have noted, the blessing of Japheth makes excellent sense as an explanation of why the Israelites had not taken control of all the Promised Land, some being left for the Philistines.[31] Noah's words imply that this had been God's intention from the beginning. Thus we remarkably have here, in this seemingly unedifying story, one of the most enlightened and tolerant attitudes towards the Philistines in the whole of the Old Testament.

5. A History of Misinterpretation: From the Cursing of Canaan to the Cursing of Ham

As noted earlier, the story of the curse of Canaan later got misinterpreted as a curse on Ham, and subsequently on the so-called Hamitic nations of the world, with devastating effects for black people. How exactly did this come about? The beginnings of this process have been traced in detail by David Goldenberg.[32] He is able to show that—in spite of the clear statement of the Bible to the contrary—already in the first millennium C.E. various Jewish rabbinic, patristic Christian and Muslim sources can be found claiming that Noah's curse affected Ham and/or all Ham's children, and not just Canaan. The sheer unreasonableness of the biblical story in which Ham is the guilty party but his son Canaan is condemned, as well as understandable misremembering of the story, contributed to the idea that it was Ham and/or all Ham's children who were cursed. Further, the Near Eastern environment in which black people were often

Phéniciens?," *RB* (1992): 70–97 (94–96), who sees this passage as late but rejects a connection with Alexander.

30. In the J narrative about Nimrod in Gen 10:12, Calah (modern Nimrud) appears to be called "the great city." It was in fact from c. 880–c. 700 B.C.E. that Calah was the capital of Assyria. This might suggest that the date of J is most likely in the ninth or eighth century. So far as I can see, this point has not previously been noted; I intend to discuss it in more detail in another place.

31. Von Rad, *Das erste Buch Mose: Genesis*, 115 (ET *Genesis*, 134–35); Zimmerli, *1. Mose 1–11*, 361–62.

32. D. M. Goldenberg, *The Curse of Ham: Race and Slavery in Early Judaism, Christianity, and Islam* (Princeton: Princeton University Press, 2003), 141–77.

slaves also tended to encourage the view that it was black people who had been cursed. The notion that Ham himself was black (as one of his sons, Cush, certainly was), though something not implied in the Bible, was encouraged by a false etymology according to which the name Ham was associated either with the Hebrew root חמם, "to be hot," or with חום, "to be dark, black."[33] This is already reflected in two rabbinic passages, one in the Palestinian Talmud (*y. Ta'an.* 1.6, 64d), which states that "Ham went forth darkened (מפוחם)," and another in the Babylonian Talmud (*b. Sanh.* 108b), which declares more vaguely that "Ham was punished in his skin." However, it should be noted that these two rabbinic statements are totally unrelated to Noah's curse in Gen 9 but represent rather a punishment for Ham's disobedience in having had sexual relations in the Ark.

The first explicit connection between Noah's alleged curse of Ham and black slavery is found in Islamic sources from the seventh century onwards, a period which witnessed the Muslim conquest of parts of Africa when native peoples were enslaved by Arabs. We find this connection expressed, for example, by 'Aṭā' (died 732/3) and an anonymous source, both quoted by Ṭabarī (died 923), in a tenth- or eleventh-century work called *Akbār al-zamān*, and by "genealogists" cited by Ibn Khaldūn (died 1406).[34] In some Islamic sources Canaan himself is envisaged as the ancestor of black people, a view perhaps influenced by an eastern Christian work, *The Cave of Treasures*, a book originally compiled in Syriac in the third or fourth century C.E. in which the connection between black people and slavery is implicit, and becoming more explicit in later recensions.[35]

During the later mediaeval period Christian interpretation understood the curse of Canaan as providing an aetiology of serfdom, rather than anything with racial overtones.[36] However, during the sixteenth and

---

33. Although the precise scientific etymology of the name Ham is unknown, both these proposed etymologies are certainly wrong. Goldenberg notes that the name Ham started with *ḥ*, as is shown by its representation in the LXX by the letter χ, whereas the roots "to be hot" and "to be dark, black" both have *h*. Incidentally, Egyptian *km(t)*, "black," an Egyptian term for Egypt sometimes regarded as the etymology of Ham in more recent times, similarly has the wrong first letter (Egyptian *k* is always represented in Hebrew by kaph or qoph). On all this, see Goldenberg, *The Curse of Ham*, 144–49.

34. For full details, see ibid., 170, with pp. 350–51 nn. 10–17.

35. See ibid., 172–74.

36. See D. M. Whitford, *The Curse of Ham in the Early Modern Era: The Bible and the Justifications for Slavery* (St. Andrews Studies in Reformation History; Farnham: Ashgate, 2009), 19–42.

especially the seventeenth century Canaan essentially dropped out of the story and it started to become common among Christian biblical commentators and preachers for Noah's curse to be understood as being uttered directly against Ham, who was understood to be black.[37] Coming alongside the development of the African slave trade, this interpretation was to have devastating consequences. Thomas Newton (1704–1782), an English cleric and biblical scholar who eventually became Bishop of Bristol, went so far as to emend the Hebrew text of Gen 9:25 so as to read "Ham, the father of Canaan" rather than "Canaan" as the object of Noah's curse. This was in the first volume of his *Dissertations on the Prophecies*, published in 1754. In support of his view he appealed to the Arabic version of the Bible, certain Septuagint manuscripts, the alleged opinion of the sixteenth-century scholar François Vatablus, and Hebrew metre, but his arguments were weak.[38] Nevertheless, Newton's work was one of those appealed to by Americans in the southern states seeking to defend black slavery. It was indeed in the nineteenth century, up to the time of the Civil War, that the notion of Noah's curse of Ham became particularly prominent and was highly influential in the American south in providing an apparent scriptural basis for the enslavement of black people.[39] This continued even after the Civil War, as, for example, in the case of Benjamin M. Palmer, a prominent Presbyterian pastor in New Orleans from 1856 to 1902, who proclaimed throughout this period the mental and moral degradation of Ham's black progeny and their divine sentence to perpetual servitude.[40] Over against this, those in favour of the abolition of slavery argued that the use of Gen 9 in this connection was unjustified, noting among other things that the curse was directed at Canaan rather than Ham, and that it was Cush, not Canaan, who was the ancestor of the black African nations. Moreover, it was pointed out that Nimrod, a grandson of Ham, was a mighty man, and clearly not cursed! However, even in the twentieth century the so-called curse of Ham

37. See ibid., 77–104.

38. On Newton and the curse of Ham, see ibid., 140–69, who highlights the weaknesses in Newton's arguments on pp. 150–60.

39. On this see especially S. R. Haynes, *Noah's Curse: The Biblical Justification of American Slavery* (Religion in America Series; New York: Oxford University Press, 2001). Other studies include T. V. Peterson, *Ham and Japheth: The Mythic World of Whites in the Antebellum South* (ATLA Monograph Series 12; Metuchen, N.J., and London: The Scarecrow Press and the American Theological Library Association, 1978), and S. A. Johnson, *The Myth of Ham in Nineteenth-Century American Christianity: Race, Heathens, and the People of God* (New York: Palgrave Macmillan, 2004).

40. On Palmer, see Haynes, *Noah's Curse*, 125–60.

continued to be appealed to by American segregationists, as well as by some Boers and the Dutch Reformed Church in South Africa in justification of apartheid. All this goes to show how people are capable of finding support in the Bible for anything they fancy, and it also highlights the necessity for responsible biblical exegesis.

It is a great pleasure to dedicate this essay to Andrew Macintosh, whom I have known since 1967 when he became my very first Hebrew teacher. As a lecturer he is lively and entertaining, while as a scholar his mastery of the mediaeval Jewish commentators surpasses that of other *Alttestamentler* known to me.

DIVIDING UP THE PENTATEUCH:
SOME REMARKS ON THE JEWISH TRADITION*

Graham Davies

The division of the biblical text into sections is an ancient and important feature of both the textual tradition and biblical commentary. In the latter case it may serve simply for convenience, to create a manageable extent of text for closer examination, or it may be a vital stage in exegetical method, as in studies based on form criticism and other types of literary analysis. Recently a new name, "Delimitation Criticism," has been coined for the study of such divisions and it has become a popular focus of contemporary scholarship.[1] There is the hope that traditional markers of the structure of a text may not only shed light on the history of biblical study and interpretation but may be useful in modern scholarly interpretation of the Bible and even in establishing some new understanding of the intentions of the original authors and compilers of the biblical books.

It is a well known fact that at certain points the chapter-divisions of the Hebrew and most English texts of the Old Testament differ, and modern English translations commonly indicate where such variations occur.[2] As a result the numbering of individual verses differs until a new

*   I am indebted to Professor Stefan Reif of the University of Cambridge and to Dr. Noam Mizrahi of Tel Aviv University for their advice, and to Mr. Mark Statham, Librarian of Gonville and Caius College, Cambridge, and the staff of the Cambridge University Library and the British Library for facilitating access to items in their collections, during the preparation of this essay. I offer it to a dear friend and colleague of many years as a tribute to his daunting standards of scholarship and his love for the Hebrew language, which he has so conscientiously transmitted to both the scholarly world and his many pupils.
  1.   See M. C. A. Korpel and J. M. Oesch, eds., *Delimitation Criticism* (Pericope 1; Assen: Van Gorcum, 2003), and subsequent volumes in this series.
  2.   The 29 instances outside the Pentateuch are at the beginnings of the following chapters: 1 Sam 21; 24; 2 Sam 19; 1 Kgs 5; 2 Kgs 12; Isa 9; 64; Jer 9; Ezek 21; Hos 2; 12; 14; Joel 3; 4; Jonah 2; Mic 5; Nah 2; Zech 2; Mal 4; Job 41; Song 7; Qoh 5; Dan 4; 6; Neh 4; 10; 1 Chr 6; 2 Chr 2; 14. German Bibles follow the "Hebrew" divisions, as understandably do editions of the Targums and the NJPS among English

chapter begins. There are ten such cases in the Pentateuch, and details of these are tabulated below.

Table 1. *Differences between Hebrew and English Chapter-Divisions in the Pentateuch (all verse numbers are according to the Hebrew)*

Hebrew chapter beginning	English chapter beginning	Traditional support for Hebrew chapter beginning	Traditional support for English chapter beginning
Gen 32:1	Gen 32:2		
Exod 8:1	Exod 7:26		Petuchah
Exod 22:1	Exod 21:37		Setumah
Lev 6:1	Lev 5:20	Petuchah	Petuchah
Num 17:1	Num 17:16	Petuchah *or* Setumah	Petuchah
Num 26:1	Num 25:19	Petuchah	
Num 30:1	Num 30:2		Petuchah
Deut 13:1	Deut 13:2		Petuchah
Deut 23:1	Deut 23:2	Setumah	Setumah
Deut 29:1	Deut 28:69	Petuchah	Setumah

Since the Hebrew is the original language and the "English" chapter-divisions occur only in translations, it is tempting to suppose that the Hebrew chapter-divisions carry the greater authority where the two differ. At the same time, the fact that the beginnings of only ten chapters out of the 187 into which the Pentateuch is divided actually diverge means that the other 177 (i.e. some 95%) agree, and this can hardly be a coincidence: there must be some historical connection between the two systems. The "English" chapter-division has been traced back to the work of Stephen Langton in the thirteenth century on the Latin text of the Vulgate. But the standard textbooks provide no information about the origin of the "Hebrew" system, with its variations. It will be the task of this essay to try to fill this gap on the basis of the examples in the Penta-teuch. When, why and on what basis were the Hebrew chapter-divisions introduced into the text? The first conclusion must be that they are not of great antiquity, since they did not appear in the great early mediaeval manuscripts of the Hebrew Bible, such as the Leningrad Codex B19a on

versions. The "English" pattern is based on that of the Latin Vulgate (see further below), but it diverges at a few points, mainly in the numbering of the Psalms but also at Num 30, where the Hebrew and Vulgate divisions agree (William Tyndale's translation of the Pentateuch [1530] already has the "English" division here). So there are only nine points of divergence between the Vulgate and the Hebrew in the Pentateuch.

which the third edition of R. Kittel's *Biblia Hebraica* and its successor *Biblia Hebraica Stuttgartensia* were based. There the text is divided up in the traditional ways that will be briefly explored at the end of this essay. These of course included the division of the text into verses which was reflected in, and probably the basis for, the Masoretes' system of accentuation.

The evidence shows that the distinctive Hebrew chapter-divisions were first given wide circulation in printed Hebrew Bibles of the sixteenth century.[3] The first Bible to include them was Bomberg's Second Rabbinic Bible of 1524–25, and there was, as we shall see in a moment, a good reason for this. The earliest printed Hebrew Bibles had only the Masoretic divisions of the text. A change began to appear in the Madrid (Complutensian) Polyglot of 1514–17, where the Masoretic section-divisions were discarded and the "English" chapter-numbers appeared in the columns of the Greek and Latin translations and in the margin of the Hebrew. In Bomberg's First Rabbinic Bible of 1517, whose production was overseen by Felix Pratensis, the Masoretic divisions were retained but chapter-divisions corresponding to the "English" system were also included: in other words, the "Hebrew" variations did not yet appear.[4] From then on, the combination of Masoretic divisions and chapter numbers became standard practice, as it has continued to the present day.[5] But from 1524–25 the distinctive "Hebrew" divisions gradually began to appear. In the first printing of the Second Rabbinic Bible eight of the ten variations in the Pentateuch are present in the text: at the beginning of Gen 32 the division agrees with the "English" and at the beginning of Deut 23 there is no chapter mark at all.[6] The bilingual Hebrew–Latin edition of Sebastian Münster (1534–35) continued to use the "English"

3.   A useful account of the introduction of chapter-divisions into the Hebrew text is given by C. D. Ginsburg, *Introduction to the Massoretico-Critical Edition of the Hebrew Bible* (London: Trinitarian Bible Society, 1897), 25–31, and also by H. B. Swete, *Introduction to the Old Testament in Greek* (2d ed.; Cambridge: Cambridge University Press, 1902), 342–43. But neither deals with the divergences from the "English" system like those noted in the table above.

4.   There is one exception: in both the Madrid Polyglot and the first Bomberg Bible Num 30 begins according to the "Hebrew" division, as in the Vulgate.

5.   Ginsburg cites editions of 1517, 1521, 1525 and on to 1570.

6.   The omission in the latter case was soon remedied. At the front of the 1524–25 edition a list of all the chapter-beginnings was printed, and here both Gen 32 and Deut 23 conform to the "Hebrew" pattern. Curiously, in the later editions of the Venice Rabbinic Bible (1546–48, 1568, 1617–19 and even 1724–28) not only Gen 32 but also Deut 13 and 29 begin according to the "English" divisions.

system, except in the Hebrew column at the beginning of Deut 23.[7] In fact it was only in the mid-seventeenth century that the full set of the ten "Hebrew" divisions in the Pentateuch established itself in printed Bibles.[8]

The reason why at least most of the distinctive "Hebrew" chapter-divisions appeared in the Second Rabbinic Bible is fortunately made clear by Jacob ben Chayim in his Introduction, which was reprinted and translated by C. D. Ginsburg in 1865. In the course of his account of the preparation of the Masorah, Jacob ben Chayim refers to an important aid which had enabled him to check the biblical references given in older copies of the text. He writes (I cite Ginsburg's translation):[9]

> But for a certain book called *Concordance*, the author of which is the learned R. Isaac Nathan, who lived some forty years ago, and which was published in our printing-office in Venice, I could not have corrected the verses. This is a precious work; it embraces all the points of the Holy Bible, and explains all the sacred Scriptures by stating all nouns and verbs with their analogous forms, and giving at the heading of every noun and verb an explanation, saying the meaning of the word is so and so, or branches out in such and such a manner, and comments upon each one separately. It also marks the division of each chapter, and the number of chapters in every prophetical book, and tells in which chapter and verse every word occurs...

Later Jacob ben Chayim indicates a further use that he had made of R. Isaac Nathan's work:[10]

7. This may be an accident, with the marginal number being placed one line higher than intended. The Antwerp Polyglot of Arias Montanus (1571) also followed the "English" divisions for the most part, but Num 30 has the "Hebrew" beginning.

8. The earliest instance known to me is the Hebrew Bible printed by Joseph Athias in Amsterdam in 1661.

9. C. D. Ginsburg, *Jacob ben Chajim's Introduction to the Rabbinic Bible, Hebrew and English, with explanatory notes* (London: Longman, Roberts and Green, 1865), p. 13 of the text; para. 48 (p. 36) of the translation.

10. Ibid., 13–14; para. 49 (p. 37) of the translation. At the end of the paragraph the text continues: "Had I at that time the Massoretic division of the chapters on the whole Bible I would have preferred it, but I did not get it till I had almost finished the work. I have, nevertheless, published it separately, so that it may not be lost to Israel." Ginsburg, *Introduction to the Hebrew Bible*, 32–33, thought that this referred to the Sedarim (the division of the text for the triennial reading cycle), which would have provided a convenient means of reference in Jewish Bibles and which in fact quite frequently correspond to the modern chapter divisions. Ginsburg also makes it clear that R. Isaac Nathan's system, which Jacob ben Chayim used, was "the Christian chapters" (p. 33; cf. p. 25).

As the prophetic books are large, every prophet having on an average twenty-five chapters, my labour would have been in vain if I had simply said the word is found in such and such a prophet, since the reference could not be found without great exertion, and the student would soon have grown weary and left it off altogether. I have therefore adopted the division of the chapters which R. Isaac Nathan made, and said it occurs in such and such a prophet, and in such and such a verse.

So the reason why Jacob ben Chayim put the chapter-divisions in was to facilitate the use of the Masoretic lists of passages in the form in which he presented them.

A copy of R. Isaac Nathan's *Concordance* is in the Cambridge University Library, so it has been possible to see what Jacob ben Chayim had before him.[11] Before the concordance itself, there is an Introduction and a listing of the chapter beginnings which R. Isaac Nathan used. The latter mainly correspond to the "English" divisions, but at all the points in the Pentateuch where the "Hebrew" divisions diverge R. Isaac Nathan agrees with them. The *Concordance* was published in 1523, but Ginsburg states in a footnote that it had been prepared by R. Isaac Nathan between 1437 and 1445.[12] It seems clear that R. Isaac Nathan had access to the Christian division of the Old Testament into chapters, which he largely followed, but that at a number of points he put the break between chapters in a different place. Two questions then arise, both of which may be answered by a study of the Introduction to his *Concordance*: how did he gain access to the Christian system? And why did he diverge from it at certain points?

It is already clear from the widespread agreement between R. Isaac Nathan's divisions and the standard Christian pattern that he made use of Christian texts that were divided into chapters, either directly or through earlier Jewish borrowing from them. Aspects of the *Concordance* itself indicate that he made direct use of Christian texts. First, his listing of the beginnings of chapters is given in the order of the Christian Bible, not the Jewish Bible (Tanakh). So Ruth follows Judges, and the prophets, including Daniel, are at the end. Secondly, the final page of the Hebrew introduction contains several references to R. Isaac Nathan's knowledge, admiration and use of Latin books. He speaks of being in the company of

---

11. R. Isaac Nathan, מאיר נתיב הנקרא קונקורדאנשיש = *A Light to the Path*, or *Concordances* (Venice: D. Bomberg, 1523).

12. Ginsburg, *Jacob ben Chajim's Introduction*, 36 n. 41. See also *The Jewish Encyclopaedia*, 6:628, which locates him at Arles and Avignon and says that he associated with Christians. Cf. E. Mangenot, "Concordances de la Bible," *DB*, vol. 2, cols. 892–905 (899–900).

Christian scholars (חכמי הנצרים) and of his acquaintance with a valuable Latin book, a concordance, and of his resolve to make a similar aid to study (כלי) in Hebrew (בלשוננו).[13] And then he says: "So as not to depart from its practice and to make it easy to find every verse that we should seek in the two languages I listed all the twenty-four [books of the Tanakh] according to the number of chapters of the Christians, so that we should not toil to find what we wanted from them."[14] At the very end of his Introduction he adds: "Because I saw that the translator of the Holy Books into Latin divided up the books according to the number of the chapters in a way different from what is in our books, I listed all the verses according to their number, according to the number of the chapters. Also I listed the number of the verses according to our practice, so that they may easily be found in their places, according to their usual number."[15] This is exactly what is found in the pages that follow the Introduction, with each chapter number followed by its opening words (in Hebrew) and then the number of verses that it contains, for each book of the Hebrew Bible.

As a brief digression it may be noted that R. Isaac Nathan was evidently not the only person of the time to sense the need for such a reference system in the Hebrew Bible, as two volumes in Cambridge libraries show. In the University Library there is a thirteenth- or fourteenth-century Hebrew Bible with a list of the Christian chapter-divisions at the

---

13. Concordances of the Vulgate were apparently being produced already in the thirteenth and fourteenth centuries, by Hugo de Sancto Claro, or St. Cher (c. 1244), and Conrad of Halberstadt (1310), and were first printed, respectively, in 1479 and 1496 (S. L. Greenslade, ed., *The Cambridge History of the Bible.* Vol. 3, *The West from the Reformation to the Present Day* [Cambridge: Cambridge University Press, 1963], 526; on Hugo see also B. Smalley, *The Study of the Bible in the Middle Ages* [3d ed.; Oxford: Blackwell, 1983], 334). See more fully Mangenot, "Concordances de la Bible," cols. 895–97. Closer study would no doubt reveal which of them was used by R. Isaac Nathan. The earlier concordance of Hugo is the more likely source for the variant divisions, as Conrad would probably have used the standard Latin system.

14. ולמען לא אצא מדרכו ויקל למצא כל פסוק נדרשהו בשתי הלשונו' רשמתי כל עשרים וארבע' למספר פרשיות הנצרים למען לא ניגע למצא מה שנרצהו מהם.

15. ולמה שראיתי שהמעתיק ספרי הקדש בלאטי״ן חלק הספרים למספר הפרשיות מה שאין כן בספרינו רשמתי הפסוקים כלם לפי מספרם למנין הפרשי״ות גם רשמתי מספר הפסוקים לפי מה שהם אצלנו למען ימצאו בנקלה מקומותיהם במספרם כמשפטם. The listing of the verses according to Jewish practice is not included in the printed version. It may be the document whose absence Jacob ben Chayim regrets (see above, n. 10).

end, with notes at the beginning and the end of it which indicate both its purpose and its author:[16]

> These are the chapters of the Gentiles, which are called *capitulus*, of the twenty-four books, with the names of each individual book in their language. I have copied/translated them from their book, so that a man may be able to return an answer to them quickly about their questions which they ask us all the time about the subject of our belief and our holy Law and bring proofs from verses in the Law or from the Prophets or from the other Writings and say to us: See, read in such and such a verse, which is in such and such a book in such and such a chapter of the book, and we do not know what the chapter is and (how) to make a quick answer to them. Therefore I have copied them out.[17] The book Bereshith is called Genesi in their language; the first chapter (begins) בראשית ברא אלהים, the second ויכלו השמים etc.[18]

> The chapters of the Gentiles for all the 24 books are completed, and R. Salomoh ben Ismael copied them, from their books, so that a man could make a quick reply to all their questions.[19]

It is clear that the context of this enterprise was in disputations between Jews and Christians, and in fact the biographical section of R. Isaac Nathan's Introduction to his *Concordance* suggests a similar reason for his work. It is difficult to discover anything about the specific date and situation of R. Salomoh ben Ismael. S. C. Reif dates his work in the fifteenth or sixteenth century.[20] The informal hand in which the list and its framing paragraphs are written is certainly quite different from that of the main biblical text. In the latter, "Christian" chapter-divisions are marked in the margin by letters of the Hebrew alphabet and a symbol in

16. CUL Ms Add. 465: cf. S. C. Reif, *Hebrew manuscripts at Cambridge University Library: A Description and Introduction* (Cambridge: Cambridge University Press, 1997), 54–55. See also Ginsburg, *Introduction to the Hebrew Bible*, 25–26.

17. At this point the Hebrew letters פס occur: they are a common abbreviation for "verses" and may perhaps be a heading for the list that follows, as Dr. Noam Mizrahi has pointed out to me.

18. Original text in Ginsburg, *Introduction to the Hebrew Bible*, 25 n. 1. The pattern of the final sentence is followed for the title and first two chapters of each book (the books are in the traditional Jewish order), and subsequent chapter numbers are indicated by letters of the Hebrew alphabet.

19. Original text in Ginsburg, loc. cit.

20. Reif, *Hebrew Manuscripts*, 54. S. M. Schiller-Szinessy, in the earlier *Catalogue of Hebrew Manuscripts Preserved in the University Library, Cambridge* (2 vols.; Cambridge: Cambridge University Press, 1876), 1:17–18, had dated the list no later than the early fourteenth century and the divisions marked in the text to the late fifteenth century.

red ink. The points at which some of the divisions are marked provide further evidence of the lack of uniformity in this regard in early copies of the Hebrew Bible.[21]

Earlier still, the remaining two-thirds of a small thirteenth-century (or perhaps twelfth-century) Hebrew Bible, which is now in the library of Gonville and Caius College, has the Christian chapter-numbers added in the margin, and here the books themselves are written out in the order of the Christian Bible.[22] This has led scholars to conclude that the volume was prepared for the use of Christian scholars who could read Hebrew.[23] The manuscript unfortunately lacks the Torah, which was presumably bound separately: the surviving text, which runs from Joshua to Malachi, has blank pages between Job and the Psalms (and not elsewhere), evidently marking the break between what were once the second and third volumes. While it is therefore no longer possible to check the Pentateuchal chapter-divisions mentioned at the beginning of this essay, the evidence from three of the prophetic books (Hosea, Joel and Malachi) shows the consistent use of the standard Latin/English divisions and no trace of the "Hebrew" system. This is significant, as M. R. James concluded that the Latin hand in which the chapter-divisions were marked was of the thirteenth century and probably English. Although a fuller study of the manuscript might bring to light some variations elsewhere, at present the implication seems to be that something close or identical to the later standard system was known to the scribe involved.

A further point of interest is that at the end of the manuscript the Hebrew alphabet is written out in different hands, probably as a teaching aid. The first hand continued with a prayer in Hebrew addressed to "the God of Abraham," "Jesus the King of the Jews" and the Virgin Mary (the concluding lines are the words of the *Ave Maria*).[24]

21. I have checked the chapter-divisions given in the list for the ten Pentateuchal passages mentioned above, and, curiously, they represent neither of the standard patterns in their entirety. Four follow the English divisions, five follow the "Hebrew" and one is difficult to read. More curious still is the fact that at some of these points the divisions marked in the main text differ from those in the list: the beginnings of Exod 8 and Num 30 agree with the English in the text but with the "Hebrew" in the list, while the reverse is true at the beginning of Deut 29.

22. Ms 404/625 (James 1:33): cf. M. R. James, *A Descriptive Catalogue of the Manuscripts in the Library of Gonville and Caius College* (3 vols; Cambridge: Cambridge University Press, 1908), 2:471. The earlier date has been suggested by the Israeli palaeographer Dr. Edna Engel (information courtesy of Dr. Noam Mizrahi).

23. On Christian Hebrew scholarship in the thirteenth century and other texts which reflect it, see Smalley, *The Study of the Bible*, 329–55.

24. The discovery was made in 2006 by Dr. Noam Mizrahi, then of the Hebrew University Bible Project, who identified its hand with that of the vocalizer of the

The God of Abraham is my help(er).	אֱלֹהֵי אַבְרָהָם בְּעֶזְרִי
Jesus of Nazareth, king of the Jews, have mercy on us.	יֵשׁוּ הַנֹּצְרִי מֶלֶךְ הַיְהוּד יִם ו רַחֲמֵינוּ
Peace be with Miriam/Mary, full of grace.	שָׁלוֹם מִרְיָם חֵן מְלֵאָה
The Lord is with you, you are blessed among women,	אָדוֹן עִמָּךְ בְּרוּכָה אַתְּ ו בְּאִשׁוֹת
And blessed is the fruit of your womb. Amen.	וּבָרוּךְ פְּרִי בִטְנֵךְ אָמֵן

This combination must derive from a Jewish convert to Christianity, who at least contributed to the production of the manuscript, and the evidence illustrates beautifully Beryl Smalley's view that "Jewish converts were regularly employed by Christian scholars to write Hebrew."[25]

To return to our main theme, why then are some of the "Hebrew" chapter-divisions which R. Isaac Nathan presented in his *Concordance* different from the Latin and English divisions that are now familiar? There are two kinds of possible reasons for this. One possibility is that he had reasons for amending what he received at certain points, for example because he wanted to bring the divisions into closer conformity with either the Masoretic divisions or traditional Jewish exegesis. But an examination of the ten cases in the Pentateuch (see Table 1) shows that in only one of them is the "Hebrew" division supported by a Masoretic division when the "English" is not, while in four cases the "English" divisions are so supported when the "Hebrew" are not. In four cases both systems have Masoretic support and in one neither does. This hardly supports the idea that R. Isaac Nathan had a general policy to adhere more closely to the Masoretic divisions. Of course R. Isaac Nathan may have had other kinds of reasons for amending what he received, including his own judgment about where a division might most appropriately be placed. But in the extracts cited above he says nothing about any modification of what he had received, or about reasons why he felt it to be necessary, and there is equally no sign of such an intention elsewhere on the final page of his Introduction.

So it is worth considering the other possibility, which is that what R. Isaac Nathan had access to was a slightly different Christian system from the one that became standard. It is clear that in the twelfth and thirteenth centuries, when Stephen Langton was at work, "his" was not the only

manuscript. I reproduce the text of the prayer and a slightly modified version of Dr. Mizrahi's translation with his permission. The vocalization does not distinguish between sin and shin or between qamets and pathach; dagesh is not used, but raphe marks some instances where a softened pronunciation of the Begad Kefat letters would be expected.

25. Smalley, *The Study of the Bible*, 348–49.

system of divisions that was in use. Beryl Smalley writes of "the lack of a standard chapter-division in twelfth-century Bibles" and states that, in addition to other types of sub-division:

> There were also various systems of capitulation, some giving fewer, others many more chapters than our present system. The official text of Paris was divided into chapters, closely corresponding to ours; they were gradually modified during the thirteenth century until the correspondence was complete; through the Paris text this particular division became the standard everywhere.[26]

She continues by giving examples of the use of chapter-divisions in teaching and the gradual development in the practice of Peter Comestor, Peter the Chanter and Stephen Langton.[27] The former two were using various older systems, which had not yet been standardized, and Peter the Chanter says at one point that it is better to begin ch. 22 of the book of Joshua where the division is now made than earlier. Early chroniclers and lists of chapters attributed to Langton are the basis for the general view that he was the decisive figure in the establishment of the divisions set out in the Paris edition of the Vulgate. He certainly made many references to specific chapters by their numbers. But the evidence is confusing, because he uses two different systems in his writings, and there is also doubt whether in some cases the numbering derives from him rather than from scribes or pupils. Nevertheless, the "new" system is firmly associated with him in a manuscript dated 1203, and Smalley suggests that "it was the outcome of his teaching experience."

In a classic study of the Paris text, published in 1889 and 1890, J. P. P. Martin drew attention to a manuscript from the Abbey of St. Victor which purports to give Langton's chapter-divisions for the whole Bible.[28] Martin's conclusion is that they are "substantially the same as the modern system of divisions," with "only" 231 differences out of 1,159 instances. Some of the variations are very small, affecting merely the headings to

---

26. Ibid., 221–22. By "the official Paris text" Smalley will mean the edition of 1226 known as the *Correctorium Parisiense* (see B. J. Roberts, *The Old Testament Text and Versions* [Cardiff: University of Wales Press, 1951], 260). On this see further Smalley, 331–36; O. Schmid, *Über verschiedene Eintheilungen der heiligen Schrift insbesondere über die Capitel-eintheilung Stephen Langtons im XIII. Jahrhunderte* (Graz: Leuschner & Lubensky, 1892); and J. P. P. Martin, "Le texte parisien de la Vulgate latine," *Le Muséon* 8 (1889): 444–66; 9 (1890): 301–16. For a table showing the extent of the variations in earlier manuscripts, see Martin, *Le Muséon* 8 (1889): 448; in one (B.N. 3) Genesis has 138 divisions, Exodus 89, Leviticus 75, Numbers 155 and Deuteronomy 33.
27. Smalley, *The Study of the Bible*, 222–24.
28. B.N. 14417, fol. 125–26. See Martin, *Le Muséon* 8 (1889): 460–66.

lists, and they also tend to be concentrated in particular books: there are especially large numbers of them in Chronicles, Ezra and Nehemiah. In the Pentateuch the numbers of chapters are exactly the same as now, and variations in the points of division are relatively few: 8 in Genesis, 5 in Exodus, 6 in Leviticus, 4 in Numbers and 2 in Deuteronomy.[29] Martin gave more details of these variations in the chapter-divisions in his published lectures.[30] Many of those in the Pentateuch are, as elsewhere, at a surprising point in the text, for example separating the opening of direct speech from its introductory formula (e.g. Lev 8; 17; 19; 25). In Exodus the beginnings of chs. 1 and 16 are both placed halfway through a sentence. It is possible that whoever compiled the list made mistakes in correlating marginal marks of chapter numbers with the text alongside. However, two of the divisions of the Pentateuch in this list do coincide exactly with what later became the variant "Hebrew" chapter-divisions. Exodus 22 is made to begin: *Si effringens fur domum, sive*; and Deut 23 begins: *Non accipiet homo uxorem fratris* [a mistake for *patris*] *sui*. This confirms that at least some of the variant "Hebrew" divisions could have been taken directly from a Christian source. Whether or not this document actually represents a system used by Langton himself, it evidently reflects quite an advanced stage in the process that led, by about 1300, to the divisions familiar today. But the process still had some way to go, and in the second part of his article Martin includes a table which shows how in various thirteenth-century manuscripts the total number of chapters in each book gradually came to agree with the modern numeration.[31] Moreover, O. Schmid compiled a list of places where the chapter-divisions in some thirteenth-century manuscripts diverge from those in the "Langton" list, and it turns out that among these are four cases which agree with the later Hebrew divisions (Lev 6; Num 17 [in effect]; Deut 13; 29).[32] It has also been observed that in his *Postillae*, or commentaries on the Old and New Testaments, Hugo de Sancto Claro (c. 1200–1263) used a chapter-numbering system that comes somewhere between Langton's and the standard Latin/English divisions.[33] An early printed

29. See the table on p. 466.
30. J. P. P. Martin, *Introduction à la critique générale de l'ancien testament* (3 vols.; Paris: Maisonneuve et Leclerc, 1887–89), 2:464–71. The Pentateuchal variations are given on pp. 464–65. Cf. Schmid, *Über verschiedene Eintheilungen*, 59–92.
31. See *Le Muséon* 9 (1890): 58–59.
32. Schmid, *Über verschiedene Eintheilungen*, 99–103. Some of these divergences were still present in German printed editions of the Vulgate from the late fifteenth century (ibid., 104).
33. E. Mangenot, "Chapitres de la Bible," *DB*, vol. 2, cols. 559–66, esp. 565.

edition of this work appeared in 1499.[34] At two points in the Pentateuch the chapter-division is at the "Hebrew" position rather than the standard "English" position. Thus Num 30 begins: *Narravitque Moyses filiis Israel omnia quae ei dominus imperarat*; and Deut 23 begins: *Non accipiet homo uxorem patris sui* (only the second of these is a deviation from the Vulgate). It is possible that the original text of Hugo's *Postillae* had more divergences from the standard Christian chapter-divisions, but the only way to know whether or not this was the case would be to consult older manuscript copies (if they exist). Further exploration of this trail will have to be left to mediaevalists. In any case there is now evidence that seven (six in the Vulgate) out of the ten (nine in the Vulgate) variations in the Hebrew divisions were anticipated in Latin texts of the thirteenth century.

We may note that Martin also has an interesting, and plausible, explanation for the gradual standardization of the chapter-divisions which he identifies as the distinctive characteristic of the Paris text. He argues that it arose from the teaching of detailed exegesis of the biblical text in the twelfth- and thirteenth-century Paris schools to students who had come from all over Europe and probably brought with them Bibles divided in a variety of ways. If the lecturer was to point them clearly to the passage on which he wished to comment, there needed to be an agreed reference system, and this is what the standardization of the chapter-divisions came to provide.[35]

In view of the variations in Latin Bibles and the absence, in the Pentateuchal examples at least, of any consistent Jewish rationale for the differences between the "Hebrew" and "English" divisions, it would seem most likely that R. Isaac Nathan made use of a different version of the Vulgate divisions from the one which became standard and that this is the explanation for the differences which are still present in printed Hebrew and English Bibles today.

The authentically Jewish subdivisions of the biblical text are the two systems of lectionary readings, annual and triennial, and the "open" and "closed" sections (פתוחות and סתומות) which were marked originally only by empty spaces in the text but are identified in modern biblical texts also by the letters פ and ס. Both kinds of subdivision have been extensively studied in the past and evidence of them can be traced back well before the mediaeval period. For both lectionary systems an origin in the first few centuries C.E. is established, while the system of פתוחות

34. *Textum bibliae cum postilla domini Hugonis Cardinalis: Prima pars* (Basel: Johann of Amorbach, 1499).

35. *Le Muséon* 8 (1889): 450–58.

and סתומות is already presupposed in the probably third-century "minor tractate" *Sefer Torah*.[36] There is no space here to give even a summary of the general discussion about them. But what has emerged clearly in recent years is that the division into (open and closed) sections has an even older origin than previously thought, for many of the divisions known from mediaeval manuscripts (which, it must be said, do not entirely agree with each other in this matter) already appear in biblical scrolls from Qumran and the neighbouring area.[37] The following brief remarks will examine some of the relevant evidence for the book of Exodus and make some preliminary observations on its implications.[38] For the mediaeval section-divisions I have limited my own comparisons to three especially early and fine examples, *Codex Petropolitanus* (or *Leningradensis*) B19a, the basis for *BH³* and *BHS*, British Museum Ms. Or. 4445 and the list of sections given by Maimonides, *Mishne Torah, Ahaba, Hilkot Sefer Torah*, 8, which was based on a then well known manuscript that is now recognized to have been what is known today as the *Aleppo Codex*.[39] According to my reckoning there are 47 places in Exodus where a section-division in one of these manuscripts differs from those in the other two. Many of the differences are "qualitative," where one manuscript has an "open" section whereas the others have a "closed" one, or vice versa. But there are a dozen quantitative variants, where

36. E.g. J. M. Oesch, *Petucha und Setuma: Untersuchungen zu einer über-lieferten Gliederung im hebräischen Text des Alten Testaments* (OBO 27; Freiburg: Universitätsverlag; Göttingen: Vandenhoeck & Ruprecht, 1979), 32–33, 61–63; also idem, "Skizze einer formalen Gliederungshermeneutik der Sifre Tora," in *Unit Delimitation in Biblical Hebrew and Northwest Semitic Literature* (ed. M. C. A. Korpel and J. M. Oesch; Pericope 4; Assen: Van Gorcum, 2003), 162–203, where the relevant portions of *Sefer Torah* and other rabbinic rulings are conveniently collected. For the date of *Sefer Torah*, see also G. Stemberger, *Introduction to the Talmud and Midrash* (trans. and ed. M. N. A. Bockmuehl; 2d ed.; Edinburgh: T. & T. Clark, 1996), 232.

37. See already Oesch, *Petucha*, 165–291 (and pp. 144–64 on the variations in mediaeval manuscripts and lists); the most up-to-date treatment is in E. Tov, *Scribal Practices and Approaches Reflected in the Texts Found in the Judean Desert* (STDJ 54; Leiden: Brill, 2004), 143–63. On the other hand, no evidence of the lectionary divisions has been found in the biblical scrolls.

38. I hope to publish a much fuller study of this material at a future date.

39. Since the work of M. H. Goshen-Gottstein, "The Authenticity of the Aleppo Codex," *Textus* 1 (1960): 17–58, and "A Recovered Part of the Aleppo Codex," *Textus* 5 (1966): 53–59. Most of the Pentateuch of the Aleppo Codex was lost in modern times, but some of its readings have been recovered in a brilliant piece of detective-work by J. S. Penkower, נוסח התורה בכתר ארם־צובה (Ramat Gan: Bar-Ilan University, 1992).

there is no section-division at all in one or two of the three manuscripts (e.g. Or. 4445 at 6:14 and Or. 4445 and Maimonides/Aleppo at 16:6).

The Judaean Desert manuscripts of Exodus (which are all more or less fragmentary) exhibit numerous section-divisions of several different kinds, among which by far the most common are "open-ended" lines and empty spaces within lines. Entirely empty lines are comparatively rare, except in the palaeo-Hebrew manuscripts 4QpaleoGenesis–Exodus[l] and 4QpaleoExodus[m]. The location of divisions (which are helpfully tabulated in the relevant volumes of *Discoveries in the Judaean Desert*) frequently but by no means always corresponds to the location of divisions in the mediaeval manuscripts. Leaving to one side for the present the different kinds of division in both bodies of material, I count 62 instances where at least one of the mediaeval manuscripts agrees with the location of a division in the Judaean Desert manuscripts, but 48 instances where none of them does. There are also a few places where the Judaean Desert manuscripts do not have a division but the mediaeval manuscripts do. This suggests that there was considerable continuity in the placing of divisions but that the overall number of divisions in the earlier manuscripts was significantly larger.[40] Of course this global picture conceals the differences among the earlier manuscripts as well as the later ones, and it is also possible that agreements could be due to independent rather than connected scribal activity, especially when the divisions are "obvious" ones.[41] But there are some cases where a connection seems more probable, and I will conclude with two from Exodus which are striking. Part of the Song of Moses (Exod 15:1–18[19]) survives in 4QExod[c] and 4QReworkedPentateuch[c] (4Q365). In both cases the poem is not laid out stichometrically but as continuous text, with short divisions between the individual phrases that make up each verse.[42] In the Leningrad Codex and BM Or. 4445 there are similar divisions throughout

---

40. The fact that substantial sections of the text of Exodus are not represented at all in the Judaean Desert manuscripts prevents this from being more than a suggestion. But so far as it goes it implies that Oesch's view, based on a smaller sample, that the Judaean Desert manuscripts of the Pentateuch had fewer divisions than the mediaeval ones (see *Petucha*, 354) is mistaken. Our figures also call in question the common view that the Masoretic divisions exhibit "around 80% agreement with texts found at the Dead Sea" (cited in J. W. Olley, *Ezekiel* [Septuagint Commentary Series; Leiden: Brill, 2009], 43).

41. Cf. E. Ulrich, "Impressions and Intuition: Some Divisions in Ancient Manuscripts of Isaiah," in Korpel and Oesch, eds., *Unit Delimitation*, 279–307 (301–2).

42. The spaces survive in 4QExod[c] after vv. 14a and 16bα and there is said to be room for them in the lacunae elsewhere in the passage (*DJD*, 12:118); in 4Q365 they survive after vv. 17a and 19aβ[1].

the poem, but the layout is more formal, with larger spaces and a regular alternating pattern of line structure.[43] The second example comes from a regular narrative text. All three mediaeval sources curiously mark a division before Exod 6:29, although the most natural interpretation of the text would see vv. 28 and 29 as parts of a single sentence.[44] The oddness of the division is not just due to modern thinking: both Rashi and Ibn Ezra found it unacceptable. Its presence in the form of an "open" line in 4QpaleoExodus[m] (the only Qumran manuscript to survive at this point)—and also in fact in the Samaritan text—is therefore all the more noteworthy. These two cases, at least, lend impressive support to the view that there was a continuous line of tradition linking the divisions in the mediaeval manuscripts with the scribal practice and section-division that are observable in the Judaean Desert manuscripts.[45]

43. This arrangement of the text is not fully reflected in *BHS* (which may account for the statement that there is "no interval" in MT in *DJD*, 12:100, 118), but the Dotan edition shows it (and its presence is recognized in *DJD*, 13:269).

44. It is in fact an "open" division in L and Or. 4445, but a "closed" one in the Maimonides list.

45. What has been said earlier is sufficient to indicate that this by no means implies that it was an unchanging tradition. The biblical manuscripts from the Cairo Genizah might well shed valuable light on the intervening period.

Part II

THE LANGUAGE AND LITERATURE
OF THE HISTORICAL BOOKS

CAN THE SAMSON NARRATIVE PROPERLY BE CALLED HEROIC?*

Charles L. Echols

1. *Introduction*

The number of approaches by which the Samson narrative[1] has been studied is rather astonishing, including, to name simply a few, its relation with comparative ancient Near Eastern iconography,[2] mythology,[3] Samson's riddle (Judg 14:12–14),[4] and its use by Josephus and Milton.[5] It has also been analysed as heroic literature. Othniel Margalith, for example, has examined parallels between the deeds of Samson and Heracles.[6] To date, the most thorough work is the fine study by Gregory Mobley.[7] Indeed, the presumption of researchers in this area is that the Samson narrative is heroic. Is this, however, the case? Given the paucity

* It is a pleasure to dedicate this essay to Dr. Macintosh, whose insights, warmth and wit I have valued since my doctoral work at Cambridge.

1. The term "narrative" is used for convenience, irrespective of the unity of Judg 13–16 (see below).

2. R. Mayer-Opificius, "Simson, der sechslockige Held?," *UF* 14 (1982): 149–51.

3. See G. F. Moore, *A Critical and Exegetical Commentary on Judges* (Edinburgh: T. & T. Clark, 1895; repr. 1989), 364–65; G. G. Cohen, "Samson and Hercules: A Comparison between the Feats of Samson and the Labours of Hercules," *EvQ* 42 (1970): 131–41.

4. E.g. O. Margalith, "Samson's Riddle and Samson's Magic Locks," *VT* 36 (1986): 225–34; A. Yadin, "Samson's *ḤÎDÂ*," *VT* 52 (2002): 407–26; J. Schipper, "Narrative Obscurity of Samson's חידה in Judges 14.14 and 18," *JSOT* 27 (2003): 339–53.

5. Respectively, M. Roncace, "Another Portrait of Josephus' Portrait of Samson," *JSJ* 35 (2004): 185–207; D. Gay, "Milton's Samson and the Figure of the Old Testament Giant," *Literature and Theology* 9 (1995): 355–69.

6. O. Margalith, "The Legends of Samson/Heracles," *VT* 37 (1987): 63–70.

7. G. Mobley, *The Empty Men: The Heroic Tradition of Ancient Israel* (New York: Doubleday, 2005), particularly pp. 171–223; see also *Samson and the Liminal Hero in the Ancient Near East* (LHBOTS 453; New York: T&T Clark International, 2006); and "The Wild Man in the Bible and the Ancient Near East," *JBL* 116 (1997): 217–33.

of heroic literature in the Hebrew Bible, one could question whether the presupposition is built upon an adequate foundation. Fortunately there is an abundance of heroic literature from cultures ancient and modern throughout the world which can be used as a basis for comparison with the Samson narrative. This exercise has been performed in earlier studies, but with a rather narrow "control group" of extrabiblical literature.[8] Moreover, such studies have sought to identify the heroic characteristics of the Samson narrative without considering adequately its potential non-heroic factors.

The present aim is thus to survey the Samson narrative for non-heroic traits and, through an enlarged control group of extrabiblical heroic literature, to establish definitively whether or not the Samson narrative can be properly considered as heroic. For this the studies by H. Munro Chadwick and Nora K. Chadwick and by C. M. Bowra are especially important because they distinguish heroic from non-heroic literature.[9] Although somewhat dated, they remain germane and provide the necessary scope.

A few methodological remarks are in order before proceeding. Judges 13–16 is narrative, but the works by the Chadwicks and Bowra draw on both narrative and poetry. Lest there be any question of comparing apples with oranges in what follows, heroic and non-heroic features occur in both narrative and verse: "Heroic literature consists partly of stories, prose or verse, of exploits and adventures, and partly of poems, panegyrics or elegies, in which exploits and adventures are celebrated."[10] The assumption here is that it is possible to distinguish features within genres. Second, to draw on extrabiblical literature for support is to use the comparative method, an approach which has precedent in studies on Samson. Victor H. Matthews, for example, uses a "trickster scale" comparable to that of Karl Luckert, which is evidently based on the Navajo tribe of North America.[11] The scale has the divisions of "fool," "gambler," "evil trickster," "fellow trickster," "exemplary trickster," and "hero," and Matthews evidently feels justified in appropriating it to the

8. Mobley, *Samson and the Liminal Hero*, for example, makes extensive recourse to extrabiblical texts, but his concern is to establish Samson both as a "wild man" (especially vis-à-vis Enkidu of the *Gilgamesh Epic*) and as a "liminal" figure, positioned between thresholds such as his home and the battlefield.

9. H. M. Chadwick and N. K. Chadwick, *The Growth of Literature* (3 vols.; Cambridge: Cambridge University Press, 1932–40; repr. 1968); C. M. Bowra, *Heroic Poetry* (London: Macmillan, 1952; repr. 1964).

10. Chadwick and Chadwick, *Growth of Literature*, 3:727.

11. V. H. Matthews, *Judges and Ruth* (Cambridge: Cambridge University Press, 2004), 137.

Samson narrative without further explanation. The presumption here is that the comparative method is sound as long as the analogies do not overreach. Moreover, the greater the number of parallels, the greater the confidence in the accuracy of the comparison.[12] Third, the Chadwicks and Bowra also incorporate as non-heroic criteria the role of women and the use of humour, both of which appear in the Samson narrative. The problem, methodologically, is that whether or not they are heroic depends, to some extent, on where the work in which they occur lies in the societal development of the culture that produced it; but their analyses of the various stages of a society's development lead to equivocal results.[13] Hence, these aspects are excluded from consideration here. A further assumption is that Judg 13–16 is not myth. The opposite was the view of earlier scholarship, but G. F. Moore, one of the earliest critics of this opinion, countered that the narrative "has its roots in the earth, not in the sky."[14] Indeed, few scholars now regard the Samson narrative as myth.

The final methodological issue is whether the Samson narrative should be evaluated as a unity. The general critical understanding is that Judg 13–16 is mostly an amalgam of originally discrete, independent units which over time were grouped into still larger units. This judgment was common even before Martin Noth's paradigm-shifting monograph.[15] C. F. Burney, for example, regarded ch. 13 as from the J source and as introducing chs. 14–16, which were "entirely *sui generis*" and lacked the religious tones in ch. 13, while yet having interpolations from J.[16] Judges 13–16 was ultimately the product of several hands, for example, R^{E2}, J^1, J^2, R^{JE}.[17] According to Noth, the period of the judges was one of the major epochs of the Old Testament, beginning after Josh 23 at Judg 2:6 and concluding at 1 Sam 11:15, viz., from the end of the securing of the land until the beginning of the reign of Saul, the first king, which began

12. For concerns with the comparative method in biblical studies, see, e.g., S. Talmon, "The 'Comparative Method' in Biblical Interpretation—Principles and Problems," in *Congress Volume: Göttingen 1977* (ed. J. A. Emerton; VTSup 29; Leiden: Brill, 1978), 320–56. On the reliability of the method in general, see R. A. Segal, "In Defense of the Comparative Method," *Numen* 48 (2001): 339–73.

13. C. L. Echols, *"Tell Me, O Muse": The Song of Deborah in the Light of Heroic Poetry* (LHBOTS 487; New York: T&T Clark International, 2008), 149–51, 154.

14. Moore, *Judges*, 364–65.

15. M. Noth, *The Deuteronomistic History* (trans. J. Doull; JSOTSup 15; Sheffield: JSOT, 1981).

16. C. F. Burney, *The Book of Judges* (New York: Ktav, 1970), 337.

17. Ibid., 337–38.

the period of the monarchy.[18] The stories of the individual judges were from discrete sources which were probably redacted before the DtrH.[19] The notices of the minor judges came from a second source. Noth equivocated on whether Judg 13:2–16:31 was from the Dtr or was a subsequent addition.[20] In the Samson narrative, several verses have been identified as redactions, for example, 13:1,[21] 19–20 as post-Dtr;[22] 14:4b (ובעת ההיא פלשתים משלים בישראל) as deriving from J,[23] or the DtrH,[24] with vv. 1–3 as a "secondary opening" to chs. 14–15;[25] 15:20 could be from "redactors,"[26] the Dtr,[27] or a post-Dtr addition;[28] and 16:31b (והוא שפט את־ישראל עשרים שנה) might be from the Dtr.[29]

There is thus ample attestation to literary growth in Judges in general, and in the Samson narrative in particular, but different scholars attribute the development to different redactors.[30] Moreover, the additions can be of a religious nature (see below). The accrual of religious material in what was originally a secular work is a phenomenon known in extra-biblical literature. The Indian *Mahābhārata* probably began as heroic literature, with secondary, Brahmanic additions.[31] The addition of religious material has also been found in Russian, Irish, and Tatarian literature.[32] It seems best, therefore, to proceed cautiously by analysing the Samson narrative as a unity, and considering the matter of literary growth—and its potential influence on the heroicity of the story—in the course of examining the possible non-heroic factors.

18. Noth, *Deuteronomistic History*, 42. I will use the abbreviation "Dtr" for the Deuteronomistic Historian, and "DtrH" for the Deuteronomistic History.

19. Ibid., 42.

20. Ibid., 52–53.

21. Ibid., 21; W. Richter, *Traditionsgeschichtliche Untersuchungen zum Richter-buch* (Bonn: Hanstein, 1963), 140 n. 92; J. A. Soggin, *Judges: A Commentary* (Philadelphia: Westminster, 1981), 233.

22. Noth, *Deuteronomistic History*, 142 n. 5; W. Gross, *Richter: Übersetzt und ausgelegt* (Freiburg: Herder, 2009), 648.

23. Burney, *Judges*, 337.

24. Soggin, *Judges*, 239.

25. Gross, *Richter*, 657.

26. Soggin, *Judges*, 250.

27. Noth, *Deuteronomistic History*, 52.

28. Gross, *Richter*, 651–52.

29. Noth, *Deuteronomistic History*, 52; Gross, *Richter*, 659. For the case against the Dtr as the author/editor of the book of Judges, see, e.g., D. I. Block, *Judges, Ruth* (Nashville: Broadman & Holman, 1999), 49–50.

30. For a recent, detailed survey, see T. C. Butler, *Judges* (Nashville: Thomas Nelson, 2009), xliii–li.

31. Chadwick and Chadwick, *Growth of Literature*, 3:742.

32. Ibid., respectively, 2:190, 248; 1:602–7; 3:744.

2. *Non-Heroic Indicators*

a. *Community Orientation, Patriotism/Nationalism*

The first indicator to examine is the extent, if any, to which a community orientation (i.e. patriotism or nationalism) factors in the Samson narrative. According to the Chadwicks, literature which chiefly has this sort of perspective is non-heroic, because the interest is primarily in the nation rather than in the hero.[33] They find concern for the welfare of the community often occurring in conjunction with the "national religion," and they identify the pre-monarchical era, when the prophet was the ruler, as an example of the non-heroic age in the Old Testament.[34]

Regarding the book of Judges, Noth remarks: "Obviously the old heroic stories had already been collected to illustrate Israel's disputes with her hostile neighbours in the period after the conquest, disputes which took the form of isolated battles between individual tribes or groups of tribes and their foreign neighbours."[35] The redaction of the Dtr involved extending the scope of the battles such that they took on national significance.[36]

Does the Samson narrative fall foul of this criterion? The introduction to the narrative, Judg 13:1, establishes a community orientation by associating the community (בני ישראל) with the problem of Philistine dominion (ביד־פלשתים). Hence the deeds of the protagonist, Samson, are circumscribed within the ethnic community of origin, which appears to be the focus of the narrative that follows. Judges 13:5, narrated from YHWH's perspective, states that Samson's *raison d'être* was to deliver his people from Philistine domination—again a national concern. Next, in 14:3 Samson's parents press him not to take a Philistine for a wife, but a woman from his kin and people (אחיך ובכל־עמי).[37] The national factor intensifies in v. 4, where the narrator explains Samson's desire for a foreign wife as the imperceptible design of YHWH to confront the Philistines. Finally, Judg 15:10 contains the phrase "the men of Judah" (איש יהודה),[38] which, although not national in scale, certainly appears to

---

33. Ibid., e.g., 1:80–85; 2:92–100.
34. Ibid., 3:729–30.
35. Noth, *Deuteronomistic History*, 44.
36. Ibid.
37. On עם as denoting the larger social entity, e.g., "people," "nation," as well as the smaller-scale kinship unit, see, e.g., s.v., עַם, *HALOT* 1:837; R. H. O'Connell, "עַם," *NIDOTTE*, 3:429–32 (430).
38. Taking איש as a collective singular.

be community oriented. There are thus several elements which contribute towards a national perspective.[39]

On further consideration, however, such a perspective is misleading. What was "Israel" at the time, and how federated was it? Primary and secondary sources point to a precarious affiliation of tribes.[40] Moreover, in 13:2 the focus immediately narrows to a specific tribal context, viz., the Danites, and the chapter ends with one of its members in a remote place; that is, there is no coda restating any relevance of Samson to the community. The term עם (14:3) has national overtones, but is patriotism the concern of the parents rather than simply their desire for endogamous marriage? Similarly, 14:4 reflects YHWH's desire, but it is not necessarily Samson's; and, as discussed above, the verse is commonly identified as secondary. Even in 15:10, the focus is on one tribe, and not Samson's at that, so that it is difficult to make the case for a national dimension. Moreover, once the fighting actually begins, the tribe is nowhere in view—it is strictly between Samson and the Philistines. That the common enemy in the Samson narrative is the Philistines might indicate nationalism; however, they are not engaged by Israel, but by Samson, an individual, with no clear patriotic fervour. In fact, his rejection of a Hebrew wife for a Philistine undermines further the case for nationalism. Another factor is the description of Samson's death. Samson does not exclaim the ancient Israelite equivalent of "*vive la France,*" but "let me be avenged!"—a sentiment that J. Clinton McCann attributes to "personal revenge."[41] It is thus difficult to see why the narrator or editors would have shaped the denouement this way had nationalism been the emphasis. On balance, patriotism plays little or no role in the Samson narrative.

b. *Defensive Warfare*
A second factor to consider is the type of warfare in Judg 13–16. According to the Chadwicks, defensive warfare is non-heroic since it

39. Judg 16:31 states that Samson's brothers and his "father's family" (בית אביהו; cf. I. בֵּית, *HALOT* 1:125, A:4, 5) recovered his body for burial; but if the narrator's purpose was to trumpet nationalism, he surely would have made the burial on a wider societal scale.

40. Judg 5:14–18 and 1 Sam 11:7 are but two allusions to the difficulty of an all-tribe alliance. See, e.g., R. de Vaux, *The Early History of Israel* (trans. D. Smith; 2 vols.; London: Darton, Longman & Todd, 1978), 2:717–49; R. Albertz, *A History of Israelite Religion in the Old Testament Period* (trans. J. Bowden; 2 vols.; Louisville: Westminster John Knox, 1994), 1:72–76.

41. J. C. McCann, *Judges* (Louisville: Westminster John Knox, 2002), 95.

lacks the heroic focus on the individual and the desire for spoil.[42] Since the Samson narrative is cast in an era when the Philistines predominated, one could conceive of Samson's fighting as defensive in response to a superior power. Indeed, YHWH's prenatal commission of Samson, as relayed to his mother, presumes a defensive Israelite posture (והוא יחל להושיע את־ישראל מיד פלשתים, Judg 13:5; cf. also 13:1; 15:11, 20).[43]

That posture notwithstanding, Samson shows little sign of being intimidated by the Philistines. His actions against them may be responsive on occasion (e.g. 15:7), but they are not defensive. Indeed, by throwing down the gauntlet, the Philistines provide Samson with opportunities for glory and honour—two of the central motivations of the hero.[44] Moreover, the battles are between the Philistines and Samson, so that the focus of the narrative is on Samson the individual. Whether Samson has a desire for spoil, however, is less clear. He takes no armour from the Philistines whom he slays; but in the wedding scene (14:10–20) he wagers thirty "linen wraps" (סדינים, v. 12,) and "changes of clothes" (חלפת בגדים, v. 12), which become truncated (החליפות, v. 19) in the payoff. The possibility that the garments constitute spoil is strengthened by their appearance in proximity to an unambiguous term for spoil, חליצותם, in v. 19 (cf. 2 Sam 2:21). In a midnight operation against Gaza (16:3), Samson removes "the doors of the city gates and their posts" (בדלתות שער־העיר ובשתי המזוזות), which could be another example of spoil, albeit in an unusual form. If Samson's thirst for spoil is somewhat ambiguous, his depiction as an individual is unquestionable. On balance, therefore, the label of defensive warfare may apply to the Israelites in general, but not to Samson the individual.

c. *Didactic Orientation*
According to the Chadwicks, literature which is polemic is inherently non-heroic.[45] Bowra remarks that the "poet wishes not to instruct but to delight his audience."[46] A challenge to the heroicity of the Samson narrative is thus that some scholars understand the book of Judges as a polemic on behalf of Judah. Perhaps the most detailed study in this

42. Chadwick and Chadwick, *Growth of Literature*, 3:731–32.

43. On the Israelites as underdogs, see also S. Niditch, *War in the Hebrew Bible: A Study in the Ethics of Violence* (Oxford: Oxford University Press, 1993), 113, 119; Butler, *Judges*, lx.

44. Chadwick and Chadwick, *Growth of Literature*, 3:731–32; Bowra, *Heroic Poetry*, 1–2, 4–5; D. A. Miller, *The Epic Hero* (Baltimore: The Johns Hopkins University Press, 2000), 225–30, 332–33; Mobley, *Empty Men*, 48–55.

45. Chadwick and Chadwick, *Growth of Literature*, 3:748.

46. Bowra, *Heroic Poetry*, 29.

respect is that by Robert H. O'Connell.[47] In Judg 13–16, Samson represents the tribe of Dan, which in turn represents the northern tribes; and
the fact that the final deliverer story entails a protagonist who acquits his
responsibilities so poorly conveys the editorial stamp of condemnation of
the northern tribes.[48] The rhetorical purpose of Judges plays out in the
Samson narratives in various ways.[49] In O'Connell's multiple-plot
scheme, "[t]he development of Plot C [14:1–15:6], wherein Samson
attempts to secure a bride from among the Philistines, competes with the
development of Plot A [the primary plot in chs. 13–16], wherein YHWH
attempts to deliver Israel from the Philistines through Samson."[50] Regarding cultic impurity, there "may be an escalated parallelism" between
Samson and the tribes in that, as Samson fails to observe the conditions
of his Nazirite vow, so the tribes dishonour the covenant through cultic
impurity and "by neglecting to expel foreigners from the land."[51] Anti-
northern polemic also appears structurally in the contrasting estimations
of Judah. In 15:11–13, wherein Judah is "representative of 'Israel'," it is
negative, whereas it is positive in the framework (1:1–20; 20:18).[52]
Similarly, the first judge, Othniel, a Judahite, executed his duties respon-
sibly, whereas the last judge, Samson, a Danite, disgraced his office.[53]

The polemic theory is problematic for several reasons. Nothing in
15:11–13 points unambiguously to the identification of Judah as figurative for all Israel. Also, Samson's pursuit of foreign women compares
well with the heroic exogamous bride quest.[54] It is, furthermore, an
intentional move to provoke heroic opportunities. More broadly, if there
is any sustained polemic in the Samson narrative, it is anti-Philistine,

---

47. R. H. O'Connell, *The Rhetoric of the Book of Judges* (Leiden: Brill, 1996), 1.
See also E. T. Mullen, "Judges 1:1–36: The Deuteronomistic Reintroduction of the
Book of Judges," *HTR* 77 (1984): 33–54; M. Brettler, "The Book of Judges:
Literature as Politics," *JBL* 108 (1990): 395–418 (408); McCann, *Judges*, 8; R. G.
Boling, *Judges* (AB 6A; New York: Doubleday, 1975), 30–31. For criticism of the
pro-Judah interpretation, see G. T. K. Wong, "Is There a Direct Pro-Judah Polemic
in Judges?," *SJOT* 19 (2005): 84–110.
48. O'Connell, *Rhetoric of the Book of Judges*, 224.
49. Ibid., 215.
50. Ibid., 219.
51. Ibid., 223.
52. Ibid., 223 n. 320.
53. Ibid.
54. For Mongol and Uzbek literature, for example, see the essays by C. R.
Bawden and K. Reichl in A. T. Hatto, ed., *Traditions of Heroic and Epic Poetry*
(PMHRA 9, 13; London: The Modern Humanities Research Association, 1980–89),
1:268–99 (276); 2:94–120 (97), respectively.

which O'Connell himself recognizes (e.g. 14:19; 15:4–5; 16:3, 23–30).[55] Similarly, the structural arguments depend largely on material that is outside of the Samson narrative. Finally, most scholars who claim that the Samson narrative contains anti-northern polemic allow that such polemic is secondary. It follows that any anti-northern polemic is subordinate to the original function of the narrative, which was to entertain.[56]

d. *Supernatural Assistance*

The various supernatural elements, regarded as non-heroic, are the final obstacle to a heroic classification.[57] At issue is whether the protagonist, Samson, resorts to supernatural means to achieve his aims. The consistent use of such means is non-heroic because it obviates one of the principal characteristics of the hero, viz., self-reliance, and particularly strength. The supernatural intersects with the Samson narrative in four areas: Samson's Nazirite status, his prayer, direct divine assistance from YHWH, and various other evidences of supernatural involvement.

Non-heroic literature often revolves around individuals such as "saints," "prophets," and "wizards," since such figures are integral to the supernatural.[58] According to Judg 13:5, Samson was designated prenatally a Nazirite, this according him a special relationship with YHWH not shared by the typical Israelite. Should the Samson narrative thus be rejected as heroic because of the protagonist's Nazirite status? There are no explicit indications that the proscriptions of the vow—consumption of alcohol, cutting of hair, and contact with a corpse (Num 6:3–6)—would bring supernatural ability. Samson's indiscretion to Delilah regarding his secret (16:17) could perhaps connect with 13:5, indicating a connection between unshorn hair and strength. If so, it is no more problematic than the power afforded to earthly heroes such as Achilles from their semi-divine parentage.[59] Another consideration is that Samson violated each component of the vow early in the narrative, which may have impinged upon his relationship with YHWH, and thus upon YHWH's willingness to lend him aid.[60] Hence, any power deriving from his

---

55. O'Connell, *Rhetoric of the Book of Judges*, 227.

56. Cf. Matthews, *Judges and Ruth*, 166.

57. Chadwick and Chadwick, *Growth of Literature*, 3:729, 731–32; Bowra, *Heroic Poetry*, 5.

58. Chadwick and Chadwick, *Growth of Literature*, 1:96.

59. Cf. Bowra, *Heroic Poetry*, 94–95.

60. Samson touches the carcass of a lion (14:8), almost certainly consumes alcohol at his wedding feast (14:10), and has his hair cut (16:19). For the case that Samson partook of alcohol at the feast, see, e.g., J. Blenkinsopp, "Some Notes on the Saga of Samson and the Heroic Milieu," *Scripture* 11 (1959): 81–89 (84).

Nazirite status could have been undermined by these violations. By contrast the "chief characters" of the non-heroic poems in the *Kalevala* "are not warriors who prevail by strength and courage but magicians who prevail by craft and special knowledge."[61] Samson's primary heroic attribute is great strength; and, even if it is divinely imparted or accentuated, he would be no different in this regard from any number of extrabiblical heroes.

Regarding the second intersection, there are two occasions when Samson prays to YHWH. In 15:18, following his dispatch of 1,000 Philistines at Lehi, Samson prays to YHWH for water. Although the language of the prayer is somewhat hyperbolic (אָמוּת), the sense is that Samson believed that he would be mortally vulnerable to the remaining Philistines without immediate hydration (cf. the effect of the drink: וַתָּשָׁב רוּחוֹ וַיֶּחִי, v. 19b).[62] The second prayer occurs near the end of the narrative (16:28), where Samson is a blind prisoner of the Philistines, on display for their amusement. He prays to God, then pushes on the two middle columns of the temple (v. 29) so that it collapses with deadly effect. Although YHWH never directly answers Samson, the implication is that he empowers him for the demolition. In both instances Samson ostensibly achieves his objectives through prayer for divine intervention, a non-heroic characteristic. Importantly, it is not prayer *per se* that renders a piece non-heroic; rather, the consistent recourse to prayer by the hero to achieve his means is non-heroic.[63] Petitions occur in much literature that is regarded as heroic. In the *Gilgamesh* story, the eponymous hero prays for divine assistance in defeating the monster Humbaba.[64] Outside the ancient Near East, examples appear in the German *Nibelungenlied*, the Anglo-Saxon *Beowulf*, and in Tatar panegyric.[65] Since prayer features minimally in the Samson narrative, there is no reason to classify it as non-heroic on the basis of this criterion, even if 15:18 and 16:28 are original.

Arguably the most significant supernatural involvement is the direct assistance which Samson receives from YHWH, as expressed in the thrice-occurring clause, "and the Spirit of YHWH 'rushed' upon him"

---

61. Bowra, *Heroic Poetry*, 92.

62. So J. C. Exum, "The Theological Dimension of the Samson Saga," *VT* 33 (1983): 30–45 (40).

63. See, e.g., Chadwick and Chadwick, *Growth of Literature*, 1:242; 3:785.

64. Bowra, *Heroic Poetry*, 173; cf. p. 185.

65. See, respectively, strophes 2122, 2199–200. For the Tatar text, see V. V. Radlov, *Die Sprachen der türkischen Stämme Süd-Sibiriens und der dsungarischen Steppe* (10 vols.; St. Petersburg: Eggers, 1866–1904), 3:231.

(ותצלח עליו רוח יהוה, 14:6, 19; 15:14). The "rushing" enables Samson to shred a lion as easily as a kid (14:6), slay thirty men of Ashkelon (14:19), and snap the ropes which bound him at Lehi (15:14, which uses the simile of fire burning flax [כפשתים אשר בערו באש] to describe the ease of Samson's action). Does this direct involvement of YHWH undermine the heroicity of Samson's feats and thus render the narrative non-heroic? The question is complex, and requires consideration of the broader context.

First, the narrative recounts several heroic feats by Samson which he accomplishes without explicit help from YHWH. In Judg 15:4, he catches 300 foxes; and although this may not have required superhuman strength, the quantity points to superhuman ability, perhaps including strength. The slaying of 1,000 Philistines with the jawbone of an ass (15:15) is clearly a heroic deed even if the number is hyperbolic,[66] although one might object that he was still under the influence of the Spirit. That Samson can remove the doors and door posts of the city gates of Gaza and carry them to Hebron (16:3) is unambiguously heroic, requiring stealth, strength, and stamina.

Further heroic deeds occur in the Delilah episode (16:4–30). In v. 9 Samson snaps the seven fresh "bowstrings" (היתרים) that bound him as fire disintegrates a "thread of flax" (פתיל־הנערת). In v. 12 he snaps new "ropes" (עבתים) "like a thread" (כחוט), then he escapes from the "hair lock" (אם־תארגי את־שבע מחלפות ראשי עם־המסכת, v. 13). Even if this last act did not require heroic strength, meeting the onrushing Philistines would have. Most famously, he causes the Philistine temple to collapse by leaning on its central pillars (vv. 29–30).

One might argue that Samson's acts in these episodes presuppose divine assistance, but a series of alternating factors in 16:19–30 calls this into question. First, the sequence in v. 19 is sleep, head shave, torment, loss of strength. What robbed Samson of his strength—the haircut or the torment? Support for the latter comes if the conjunction in ויסר is taken to express result, viz., "so that." Also, the *athnach* is under ראשו, so that the Masoretes at least understood that the first half of the line ended there—a punctuation with semantic importance. Conversely, while v. 20b suggests that Samson's strength was contingent on the presence of YHWH, v. 22 implies that the regrowth of hair restored his strength. Then again, Samson's petition in v. 28 supports YHWH as the source of his power; yet even here there is ambiguity since there is no following statement that YHWH heard and granted his petition, and the focus is

---

66. Cf. the hero Siegfried, who slays 700 warriors singlehandedly (*Nibelungenlied*, st. 94).

exclusively on Samson. Clearly, the storyteller could have emphasized the divine role had he or she desired. Judges 13–16 thus contains considerably more heroic deeds without explicit supernatural aid than those in which such aid may feature.

A second factor to consider in evaluating the role of the Spirit of YHWH is whether the three passages in which the Spirit occurs are secondary. J. Alberto Soggin remarks: "a tenuous theological thread has been woven into the general pattern where it was clearly originally absent: all of ch. 13, then 14:4; 15:19; 16:28 and also those texts which present his strength as the product of the work of the spirit."[67] Obviously, if the Yahwistic material is secondary, then the pre-Yahwistic form of the Samson narrative is even more heroic.

The third consideration is assistance from deities to heroes in extrabiblical heroic literature. In the Sumerian version of *Gilgamesh*, Shamash sends winds to assist the eponymous hero who is thereby able to defeat the monster Humbaba.[68] In the classical tradition, "in the two most important combats in the *Iliad*, between Hector and Patroclus in xvi:731ff. and between Achilles and Hector in xxii:226ff., the issue is decided by the intervention of deities, Apollo and Athena."[69] In the same epic (xvi:698–712), Apollo repulses four times the attempts of the Achaeans led by Patroclus to breach the walls of Troy, with the deity even throwing Patroclus off the wall. In Yugoslavian heroic verse, *Vile* (ferocious female spirits) nurse wounded warriors back to health.[70] In the German *Nibelungenlied* (st. 97), the hero, Siegfried, dons a cloak that renders him invisible to his opponents. Samson's heavenly help is thus comparatively paltry.

It is now possible to make a judgment on the effect of the Spirit of YHWH on the heroicity of the Samson narrative. The narrative manifests three instances of direct recourse to YHWH on the part of Samson (14:6, 19; 15:14). Alternatively, Judg 13–16 has at least seven heroic feats that lack any explicit mention of divine assistance (15:4, 5; 16:3, 9, 11–12,

---

67. Soggin, *Judges*, 258. He regards 16:20b (והוא לא ידע כי יהוה סר מעליו) as a clarification from "redactors" (p. 257). See also, e.g., J. A. Wharton, "The Secret of Yahweh: Story and Affirmation in Judges 13–16," *Int* 27 (1973): 48–66 (54–55). For Blenkinsopp, "Some Notes," 83, the stories in the Samson narrative are "essentially secular" and for the purpose of entertainment. On the question of how a theologically oriented recasting of the narrative could leave the original stories largely intact, see, e.g., Wharton, "Secret of Yahweh," 58.

68. S. Dalley, *Myths from Mesopotamia: Creation, the Flood, Gilgamesh, and Others* (Oxford: Oxford University Press, 2000), 128 n. 43. See also p. 340.

69. Chadwick and Chadwick, *Growth of Literature*, 1:187.

70. Bowra, *Heroic Poetry*, 85.

13–14, 29–30). Admittedly, three are somewhat ambiguous on this point
(15:4, 5; 16:29–30), and one could perhaps debate over the heroic
significance of the feats which did or did not involve divine assistance.
Still, on balance the Samson narrative should qualify as heroic literature,
and unequivocally so if passages such as 14:6, 19 and 15:14 are secondary; but even if they are original, the examples from the wider corpus of
heroic literature provide comparative support for classifying the narrative
as heroic.

There remain for consideration other elements in the Samson narrative
which are not discussed specifically by the Chadwicks or Bowra, and
which may be considered under the rubric of other supernatural involvement. For convenience, ch. 13 can be considered as a whole, because of
its overall theological nature and because the adventures of Samson
begin properly in ch. 14. Verse 1 is clearly an editorial addition (cf. Judg
2:14; 3:8; 4:2; 6:1; 10:6–7). In the rest of ch. 13, the relevant supernatural involvement consists of (1) the proclamation by the "messenger/
angel of YHWH" (מלאך־יהוה, v. 3) to Manoah's wife about a forthcoming
son who would be a Nazirite from birth, and would "begin to deliver" the
Israelites from Philistine oppression (vv. 2–7), (2) a statement of the
blessing of Samson by YHWH (v. 24), and (3) the transitional statement
that "the Spirit of YHWH began to impel (לפעמו) him" in Mahaneh-dan
(v. 25). Clearly, there is divine involvement, but it is not connected
directly with any action.[71] Next are the references by the narrator in 14:4a
(ואביו ואמו לא ידעו כי מיהוה היא כי־תאנה הוא מבקש מפלשתים) and 16:20c
(והוא לא ידע כי יהוה סר מעליו), which, respectively, give the reader privileged information unknown to Samson's parents and/or Samson. The
parenthetical form of both makes it possible that they are secondary; yet
even if this is not the case, they simply allude to YHWH's involvement
behind the scenes.

Looking at supernatural assistance as a whole, then, the picture is
complex. If Samson's strength derives from his Nazirite status, it is
consistent with what one finds in extrabiblical heroic literature. Samson
receives divine aid through prayer, but only twice; and, again, such
petition is commonplace in heroic literature. The role of the Spirit of
YHWH is the most intricate of the supernatural criteria. Samson's feats

---

71. For the interpretation that the angel of YHWH impregnates Manoah's wife,
see R. Bartelmus, *Heroentum in Israel und seiner Umwelt: eine traditionsgeschichtliche Untersuchung zu Gen. 4,1–6 und verwandten Texten im Alten Testament und
der altorientalischen Literatur* (Zurich: Theologischer Verlag, 1979), 79–102, and
O. Margalith, "More Samson Legends," *VT* 36 (1986): 397–405. Even if Samson has
semi-divine paternity, this is the case with Achilles and many other heroes.

include those which directly involve YHWH through the onrushing of his Spirit. A few deeds are somewhat ambiguous in this regard, while others involve no explicit divine assistance. If the narrator had intended a more prominent role for YHWH in Judg 13–16, there was ample opportunity to provide such. Instead, the focus is predominantly on Samson, as is consistent with extrabiblical heroic literature; and when divine empowerment occurs, it is, again, the type that is found regularly in extrabiblical heroic literature. In his battles against the Philistines, Samson functions neither as a magician nor as an incinerating prophet (cf. 2 Kgs 1:10). The Samson narrative is thus heroic with respect to supernatural assistance.

3. *Conclusion*

A number of studies have assumed that the Samson narrative is heroic in the course of identifying heroic characteristics in the story. Methodologically, then, such studies are built on an unstable foundation, since they have not considered whether there are non-heroic characteristics in the narrative, and, if so, to what extent. The present effort has thus been to identify any such features in Judg 13–16 and to assess, through recourse to extrabiblical heroic literature, whether they are sufficient, quantitatively and/or qualitatively, to classify the Samson narrative as non-heroic literature. The evaluation has centred on four non-heroic indicators: community orientation, defensive warfare, didacticism, and supernatural assistance of Samson. Of these only the fourth has the potential strength to bring a non-heroic classification to the narrative: there are occasions when YHWH does extend direct aid to Samson, namely, in the inspiration of Samson in Judg 14:6, 19, and 15:14. Apart from these occurrences, there is no explicit mention of YHWH's involvement; and the inspiration is no more than what Homer describes as occurring routinely on the long slope of Troy. Indeed, both the Greeks and the Achaeans receive substantially more assistance than Samson, as do heroes outside biblical and classical heroic literature. In short, the divine footprint is comparatively faint in the Samson narratives. Moreover, in Judg 13–16 there is no non-heroic material which is either of an undisputed provenance or of a type that does not occur in extrabiblical heroic literature. The foregoing analysis thus establishes that Judg 13–16 is indeed heroic, and thereby provides a solid foundation for future work on the narrative.

TRANSLATING POLITICS INTO RELIGION: THEOLOGICAL ENRICHMENT IN 1 KINGS 5–9

Gönke Eberhardt

1. *Introduction*

The Hebrew Bible is not only a book about God's love towards human-kind or about the history of the people of God, nor is it merely a collection of ancient stories and prayers. It is also a document of the power of language and literature.

It is a commonplace observation that history is a construct. In the same way, Israel's history as described in the Hebrew Bible is a theological construct. It was language and literature that, in the process of interpretation, almost made a saint of a perhaps religious, but certainly a politically calculating, king. It was language and literature that made his time a golden age and his temple—even its remnants—the centre of a religion that has spread worldwide. And it is the language and literature of the Hebrew Bible that still has influence on politics in the modern state of Israel.

The power of language, literature and interpretation has always been present in the teaching and the written work of Andrew Macintosh. Therefore, I would like to deal with the impact of interpretation on the formation of biblical literature, particularly the process of theologization—that is, of "theological enrichment."[1] The idea of theological enrichment does not mean that the history of ancient Israel as such was without any theological facets. It only means that the selection of certain events and their theological interpretation and reinterpretation in the formative history of the Hebrew Bible continually added to the theological significance of the original events, people and places. One of the

---

1. Cf. M. A. Sweeney, *I & II Kings: A Commentary* (OTL; Louisville: Westminster John Knox, 2007), 5. He speaks here of 1–2 Kings as a "highly theologized account of Israel's and Judah's history."

most prominent examples of this process is the story of Solomon's building of the Temple.

There is no doubt that the Solomon of the Hebrew Bible is not identical with the historical Solomon, but rather an idealized figure of fabulous wealth, wisdom, and—although not consistently—piety.[2] The temple of Solomon also seems to have been subject to idealization. As the temple of Jerusalem was subjected to substantial alterations, the story of its construction likewise underwent a process of modification.[3] Besides some literary adjustments to the changing shape of the actual sanctuary, new theological ideas and concepts were integrated into the story.

It is neither possible nor reasonable to present a conclusive literary and redactional account of 1 Kgs 5–9 in this essay, especially since the discussion around the Deuteronomistic History has been very lively for decades. I will rely on some textual examples and general considerations in order to illustrate, somewhat sketchily, the process of theological enrichment of this text.[4] Apart from the process of theologization as such, there is the question of its starting point in history. What building, what king, what text stood at the beginning of the theological and textual development?

The abundance of literature concerning the Solomonic temple reveals manifold approaches to the topic, especially on the question whether the description of the temple permits a reconstruction of the historical temple. Scholars have attempted to deal with the measurements in 1 Kgs 6–7 as one might deal with archaeological data, by interpreting them in the light of archaeological finds from the end of the second or the beginning of the first millennium B.C.E. One important example of this approach is the 1999 work of Wolfgang Zwickel.[5] Others have preferred

---

2. 1 Kgs 11 presents a different picture of Solomon in accordance with the Deuteronomistic interpretation of the exile as caused by Israel's idolatry (see below).

3. V. A. Hurowitz, *I Have Built You an Exalted House: Temple Building in the Bible in Light of Mesopotamian and Northwest Semitic Writings* (JSOTSup 115; Sheffield: Sheffield Academic, 1992), 320, considers a connection between the two kinds of alteration: "Possible changes in the temple architecture may have occasioned changes in the description at any time in the process of the account's development."

4. Ibid., 171–73, concerning the extent of the "Deuteronomic" reworking.

5. W. Zwickel, *Der salomonische Tempel* (Kulturgeschichte der antiken Welt 83; Mainz: von Zabern, 1999); also B. Herr, "*Deinem Haus gebührt Heiligkeit, Jhwh, alle Tage*": *Typen und Funktionen von Sakralbauten im vorexilischen Israel* (BBB 124; Berlin: Philo, 2000). For further literature and recent scholarly discussion see Hurowitz, *Exalted House*, and "YHWH's Exalted House—Aspects of the Design and Symbolism of Solomon's Temple," in *Temple and Worship in Biblical Israel* (ed. J. Day; LHBOTS 422; London: T&T Clark International, 2005), 63–110.

to understand the text as mirroring the political and cultic circumstances of later times, when its "first drafts"—or even the latest redactional passages—were written.[6] Hurowitz has taken into account the similarity of 1 Kgs 5–9 to ancient Near Eastern royal building accounts. He has been cautious concerning the historicity of the textual data, although he does not exclude the possibility of their reliability.[7] McCormick even goes so far as to postulate that the text is a "verbal icon," not referring to a real pre-exilic temple but providing a literary temple for the exilic community and embodying "the historian's own ideology regarding proper religious practice and relationship between humanity and the deity."[8] According to McCormick, the structure, as described in 1 Kgs 6–7, "is the creation of the historian, and in many respects is influenced by the architectural forms he and the rest of the nation met in exile. These forms are used by the historian to present what was a truly innovative concept of divine presence and to fuel a religious reform that sought to reshape Israel's basic notions about YHWH."[9]

Despite the question of how the Solomonic temple looked, there is little doubt about its existence. Furthermore, its construction was obviously very much connected to the name of Solomon. Otherwise one would perhaps have attributed its building to David, since this would have suited the royal ideology much better (see below). Thus we have good reason to assume that it was the Davidic king Solomon who was responsible for the project—whatever his true relationship to David may have been. So, for the present, I will begin with a rather minimalistic assumption: King Solomon built or renovated a temple at some point in the tenth century B.C.E. That is the historical kernel in the literary and theological history of 1 Kgs 5–9. Is there also a "theological kernel"?

---

6. Cf. J. C. Gertz, "Konstruierte Erinnerung: Alttestamentliche Historiographie im Spiegel von Archäologie und literarhistorischer Kritik am Fallbeispiel des salomonischen Königtums," *Berliner theologische Zeitschrift* 21 (2004): 3–29.

7. Hurowitz, "YHWH's Exalted House," and *Exalted House*.

8. C. M. McCormick, *Palace and Temple: A Study of Architectural and Verbal Icons* (BZAW 313; Berlin: de Gruyter, 2002), 41.

9. Ibid., 41. One may ask, however, whether indeed it was possible to create a "verbal icon" shortly after the destruction of the real temple by describing something totally different. See J. Kamlah, "Der salomonische Tempel: Paradigma der Verknüpfung von biblischer Exegese und Archäologie für eine Rekonstruktion der Religionsgeschichte Israels," *Verkündigung und Forschung* 53 (2008): 40–51 (50–51). It seems more likely that there were at least some similarities between the real temple and the "icon."

2. *Solomon's Political and Religious Reasons*

We can only guess why Solomon built a temple for YHWH in Jerusalem.
"As the ambitious and successful king of a young nation, he had political
and religious reasons to build a temple, as well as the necessary resources
and political connections."[10] It seems as if it was not so much YHWH who
needed the temple, but rather Solomon himself. That is also an implication of the Deuteronomistic redaction, which seems to ascribe serious
doubts about the building project to Solomon: "But will God indeed
dwell on the earth? Even heaven and the highest heaven cannot contain
you, much less this house that I have built!" (1 Kgs 8:27, NRSV). That the
temple was more important for the king than for YHWH is, of course, not
the text's intended message, but nevertheless there may be an element of
truth in this assessment.

Solomon did in fact need a temple in order to establish fully the—
still—newborn state of Israel. It seems as if David's *not* having built a
temple for YHWH was seen in later times as a blemish in the glorious
undertaking of the first "proper" king of Israel.[11] The later traditions tried
to explain David's "failure" by talking of his intention to build a temple,
and of its rejection by YHWH (2 Sam 7; 1 Kgs 5:17–19 [implicitly];
8:17–19). The aetiological story of David's building an altar on
Araunah's threshing floor probably also belongs in this context.

At least the reputation of the dynasty could be saved by YHWH's
announcing a Davidic scion who would build "a house for my name"
(2 Sam 7:13; 1 Kgs 5:19; 8:19). The biblical records concerning YHWH's
unwillingness to allow David to build him a house also function as a
defence for David in that they affirm his integrity in relation to YHWH.[12]
David's having "no time because of his enemies" (1 Kgs 5:17–19), by
contrast, may indeed have been the main reason why he did not build a
temple.[13] Despite the many uncertainties concerning the true origin and

10. E. Bloch-Smith, "Solomon's Temple: The Politics of Ritual Space," in
Sacred Time, Sacred Place: Archaeology and the Religion of Israel (ed. B. M.
Gittlen; Winona Lake: Eisenbrauns, 2002), 83–94 (83).

11. O. Keel, E. A. Knauf and T. Staubli, *Salomons Tempel* (Fribourg, Schweiz:
Academic, 2004), 9: "scandal."

12. Otherwise W. Dietrich, *Von David zu den Deuteronomisten: Studien zu den
Geschichtsüberlieferungen des Alten Testaments* (BWANT 156; Stuttgart: Kohl-
hammer, 2002), 191, who assumes that the biblical record of YHWH's rejection of
David's proposal tried to avoid a "classical oriental 'do ut des' relationship" between
YHWH and David.

13. The passage does not necessarily belong to an inscription pattern as one
could suppose from the Babylonian "parallel" cited by Hurowitz, *Exalted House*,
133–34. See also Hurowitz, "YHWH's Exalted House," 91–92.

further development of the monarchy in Israel and Judah during the tenth and ninth centuries B.C.E., the archaeological and textual material points towards a scenario that has certain similarities with the biblical view.[14] At the end of a long process of sedentarization, there was the formation of city states on the basis of military groupings. This roughly matches the biblical description of the period of Saul and David. It is likely that the historical David was indeed busy with basic measures during his lifetime: establishing the state by "defining" and defending its territory, and perhaps turning Jerusalem into the kingdom's capital. In the course of time, the different "chiefdoms" in Palestine were bound together in the form of an ancient Near Eastern state, a process that was initiated by David's territorial rearrangements and continued by his successors' political programmes of internal and external stabilization.[15]

Only after the kingdom was settled could the respective kings concentrate on questions of administration and representation, diplomacy and dynasty, as also on questions of a national cult. A residence city without a sanctuary would have been unthinkable in the ancient Near East. In the city states of the period, the city gods ensured blessing, military protection, and food and water, as well as law and order, for the inhabitants. The king was responsible for the maintenance of the cult.[16] Since it is unlikely that Jerusalem lacked a temple prior to its conquest by David (see below), it is evident that it was not a temple as such that Solomon needed. It was a representative project[17] and a national symbol that he required.[18] The newborn state, which was to unite different groups of people who had their own histories and distinctive traditions, needed the unifying cult of a national deity, or at least a deity who protected the monarch and the ensuing dynasty.[19] It may be for this reason that the new temple was built outside the old city fortifications. Zwickel proposes that David allowed the new YHWH sanctuary, housing the ark of the covenant (cf. 2 Sam 6), to reside outside the city walls in order to avoid a competition between YHWH and the long-established city god(s), possibly Shalim

14. See Gertz, "Konstruierte Erinnerung," 19–21.
15. Ibid., 27.
16. Zwickel, *Der salomonische Tempel*, 34.
17. For the importance of royal building projects, see Hurowitz, *Exalted House*, 313, also with n. 1.
18. I doubt that the temple was at first "a foreign body" in Israel; cf. H. Donner, *Geschichte des Volkes Israel und seiner Nachbarn in Gründzügen. Teil 1: Von den Anfängen bis zur Staatenbildungszeit* (2d ed.; Grundrisse zum Alten Testament; ATD 4/1; Göttingen: Vandenhoeck & Ruprecht, 1995), 250.
19. YHWH as the protective deity of the Davidic dynasty is, for example, assumed by M. Köckert, "Wandlungen Gottes im antiken Israel," *BThZ* 22 (2005): 3–36 (28).

and Zedeq, and perhaps also El.[20] After the monarchy had become more firmly established and certain elements of the YHWH cult and the cult of the city gods had begun to conflate,[21] the provisional sanctuary was replaced by a proper temple which, thanks to new fortifications, now lay inside the city walls.[22] Whether or not Zwickel is right about a Davidic YHWH sanctuary outside the walls, only Solomon experienced the right conditions for establishing a symbol of the king's and the state's religious and political status.

It would be an interesting question whether the decision to identify YHWH as the national god was in fact as self-evident as it was seen in retrospect—and whether YHWH was as easily accepted as the national god by the population as the biblical account implies.[23] These questions must remain unaddressed in this context, even more so as Solomon's personal religious motivations can only be a subject of speculation and can hardly be divided from political considerations. The desire for the state's and also the dynasty's divine protection may with some probability have been part of his motivation. Whatever the extent of the connection between the god YHWH and the early "people" of Israel may have been, now YHWH's connection with the dynasty became dominant.[24] Thus the first theological aspects of the history of the Temple—and of 1 Kgs 5–9—were likely to have been dominated by political reasoning. This also seems to have been the case in the first stages of the literary development.

3. *First Elements of the Building Account*

We do not know what, if any, contemporary literary accounts remained from Solomon's time. Perhaps there was not more than an oral tradition about Solomon having built the temple. Perhaps pieces of Solomon's

20. Cf. Zwickel, *Der salomonische Tempel*, 15, 25.

21. Ibid., 28. The questions relating to a possible predecessor of the temple and of syncretism ("was YHWH a sun deity?") are still disputed.

22. Ibid., 21–23.

23. H. Schmid, "Der Tempelbau Salomos in religionsgeschichtlicher Sicht," in *Archäologie und altes Testament: Festschrift Kurt Galling zum 8. Januar 1970* (ed. A. Kuschke and E. Kutsch; Tübingen: Mohr Siebeck), 241–50 (245), considers Solomon's building a temple for YHWH "surprising," because he supposes Jebusite opposition to it, referring to Nathan's words in 2 Sam 7:1–7. He interpreted Nathan's words as having been influenced by Jebusite interests. It is doubtful, however, whether 2 Sam 7:1–7 allows one to assume such opposition.

24. Cf. E. Zenger, "Der Monotheismus Israels: Entstehung–Profil–Relevanz," in *Ist der Glaube Feind der Freiheit? Der neue Debatte um den Monotheismus* (ed. Thomas Söding; QD; Freiburg: Herder, 2003), 9–52 (24).

correspondence with Hiram of Tyre had survived somewhere for some hundreds of years until later writers used them for an expanded building account.[25] In any case, the "archival" practices of the time certainly were different from modern ones.[26] With some greater probability, there may have been administrative records (concerning the temple vessels, for example), texts of prayers, etc.[27] It is not unlikely that there also existed a dedicatory inscription or a short notice similar to one that has emerged from Assyria and is dated to the twelfth or eleventh century, found on paving bricks from the fountain courtyard of the Anu-Adad Temple at Ashur: "Tiglath-pileser, vice-regent of Ashur, son of Ashur-resha-ishi (who was) also vice-regent of Ashur, built and reconstructed the temple of the gods Anu and Adad, his lords."[28] Again, all this is mere speculation and based on questions of probability. Although we can assume that annals were written in Jerusalem at the end of the tenth century B.C.E.,[29] nothing indicates that such annals were used for describing the reign of Solomon in 1 Kings.[30]

There are certain details in the biblical text of the Solomon story that indicate the existence of, at the least, strong oral traditions concerning Solomon and his building projects. Such details include, for example, the references to the "House of the Forest of Lebanon" and the "hall for Pharaoh's daughter,"[31] and, above all, the temple's connection with Solomon instead of David (see above). If there had not been an oral tradition behind them, there would be no reason for a later author to invent them.

---

25. Cf. Hurowitz, *Exalted House*, 134. On the likelihood of a real correspondence, see the ancient Near Eastern parallels in ibid., 223. The view that 1 Kgs 5–9 includes contemporary material that survived in the royal archives was prominently taken by M. Noth in his *Könige* (BKAT 9/1; Neukirchen–Vluyn: Neukirchener, 1968). Otherwise V. Fritz, "Monarchy and Re-urbanization: A New Look at Solomon's Kingdom," in *The Origins of the Ancient Israelite States* (ed. V. Fritz and P. R. Davies; JSOTSup 228; Sheffield: JSOT, 1996), 187–95 (189), who takes only the list of royal officials in 1 Kgs 4:1–6 and the list of the administrative districts in 1 Kgs 4:7–19 as original documents from the royal chancellery.

26. Cf. J. Van Seters, "Solomon's Temple: Fact and Ideology in Biblical and Near Eastern Historiography," *CBQ* 50 (1997): 45–57 (49).

27. Hurowitz, *Exalted House*, 319. He also considers that building plans could have survived from Solomon's time.

28. A. K. Grayson, *Assyrian Rulers of the Early First Millennium BC* (2 vols.; RIMAP 2; Toronto: University of Toronto Press, 1991), 1:A.0.87.22.

29. N. Na'aman, "Sources and composition in the history of David," in Fritz and Davies, eds., *The Origins of the Ancient Israelite States*, 170–86 (170–71).

30. Cf. Gertz, "Konstruierte Erinnerung," 19, 22.

31. Ibid., 24.

4. *The Building Account from Hezekiah's Time*

A long time later, pieces of text (if any) and traditional material would have been bound together in a "proper" building account. This account probably included already the main passages of 1 Kgs 5–9, and perhaps even the whole text, apart from Deuteronomistic additions (see below). Many scholars have shown from different perspectives that various details of the building account point to the Assyrian period:[32]

Solomon's trade connections and the cultural contact with Egypt. According to Schipper, both of these point to the time of Hezekiah's reign (725–697 B.C.E.) rather than to the time of Solomon.[33]

The "store cities" in 1 Kgs 9:19. The Hebrew word מסכנות is an Akkadian loan word.[34] The verse does not belong to the temple building account, but stems from its direct context. The use of such a loan word forms a *terminus post quem* for the respective text. Despite the possibility of the text preserving older elements, the loan word is another argument against dating the composition of 1 Kgs 5–9 prior to the Neo-Assyrian period.

The similarity with other building accounts of the Assyrian period. On the basis of comparison with several ancient Near Eastern building accounts, Hurowitz has shown that the main structure of the building account in 1 Kgs 5:15–9:9, including the dedication ceremonies, is that of "a typical ancient Near Eastern building story"[35] representing "a scribal convention rehearsing a literary stereotype rather than a habitual adhering to the actual course of events,"[36] and reflecting "the literary environment of the Assyrian period."[37] The structure is as follows:[38]

5:17–19	Decision to build and divine approval
5:20–32	Preparations for the building (materials, drafting workmen, laying foundations)

---

32. Most of the following arguments are discussed by Gertz (ibid., 22–27).

33. B. U. Schipper, *Israel und Ägypten in der Königszeit: Die kulturellen Kontakte von Salomo bis zum Fall Jerusalems* (OBO 170; Fribourg: Universitäts-Verlag; Göttingen: Vandenhoeck & Ruprecht, 1999), esp. 115–16, 283–86; cf. S. Wälchli, *Der weise König Salomo* (BWANT 141; Stuttgart: Kohlhammer, 1999), 195–203.

34. Gertz, "Konstruierte Erinnerung," 24.

35. Hurowitz, *Exalted House*, 110.

36. Ibid., 128.

37. Ibid., 314; cf. also pp. 313–16. See also p. 259, where Hurowitz claims that the writer "was influenced from some already existing literary form, and did not invent his style of description *ex nihilo*."

38. Ibid., 109–10.

6:1–7:51   Description of the construction process and the buildings
            and furnishings
8:1–11   Dedication festivities; the ark and God's glory enter the
            Temple
8:12–61   Dedication prayers
8:62–66   Dedication festivities (popular festivities)
9:1–9   Divine promises/revelation; blessings and curses for the
            future

Concerning the Deuteronomistic passages (see below), Hurowitz reckons with a later "Deuteronomic" redactor or several redactors who "added their glosses to certain parts of the story and rewrote others, so as to reflect their own views about the nature of the Temple and about the place its building occupied in their view of Israelite history."[39]

The relatively great number of building accounts in the ancient Near East first indicates that building or restoring temples belonged to the duties of an ancient Near Eastern king.[40] Secondly, it is probable that the building accounts not only fulfilled an administrative purpose but also functioned to glorify the king (even if the "glorification" here was reduced to preserving the memory of one's merits for later generations).[41] Whether a king indeed had strictly *religious* reasons to erect or restore a temple, or whether the building programme was in fact merely politically motivated, the building inscriptions provided a concrete and literary manner of documenting the king's piety—and divine acceptance. This

39. Ibid., 316.
40. See also A. S. Kapelrud, "Two Great Rulers and Their Temple Buildings," in *Text and Theology: Studies in Honour of Prof. Dr. Theol. Magne Saebø* (ed. A. Tangberg; Oslo: Verbum, 1994), 135–42, who compares the biblical building account with a Sumerian hymn on Gudea's building a temple for Ningirsu. He detects the following parallels between the two independently written texts: "1. Some indications that a temple has to be built. 2. The king visits a holy place overnight and has a dream. 3. A god tells him what to do, indicates plans. The wisdom of the ruler is emphasized. 4. The king announces his intention to build a temple. 5. Master builder is engaged, cedars from Lebanon, building stones, gold, silver, etc. procured for the task. 6. The temple finished according to the plan. 7. Offerings and dedication, fixing of norm. 8. Assembly of the people. 9. The god comes to his new house. 10. The king is blessed and promised everlasting domination for himself and/ or his descendants" (p. 141). Kapelrud comes to the conclusion that nothing "in King Solomon's undertakings during his temple building was surprising. It was all in full accordance with well known ways to accomplish such tasks" (pp. 141–42).
41. Cf. Hurowitz, *Exalted House*, 312: "The 'building account' was an important, prominent and even formative element in the historical writings of the kings of Mesopotamia, and the prominence it has achieved in biblical writings as well can be taken as a sign of connections between historical writing in Israel and historical writing in neighbouring cultures." See also ibid., 313: "suitable for glorifying kings."

means that the texts "proved" that the king was accepted by the respective deity.[42] Without this acceptance he might not have been given the divine command to restore or construct a temple.[43] In this respect, the building account often provided a form of theological legitimation.[44]

It is a difficult question whether the first building account contained a description of the temple like the one we have in 1 Kgs 6–7. As has been mentioned briefly in the introduction to this essay, the kinds of interpretation range from "building plans,"[45] through "contemporary description," "later description of the historical Solomonic temple,"[46] "report of an eye-witness of the 9./8. century BC"[47] and "exilic memory"[48] to "verbal icon."[49] Although the comparison with other archaeological evidence, as well as the unrealistic measurements, indicates that the description of 1 Kgs 6–7 does not depict the temple from the tenth century B.C.E.,[50] and although a detailed description does not belong to the "classical" ancient Near Eastern building accounts, it is still possible that the account from Hezekiah's time did contain some description that was subject to later redactional work. Since there are almost no true parallels to the biblical temple description of 1 Kgs 6–7, not even from the exilic or postexilic periods, as Van Seters has pointed out,[51] the *argumentum e silentio* does not work. The dating of the description has to rely on considerations other

42. Cf. Sweeney, *I & II Kings*, 133.

43. Cf. the section "Building Temples upon Divine Command," in Hurowitz, *Exalted House*, 135–63. According to Hurowitz, the pre-Deuteronomic passage recording Solomon's correspondence with Hiram of Tyre already contained the indispensable divine permission to build the temple (ibid., 166). See also the biblical records of renovation works on the temple in 2 Kgs 12 (Jehoash) and 22 (Josiah; cf. 2 Chr 34).

44. Several of the ancient Near Eastern building accounts report a divine order or explicit permission to build or restore a sanctuary, for example in a dream. In the context of the later Deuteronomistic History, this function is served by YHWH's announcement of a Davidic descendant who would build the temple (2 Sam 7:12–13), and by YHWH's acceptance of the temple (1 Kgs 9:3). In the Deuteronomistic History, Solomon receives still further proofs of divine legitimation: YHWH's dynastic promises to him (1 Kgs 9:4–5), and his dream in Gibeon (1 Kgs 3:5–15). The permission to build the temple thus takes its place among several other positive elements relating to Solomon.

45. Noth, *Könige*, 104, 125.

46. Zwickel, *Der salomonische Tempel*, passim.

47. Gertz, "Konstruierte Erinnerung," 23.

48. Van Seters, "Solomon's Temple," 45–57.

49. See the introduction, above. For the recent discussion see Kamlah, "Der salomonische Tempel," 40–51.

50. Ibid., 50.

51. Van Seters, "Solomon's Temple," 49–51.

than extrabiblical parallels. The exilic desire to preserve the memory of the destroyed temple or to provide a model for a new one could indeed have provided strong motivation for inserting a description into the text.[52] That does not explain, however, the unrealistic measurements, nor does it exclude the possible existence of older descriptions, whatever their purpose may have been.

As regards the glorification of the monarch, the first version of the building account of 1 Kgs 5:15–9:25 will certainly have served its purpose in this respect, with or without a detailed description.[53] Solomon was depicted as the pious and divinely accepted king of Israel, equal to his neighbour kings and knowing his kingly duties, this latter point being deducible from the text's similarities with ancient Near Eastern royal inscriptions. Even if Solomon's reasons for building the temple had been mainly political, the building account in its first stages provided the proper religious framework for them. The main parts of the Solomon passages in 1 Kings, written *ad maiorem gloriam Salomonis*,[54] were a piece of court literature that was written in order to describe the mighty position, the wisdom, the righteousness, and the piety and divine acceptance of the Davidic king. But this was not the only motivation for the text's composition.

It certainly was no coincidence that the building account, together with other texts on "Israel's" history, was composed at a time when Judah's political and religious future was more uncertain than it had been for a long time. After 701 B.C.E., the state of Judah had ceased to exist. Although the Davidic dynasty continued to exist, Hezekiah's territory was reduced by the Assyrians to the confines of Jerusalem alone. It is possible that these measures were soon revoked, because Assyria was interested in stabilizing the southern part of Palestine against Egyptian interests. This was done during Manasseh's reign at the latest (696–642 B.C.E.), and perhaps already during the reign of Hezekiah himself.[55] Without doubt, the end of the eighth century B.C.E. forced Judah into a tightrope walk between loyalty towards the Assyrian rulers and the need to stabilize its own political and religious identity. It is possible that hope of a new political independence spurred on the authors of the pre-Deuteronomistic Solomon story.[56] Yet it might as well have been grief over the

---

52. Ibid., 57.

53. Cf. ibid., 55.

54. Cf. Gertz, "Konstruierte Erinnerung," 23, referring to the reliability of the text.

55. Donner, *Geschichte des Volkes Israel*, 359.

56. Cf. Gertz, "Konstruierte Erinnerung," 28: "The [Solomon story of the eighth century B.C.E.] mirrors the wish for legitimation of the rising kingdom of Judah. Still

(temporary) loss of Judah's independence that made the authors describe Solomon's glory in even brighter colours. We do not know.

What we do know is that the Assyrian influence on the population in Judah and Jerusalem was reflected also in terms of religion. Cylinder seals depicting astral symbols and the moon god[57] have been found, for example, where there had been no substantial astral tradition before. Yet the extent to which the Assyrians exerted their political influence also on religious matters in Palestine is a contested matter. At any rate, some genuine or pre-Assyrian elements of the YHWH cult survived,[58] and the Assyrian influence on religious life in Judah and Jerusalem never became as strong as it had been earlier in Israel. The "orthodox" tendencies that can be detected in the iconography of the period[59] may belong to the same back-to-roots ideas as are reported in connection with the so-called reform of Josiah (2 Kgs 22–23), although the historical reliability of the text is a still disputed question. It is likely that the attempt to discover the original form of worship inspired a new interest in the origins of the YHWH cult in Jerusalem.

Finally, there was another reason for the special significance of the Jerusalem temple and its builder during the reign of Hezekiah. After the fall of Samaria in 720 B.C.E., Judah had been filled with refugees from the Northern Kingdom who brought with them their own religious traditions and experiences. If Jerusalem was to be their new religious home, it might have been useful to strengthen the Solomon tradition and the claim always to have housed the proper dwelling place of YHWH, as the first and proper cultic centre of the Davidic kingdom. In that case, the authors of the building account would have had reason to insert a more or less detailed description of the temple in order to identify the temple of the seventh century B.C.E. with the Solomonic one. The unrealistic measurements could be later modifications.

Bearing all this in mind, we have good reason to believe that the first literary expression of Solomon's building project was—at least in part—politically motivated. The oral and perhaps written traditions about the

---

being in the shadow of a real imperium, it had ventured to gain the heritage of the North since Hezekiah and to establish a state according to a Neo-Assyrian pattern" (author's translation).

57. Cf. O. Keel and C. Uehlinger, *Göttinnen, Götter und Gottessymbole: Neue Erkenntnisse zur Religionsgeschichte Kanaans und Israels aufgrund bislang unerschlossener ikonographischer Quellen* (4th ed.; QD 134; Freiburg: Herder, 1998), 339–55.

58. Ibid., 404–6; 422–29, esp. 426–28.

59. Ibid., 406–22.

fabulous king Solomon and his temple condensed into a piece of court literature that celebrated the origins of the dynasty and expressed both Jerusalem's religious claims and Judah's political hopes.

5. *The Text in the Time of Josiah*

It is unlikely that the cultic changes in Judah during the seventh century B.C.E. that are generally attributed to the reforms of Josiah left no traces in the building account from the time of Hezekiah. It was now the unity and "purity" of the central sanctuary that came into focus. From the eighth century onward, the veneration of YHWH had induced monolatrous tendencies in (former) Israel and Judah. It seems as if, with his growing universalism, YHWH extended his claim to exclusive worship. The idea of a single and central sanctuary corresponds to these tendencies. Both claims—of monolatry and of a central sanctuary—find their expression in what was later understood as the "Josianic reform." In these circumstances the building account of 1 Kgs 5–9 must gain new significance. Donner even goes so far as to say: "In the light of Deuteronomy, Solomon appeared as the great builder of the temple...and, if one wanted to say so, as the first one who fulfilled the claim of cult centralization in Deut 12."[60] But what impact did this have on the building account itself?

The hypothesis that there existed during the late monarchy a pre-exilic Deuteronomic version of the otherwise exilic or post-exilic "Deuteronomistic History" has received growing support recently, and it is the very idea of the unity of the central sanctuary that provides the focus of such a pre-exilic Deuteronomic version.[61] Unfortunately, attempts to identify certain Deuteronomic texts from pre-exilic times and to distinguish them from exilic Deuteronomistic layers are in most cases rather speculative. It is possible that the references to YHWH's *dwelling* in the temple (e.g. לשבתך עולמים, "to dwell for ever," 8:13) which stand in direct contrast to 8:39, 43, 49—the allusions to Israel's years in the desert and the guiding cloud—were composed or at least strengthened under Deuteronomic influence. If the temple in pre-exilic times was understood as the place in which YHWH dwelt, then its significance did not need to be disputed. All in all, it seems that theological questions prevailed over political ones in the understanding of the building account during the seventh century B.C.E.

60. Donner, *Geschichte des Volkes Israel*, 256 (author's translation).
61. Cf. G. Hentschel, *1 Könige* (Neue Echter Bibel 10; Würzburg: Echter, 1984), 7.

But again, all this is uncertain. The exilic or post-exilic Deuteronomistic revision so dominates the respective texts that the attempt to distinguish pre-exilic, exilic, and post-exilic Deuteronom(ist)ic layers is almost bound to end up in *a priori* argument or, if not so, in heuristic circumambulation. There is no room here for entering the lively discussions around the Deuteronomistic History, the Deuteronomists, their predecessors, and the question of their dating. Despite the abundance of literature on the Deuteronomists, and particularly on the formation of the dedication prayer in 1 Kgs 8, space permits only a short look at some new theological ideas that were successively incorporated into the eighth-century building account by the Deuteronomists. In most of the passages discussed here an exilic or perhaps even post-exilic perspective is evident.[62]

6. *The Exilic Deuteronomist's Version*

With the catastrophe of 587/586 B.C.E., everything changed. What in Hezekiah's times had been described as the Golden Age of the kingdom, full of promises and blessing, now appeared in a new light. What had gone so terribly wrong? One attempt to answer this question can be seen in some passages and ideas that are, according to a broad consensus, Deuteronomistic, notably 1 Kgs 5:17–19, 21 (disputed), 26a; 8:15–61, and 9:2–9. The passages are not necessarily simple additions to a previous text. They might as well be revised parts of the pre-Deuteronomistic version. Whether this pre-Deuteronomistic version was identical with the "book of the acts of Solomon" (ספר דברי שלמה) from 1 Kgs 11:41, as Gertz suggests,[63] remains an open question. It seems unlikely, however, that redactors should revise a text and afterwards refer to the original as a sort of supplement to their revised version.

At any rate, in their interpretation of political events the Deuteronomists developed their characteristic theological ideas. Several of them

---

62. As regards the dedication prayer, Sweeney presupposes a pre-exilic version of the dedication prayer in 1 Kgs 8 that originally referred to the Assyrian exile of the Northern Kingdom and that was reread by later Deuteronomists against the background of the Babylonian exile; Sweeney, *I & II Kings*, 130. G. N. Knoppers, "Prayer and Propaganda: Solomon's Dedication of the Temple and the Deuteronomist's Program," in *Reconsidering Israel and Judah: Recent Studies on the Deuteronomistic History* (ed. G. N. Knoppers and J. G. McConville; SBTS 8: Winona Lake: Eisenbrauns, 2000), 370–96, even proposes the unity of the prayer and its *Sitz im Leben* in the context of the Josianic reform. His arguments, however, are not adequate to such an interpretation.

63. Gertz, "Konstruierte Erinnerung," 22–23.

are represented in the Deuteronomistic building account, particularly in the dedication prayer in 1 Kgs 8.

Disobedience Against the Law

After the events of 587/6 B.C.E., confidence in YHWH's faithfulness and in the reliability of his covenant was lost. The state of Judah, the last remains of the great kingdom, was gone. The capital and the national sanctuary had been destroyed. Yet the Deuteronomists managed to avoid the conclusion that it was the national god who had failed to act for his king and his people. According to them, blame lay with the people because of their deficient righteousness and the absence of the fear of God (cf. 1 Kgs 8:46–50; 9:6–9). The political catastrophe was nothing other than God's punishment for Israel's religious failure. YHWH's promises to David had depended on the obedience of Israel and its kings to YHWH's law (1 Kgs 9:4–5, 6–9).[64] Solomon's desire that Israel might "walk in all his ways" (ללכת בכל־דרכיו, 1 Kgs 8:58; see also 8:61) had in the end not been fulfilled.

In their deployment of pre-exilic Deuteronomic ideas, the exilic Deuteronomists identified Israel's "idolatry" as the main symptom of the nation's disobedience with regard to the law.

Monotheistic Ideas

The pre-exilic tendencies towards a monolatrous YHWH-cult within the context of a polytheistic society had been taken up and further developed by the Deuteronomists. Although YHWH held an eminent position, several deities were worshipped in Israel and Judah during pre-exilic times. The concept of "idolatry," perhaps a prophetic idea from the eighth century, became the basis of Deuteronomistic reasoning and forms the climax of YHWH's admonitions in 1 Kgs 9:1–9: "Because they have forsaken (עזבו) the LORD their God (אלהיהם), who brought their ancestors out of the land of Egypt, and embraced other gods (ויחזקו באלהים אחרים), worshipping them (וישתחוו להם [qere]) and serving them (ויעבדם); therefore the LORD has brought this disaster upon them" (NRSV). YHWH had required that he be Israel's only god, but Israel had not obeyed. In fact, YHWH *was* the only god and there was no other: יהוה הוא האלהים אין עוד (1 Kgs 8:60). While 1 Kgs 9:9 leaves unanswered the question whether other gods exist—concentrating instead on the prospect of veneration of them—and 1 Kgs 8:23 is ambiguous regarding their existence (אין כמוך אלהים), 1 Kgs 8:60 can be seen as a truly monotheistic text. Its authors left no doubt about "the true deity," and it seemed to be just a matter of

---

64. 1 Kgs 6:11–13 contains the same idea, but is a later addition.

time before "all the peoples of the earth" (כל־עמי הארץ) would come to
know this. More than ever, "our god" (אלהינו) stands as the true god over
against idolatrous pretenders (באלהים אחרים). YHWH had become the
deity on account of whom Israel was distinguishable from other peoples.
In this respect, he was now *God of Israel* more than ever.

"God of Israel"

The monotheistic interpretation enabled the Deuteronomists to gain a
new perspective on YHWH's relationship with what remained of the
kingdoms of Israel and Judah. YHWH was neither bound to the kingdom
nor dependent on a national sanctuary. He was bound neither to the
dynasty nor to the state as an institution. The one true god had bound
himself to the people itself, despite all its failures. Thanks to this new
understanding, the national god became "God of Israel" in a new manner. The cult of the dynasty's god acquired elements that were almost
"democratic."[65]

The name "Israel" also gained a new meaning in this context and
enjoyed growing importance during the following decades and centuries.[66] After the catastrophe of 720 B.C.E., it had been brought to Judah by
the refugees from the Northern Kingdom. As the kingdom of Israel had
ceased to exist, the name could be used to designate the people of God.[67]

It is noticeable that the term "God of Israel" (אלהי ישראל) occurs only
in the framing passages of 1 Kgs 1–11 (namely, 1 Kgs 1:30, 48; 11:9, 33)
and in Solomon's dedicatory prayer (8:15, 17, 20, 23, 25, 26). The term
is well represented in the Deuteronomistic History as well as in the
Chronistic History and other exilic or post-exilic texts. Similarly, within
1 Kgs 5–9, the phrase עם ישראל occurs almost exclusively in the
Deuteronomistic prayer of dedication in 1 Kgs 8:15–61. First Kings 6:13
is an even later addition. The people of Israel explicitly belong to God:
1 Kgs 8:16, 30, 33, 34, 36, 38, 41, 43, 51, 52, 56, 59. The phrase עם
ישראל, with the possessive suffix, that occurs in these verses and in
similar phrases may have its origin in the pre-exilic prophecy and traditions of the Northern Kingdom (cf. Exod 3:10; Amos 7:8, 15;[68] 8:2, etc.).

---

65. According to R. G. Kratz, "Israel als Staat und als Volk," *ZThK* 97 (2000):
1–17 (15–17), this process already began after the downfall of Samaria in 720 B.C.E.

66. See, for example, the development in the Chronistic *relecture* of earlier texts;
cf. ibid., 6–8.

67. U. Becker, "Von der Staatsreligion zum Monotheismus: Ein Kapitel
israelitisch-jüdischer Religionsgeschichte," *ZThK* 102 (2005): 1–16 (11); cf. Kratz,
"Israel als Staat und als Volk," 1–17.

68. Amos 7:15 belongs to a later, perhaps exilic, passage in the book of Amos
and uses the older phrase.

Yet the overwhelming majority of occurrences in the Bible as a whole belong to exilic or post-exilic texts, mainly from Deuteronomistic or Chronistic contexts as well as from exilic prophetic and priestly texts. Alongside the phrases connecting God and Israel, there is another element that accentuates the bond between YHWH and Israel, namely the allusions to "Egypt" that, in the context of the building account, occur only in the framing verse 1 Kgs 6:1, in the dedication prayer (1 Kgs 8:16, 21, 51, 53) and in YHWH's final admonition to Solomon (1 Kgs 9:9). It seems that the Deuteronomists never wearied of emphasizing the continuous and direct relationship between YHWH and the people. It was one of their main interests to show that the exclusive relation between YHWH and Israel continued to exist even during the exile.[69] So, after the loss of national identity, Israel could form a new, more theologically defined, identity.[70] Ironically, YHWH seems to have become more of a national deity *after* the end of Israel and Judah than he had been prior to their destruction.[71]

But the concept of the deity was changing in another respect, too. For if the relationship between YHWH and Israel was to hold up after the temple's destruction, YHWH had to be understood in a more transcendent manner.

Transcendence of YHWH
The Deuteronomic passages of the temple building account called into question the temple as a proper dwelling place for YHWH. How could a temple built by human beings contain God (1 Kgs 8:27)? The text repeatedly says that heaven is the place in which YHWH dwells: השמים מכון שבתך (1 Kgs 8:39, 43, 49). The same idea occurs in 1 Kgs 8:30, 32, 34, 36, 45.[72]

---

69. Dietrich, *Von David zu den Deuteronomisten*, 196.

70. Cf. McCormick, *Palace and Temple*, 41.

71. A similar perspective is advanced by W. Dietrich, "Gott als König: Zur Frage nach der theologischen und politischen Legitimation religiöser Begriffsbildung," in *Theopolitik: Studien zur Theologie und Ethik des Alten Testaments* (Neukirchen–Vluyn: Neukirchener), 58–70 (67–78). Analysing the idea of YHWH as king, Dietrich observes that the idea of YHWH as *king of Israel* becomes important especially during exilic times, namely in the writings of Deutero-Isaiah and the Deuteronomistic History.

72. See B. Janowski, "'Ich will in eurer Mitte wohnen': Struktur und Genese der exilischen *Schekina*-Theologie," in *Gottes Gegenwart in Israel: Beiträge zur Theologie des Alten Testaments* (Neukirchen–Vluyn: Neukirchener, 1993), 119–47 (131 n. 52).

What in fact could be found in the temple was, according to the Deuteronomists, YHWH's *name*.[73] The temple is built for it: 1 Kgs 5:17, 19 (MT); 8:16, 17, 18, 19, 20, 29, 44, 48; 9:3, 7. The name is "called upon the temple" (1 Kgs 8:43). The name is acknowledged in the temple (1 Kgs 8:33, 35), and foreigners will hear of it (1 Kgs 8:41–42) and will come from a distance because of it (למען שמך, 1 Kgs 8:41). This is why the temple continues to be a special place where people can come into contact with YHWH. It is also why the people's prayers are directed towards the temple, towards the city of Jerusalem, or even towards the land (1 Kgs 8:48), albeit they are heard in heaven. Solomon's dedicatory prayer "anticipates" the situation of the exile and provides the possibility of God's proximity[74] even after the destruction of temple and city, and even in a foreign country (1 Kgs 8:46–51).

The Deuteronomistic redaction(s) may be seen as the climax of the process of theological enrichment. To the Deuteronomists the building account of the Solomonic temple became a key text in the interpretation of Israel's history.[75] It was not just Solomon's glory, piety and personal history that drew from the redactors a new version of the story. It was not only the memory of the temple's appearance that had to be preserved for further generations.[76] The temple was the embodiment of the veneration of YHWH—and YHWH was all that Israel had left after 587/6 B.C.E. The YHWH cult had become not only the connecting element for the scattered remnants of the people, but also the basis of Israel's self-perception as the people of God. Aspects of religion had now replaced the political definition, at least for a time.

---

73. G. Braulik, "Spuren einer Neubearbeitung des deuteronomistischen Geschichtswerkes in 1 Kön 8,52–53:59–60," in *Studien zur Theologie des Deuteronomiums* (ed. G. Braulik; Stuttgarter Biblische Aufsatzbände 2; Stuttgart: Katholisches Bibelwerk, 1988), 39–52 (50), sees the main motivation for developing a theology of God's name in the Deuteronomistic fear of God's "disposability" rather than in the needs of a community without a temple. For the theology of the name in general, and in the dedication prayer in particular, see Janowski, "Ich will in eurer Mitte wohnen," esp. pp. 127–34.

74. For the exilic concept of God's proximity, see Janowski, "Ich will in eurer Mitte wohnen," 133–34.

75. Cf. Dietrich, *Von David zu den Deuteronomisten*, 188, who detects a basic rule in the development of redactional work: the later a redactional layer or historiographic description, the more general it is. The historical horizon is continually widening. This may be questioned, however, in the case of 1 Kgs 5–9. Post-Deuteronomistic redaction seems to concentrate on particular matters as, for example, the temple decoration (see below).

76. Otherwise Van Seters, "Solomon's Temple," 45–57, who dates the temple descriptions to exilic times.

7. Post-Deuteronomistic Textual History

The redactional work on 1 Kgs 5–9 that followed after the Deuteronomistic revision did not leave many marks. First Kings 6:11–13 unifies priestly ("if you will follow my statutes and obey my rules," "I will dwell among the Israelites") and Deuteronomistic ("keep my commands," "fulfil my promise") language.[77] The absence of these verses in the LXX seems to indicate a very late insertion. Perhaps also the gold-laden verses in 6:20–22 are late additions, deriving from the post-exilic interest in temple texts and intended to add to the glory of the first temple.[78] On the one hand, prophetic ideas about a new temple (Ezekiel) and the actual building of one will have modified the theological interest in the Solomonic temple. On the other hand, the ongoing process of canonization, the reception of 1 Kgs 5–9 and its context in the Chronicler's work,[79] the translations, and scribal and, even later, rabbinical interpretation caused smaller modifications on a different level. The process of modification of the literature eventually ceased and made way for the text's conservation and its further interpretation.

8. Conclusion

Under the influence of political and religious developments in Israel and Judah, the power of language had fashioned a work of permanently influential theological literature. Interpretation, reinterpretation, and reformulation had made the temple of Solomon an ideal. The reports of its construction now contained the theological essence of several centuries of theological development. In this respect, McCormick's idea of 1 Kgs 5–9 as a "verbal icon" is correct. In exilic and post-exilic times, and even many centuries later, the stories surrounding the Solomonic temple repeatedly have served as a verbal icon for Israel, Judaism and

---

77. This is why it is often regarded as a late Deuteronomistic insertion. For the text and its significance in relation to YHWH's "dwelling," see also Janowski, "Ich will in eurer Mitte wohnen," 134–40, and also p. 144 for the religio-political dimension: "The theology of 'shekhinah' now gains a national dimension that is referring to Israel's restitution and is of almost ecclesiological significance" (author's translation).

78. Hentschel, *1 Könige*, 9.

79. For the Chronistic reception of the text see, among others, Zipora Talshir, "The Reign of Solomon in the Making: Pseudo-Connections between 3 Kingdoms and Chronicles," *VT* 50 (2000): 233–49.

Christianity, respectively. Throughout the history of its origin, development and reception the story of the building of Solomon's temple in 1 Kgs 5–9 has never ceased to reflect the tension inherent in the interplay of politics and religion.

BEHIND CLOSED DOORS:
THE HIDDEN WORLD OF JERUSALEM'S ROYAL PALACE

Ronald E. Clements

Increasingly, an established feature of the contemporary political scene for major figures of public life, after they leave office, is to publish memoirs of their years in power. The story of what went on behind closed doors in royal palaces, cabinet offices and less public places has become a well-established class of historical writing. A wealth of private conversations, secret plans and unrealized hopes are brought to light through the diaries and recollections of men and women who held high public office. There is no reason for doubting that a comparable realm of intrigue and plotting was current in the world of the Bible and that, had it been possible for some of the leading figures of ancient Israel to tell their personal stories, a remarkably enlightening series of biographies might have come into being. Not until Roman times did literacy become sufficiently popular and widespread to create authors willing and able to tell the truth about the private lives of the leaders and persons they served.

1. Hamutal and the Fall of the Royal House of David

The primary focus for this study falls upon a remarkable participant in the inner world of palace life who was mother to King Zedekiah, the last of ancient Jerusalem's Davidic kings. Her name was Hamutal, the widow of Josiah—one of the most celebrated rulers of the dynasty, who was killed in conflict with the Egyptian Pharaoh Necho after 31 years of rule. In the sixth century B.C.E. Hamutal's son Zedekiah became the last ruler of the Davidic family to occupy the throne in Jerusalem (2 Kgs 24:18), but was actually the second of her sons to achieve this honour (cf. 2 Kgs 23:31). This rare distinction occasions a lament for her in Ezek 19:1–14.[1] Had she lived with the conventions and resources of more recent times

---

1. For the text of the lament, see W. Zimmerli, *Ezekiel 1–24* (Hermeneia; Minneapolis: Fortress, 1980), 388–98; D. I. Block, *Ezekiel 1–24* (NICOT; Grand Rapids: Eerdmans, 1997), 591–610; I. Kottsieper, "'Was ist deine Mutter?': Eine Studie zu Ezek. 19:2–9," *ZAW* 105 (1993): 444–61.

she would undoubtedly have made a fascinating informant on the realities of life "behind closed doors" in Jerusalem's ancient royal palace. Moreover, it is evident from the language of Ezekiel's lament that Hamutal was a remarkable woman—a "lioness...among lions" (Ezek 19:2), and her life, were it more adequately documented, would surely have revealed her formidable character. Her story is also remarkable in that when its basic features are examined they reveal a person who was evidently a significant power behind the men who occupied the centre of the stage in a world that was dominated by a patriarchal social structure. Ezekiel's portrait certainly confirms such an assessment of her life. There is, in any case, no necessity to emphasize that the events through which she lived represent one of the most remarkable periods in the entire biblical story. Had she been able to record the story of her life it would not only have provided an important insight into the problems and jealousies caused by sibling rivalries within an ancient royal palace, but would also have shown the merciless nature of the international conflicts which led to the downfall of the Davidic royal house in ancient Israel's first kingdom.

The significance of Hamutal's story makes it necessary to consider closely the political background to the century of disastrous decline that preceded this downfall. All five of the last rulers who occupied the throne in Jerusalem suffered violent ends to their reigns, three of which were remarkably brief. Hamutal became a widow when her husband, King Josiah, was killed in battle at Megiddo while confronting the Egyptian ruler, Pharaoh Necho, in 609 B.C.E. (2 Kgs 23:29; 2 Chr 35:20–27).[2]

Josiah had come to the throne in Jerusalem as a mere boy of eight and, apart from the dynasty's founder, he is credited with being the most praiseworthy of its members (2 Kgs 23:25; 2 Chr 35:26). Although not the first to taste the bitterness of the dynasty's misfortunes, his untimely death marked a critical turning-point in the decline that ended its three centuries of rule. It was to survive little more than another twenty years.

2. *Conflict in the Near East in the Seventh Century B.C.E.*

Throughout the seventh century B.C.E., and for much of the preceding one, control of the eastern Mediterranean coastlands was contested by

2. The political background to this disaster is discussed in A. Malamat, "Josiah's Bid for Armageddon: The Background of the Judean-Egyptian Encounter in 609 B.C.," in *History of Biblical Israel: Major Problems and Minor Issues* (CHANE 7; Leiden: Brill, 2001), 282–98.

the two "Superpowers" of the region—Egypt and Mesopotamia.[3] This conflict passed through several violent changes and inevitably brought plotting and division into the heart of the royal palaces of its many minor kingdoms. Among these Jerusalem was not exempt, and Ezekiel's lament shows that Jerusalem's Queen Hamutal and her sons were participants in such activities. The divided loyalties of the region were mirrored in divided loyalties within the royal palace. Ezekiel 19:5–6 describes a situation in which, after an attempt by a royal prince to claim the throne was thwarted, a second son made a more successful bid. As a reflection, however partial, of life in Jerusalem's royal palace during the years of Jehoiakim's rule (609–598 B.C.E.), it lifts the veil of secrecy from off the personal rivalries that flourished behind palace walls. By implication, it reveals the remarkable power that women could exercise in a royal palace, besides showing up the indecision and the changes of international allegiance that prevailed in Jerusalem during these momentous years. Rivalry to secure the right of succession to the throne became interwoven with conflict between a party that sought to maintain Judah's commitment to Assyria, which King Hezekiah had been compelled to accept in 701 B.C.E. as the price of surrender and submission, and an opposing party which sought to re-establish Jerusalem's traditional allegiance to Egypt. The tensions and bloodshed this generated lasted throughout the following century and shaped events in the city's royal palace.

Conflicts over royal succession were evidently not a new or isolated phenomenon; stories about the conflict over Solomon's succession to David show the potential for such situations to generate a legacy of lasting political division. From early years Hamutal would have been well aware of the international tensions that governed the fact that she had been chosen to become consort to a king who had been elevated to the throne in order to secure a precarious political agenda. She is described as the "daughter of Jeremiah of Libnah" (2 Kgs 23:31), identifying her as coming from a family of Judaean rural nobility. As a mere child, Josiah had been made king by "the people of the land" after his father, King Amon, had been murdered (2 Kgs 21:19–26; 2 Chr 33:21–25). The assassins were brought to account by the same "people of the land" who made this choice. We can assume that there were in existence other potential candidates for the throne among the various princes and royal siblings. Before King Amon's assassination his predecessor Manasseh had earned an unrivalled reputation for violence. His long 45-year reign is reported as the bloodiest of all that had gone before (2 Kgs 21:1–18;

---

3. Cf. especially A. Malamat, "The Twilight of Judah in the Egyptian–Babylonian Maelstrom," in *History of Biblical Israel*, 299–321.

2 Chr 33:1–20), although this is softened by the Chronicler's story of the king's repentance and return to commitment to YHWH as God. However, this may be no more than the author's desire to justify the great length of Manasseh's reign (2 Chr 33:12–13).

The later biblical authors who recorded these events looked for specific religious offences to explain the outbreak of bloodletting in the royal palace (2 Kgs 21:2–9; 2 Chr 33:2–9). However, from the course of subsequent events the underlying cause is more convincingly explained as related to the international tensions that dominated the region.[4] Manasseh had acted fiercely to uphold Jerusalem's commitment to Assyrian allegiance in the face of a party that was working actively, and no doubt violently, to re-establish the older, more traditional loyalty to the Egyptian Pharaoh that went back to the time of King Solomon's reign. The "people of the land," by seizing and executing Amon's assassins, sought to reaffirm Jerusalem's place within the regional coalition of kingdoms committed to Assyria. Their choice of Josiah as king was clearly in line with this. The violence of the reign of Manasseh and the subsequent assassination of Amon were consequences of this wider international struggle for control of the region that continued throughout the seventh century B.C.E. The choice by "the people of the land" of the boy-prince Josiah to wear the crown in Jerusalem can only have been because he was expected to maintain the policy of his two predecessors (2 Kgs 21:24). The arrest and execution of those responsible for Amon's death (2 Kgs 21:23–24) reveals the tensions and divided loyalties that could exist within a royal palace. Josiah's elevation to the throne points to a temporary victory for those who opposed any return to alliance with Egypt. Such a victory, however, was to prove short-lived.

Inner-palace aspects of this conflict and its personal relevance for Hamutal take on a special interest with the evidence that she almost certainly was not the first young woman to have been chosen as consort to Josiah. Her marriage probably took place c. 630 B.C.E. when there already existed a rival consort, Zebidah, as subsequent events reveal. That Zebidah had been chosen before Hamutal becomes apparent from events that took place after Josiah's death at Megiddo. Initially, when

---

4. Cf. A. Malamat, "The Historical Background of the Assassination of Amon, King of Judah," in *History of Biblical Israel*, 277–81; for alternative interpretations, see F. Stavrakopoulou, "The Blackballing of Manasseh," in *Good Kings and Bad Kings: The Kingdom of Judah in the Seventh Century B.C.E.* (ed. L. L. Grabbe; LHBOTS 393; ESHM 5; London: T&T Clark International, 2007), 248–63; eadem, *King Manasseh and Child Sacrifice: Biblical Distortions of Historical Realities* (BZAW 338; Berlin: de Gruyter, 2004).

this occurred Hamutal's son Jehoahaz was elevated to the throne and was evidently the heir apparent and the choice of both his father and "the people of the land." However, after a mere three months he was summoned to Riblah in Syria by command of the Egyptian Pharaoh and from there he was taken into exile in Egypt, from which he did not return. In his place the Egyptian ruler installed the son of Hamutal's rival Zebidah on the throne in Jerusalem. His name is recorded as Eliakim, which was changed on his enthronement to Jehoiakim. He now became the new ruler, as the subordinate and ally of Egypt, being forced to pay the fine of a hundred talents of silver and one of gold, which he exacted from "the people of the land" (2 Kgs 23:33–35; 2 Chr 36:3).

It is a significant feature that Zebidah came from Galilee (2 Kgs 23:36) and that her son Eliakim-Jehoiakim was two years older than Jehoahaz, his deposed rival (their ages being 25 and 23, respectively). Evidently the new king had already been passed over as the heir apparent, although he was the older of the two senior royal princes. This is almost certainly because he had shown himself supportive of renewing Jerusalem's alliance with Egypt, which was opposed by "the people of the land." The situation is elaborated even more fully in 1 Esd 1:34–38, which mentions yet another royal prince, Zarius, who was subsequently brought back from Egypt by command of Jehoiakim. His fate thereafter is not mentioned, although the silence seems ominous. Quite evidently, well before Josiah's death in 609 B.C.E. a great deal of subversive activity had been going on behind Jerusalem's palace walls, and the circumstances of King Amon's assassination confirm this. Tensions between contenders for a pro-Egyptian and for a pro-Assyrian national commitment were a major feature of life in Jerusalem's palace. Years of whispering and careful watchfulness were brought to the surface by Josiah's death. Division of allegiance between a commitment to Assyria or to Egypt had been stalking the corridors of power in Jerusalem from the days of Manasseh, and its impact on the prospects for any one of the royal princes would have been carefully weighed. For a period of three months, backed by "the people of the land," Jehoahaz claimed the royal succession, but this reckoned without the determination of the Egyptian pharaoh to pursue a different course.

3. *Jerusalem's Struggle for Survival in the World of International Politics*

These events highlight how the larger horizon of international politics shaped the ideas and policies of kingship that prevailed in ancient Judah. Kings were seldom in command of their destiny, as ample evidence from

antiquity shows. The biblical author's understandable *Schadenfreude* at
the Assyrian king Sennacherib's death when he was murdered by his
own sons confirms this judgment (2 Kgs 19:37; cf. Isa 37:38). Kings
were far from being absolute masters even in their own royal palaces.[5]
Kingship controlled national and international diplomacy, but the institution of monarchy was always a vulnerable one. The right to rule was a
cloth woven by royal upbringing, palace loyalties and international mar-
riages, but it was all too frequently torn apart by sibling rivalries and
intrigue. The dynastic principle, which appears to have prevailed in
Jerusalem and most ancient royal courts of the Near East, could never
remove all competition.[6] In a similar vein, primogeniture—the right of
the firstborn son to have the strongest claim to inherit his father's
crown—could not be established as an absolute commitment. The prize
to be won—to sit upon the throne of a proud kingdom—presented too
great a temptation for other siblings to surrender lightly and, in any case,
the cost of coming second was often either banishment or death. Administrative conventions were not so inflexible that they could never be overridden, and the consequences ultimately determined the fate of whole
populations.

These political conventions inevitably centred upon the male members
of a family, but the women of a royal court were not without influence,
which fact the later Jewish author of the book of Esther exploited when
introducing a subtle note of comedy into his story (Esth 1–3). Significant
discussion has focused on the role of the *gᵉbîrâ* (Heb. גבירה), which has
usually been translated as "queen mother," though this appears to be an
over-translation.[7] The precise status of such an important figure in palace
life is far from clear and the title is nowhere accorded to Hamutal. In
what circumstances it could be granted or withheld is not evident, since
it does not appear to have been conferred on all the royal mothers of
reigning kings. In any case, it must be taken for granted that when a
major shift of power in a royal administration took place, as happened
with the removal and exile of Jehoahaz in 609 B.C.E., then a related
change in the internal life of the palace would have occurred.

5. For further illustration of this point, see D. J. Wiseman, "Murder in Mesopotamia," *Iraq* 36 (1974): 249–60.

6. Cf. T. Ishida, *The Royal Dynasties of Ancient Israel: A Study in the Formation
and Development of Royal Dynastic Ideology* (BZAW 142; Berlin: de Gruyter,
1977).

7. Cf. N. Bowen, "The Quest for the Historical *Gebîrâ*," *CBQ* 63 (2001): 597–
618.

Hamutal was born and brought up within a privileged circle of Judaean nobility, almost certainly reckoned among "the people of the land." This brought her into the immediacy of palace life, where, as Ezekiel's lamentation avers, she flourished and exercised great influence as "a lioness among lions" (Ezek 19:2). She would have known the men who were responsible for arresting and executing the murderers of Josiah's father and for setting her husband on the throne. Nevertheless, even the power of this regional nobility was limited, as events were to show; supporters of a commitment to Egypt had clearly gained entry into the administration of Jerusalem's royal palace, since they were responsible for the death of Amon. Hamutal's reputation must have been won by her forcefulness and her determination to succeed in a world dominated by a patriarchal social structure. Her only avenue to greatness lay in her gift of motherhood and the sons she bore. That her ambitions in this direction were ultimately doomed was the result of the uncompromising ruthlessness of the international political scene.

The disaster that brought the death of her husband was the first in a sequence of events that provides a focal point for the entire Old Testament literature. It marked the downward slide to disaster and more than a hundred years of regional conflict, but, as significantly, it also marked the beginning of the end of the rule of a royal dynasty that had lasted for three centuries. More than simply a fight for territory, it marked the clash of the two rich and powerful cultures of Egypt and Mesopotamia which has left a legacy that has survived to the present day.

The new administration that took office in Jerusalem under her rival's son Jehoiakim, acting under Egyptian authority, did not survive for long. Assyria's position as the leading power in the ancient Near East had collapsed with the fall of Nineveh to Babylon in 612 B.C.E. Any hope on the part of Egypt that it could reclaim the mantle of power in the region proved to be short-lived and was decisively ended when Babylonian forces defeated those of Egypt at Carchemish on the Euphrates in 605 B.C.E. Nebuchadnezzar became master of the eastern Mediterranean. Jehoiakim was compelled to look for a new beginning under the suzerainty of Babylon, but his commitment soon wavered. No doubt the situation itself generated uncertainty, and Jehoiakim's loyalty to his new master may not have been very deep. As a bystander in Jerusalem, Hamutal would undoubtedly have had much to observe and remember! Jehoiakim's rebellion in 599 B.C.E. brought inevitable retaliation. A military force, under Babylonian command, laid siege to Jerusalem in 599–98 B.C.E., leading to the city's surrender.

During the period of this threat Jehoiakim died and was succeeded by his son Jehoiachin. With Jerusalem's surrender came Zebidah's turn to suffer the grief and humiliation that had earlier overtaken her rival, Hamutal. She and her sons were taken to Babylon, together with many officials, smiths and craftsmen (2 Kgs 24:15). Jerusalem was reduced to a city that was humiliated and stripped of wealth (cf. Isa 39:6–7). The throne was given to an older sibling within the royal family, another of Hamutal's sons. His name was Mattaniah and he was now given the new royal name of Zedekiah. The name expresses renewal of hope for the city, and probably also for Hamutal, since he was now the second of her sons to wear the crown in Jerusalem (2 Kgs 24:17–18).

A period of relative stability under Babylonian sovereignty now appeared within reach, but it was short-lived. The course eventually chosen by Zedekiah and his officials proved to be as disastrous as that of his predecessors. He reneged on his allegiance to Nebuchadnezzar, King of Babylon, choosing to become a rebel, as his predecessor had done. For this he paid the inevitable price. After a further prolonged siege by forces under the direction of Babylon, Jerusalem collapsed and the city, together with its temple and royal palace, was destroyed in 586 B.C.E. Zedekiah was compelled to witness the killing of his children and was then blinded and taken into exile. Hamutal's fate is not made clear. Whether, like her erstwhile rival Zebidah, she also was compelled to accompany her son to Babylon is not recorded, but the fact that she appears as the subject of Ezekiel's lament (Ezek 19:1–14) suggests that this was very likely the case. The lament not only mourns her passing but hints at the passing of Zedekiah, the last of the Davidic kings to rule in Jerusalem, and at the end of this long-surviving dynasty. This must be the point of the editor's concluding remark: "This is a lamentation and it has become a lamentation" (Ezek 19:14).

The downfall of the royal house of David, with its divided politics, sibling rivalries and troubled rulers, bears comparison with the chaos and jealousies that prefigured the end of most of the royal dynasties of Europe in more recent times. What future was there now for Jerusalem without an heir to the dynasty which had for so long worn the crown of divine approval? As scholars have sought to piece together a picture of the events which led ultimately to the destruction of the city of Jerusalem in 586 B.C.E., there can be no doubt that Hamutal, had she been able to recount the story of her life, would have had a startling account to give of the many intrigues, plots and secret conversations that took place "behind closed doors" in that city.

It is a pleasure to remember such a near-forgotten woman of great distinction and to present these reflections in tribute to Andrew Macintosh, who has contributed so patiently, and successfully, to the teaching and study of Hebrew in Cambridge University. It is also worthy of note that he has been a distinguished servant of St. John's College, Cambridge, founded in the sixteenth century by Lady Margaret Beaufort, mother of King Henry VII and founder of two of the University's historic colleges. She is acclaimed by historians as "the power behind the throne" in the world of sixteenth-century politics. It is not too much to claim that such a title would have been appropriate for Hamutal two millennia earlier. She was indeed "a lioness among lions," and is surely worthy of remembrance.

Part III

THE LANGUAGE AND LITERATURE OF THE PROPHETS

Israel's Sage (Psalm 1) in LXX Isaiah 31:9b–32:8: A Palimpsest

David A. Baer

When this volume's honorand published his monograph on the oracles of Isa 21, he suggested that the most adequate path to resolving the exegetical difficulties presented by the material was to view the chapter as a "palimpsest." Citing the adage *quidquid recipitur recipitur ad modum recipientis*,[1] Andrew Macintosh proposed that a text such as the one that lay before him required the interpreter to negotiate multiple historical points of reference if it was to be understood satisfactorily in the light of its inherent complexity.[2]

Seeking a way through the difficulties of establishing the precise political downfall to which the oracles of Isa 21 address themselves, Macintosh wrote:

> An attempt will be made to show that many of the words and phrases of Isa. xxi:1–10 have their origin in the eighth century but that the oracle as a whole attained its final form in the book of Isaiah as a prophecy which portrayed the fall of Babylon at the hands of Cyrus in 539 B.C. *The prophecy may then be regarded as a palimpsest.* Its reception and interpretation within the Isaianic tradition give to it its superimposed form and it is this that enables it to speak of that fall of Babylon which was of such immense importance in the history of the Jewish people. Beneath the *superimposed form*, however, we may catch at least glimpses of earlier prophecies and of the historical circumstances of an earlier age.[3]

Macintosh's deployment of the term "palimpsest" with reference to prophetic texts received in more than one context and understood to speak descriptively to them was a happy use of a potent analogy. The *New Shorter Oxford English Dictionary* defines *palimpsest* in this manner:

---

1. "Whatever is received is received according to the manner of the receiver."
2. A. A. Macintosh, *Isaiah XXI: A Palimpsest* (Cambridge: Cambridge University Press, 1980), 104.
3. Ibid., 105–6; emphases added.

> A paper, parchment, etc., on which the original writing has been effaced
> to make way for other writing; a manuscript in which a later writing is
> written over an effaced earlier writing.[4]

In antiquity the removal of the original writing was seldom complete,[5] for which reason scholars refer to the "underwriting" and "overwriting" that are often to be found on a palimpsest.[6] The early writing shows through, as it were, presenting either the unfocussed or the highly attentive reader with a mixed message.

In the present study I will argue that the wise man of Ps 1 "peeks through" the rhetoric of LXX Isa 32. As the Greek translator went about his work, the uncharacteristically sapiential language of the prophetic text before him put him in mind of the first psalm and its wise protagonist. The anonymous translator carried out his task in a way that shows the face of the first psalm's sage, even as it presents the Isaiah text's "king who rules in justice" to the Greek reader.

1. *LXX Isaiah 31:9b–32:8 as Coherent Greek Literature*

In his 2010 essay on the Greek text of Isa 31:9b–32:1–8, Arie van der Kooij applied to this text a methodologically disciplined search for a reading of the Greek Isaiah as a work that is coherent in its own right. This approach takes seriously the translation's presumed Hebrew *Vorlage*, but allows the Hebrew text a lower order of importance when compared with the Greek document that results from the translator's labours.[7]

---

4. L. Brown, ed., *The New Shorter Oxford English Dictionary*, vol. 2 (Oxford: Clarendon, 1993), 2076.

5. M. Carey et al., *The Oxford Classical Dictionary* (Oxford: Clarendon, 1966), 638.

6. E. Würthwein, *The Text of the Old Testament: An Introduction to the Biblia Hebraica* (trans. E. F. Rhodes; 2d ed.; Grand Rapids: Eerdmans, 1995), 6; K. H. Jobes and M. Silva, eds., *Invitation to the Septuagint* (Grand Rapids: Baker Academic, 2000), 37 n. 16.

7. A. van der Kooij, "The Septuagint of Isaiah and the Issue of Coherence: A Twofold Analysis of LXX Isaiah 31:9b–32:8," in *The Old Greek of Isaiah: Issues and Perspectives* (ed. A. van der Kooij and M. N. van der Meer; Leuven: Peeters, 2010), 33–48 (35). Although van der Kooij has utilized this method over a lifetime of work on the Greek Isaiah, the most extensive single example is a full-scale monograph that treats LXX Isa 23, *The Oracle of Tyre: The Septuagint of Isaiah XXIII as Version and Vision* (VTSup 71; Leiden: Brill, 1998). In this present study I will assume but will not argue for the widely held view that the Isaiah translator's *Vorlage* approximates to our MT.

Van der Kooij successfully demonstrated that the Greek text is not a "literal rendering" of the Hebrew, concluding that the evidence

> may suffice to show that the passage under discussion is not only well organized as regards syntax and style, but also that it makes good sense from a conceptual point of view. Its main topic pertains to a change of leadership in Jerusalem. Bad rulers will no longer have power; new rulers will take over. They will rule with judgment, doing justice to the humble, in line with the law. One of them, apparently the supreme leader, is referred to in v. 2. As a result, people in Sion will live in justice and peace.[8]

At the conclusion of his study, van der Kooij remarks that further investigation might uncover links between this passage and other sections of the Greek Isaiah that would shed additional light on "how the translator as a scribe reworded a Hebrew text in order to specify its meaning in the way he perceived and understood it."[9]

Building upon van der Kooij's work, I propose that the Greek text of Isa 31:9b–32:8 does indeed provide subtle hints regarding influence from outside the passage itself. However, such influence takes us beyond the Greek Isaiah to two psalms.

In principle, the appearance of influence from other biblical texts in the Greek Isaiah should not surprise us. I have argued elsewhere that the Isaiah translator's work displays evidence that he is a "biblical theologian" of sorts, with a broad familiarity with at least the Greek Scriptures.[10] I also endorse the near consensus that the book of Isaiah was one of the last biblical books to be translated and incorporated into our "Septuagint," at least in the form of the translation we know. This was probably accomplished subsequent to the translation of the Psalms, a matter of sequence that is of some pertinence to the argument being developed in this essay.[11] Here, the translator's knowledge of Ps 1, and to a lesser extent Ps 2, shows through his translation of Isa 31:9b–32:8, adding depth to the picture of wise and just rule that van der Kooij finds described in coherent fashion in the Greek Isaiah. One might describe the result as a palimpsest.

---

8.   Van der Kooij, "Septuagint of Isaiah," 47.

9.   Ibid., 48.

10.   D. A. Baer, *When We All Go Home: Translation and Theology in LXX Isaiah 56–66* (JSOTSup 318; The Hebrew Bible and Its Versions 1; Sheffield: Sheffield Academic, 2001), 25–26.

11.   Ibid.

2. Isaiah 32 as an Unusually "Sapiential" Prophetic Oracle

The strikingly non-specific rhetoric of Isa 32:1–8 is unusual in prophetic
texts. An ideal king, surrounded by equally ideal princes, is described in
a way that bedevils attempts to locate a precise, historical referent.

In addition to the non-referential sketch of righteous rulers and just
rule, one notes the proliferation of similes in v. 2 and the sustained
engagement with wisdom and folly and with the wise and the foolish in
vv. 5–8. Furthermore, פלגי־מים in v. 2 is a virtual set piece of wisdom
imagery, utilized elsewhere only in Pss 1:3; 119:136; Prov 5:16; 21:1,
and Lam 3:48, passages with indisputable wisdom credentials.

It is a cause for little wonder that scholars, independently of their
views on the broader issues of the relationship of "wisdom" motifs and
schools to prophetic literature, frequently use words such as "wisdom"
and "sapiential" to describe Isa 32.[12] Indeed, the author of a recent article
that understands Isa 32 as a "religio-political discourse within the Isaian
tradition as it tries to solve a common Near Eastern intellectual problem:
the morality of kingship" finds the passage "reminiscent of the depiction
of the sage in Psalm 1."[13]

Nor is it difficult to imagine that the LXX translator of the passage
would have detected similarities between this passage and others like it
in the Bible, probably the Greek Bible. Slight shifts of meaning and
suggestive word choices in translation indicate that he has done so, and
that he has not hesitated to signal to his readers the connection that he
has glimpsed.

3. The LXX Translator's Handiwork

We turn now to eight elements of LXX 31:9b–32:8 that appear to indicate
an association in the translator's mind with Pss 1 and 2.

a. *Blessedness in Zion*
In addition to the general similarities to wisdom discourse that have been
mentioned above, the Hebrew inadvertently provides the translator with a
kind of confirmation that his text is to be read in conjunction with the
first psalm.

12. E.g. H. Wildberger, *Isaiah 28–39* (trans. T. H. Trapp; Continental Commentaries; Minneapolis: Fortress, 2002), 234; T. L. Leclerc, *Yahweh Is Exalted in
Justice: Solidarity and Conflict in Isaiah* (Minneapolis: Fortress, 2002), 82.
13. M. W. Hamilton, "Isaiah 32 as Literature and Political Meditation," *JBL* 131
(2012): 663–84 (668). Hamilton notes that "the sapiential material serves as amplification and warrant for the basic vision of a just king and hierarchy."

It has been widely recognized that MT 31:9b concludes an oracle that promises YHWH's protection of Jerusalem against Assyrian assault with the stock oracular summation (...אשר) נאם־יהוה, but that this has been rendered in the LXX as initiating a new thematic section in which the just king is a central figure.[14]

It is almost certain that the translator understood his *Vorlage* at 31:9b as though it read—and perhaps it did!—...נאם־יהוה אשרי. What followed after אשרי we cannot know. I have argued for אשרי זרע לו בציון; van der Kooij has in response proposed that the MT's אור and תנור have generated σπέρμα καὶ οἰκείους in the light of the potential metaphorical freight that "light" and "hearth" can bear in the context of family and kinship.[15]

For our purposes, the important points are two. First, the translator produced μακάριος and was from that point already approaching the passage as one that deals with a particular kind of blessedness. He was probably regarding it at this early point as connected with the first psalm, and possibly with the first and second psalms together, with the focus upon the wise man and the centrality of Zion and its king that these two psalms convey.

Second, this apprehension of the passage before him might have made it attractive in conceptual terms to read בציון (MT בְּצִיּוֹן) as ἐν Σιων, even though it is locked in synonymous parallelism with בארץ עיפה (= ἐν γῇ διψώσῃ). That is to say, the focus of the second psalm upon Zion may have created in the translator a predisposition to find continued reference to that city.

b. *Heightened Emphasis Upon "the Man"*
In v. 2, the translator moves the protective imagery of the Hebrew text (והיה־איש כמחבא־רוח) in an unexpected and possibly sapiential direction. The Hebrew idiom והיה־איש doubtless carries forward the reference just before it to a "king...and princes." The distributive use of איש is a well-documented linguistic convention, in this case one that advances the argument by making concrete reference to the individuals that comprise the aforementioned group.[16] The rhetorical force of the idiom consists in

---

14. For example, I. L. Seeligmann in R. Hanhart and H. Spieckermann, eds., *Isaac Leo Seeligmann: The Septuagint Version of Isaiah and Cognate Studies* (FAT 40; Tübingen: Mohr Siebeck, 2004), 284; van der Kooij, "Septuagint of Isaiah," 35; Baer, *When We All Go Home*, 217–19.

15. Baer, *When We All Go Home*, 218; van der Kooij, "Septuagint of Isaiah," 36; see also "p אַשְׁרֵי(־)שְׁאַרלֹ," in *The Book of Isaiah* (ed. M. H. Goshen-Gottstein; HUBP; Jerusalem: Magnes, 1995), ad loc.

16. GK §139; P. Joüon and T. Muraoka, *A Grammar of Biblical Hebrew*, vol. 2 (Subsidia Biblica 14/2; Rome: Pontificio Istituto Biblico, 2000), §147d (p. 454).

underscoring the potency of king and princes as protective agents—every one of them!—over the people whom it is their lot to rule justly.

The translator responds with a different notion entirely. The strikingly literal καὶ ἔσται ὁ ἄνθρωπος appears to set forth a representative individual along the lines of the blessed man of Ps 1. That individual is introduced by the verbless clause μακάριος ἀνήρ. The argument for connectivity between Isa 32 and Ps 1 that I wish to develop is not based upon a slavish correspondence between the two texts, but rather upon the accumulation of subtle hints that the translator has repeatedly nudged his text in the direction of the opening poems of the Psalter. The placing of "the man" on centre stage is one such hint.

c. *Restrained Speech*

"The man" of LXX Isa 32 will be κρύπτων τοὺς λόγους αὐτοῦ. Of his 46 encounters with רוח, this is the only time that the Isaiah translator falls upon λόγος as its equivalent, suggesting a degree of intentionality about the shift from shelter to restrained speech. Because the translator manages רוח with discernible dexterity, neither accident nor wooden rigidity is an adequate explanation for his word choice at 32:2.[17]

At the point at which the Hebrew text is developing the protective capacity of king and princes—the images themselves are of course indigenous to the rhetoric of monarchy in the ancient Near East—the Greek translation is admiring the glory (ἔνδοξος) of the man who speaks with restraint in Zion. The notion is conceptually contiguous with common wisdom motifs and, if the figure is a royal one, with both the first and the second psalms.

d. *King and Rulers*

A further detail may have drawn the translator's thoughts to Ps 1 and its vicinity as he encountered the wisdom cadences of his Isaiah text. This point requires a brief digression.

Psalms scholars have long been aware of the manner in which the first two psalms are linked together by common vocabulary, leading to the conclusion that the two poems represent the first and second parts of a single introduction to the Psalter.[18] It is worth observing that it is

---

17. He has frequent recourse to πνεῦμα, but avails himself of eleven other renderings of רוח.

18. P. D. Miller is representative of the tendency to mine the juxtaposition of the two psalms for its theological import; see his "The Psalter as a Book of Theology," in *The Way of the Lord: Essays in Old Testament Theology* (Grand Rapids: Eerdmans, 2007), 217–22.

precisely "kings and rulers" (βασιλεῖς...καὶ ἄρχοντες) who are summoned to submission before YHWH and his Zion-based monarch in
Ps 2.

Although there is nothing unusual in the translator's management of
מלך and שר—βασιλεύς and ἄρχων are highly predictable conventions—
it is plausible that if the material before the translator had put him in
mind of the first two psalms, he might have found the contextual overlap
denoted by the presence of "kings" and "princes" to confirm his intuition
that the two passages are interrelated.

e. *An Adversative Uninvited by the Source Text*
The Hebrew text at vv. 3–4 engages a set of images that denote perception and the capacity to articulate—together with their counterparts,
imperception and an inarticulate condition—that is central to the discourse of the Isaianic tradition:

ולא תשעינה עיני ראים ואזני שמעים תקשבנה
ולבב נמהרים יבין לדעת ולשון עלגים תמהר לדבר צחות

> Then the eyes of those who have sight will not be closed, and the ears of
> those who have hearing will listen. The minds of the rash will have good
> judgment, and the tongues of stammerers will speak readily and distinctly
> (NRSV).

The tradition relentlessly works the possibilities inherent in this vocabulary for purposes both of judgment by decreed imperception and of
redemption by the return of perceptive faculties once lost.[19]

The translator has ample occasion, then, to become familiar with this
language and its continuum of configurations within the Isaianic rhetoric.
Indeed, he shows himself capable of competent management of it, even
of subverting the Hebrew text's meaning when YHWH's purposes as they
are registered there seem too terrible to contemplate (6:9–10).

The Hebrew text speaks of a return of perception under the wise rule
of just leaders by declaring that eyes that had been shut "will no longer
be closed" and that ears that had been deaf or inattentive "will listen"
(32:3). The Greek translator has a different idea, one that he articulates

---

19. Even a partial list must include 6:9–10; 11:3; 29:18; 35:4–6; 42:6–7; 43:8;
44:18; for a fuller treatment, see T. Uhlig, "Too Hard to Understand? The Motif of
Hardening in Isaiah," in *Interpreting Isaiah: Issues and Approaches* (ed. D. G. Firth
and H. G. M. Williamson; Nottingham: Apollos; Downers Grove: InterVarsity,
2009), 62–83. Indeed, the title of this volume derives from a moment of ironic
reversal in which לשון למודים—"the *tongue of a teacher*" (so NRSV)—is given "that I
may know how to sustain the weary with a word."

by introducing antithetic parallelism that opposes one behaviour to another: καὶ οὐκέτι ἔσονται πεποιθότες ἐπ᾽ ἀνθρώποις ἀλλὰ τὰ ὦτα δώσουσιν ἀκούειν.[20]

Van der Kooij observes that the adversative ἀλλὰ "indicates a contrast which is not found in the Hebrew text as we understand the MT. The notion of a contrast reflects a different reading of the underlying text, based on the assumption that the negation לא in the first clause does not apply to the second clause."[21] The Greek text represents a formidable reconfiguration of the conventional parallelism of the Hebrew text. It is difficult to locate in the Hebrew text itself motivation for the stark contrast that the translator is developing. But if his thoughts were drawn to the first psalm, one can imagine that he derived the antithesis between those who "trust in men" and those who are now moved to lend their ears to hear—emphasized by ἀλλὰ—from the severe lines of that psalm's structure.

The blessed state of the psalm's protagonist (μακάριος ἀνήρ) hinges upon his wholesale refusal to participate in the conviviality that is three times offered in the first verse over against his night-and-day occupation with the "law of the Lord." The deep bifurcation of human conduct and of human beings that is urged upon the reader of the first psalm is signalled by the strong adversative ἀλλά.[22] It is possible that the translator's reconfiguration of Isa 32:3 signals that his mind is operating along similar lines, and perhaps even with the first psalm in view.

f. *Tuition for Rulers*
In Isa 32:4, the translator surprises yet again by supplying the verb μαθήσονται in his portrayal of "stuttering tongues that hasten." In the translator's view they *swiftly learn*—to speak peace. It is difficult to account for the language of learning from within the Isaiah text itself. One clue to the translator's thoughts may come from the second psalm, where "kings" and "rulers of the earth" had conspired against "the LORD and his anointed" prior to YHWH's decree, "I have set my king on Zion, my holy hill." Now that circumstances have changed (ועתה), the kings and rulers[23] are urged to submit themselves to their new reality in the

---

20. "Then no longer will they trust in men, but they will lend their ears to hear" (NETS).

21. Van der Kooij, "Septuagint of Isaiah," 40.

22. LXX Ps 1:2a: ἀλλ᾽ ἢ ἐν τῷ νόμῳ κυρίου τὸ θέλημα αὐτοῦ...

23. ἄρχοντες, as in Isa 32:1. Note also ἄρξουσι ("shall rule") in 32:1 and καὶ οὐκέτι μὴ εἴπωσιν τῷ μωρῷ ἄρχειν ("and no longer shall they tell the fool to rule") in 32:5.

twin imperatives השכילו and הוסרו, for which the LXX has σύνετε and παιδεύθητε. One wonders, then, whether the translator of Isa 32 has supplied his hopeful μαθήσονται because of the influence of Ps 2.[24]

g. *The Intrusion of "Counsel" into the Greek Text*
Another unexpected LXX plus occurs at Isa 32:7, a text that explores the villainous misconduct that stands over against the rule of a righteous king and his just rulers:

וכלי כליו הוא רעים זמות יעץ
לחבל ענוים באמרי־שקר ובדבר אביון משפט

> The villainies of villains are evil; they devise wicked devices to ruin the poor with lying words, even when the plea of the needy is right. (NRSV)

With only modest warrant from his text, the translator lays hold of words for evil *counsel* and produces ἡ γὰρ <u>βουλή</u> τῶν πονηρῶν ἄνομα <u>βουλεύσεται</u> καταφθεῖραι ταπεινοὺς ἐν λόγοις ἀδίκοις καὶ διασκεδάσαι λόγους ταπεινῶν ἐν κρίσει. Apart from the possibility of attraction to the βουλή vocabulary of the verse that follows—which itself is only partially generated by the Hebrew text—it is difficult to establish from within the Isaiah text the source of this language of counsel and of taking counsel. I suggest that it comes over from Ps 1. There, memorably, the blessed man is the one who does not walk in the *counsel* (ἐν βούλῃ) of the wicked; and where, conversely and penultimately as the poem nears its climax, sinners shall not rise in the *counsel* (ἐν βουλῇ) of (the) just ones.

h. *A Moment of Judgment*
Possibly the argument that the Isaiah translator has lingered over the early lines of the Psalter is buttressed by his unanticipated way with the enigmatic ובדבר אביון משפט at Isa 32:7.[25] In the translator's hands, this becomes a reference to a moment or a venue in which justice is meted out, an occasion when according to his understanding of the Isaiah text the wicked customarily "shatter the words of the humble." The Greek uses the exact terminology employed by the writer of the first psalm to

---

24.   Such a reading, if it can be sustained, may provide evidence that the Isaiah translator is reading his passage and regarding its "man" and its "king" as messianic. In this regard, one is reminded of van der Kooij's observation that the Greek text of Isa 31:9b–32:8, understood as a coherent declaration in its own right, has in view "a particular person" (van der Kooij, "Septuagint of Isaiah," 37).

25.   The NRSV translation reads: "even when the plea of the needy is right."

speak of the moment in which YHWH's stewardship of the wicked and the just guarantees that the godless shall not stand: ἐν κρίσει (Isa 32:7; Ps 1:5).

4. *Conclusion*

Eight novelties introduced into the Greek translation of Isa 31:9b–32:8 make it plausible that the translator glimpsed in his text the face of Israel's sage (Ps 1) and possibly also its anointed king (Ps 2).

The translation can be regarded as a palimpsest. Beneath the text that comes into the translator's hands lies a pre-understanding of what this text must mean. The face of Israel's paradigmatic wise man is visible only faintly behind the lines of the Greek Isaiah text that is now presented to the reader. The outlines of sage and king merge as a translator with as much concern for the wider biblical tradition as for the details of the particular text before him prepares that text in a new language for a new reader.

FOOD FOR THE BIRDS OF HEAVEN: STAGED DEATH AND INTERCESSION IN JEREMIAH IN LIGHT OF SHAKESPEARE'S CYMBELINE

Diana Lipton

It gives me great pleasure to offer this study to a Festschrift in honour of Andrew Macintosh. Andrew taught me Biblical Hebrew during the year that I was studying for a Diploma in Theology at Cambridge University in preparation for Ph.D. research. He was an excellent teacher, always ready with precisely the right blend of correction and encouragement. I learned something important about his pedagogical methods when, in the summer term with examinations approaching, our lessons moved from a small, modern, functional classroom in what was at the time the Faculty of Oriental Studies to Andrew's elegant study at St. John's College. Alongside the portraits of (I am guessing) his illustrious predecessors as Dean of Chapel, and a sign above the door declaring "Welcome" in Hebrew, hung several blades (oars) celebrating victories by St. John's College rowers while Andrew was their coach. His teaching techniques for Biblical Hebrew owed a lot to coaching expertise gleaned on the banks of the Cam (and no doubt I, a former undergraduate rower at a college at "the other place," was especially responsive to his particular brand of motivation). I learned something else about Andrew's teaching methods when, much later, he invited me to a party at his home and I met his remarkable wife Mary. During their married life together, Andrew and Mary had been foster parents to over a hundred children, most of them from severely disadvantaged backgrounds, and many with learning and other difficulties. Having seen Mary in action with the beautiful baby girl who accompanied them to a shabbat dinner at our house some time later, I speculated that Andrew had learned as much about teaching in the home as on the river. At the very least, in Mary's company he honed his wonderful capacity to be, in one breath, kind, funny and firm.

Asked to identify the central task of prophecy, most readers of the Hebrew Bible emphasize the communication of the divine word, usually with an emphasis on future events. As traditionally understood, the prophet is God's mouthpiece, telling the people what lies ahead. A less often discussed aspect of the prophetic task is intercession,[1] when the prophet acts as mediator or go-between, interceding ever more creatively in both directions to keep alive the relationship between God and Israel.[2] On occasion, it is hard to see how these two roles can be compatible. This is a particular issue in the case of Jeremiah, where the future events predicted are so dire. How can constructive intercession sit alongside the doom-laden prophecies of death and destruction characteristic of the Hebrew Bible's least likely marriage-guidance counsellor? In the present study I will argue—counter-intuitively, I admit—that it is precisely the harsh and graphic expression of God's fury that serves in the end as Jeremiah's mechanism of intercession.

In his seminal discussion of prophetic intercession, "Who will stand in the breach?," Yochanan Muffs offers four mechanisms for averting or limiting divine anger and the punishment it generates: punishment is exacted little by little (Num 14:19); punishment is transferred (2 Sam 12:14); God limits his own anger (Ps 78:38; Hos 11:9); and divine love trumps divine anger (only post-biblical examples given). In narrative terms, Exod 32–33 (the golden calf) could serve as a manual for prophetic intercession. Moses tells God: calm down (32:11); they are *your* people (32:11); *you* brought them out of Egypt (32:11); think of what the Egyptians will say (32:12); remember the patriarchs (32:13); keep *your* promises (32:13); let the Levites kill three thousand people (32:27); kill me instead (32:32). Death is strikingly prominent in this manual of intercession. Moses' interaction with God over the golden calf seems to suggest that, when all else fails, God can be appeased by one or two (or three thousand) dead bodies. Elsewhere in the Bible, and in the ancient world more generally, death—and substitute death—intercedes: animal sacrifice, molech worship and child-sacrifice. In recent years it has been suggested that in some circumstances mourning rituals ("petitionary mourning") may function as a type of intercession,[3] and that simulated

---

1. I owe my interest in this approach to prophecy to Y. Muffs, *Love and Joy: Law, Language and Religion in Ancient Israel* (New York: Jewish Theological Seminary of America, 1992), 9–48.

2. In the present study I use "Israel" in a broad "theological" sense to refer to the people or land of Israel, even when, in relation to some (though not all) passages in Jeremiah, for example, it would be more accurate to use "Judah."

3. See S. Olyan, *Biblical Mourning: Ritual and Social Dimensions* (Oxford: Oxford University Press, 2004), on petitionary mourning, and D. Lipton, "Early Mourning? Petitionary Versus Posthumous Ritual in Ezekiel xxiv," *VT* 56 (2006): 185–220, on God's prohibition of Ezekiel's mourning his wife's death (Ezek 24) as advance resistance to intercession.

death and willingness to die may also play significant roles in post-biblical intercession, from martyrdom to Yom Kippur rituals.[4] Bearing all this in mind, we turn not in the first instance to Jeremiah, but to one of Shakespeare's less frequently performed plays, Cymbeline.

For those who have not recently read or seen Cymbeline, I shall summarize just those elements of its complex plot that concern us here. As so often in Shakespeare's plays, Cymbeline has two interwoven plots, in this case one personal and one political. In the personal narrative, Imogen, the only surviving child of King Cymbeline of Britain, has just married her beloved Leonatus. Her father and her wicked step-mother (whose dramatic punishment is to be known only as "Queen") are angry; they wanted her to marry Cloten, the step-mother's son from a previous marriage. Egged on by Queen, King Cymbeline exiles his new son-in-law Leonatus to Italy, where Leonatus foolishly enters into a Job-like wager with Iachimo (think Iago) to test Imogen's fidelity. Iachimo returns with "evidence"—a detailed description gleaned by breaking into her bedroom while she is sleeping—that he has had sexual relations with Imogen, and Leonatus writes immediately to his loyal servant Pisanio, still in Britain looking after Imogen, ordering him to kill Imogen. Although Pisanio is devoted to Imogen, he sets out to comply with his master's wishes, arranging what we think will be Imogen's date with death in Milford Haven. As the play draws to a close, both Imogen and Leonatus are lying, apparently dead, on centre stage. But all is not what it seems. Husband and wife have survived: Imogen was merely affected by a sleeping potion (think Romeo and Juliet), while the headless corpse we thought was Leonatus was in fact the wicked Cloten. All's well that ends well.

In the political plot, King Cymbeline of Britain attempts to terminate his contractual agreement with Rome, informing Cassius, Caesar's ambassador, that Britain will no longer pay taxes. Cassius declares war on Britain and fighting ensues, but it transpires that Cymbeline's change of heart about Rome was due to the influence of his Machiavellian wife, Queen, who has in the meantime killed herself over the death of Cloten, her beloved son from a previous marriage. Cymbeline reactivates his standing order to pay his taxes, and lasting peace descends upon Britain and Rome.

---

4. D. Boyarin, *Dying for God: Martyrdom and the Making of Christianity and Judaism* (Figurae: Reading Medieval Culture; Stanford: Stanford University Press, 1999); S. Weitzman, *Surviving Sacrilege: Cultural Persistence in Jewish Antiquity* (Cambridge, Mass.: Harvard University Press, 2005); Lipton, "Early Mourning?"

A notable point of contact between Cymbeline's two plots is that both concern established relationships that are abandoned by the parties involved without good reason and on the basis of insufficient or misleading evidence. Leonatus gives up on his beloved Imogen on the basis of a false report issued by a man he barely knew, and who had a compelling reason to lie to him (his "proof" was offered in the context of a wager). Cymbeline gives up on a relationship with Rome that benefitted all his subjects because Queen, his blatantly manipulative, unreliable and self-serving wife, tells him to. In both cases, as we shall see, reconciliation is achieved through the interventions of the servant.

Soon after Cymbeline has banished Leonatus, Pisanio receives a shocking letter from his absent master instructing him to kill Imogen for committing adultery:

> Enter PISANIO, with a letter
> PISANIO
> How? of adultery? Wherefore write you not
> What monster's her accuser? Leonatus,
> O master! what a strange infection
> Is fall'n into thy ear! What false Italian,
> As poisonous-tongued as handed, hath prevail'd
> On thy too ready hearing? Disloyal! No:
> She's punish'd for her truth, and undergoes,
> More goddess-like than wife-like, such assaults
> As would take in some virtue. O my master!
> Thy mind to her is now as low as were
> Thy fortunes. How! that I should murder her?
> Upon the love and truth and vows which I
> Have made to thy command? I, her? her blood?
> If it be so to do good service, never
> Let me be counted serviceable. How look I,
> That I should seem to lack humanity
> so much as this fact comes to?
> *Reading*
> "Do't: the letter
> that I have sent her, by her own command
> Shall give thee opportunity." O damn'd paper!
> Black as the ink that's on thee! Senseless bauble,
> Art thou a feodary for this act, and look'st
> So virgin-like without? Lo, here she comes.
> I am ignorant in what I am commanded.[5]

___

5. The Arden Shakespeare *Cymbeline* (London: Methuen, 1980).

Given his loyalty to his mistress and his conviction that the charges against her are trumped up, Pisanio might have been expected to conceal Leonatus's message from Imogen, or at least to temper it. Instead, he conceals it only for as long as it takes for them to reach Milford Haven, the venue chosen by Leonatus for Imogen's execution. Once they have arrived, he ensures that she knows precisely, word for word, what his master thinks of her and what he intends, by handing her the letter so that she can read it for herself.

> PISANIO
> Please you, read;
> And you shall find me, wretched man, a thing
> The most disdain'd of fortune.
> IMOGEN
> [Reads] "Thy mistress, Pisanio, hath played the
> strumpet in my bed; the testimonies whereof lie
> bleeding in me. I speak not out of weak surmises,
> but from proof as strong as my grief and as certain
> as I expect my revenge. That part thou, Pisanio,
> must act for me, if thy faith be not tainted with
> the breach of hers. Let thine own hands take away
> her life: I shall give thee opportunity at
> Milford-Haven. She hath my letter for the purpose
> where, if thou fear to strike and to make me certain
> it is done, thou art the pandar to her dishonour and
> equally to me disloyal."

Leonatus's words are all the more cutting for having been written in the third person and addressed in the first instance to a third party ("Thy mistress, Pisanio, hath played the strumpet in my bed"). Their effect would have been much milder had he sat down to write directly to Imogen, and not via his servant. Since the letter was clearly not intended for her eyes, why did Pisanio show it to her, thus exposing her to the additional pain of reading cruel and angry words that Leonatus had addressed to him? A possible answer may be read between the lines of his subsequent soliloquy:

> PISANIO
> What shall I need to draw my sword? the paper
> Hath cut her throat already. No, 'tis slander,
> Whose edge is sharper than the sword, whose tongue
> Outvenoms all the worms of Nile, whose breath
> Rides on the posting winds and doth belie
> All corners of the world: kings, queens and states,
> Maids, matrons, nay, the secrets of the grave
> This viperous slander enters. What cheer, madam?

Pisanio's speech brings a whole new dimension to the notion of paper cuts. The paper on which Leonatus's slanderous words are written substitutes for the sword. The words themselves are as poisonous as the venom of Nile serpents (a nod at Cleopatra?). Having placed the letter into Imogen's hands, thus allowing it to do its violent work, he need not murder her as Leonatus has instructed him. Consciously, half-consciously or otherwise, Pisanio has discovered a way of being perfectly loyal to his master and yet simultaneously true to his mistress. He will kill her with words on paper in response to accusations against her which have no reality beyond the words on paper that frame them.

Yet it is not enough for Pisanio to be obedient to Leonatus; he must also persuade him to change his mind. When Pisanio sets out for Milford Haven, where, according to Leonatus's instructions, he will take Imogen's life, it appears that he is being perfectly obedient to his master. Imogen appears to be lying dead on centre stage, as indeed does Leonatus. But all is not what it seems. Imogen is in fact under the influence of a sleeping potion administered by Pisanio; she only looks dead. The headless corpse that looks like Leonatus is none other than his dreadful rival Cloten, dressed in Leonatus's clothes. Cloten, on the other hand, really is dead, and his death leads Queen to take her own life in grief, paving the way for the restoration of good relations between Britain and Rome. Leonatus, however, is very much alive, and, seeing what he believes to be Imogen's corpse, he laments (unfairly one could say!) that Pisanio had obeyed his command to kill her.

> SCENE I. *Britain. The Roman camp.*
> Enter POSTHUMUS, with a bloody handkerchief
> POSTHUMUS LEONATUS
> Yea, bloody cloth, I'll keep thee, for I wish'd
> Thou shouldst be colour'd thus. You married ones,
> If each of you should take this course, how many
> Must murder wives much better than themselves
> For wrying but a little! O Pisanio!
> Every good servant does not all commands:
> No bond but to do just ones.

But of course Pisanio had been far from obedient; he had merely created the appearance of Imogen's death. Before the final curtains have closed, Imogen and Leonatus have been reconciled by their loyal servant Pisanio. And here is my main point: a crucial component of the reconciliation is death and, notably, staged death. What started out looking like a funeral ends as, if not a wedding, at least a renewal of vows.

Like Cymbeline, Jeremiah has two plots, or at least one plot with two distinct strands, one personal and one political. At the personal level, God and Israel are husband and wife:

> Thus says the LORD: I remember the devotion of your youth, your love as a bride, how you followed me in the wilderness, in a land not sown. Israel was holy to the LORD, the first fruits of his harvest... (Jer 2:2–3)[6]

At the time of writing, the marriage is on the rocks, with Israel's presumed infidelity as one of the main "issues" that lies between them:

> This is your lot, the portion I have measured out to you, says the LORD, because you have forgotten me and trusted in lies. I myself will lift up your skirts over your face, and your shame will be seen. I have seen your abominations, your adulteries and neighings, your shameless prostitutions on the hills of the countryside... (Jer 13:25–27)

At the political level, Jeremiah, like Cymbeline, addresses a relationship between two unequal powers, one subjugated to the other:

> I herewith deliver all these lands to My servant, King Nebuchadnezzar of Babylon; I even give him all the wild beasts to serve him: All nations shall serve him, his son and his grandson—until the turn of his own land comes, when many nations and great kings shall subjugate him. (Jer 27:6–7)

Ultimately, the prophet attributes Israel's political plight—subjugation to Babylon, to a personal cause—Israel's "marital" infidelity to God, and thus the two strands are intertwined.

With respect to infidelity, Cymbeline and Jeremiah differ on at least one important point: Imogen was wholly virtuous, while Israel was not. Yet it is arguable that both Leonatus and God suffer unduly, and cause undue suffering to others, by growing too angry and giving up too quickly on their partners in love when confronted by infidelity, whether real or merely suspected. This, I think, is what lies behind Jeremiah's surprising characterization of God as a man on a one-night stand:

> Although our iniquities testify against us, act, O LORD, for your name's sake; our apostasies indeed are many, and we have sinned against you. O hope of Israel, its saviour in time of trouble, why should you be like a stranger in the land, like a traveller turning aside for the night? Why should you be like someone confused, like a mighty warrior who cannot give help? Yet you, O LORD, are in the midst of us, and we are called by your name; do not forsake us! (Jer 14:7–9)

---

6. All English translations from *JPS Hebrew–English Tanakh* (Philadelphia: Jewish Publication Society, 1999).

God, according to Jeremiah, has a commitment problem. His reluctance to work at the marriage is, of course, especially problematic since, as God himself observes, precisely in the context of infidelity, people do not (usually) change: "Can the Cushite change his skin, or the leopard his spots?" (Jer 13:23). Since Israel was apparently predisposed to be unfaithful when God took her as a wife, God should have factored this disposition into their relationship. As any marriage-guidance counsellor will confirm, it is unwise in the extreme to predicate marital happiness on a partner's capacity to change. Was God then justified in rejecting Israel when her behaviour was predictable? And was he, moreover, emotionally capable of evaluating the evidence against her? Leonatus—together with other characters in Cymbeline and even members of the audience—is presented with multiple forms of evidence, from eye-witness accounts, through "tokens" of clothing and jewellery, to "dead" bodies on stage, that such and such a person is guilty of this or that crime or that such and such a person is dead. Almost all this evidence and testimony turns out to be false or misleading. Imogen was neither unfaithful nor, eventually, dead. Is it possible that, in a heightened state of anger and distress, God too misinterpreted or exaggerated the "evidence" of adultery and depravity that he thought he saw throughout the land? Was Israel really worshipping other gods on high places and under leafy trees, or was she just having a picnic? Yet in the end, as we learn from Cymbeline, not to mention human nature in general, it barely matters whether or not these accusations of infidelity are appropriate or legitimate. Just as an agoraphobe derives little comfort from the news that the countryside holds no actual threat, so a jealous lover is rarely consoled by the news that his or her suspicions are unfounded. Once feelings of betrayal and distrust set in, they take on a life of their own, and must be dealt with accordingly. In both Cymbeline and Jeremiah, the task of dealing with these feelings falls to the loyal servant. And just as Pisanio refrains from straightforward reasoning with Leonatus, seeming rather to go along with him, so Jeremiah, I shall try to show, avoids a direct attempt to change God's mind but allows the drama to play out.

One reason for Jeremiah's reluctance to intercede explicitly is that God has explicitly prohibited it:

> Therefore do not pray for this people, nor lift up a cry nor pray for them, nor make intercession to me; for I will not hear. Do you not see what they do in the cities of Judah and in the streets of Jerusalem? The children gather wood, and the fathers kindle the fire, and the women knead their dough, to make cakes to the queen of heaven, and to pour out drink offerings to other gods, that they may provoke me to anger. Do they provoke me to anger? says the LORD; Do they not provoke themselves to their own

> disgrace? Therefore thus says the LORD God: Behold, my anger and my
> fury shall be poured out upon this place, upon man, and upon beast, and
> upon the trees of the field, and upon the fruit of the ground; and it shall
> burn, and shall not be quenched. (Jer 7:16–20)

Once it is clear that God's wrath has been aroused and that all pleas for
compassion will be rejected, Jeremiah begins to address the crisis not by
trying to avert it but by hastening it towards a dramatic conclusion. He
achieves this in the first instance by fanning the flames and intensifying
God's message of anger. God, like Leonatus, is seething with jealous
rage and, again like Leonatus, wants nothing less than the death of his
beloved:

> And they have built the high places of Tophet, which is in the valley of
> Ben-Hinnom, to burn their sons and their daughters in the fire; which I did
> not command them, nor did it come into my heart. Therefore, behold, the
> days come, says the LORD, that it shall no more be called Tophet, nor the
> valley of Ben-Hinnom, but the Valley of Slaughter; for they shall bury in
> Tophet, because there is no place elsewhere. And the carcasses of this
> people shall be food for the birds of heaven, and for the beasts of the earth;
> and none shall scare them away. Then will I cause to cease from the cities
> of Judah, and from the streets of Jerusalem, the voice of mirth, and the
> voice of gladness, the voice of the bridegroom, and the voice of the bride;
> for the land shall be desolate. (Jer 7:31–34)

Instead of a wedding there will be a funeral, or rather a non-funeral.
Since a funeral would be more than Israel deserves, according to God,
her dead body will instead be left uncared for and unburied on the earth,
exposed to the elements, food for birds of prey and wild animals. This
juxtaposition of images of marriage and fertility on the one hand and, on
the other, scenes of death and mourning is characteristic of the book of
Jeremiah. Mothers of young men will be destroyed, bearers of seven will
be shamed, and widows will be more numerous than the offspring they
might otherwise have produced:

> You have rejected me, says the LORD, you are going backwards; so I have
> stretched out my hand against you and destroyed you—I am weary of
> relenting: I have winnowed them with a winnowing-fork in the gates of the
> land; I have bereaved them, I have destroyed my people; they did not turn
> from their ways: Their widows became more numerous than the sand of
> the seas; I have brought against the mothers of youths a destroyer at noon-
> day; I have made anguish and terror fall upon her suddenly. She who bore
> seven has languished; she has swooned away; her sun went down while it
> was yet day; she has been shamed and disgraced. And the rest of them I
> will give to the sword before their enemies, says the LORD. (Jer 15:6–9)

In a move unparalleled in the Hebrew Bible, life is cut off before it
begins; God prohibits Jeremiah from having children of his own or even

marrying. Those unlucky enough to be born already will die unmourned, and those who should by rights have been their mourners will not be comforted:

> The word of the LORD came also to me, saying, You shall not take a wife, nor shall you have sons or daughters in this place. For thus says the LORD concerning the sons and concerning the daughters who are born in this place, and concerning their mothers who bore them, and concerning their fathers who begot them in this land: They shall die of grievous deaths; they shall not be lamented; nor shall they be buried; but they shall be as dung upon the face of the earth; and they shall be consumed by the sword, and by famine; and their carcasses shall be food for the birds of heaven, and for the beasts of the earth. For thus says the LORD, Enter not into the house of mourning, nor go to lament nor bemoan them; for I have taken away my peace from this people, says the LORD, both loving-kindness and mercy. Both the great and the small shall die in this land; they shall not be buried, nor shall men lament for them, nor gash themselves, nor make themselves bald for them; No men shall break bread during the mourning, to comfort him for the dead; nor shall men give them the cup of consolation to drink for his father or for his mother. You shall also not go into the house of feasting, to sit with them to eat and to drink. For thus says the LORD of hosts, the God of Israel: Behold, I will cause to cease from this place before your eyes, and in your days, the voice of mirth, and the voice of gladness, the voice of the bridegroom, and the voice of the bride. (Jer 16:1–9)

The unlamented carcasses that litter these passages are, I think, Jeremiah's rhetorical equivalent of the "dead bodies" that lie on stage at Cymbeline's dramatic turning point. Pisanio "faked" Imogen's death because he understood that, for all concerned, the appearance of catastrophe was both cathartic and sufficient to render it unnecessary in reality. First, it brought Leonatus to his senses, allowing him to visualize the logical end of his destructive emotions. Secondly, and more importantly, it brought a virtual end (staged death) to a virtual nightmare (Leonatus's unfounded jealousy). Similarly, Jeremiah's graphic death scenes bring closure to God's escalating jealousy and anger and, it is to be hoped, to any behaviour of Israel's that might have caused it. When confronted by Jeremiah's devastating prophecies, Israel and God learn where their story would have ended without his intercession. Jeremiah—paradoxically identified with excessive anger by later readers such as Abraham Joshua Heschel[7]—forces divine anger to its natural conclusion, and in so doing

---

7. Abraham Joshua Heschel, *The Prophets*, vol. 1 (New York: Harper & Row, 1962). More recently see S. Joo, *Provocation and Punishment: The Anger of God in the Book of Jeremiah and Deuteronomistic Theology* (Berlin: de Gruyter, 2006).

frees God and Israel to return to the script they unwisely, but only temporarily, abandoned. Cries of lament can at last be replaced by the sound of celebration:

> Thus said the LORD: again there shall be heard in this place, which you say is ruined, without man or beast—in the towns of Judah and the streets of Jerusalem that are desolate…the sound of joy and gladness, the voice of the bridegroom and the voice of the bride, the voice of those who cry, "Give thanks to the LORD of Hosts, for the LORD is good, for his loving-kindness is everlasting…" (Jer 33:10–11)

My analysis, if correct, suggests that prophetic intercession is more varied and creative than usually assumed, and that Jeremiah is a more interested and effective intercessor than often supposed. Moreover, this reading deepens (and complicates) possible biblical foundations of martyrdom, whether understood as actual death or willingness to die. It also suggests a way in which written texts can be said to intercede; God accepts descriptions in lieu of reality.[8] Finally, it expands the notion of reusable prophecy. Jeremiah's graphic accounts of unmourned bodies reduced to bird food were valuable tools of intercession, both at the time of the Babylonian exile and for later readers in faith communities of all denominations for whom such scenes were not merely manifestations of divine anger but functioned as a mechanism for transforming that anger into love.

---

8. I have tried to articulate this idea more clearly in relation to divine kingship in "By Royal Appointment: God's Influence on Influencing God," in *The God of Israel* (ed. R. P. Gordon; Cambridge: Cambridge University Press, 2007), 73–94.

DAVID THEIR KING (WHOM GOD WILL RAISE): HOSEA 3:5 AND THE ONSET OF MESSIANIC EXPECTATION IN THE PROPHETIC BOOKS

Alexander Rofé

In his distinguished commentary on the book of Hosea, Dr. Macintosh subscribed to the view, already expressed by former exegetes, that the mention of "David their King" in Hos 3:5 had been interpolated into the text.[1] He also maintained that these words were contributed by Judaean redactors in the seventh century B.C.E. at the earliest, but they possibly are post-exilic.[2] In the present study I will elaborate upon the insight of our jubilarian in a number of ways: in the first place the expressions suspected to have been interpolated will be aligned with similar ones in other prophetic books; then the implication for the origin of these annunciations will be explored; finally conclusions will be drawn about the exact meaning of the prediction concerning David and its purport for the history of messianic expectation in Israel.

The following promises of a future David—shepherd, prince, king— whom the Lord will raise up for Israel appear in three prophetic books:[3]

> Afterward, the Israelites will turn back and will seek the Lord their God and David their king—and they will thrill over the Lord and over His bounty in the days to come. (Hos 3:5)

> In that day, declares the Lord of Hosts, I will break his yoke from off your neck and I will rip off your bonds. Strangers shall no longer put him to work. Instead they shall serve the Lord their God and David their king whom I will raise up for them. (Jer 30:8–9)[4]

---

1. A. A. Macintosh, *A Critical and Exegetical Commentary on Hosea* (ICC; Edinburgh: T. & T. Clark, 1997), 110. An alternative view considers the whole of v. 5 as secondary; cf. S. Rudnig-Zelt, "Vom Propheten und seiner Frau, einem Ephod und einem Teraphim—Anmerkungen zu Hos. 3:1–4, 5," *VT* 60 (2010): 373–99, esp. 392–94, 396, with references to earlier scholars. (This learned article, however, did not take into account the LXX readings for *ephod* and *teraphim* in v. 4).

2. Macintosh, *Hosea*, lxxi.

3. The English version has been adapted from the NJPS.

4. The shift in the use of pronouns—second singular, third singular, third plural— features in late expansions of prophetic oracles; cf. Mic 7:14–15, 17, 19; Zeph 3:19.

Then I will raise up a single shepherd over them to tend them—My servant David. He shall tend them, he shall be a shepherd to them. I the Lord will be their God, and My servant David shall be a prince among them. I the Lord have spoken. (Ezek 34:23–24)

My servant David shall be king over them; there shall be one shepherd for all of them. They shall follow My rules and faithfully obey My laws. Thus they shall dwell in the land which I gave to My servant Jacob and in which your fathers dwelt…with My servant David as their prince for all time. (Ezek 37:24–25)

The elements shared by these passages are evident. All of them speak about a future David who will appear; most of them (Jer 30:9; Ezek 37:24; Hos 3:5) define him as king; alternatively he is called prince, *nāśî* (Ezek 34:24; 37:25),[5] and shepherd (Ezek 34:23; 37:24). In any case, he is the future ruler of Israel; two of the passages, moreover, explicitly state that the Lord will raise him (*hqmty/ᵓqym*) for Israel (Jer 30:9) or over Israel (Ezek 34:23). At the same time, these passages are marked off from other "Davidic" passages in the Bible: here there is no mention of the "booth of David" (Amos 9:11) or lamp (e.g. 1 Kgs 11:36), or of a branch of his line (Jer 23:5). The prophecies here mention David himself—whatever that means—nothing less and nothing more.

How can we explain the presence of four similar predictions in three prophetic books? The plain solution that one prophet influenced the other two (or their disciples) must be ruled out. Since Hosea did not speak of Jerusalem and her king, either in reproach or in consolation, it is evident that the mention of David in Hos 3:5 did not originate with this prophet. Nor can we assume that Ezekiel influenced the compilers of the other two books. Ezekiel 34:17–31, which includes the prophecy concerning David, is a secondary expansion of the original allegory of the shepherds and the flock (vv. 1–16). In the latter, the "shepherds," namely the Davidide kings of Judah, were indicted (vv. 1–8); the Lord would dismiss them (v. 10) and take it upon himself to be the sole shepherd (vv. 11–16, especially v. 15: "I myself…I myself");[6] this means that the Lord would be the only king of Israel. Conversely, in vv. 17–24 the problem is not the negligence and gluttony of the shepherds, but rather the disarray in the flock, with strong beasts abusing the feeble ones,

5. LXX Ezek 37:24 reads *archōn* (= *nāśî*), which probably is a secondary reading, theologically motivated; cf. A. Rofé, "Qumranic Paraphrases, the Greek Deuteronomy and the Late History of the Biblical נשיא," *Textus* 14 (1988): 163–74.

6. אני ארעה צאני ואני ארביצם. On this use of the personal pronoun, see P. Joüon and T. Muraoka, *A Grammar of Biblical Hebrew. Part Three, Syntax* (Rome: Pontificio Istituto Biblico, 1996), 538–39.

which symbolizes oppression within society; the remedy for this trouble will not be the Lord assuming power as shepherd, but David. This goes to prove that the passage in Ezek 34:23–24 did not originate with the prophet Ezekiel.[7] Consequently, this will also apply to Ezek 37:24–25, which presents the same idea and imagery.

No more attractive is the possibility of Jeremianic authorship of the passage in Jer 30:8–9. The style of this prophet is well known and it is quite dissimilar from that of the verses in question. Thus, one is left with the alternative solution: all four passages were coined by one author or school of authors[8] who introduced them into the oracles of three major prophets—Hosea, Jeremiah and Ezekiel.[9]

The conclusion about authorship entails an inference as to the date of composition. The introduction of similar expressions in three distinct books implies that their author was not a disciple, near or remote, of any one of those prophets. Rather, he lived and worked after the various prophetic books had been collected, while the prophetic canon was being formed. We may reckon that his activity took place rather late in post-exilic times, towards the end of the Persian period.

7.   The first step toward this distinction was made by K. Begrich, "Das Messiasbild des Ezechiel" (Ph.D. diss., Altenburg, 1904), 21–22. Perhaps even the secondary layer is not a single piece and the text was expanded again in vv. 25–31; see G. Hölscher, *Hesekiel, der Dichter und das Buch* (BZAW 39; Giessen: Töpelmann, 1924), 169–71; G. A. Cooke, *A Critical and Exegetical Commentary on the Book of Ezekiel* (ICC; Edinburgh: T. & T. Clark, 1936). In my opinion, neither Hammershaimb nor Rembry succeeded in establishing the unity of the chapter; see E. Hammershaimb, "Ezekiel's View of the Monarchy," in *Studia Orientalia Ioanni Pedersen Dicata* (Hauniae: Munksgaard, 1953), 130–40, esp. 136–38; J. G. Rembry, "Le thème du berger dans l'oeuvre d'Ezéchiel," *Liber Annuus* 11 (1960/61): 113–44. Even Greenberg, who adopted a "holistic approach," had to admit: "Several signs, therefore, point to B [i.e. vv. 17–31, A. R.] being secondary reflections, including motifs more at home in subsequent oracles"; cf. M. Greenberg, *Ezekiel 21–37: A New Translation with Introduction and Commentary* (AB 22A; New York: Doubleday, 1997), 707.

8.   The latter possibility is favoured by the variety of literary forms: in Hos 3:5 we have a gloss to an existing text; in Jer 30:8–9, a short independent prophecy; Ezek 34:17–24 is an extensive appendix to an already extant oracle, and Ezek 37:15–28 is a fully fledged prophecy in itself. However, one should not deny the likelihood that a late scribe chose to express himself in alternative ways.

9.   The "four prophecies" have been dealt with in recent scholarship, but their significance as a single redactional layer has apparently escaped scholars' attention; cf., e.g., A. Laato, *Josiah and David Redivivus: The Historical Josiah and the Messianic Expectations of Exilic and Postexilic Times* (ConBOT 33; Stockholm: Almqvist & Wiksell International, 1992), passim.

Possibly, the pericope Ezek 34:17–24 (thus I would delimit this layer of composition) contains a hint regarding its historical-social circumstances. Verse 21 reads: "Because you pushed with flank and shoulder against the feeble ones and butted them with your horns *until you scattered them abroad.*" If we look for a reality behind this metaphor, we would find it in a process of emigration from the land caused by social oppression. Of course, this could have been an extended process over an undetermined period of time, yet a similar phenomenon of impoverished individuals, mostly peasants, subjected to slavery on account of debts and then sold abroad, is attested by Nehemiah (ch. 5, especially v. 8) during his first governorship in Jerusalem (445 B.C.E.).[10] One may infer that, in spite of the energetic measures of Nehemiah and his stern reproach, the same economic and social conditions continued to prevail in the province of Yehud until the end of the Persian Empire and even beyond.

An additional correspondence between our Davidic promises and circumstances described in the book of Nehemiah can be observed. In Jer 30:8 it is said: "Strangers shall no longer put him to work." These "strangers" are left anonymous; who are they? Probably not the Babylonians, since the book of Jeremiah abounds with hostile references to this arch-enemy. The Persians, by contrast, are never mentioned in biblical books as an oppressive power. But the great confession in Neh 9 clearly refers to them while saying:

> Today we are slaves, and the land you gave our fathers to enjoy its fruit and bounty—here we are slaves on it! It yields its abundant *crops to kings whom you have set over us on account of our sins. They rule over our bodies and our beasts as they please*, and we are in great distress.

The heavy burden of taxes and forced labour imposed by the Persian government is referred to in both Jeremiah and Nehemiah. This is consistent with the late date, assigned above by historico-literary criteria, to the four Davidic prophecies.[11]

10. See the inspiring chapter on Nehemiah in Morton Smith, *Palestinian Parties and Politics That Shaped the Old Testament* (New York: Columbia University Press, 1971; repr., London: SCM, 1987), 96–112.

11. Thus, I would answer the query posed by R. Mason, "The Messiah in Postexilic Old Testament Literature," in *King and Messiah in Israel and the Ancient Near East* (ed. J. Day; JSOTSup 270; Sheffield: Sheffield Academic, 1998), 338–64 (339): "The trouble is that the decision about the date of origin of any one passage is notoriously difficult and subjective." This he wrote with reference to our passages.

Thus four passages written late in the Persian period and heralding the rise of David as future king or prince of Israel were interpolated in the prophetic canon. What is the significance of these promises in the context of Jewish messianic expectation? Prophecies of restoration of the Davidic dynasty are not ubiquitous in the prophetic corpus—their absence from Deutero- and Trito-Isaiah speaks volumes[12]—yet they do show up in some secondary passages. Noteworthy is a series of short oracles in Jer 33:14–26 that announce the eternality of the Davidic line. Other prophecies speak about the stock of Jesse (Isa 11:10) or a true branch of David (Jer 23:5–6). Here, however, in the four passages we have discussed, one notes something different: it is David himself who will come. The Lord will raise him up. Is it a *David Redivivus*, resuscitated from death? I am inclined to this view.[13] But even if we dismiss it as being remote from the world of thought of the Hebrew Bible, one has to reckon with the alternative—a future personality, endowed with the exceptional qualities of David, whom the Lord is going to grant to Israel. Is he pre-existent, hidden in God's treasures, as assumed later in the Apocrypha?[14] This is a possibility not to be excluded. In any case, this future ruler, merely by the fact of his being called David, has a supernatural quality.

It is generally acknowledged that the essence of messianism lies in the expectation of a superhuman figure, redeemer and judge, acting for his people at first, and later for the whole world. If we are right, the seeds of this belief were already sown in the prophetic books by the diligent scribes who gathered and edited them. Their impact in the generations to come has been and will certainly be the object of inquiry.[15] No less

12. "The enduring loyalty promised to David" is transferred by Trito-Isaiah to the obedient ones in Israel (Isa 55:3–5); cf. P. Volz, *Jesaia*. Vol. 2, *übersetzt und erklärt* (KAT 9; Leipzig: Deichert, 1932), 138–43; O. Eissfeldt, "The Promises of Grace to David in Isaiah 55.1–5," in *Israel's Prophetic Heritage: Essays in Honor of James Muilenburg* (ed. B. W. Anderson and W. Harrelson; London: SCM, 1962), 196–207. The construct state of חסדי דוד can only be objective; cf. H. G. M. Williamson, "The Sure Mercies of David: Subjective or Objective Genitive?," *JSS* 23 (1978): 31–49.

13. Cf. A. Rofé, "The Battle of David and Goliath: Folklore, Theology, Eschatology," in *Judaic Perspectives on Ancient Israel* (ed. J. Neusner et al.; Philadelphia: Fortress, 1987), 117–51, esp. 141–44; previous adherents to this view are mentioned in n. 15, below.

14. Cf. W. Horbury, "Messianism in the Old Testament Apocrypha and Pseudepigrapha," in Day, ed., *King and Messiah*, 402–33.

15. H. Schmidt, *Der Mythos vom wiederkehrenden König im Alten Testament* (2d ed.; Giessen: Töpelmann, 1933); H. Gressmann, *Der Messias* (FRLANT 43; Göttingen: Vandenhoeck & Ruprecht, 1929), 232–72. This belief was noted for

important is the perception of their intellectual milieu as attested by additional genres of biblical literature. As for late narrative writing, I have tried elsewhere to establish the presence of this messianic state of mind in the story of David and Goliath.[16]

post-biblical times by G. F. Moore, *Judaism in the First Centuries of the Christian Era, the Age of Tannaim* (3 vols.; Cambridge, Mass.: Harvard University Press, 1927–30), 2:325–26; E. Schürer, *The History of the Jewish People in the Age of Jesus Christ (175 B.C.–A.D. 135)* (ed. G. Vermes et al.; 2 vols.; Edinburgh: T. & T. Clark, 1973, 1979), 2:521–23; P. Volz, *Die Eschatologie der jüdischen Gemeinde im neutestamentlichen Zeitalter* (Tübingen: J. C. B. Mohr [Paul Siebeck], 1934), 206–7. See the texts in *b. Roš. Haš.* 25a; *b. Sanh.* 98b; *y. Ber.* 82:4.

16. See above, n. 13. A condensed treatment can be found in my *Introduction to the Literature of the Hebrew Bible* (ET ed. A. A. Macintosh; Jerusalem: Simor, 2009), 123–28.

GODDESSES, TREES, AND THE INTERPRETATION OF HOSEA 14:8(9)*

Judith M. Hadley

Introduction

The translation and interpretation of Hos 14:8(9) has been a point of interest for scholars for many generations. This essay will look at the numerous ways this text has been translated since the proposed emendation of Wellhausen,[1] with a view to contributing to the interpretation of the text. A full discussion of the dating of the verse is beyond the scope of this study. In summary, most scholars see no reason to doubt Hosean authorship,[2] although this view is not without its critics.[3] Fortunately, the

* I am pleased and honoured to be able to offer this small piece in gratitude for the work of A. A. Macintosh. I also wish to thank David Kiblinger, Mary Catherine O'Reilly-Gindhart and Elizabeth Hollenbach, of Villanova University, for their help in the typing of this article.

1. See n. 26.

2. T. Naumann, *Hoseas Erben: Strukturen der Nachinterpretation im Buch Hosea* (BWANT 131; Stuttgart: Kohlhammer, 1991), 130, "ist nicht zu zweifeln"; G. I. Emmerson, *Hosea: An Israelite Prophet in Judean Perspective* (JSOTSup 28; Sheffield: JSOT, 1984), 49–50; cf. also most of the commentaries on Hosea in English.

3. G. A. Yee, *Composition and Tradition in the Book of Hosea: A Redaction Critical Investigation* (SBLDS 102; Atlanta: Scholars Press, 1987), 131–32; R. Vielhauer, *Das Werden des Buches Hosea: Eine redaktionsgeschichtliche Untersuchung* (BZAW 349; Berlin: de Gruyter, 2007), 199; P. A. Kruger, "Yahweh's Generous Love: Eschatological Expectations in Hosea 14:2–9," *Old Testament Essays* 1 (1988): 27–48 (43); I. Cornelius, "Paradise Motifs in the 'Eschatology' of the Minor Prophets and the Iconography of the Ancient Near East: The Concepts of Fertility, Water, Trees and 'Tierfrieden' and Gen 2–3," *JNSL* 14 (1988): 41–83 (45); and see also C. Frevel, *Aschera und der Ausschliesslichskeitsanspruch YHWHs* (BBB 94/1; Weinheim: Beltz Athenäum, 1995), 329, and the references there, for an overview of the arguments concerning dating up until 1995; also W. R. Harper, *A Critical and Exegetical Commentary on Amos and Hosea* (ICC; Edinburgh: T. & T. Clark, 1979), 408–9.

precise authorship of the verse does not have a vital bearing on the discussion here.

The MT of Hos 14:8(9) reads, אפרים מה־לי עוד לעצבים אני עניתי ואשורנו אני כברוש רענן ממני פריך נמצא, and can be translated, "O Ephraim, what have I to do with idols? / It is I who answer and look after you, / I am like an evergreen cypress; / your faithfulness comes from me" (NRSV), or "Ephraim [shall say]: / 'What more have I to do with idols? / When I respond and look to Him, / I become like a verdant cypress.' / Your fruit is provided by Me" (JPS). The present study will first examine each of the four lines before turning to Wellhausen's emendation.

Line 1

As it stands, the first line, אפרים מה־לי עוד לעצבים, can be translated "Ephraim, what have I to do with idols any more?" Although the MT has מה־לי, many scholars prefer to emend the text to מה־לו, following the LXX.[4] Day notes that this emendation is preferable, "since it is Ephraim, not Yahweh, who is joined to idols."[5] Wolff believes that the text as it stands makes sense only if the verse began with ויאמר אפרים. But since the rest of that verse is a speech by YHWH, Ephraim must have been added as a clarification. "Therefore, 'Ephraim' should be understood as *casus pendens*, which is again referred to by לו."[6] Similarly, Harper notes that if the לי of the MT were to be retained, the translation should read "Ephraim (shall say): What have I to do any more with idols?"[7] This is the interpretation preferred by Macintosh, who interprets this verse as a dialogue between Ephraim and YHWH, with Ephraim reciting the first and third lines, and YHWH the second and fourth.[8] He notes the common

4. Cf. J. Day, "A Case of Inner Scriptural Interpretation," *JTS* NS 31 (1980): 309–19 (314); idem, "Asherah in the Hebrew Bible and Northwest Semitic Literature," *JBL* 105 (1986): 385–408 (404); Harper, *Amos and Hosea*, 414; G. I. Davies, *Hosea* (NCB; Grand Rapids: Eerdmans, 1992), 308; J. L. Mays, *Hosea* (OTL; Philadelphia: Westminster, 1969), 184; H. W. Wolff, *Hosea* (trans. G. Stansell; Hermeneia; Philadelphia: Fortress, 1974), 233; H. McKeating, *The Books of Amos, Hosea and Micah* (CBC; Cambridge: Cambridge University Press, 1971), 153; D. Stuart, *Hosea–Jonah* (Word Biblical Themes; Dallas: Word, 1989), 34; J. M. Ward, *Hosea: A Theological Commentary* (New York: Harper & Row, 1966), 227–28.

5. Day, "Asherah in the Hebrew Bible," 404 n. 59.

6. Wolff, *Hosea*, 233.

7. Harper, *Amos and Hosea*, 414; and cf. the JPS translation noted above.

8. A. A. Macintosh, *A Critical and Exegetical Commentary on Hosea* (ICC; Edinburgh: T. & T. Clark, 1997), 576.

difficulty with considering YHWH to be the speaker since YHWH "never had anything to do with idols and hence the exclamation is otiose."⁹ In Macintosh's interpretation, the first line is a rhetorical question, where Ephraim is described in the following question, so that the question sets forth the national situation that now exists. "What, then, the prophet intends to convey is as follows: 'Ephraim('s attitude is): what need more have I of idols?'"¹⁰ Couturier also keeps the מה־לי of the MT, and notes that the two stichoi of the verse are set in a chiastic structure.¹¹

Wagenaar presents a good overview of the arguments concerning the proposed emendation of לי to לו, but notes that "[i]n view of the absence of formal criterion to indicate an alternation of speakers the interpretation of v. 9 as a dialogue would…result in complete confusion with regard to the identity of the speaker and addressee."¹²

A full discussion of the word "idols" here, עצבים, is beyond the scope of this essay. It may be that it is not "foreign" idols that are meant, but rather "calf images" that are known to have occurred in the Northern Kingdom (cf. Hos 8:4–5; 10:5) and that were used in the worship of YHWH.¹³

Line 2

The next line, אני עניתי ואשורנו, can be translated, "It is I who answer and look after him," although JPS places this line in Ephraim's mouth. The NRSV treats this verse as a speech of YHWH to Ephraim, and so has "you" rather than "him." Mays translates, "It is I who answer and make him happy."¹⁴ Yee believes that *waᵃšûrennû* here in 14:8(9) continues a

---

9. Ibid.

10. Ibid., 577; cf. F. I. Andersen and D. N. Freedman, *Hosea* (AB 24; New York: Doubleday, 1980), 644.

11. G. Couturier, "Yahweh et les déesses cananéennes en Osée 14,9," in *Communion et réunion: Mélanges Jean-Marie Roger Tillard* (ed. G. R. Evans and M. Gourgues; Leuven: Leuven University Press, 1995), 245–64 (250).

12. J. A. Wagenaar, "'I Will Testify Against Them and Challenge Them': Text and Interpretation of Hosea 14:9," *JNSL* 26 (2000): 127–34 (130); and cf. Frevel, *Aschera*, 331 n. 1108, for a list of the various interpretations. See also E. Ben Zvi, *Hosea* (FOTL 21A/1; Grand Rapids: Eerdmans, 2005), 299, for a list of several possible meanings of the phrase if the opening word is "Ephraim."

13. Cf. J. M. Hadley, "עצב," *NIDOTTE* 3:483–84, and the references there. See also A. A. Keefe, *Woman's Body and the Social Body in Hosea* (JSOTSup 338; Sheffield: Sheffield Academic, 2001), 121–22.

14. Mays, *Hosea*, 184, reading *waᵃᵃššᵉrennû* with L. Köhler and W. Baumgartner, *Lexicon in Veteris Testamenti Libros* (Leiden: Brill, 1958), 957.

pun begun earlier in 14:3(4) and featuring "Assyria" as well as "happiness": "Assyria (*ʾaššûr*), which Israel thinks is a source of happiness (*ʾešer*) or good fortune, will not save them (*lōʾ yôšîʿēnû*). The paronomasia on *ʾšr* is extended further to 14:9: Assyria will not save Israel/ Ephraim but 'I (YHWH) will look after him'."[15]

עניתי, "I will answer," is used in Hos 2:21(23), where YHWH is responding to a need.[16] Ward translates v. 8(9): "What further need has Ephraim of idols? It is I who afflicted and I who watch for him. I am like a luxuriant juniper tree; your fruit is found in me."[17] Ward presents many previous translations of line 2. Retaining the MT, "the first verb means either 'I answer(ed), hearken(ed)'…or 'I afflict(ed), humble(d)'…and the second, 'I (will) regard, watch'."[18] Ward is taken by the "slight change of שׁור to שׁוב, with the sense of 'affirm,' 'establish,' or 'restore'… The resulting statement is eloquent: 'It is I who afflict(ed) and I (shall) restore.' Yet, שׁור occurs in 13:7 in a negative sense ('lurk, watch'), and its positive use here is thus especially meaningful. God, the Watcher, is both disciplinarian and benefactor."[19] Ward believes that Köhler's minor emendation of ואשׁורנו to ואאשׁרנו "yields a good line: 'I have afflicted and I will lead him in the straight way'."[20] Wolff notes that, if Hosea "has used the same word here as in 13:7, he then further declares that Yahweh, who grants Israel's prayer and thus saves her, is also constantly awake, looking out for his people (cf. Nu 24:17; Job 7:8)."[21] McComiskey notes that the verb שׁור in 13:7 is used in the sense of an animal closely watching its prey, but its use here with ענה "influences the word in the direction of watchful care."[22] Wagenaar takes ענה as "give evidence, testify" and שׁור as "lurk, challenge," which would retain the meaning of שׁור as in Hos 13:7, instead of taking the verb here in a more positive way, as others have done. Therefore, in Wagenaar's opinion, this part of the

15. Yee, *Composition and Tradition*, 134; cf. T. E. McComiskey, "Hosea," in *The Minor Prophets: An Exegetical and Expository Commentary* (ed. T. E. McComiskey; 3 vols.; Grand Rapids: Baker, 1992), 1:1–237 (236); and see F. Gangloff, "'Je suis son ʿAnat et son ʾAšerâh' (Os 14,9)," *EThL* 74 (1998): 373–85 (374), for suggested derivations of the root, and p. 375 for the rendering of *aʾašûrennû* in the ancient versions.

16. McComiskey, "Hosea," 236.

17. Ward, *Hosea*, 226–27.

18. Ibid., 228.

19. Ibid.

20. Ibid.; cf. H. D. Beeby, *Grace Abounding: A Commentary on the Book of Hosea* (Grand Rapids: Eerdmans, 1989), 184.

21. Wolff, *Hosea*, 237.

22. McComiskey, "Hosea," 236.

verse refers to the idols; YHWH will testify against the idols and challenge the idols.[23] He therefore interprets the first two lines to read: "Ephraim, what have I to do with idols any more? I will testify against them and challenge them."[24] On a more minor note, Stuart translates this line, "I will have responded and I will bless him."[25]

In 1892, Wellhausen proposed an alternative reading for this line: אני ענתו ואשרתו, "I am his Anat and his Asherah."[26] Reactions to this emendation have covered the spectrum, from Harper's "a freak of the imagination" to Wolff's "much too audacious," Olyan's "fanciful and unfounded," Macintosh's "daringly," Ackroyd's "attractive though purely hypothetical" and Zevit's "clever but conjectural," through to full acceptance.[27] We will return to a fuller discussion of this emendation below.

Line 3

The third line, אני כברוש רענן, can be translated, "I am like an evergreen cypress" (NRSV). There have been numerous suggestions concerning what type of tree ברוש is. It is clear that some type of coniferous tree is

23. Wagenaar, "I Will Testify Against Them and Challenge Them," 130–31.
24. Ibid., 131.
25. Stuart, *Hosea–Jonah*, 34; and cf. Couturier, "Yahweh et les déesses cananéennes," 262–63.
26. J. Wellhausen, *Die kleinen Propheten übersetzt und erklärt* (3d ed.; Skizzen und Vorarbeiten 5; Berlin: Reimer, 1898), 134.
27. Harper, *Amos and Hosea*, 415; Wolff, *Hosea*, 233 n. w (where he also notes Sellin's response: "more ingenious than correct"); S. M. Olyan, *Asherah and the Cult of Yahweh in Israel* (SBLMS 34; Atlanta: Scholars Press, 1988), 21; Macintosh, *Hosea*, 581; P. R. Ackroyd, "Goddesses, Women and Jezebel," in *Images of Women in Antiquity* (ed. A. Cameron and A. Kuhrt; rev. ed.; Detroit: Wayne State University Press, 1993), 245–59 (252); Z. Zevit, "Proclamations to the Fruitful Tree and the Spiritualization of Androgyny," in *The Echoes of Many Texts: Reflections on Jewish and Christian Traditions: Essays in Honor of Lou H. Silberman* (ed. W. G. Dever and J. E. Wright; BJS 313; Atlanta: Scholars Press, 1997), 43–50 (49). For those who accept Wellhausen's emendation, see, e.g., J. McKinlay, "Bringing the Unspeakable to Speech in Hosea," *Pacifica* 9 (1996): 121–33 (130); M. Weinfeld, "Kuntillet 'Ajrud Inscriptions and Their Significance," *Studi epigrafici e linguistici* 1 (1984): 121–30 (122–23); F. Gangloff, "YHWH ou les déesses-arbres? (Osée XIV 6–8)," *VT* 49 (1999): 34–48 (48), who gives a list of those who accept the emendation in n. 58; [M. Dietrich and] O. Loretz, *"Jahwe und seine Aschera": Anthropomorphes Kultbild in Mesopotamien, Ugarit und Israel: Das biblische Bilderverbot* (Ugaritisch-Biblische Literatur 9; Münster: Ugarit Verlag, 1992), 110; cf. Gangloff, "Je suis son 'Anat," 375–77.

indicated, but exactly which one is unclear. Space does not allow a full discussion here, but a few comments are in order. It is generally considered to be a cypress[28] or juniper.[29] Also suggested are fir[30] and pine.[31] Gangloff notes that each of the ancient versions chooses a different species of tree.[32]

The majority of commentaries point out that this verse is the only one in the Hebrew Bible that likens YHWH to a tree.[33] This has caused some scholars (as well as JPS noted above) to interpret ברוש as referring to Ephraim. Macintosh notes that "elsewhere in this chapter it is Ephraim who is likened to the luxuriant, arboreal growth of Lebanon (vv. 6f) in which, indeed, a number of species (lily, olive, vine) are subsumed."[34] Therefore, Macintosh prefers the interpretations of the Vulgate, Targum and Ibn Ezra, which see Ephraim as the referent for the tree. He thus interprets v. 8(9) as a "rapid dialogue" where the first and third lines are "sentiments expressed by Ephraim" and the second and fourth are

---

28. E.g. Harper, *Amos and Hosea*, 415; McComiskey, "Hosea," 236; E. J. Pentiuc, *Long-Suffering Love: A Commentary on Hosea with Patristic Annotations* (Brookline, Mass.: Holy Cross Orthodox, 2002), 205; B. C. Birch, *Hosea, Joel, and Amos* (Westminster Bible Companion; Louisville: Westminster John Knox, 1997), 117; D. J. Simundson, *Hosea, Joel, Amos, Obadiah, Jonah, Micah* (Abingdon Old Testament Commentaries; Nashville: Abingdon, 2005), 113; P. J. King, "Hosea's Message of Hope," *BTB* 12 (1982): 91–95 (95); Gangloff, "Je suis son ʿAnat," 382, "*Cupressus sempervirens.*"

29. Macintosh, *Hosea*, 579, "*Juniperus phoenicea*," following LXX; Ben Zvi, *Hosea*, 307, "*Juniperus excelsa*," following B. Oestreich, *Metaphors and Similes for Yahweh in Hosea 14:2–9 (1–8): A Study of Hoseanic Pictorial Language* (Frankfurt am Main: Lang, 1998), 192–95; Wolff, *Hosea*, 233; Ward, *Hosea*, 227; Yee, *Composition and Tradition*, 139; Naumann, *Hoseas Erben*, 130.

30. Andersen and Freedman, *Hosea*, 643; Mays, *Hosea*, 184; K. A. Tångberg, "'I am Like an Evergreen Fir; From Me Comes Your Fruit': Notes on Meaning and Symbolism in Hosea 14,9b (MT)," *SJOT* 2 (1989): 81–93 (85); followed by Zevit, "Proclamations to the Fruitful Tree," 48.

31. McKeating, *Amos, Hosea and Micah*, 153.

32. Gangloff, "Je suis son ʿAnat," 375; and cf. Tångberg, "I am Like an Evergreen Fir," 83–85.

33. E.g. Macintosh, *Hosea*, 577; Mays, *Hosea*, 189; Pentiuc, *Long-Suffering Love*, 205; Harper, *Amos and Hosea*, 415; Wolff, *Hosea*, 237; Beeby, *Grace Abounding*, 184; Yee, *Composition and Tradition*, 138; Davies, *Hosea*, 309; Cornelius, "Paradise Motifs," 46; King, "Hosea's Message of Hope," 95; Emmerson, *Hosea*, 46; Gangloff, "Je suis son ʿAnat," 375; Tångberg, "I am Like an Evergreen Fir," 82. For a fuller discussion of the tree metaphor in Hos 14:8(9), see Oestreich, *Metaphors and Similes*, 191–225, and the references there.

34. Macintosh, *Hosea*, 577.

"responses of Yahweh."[35] This dialogue, in Macintosh's opinion, expresses "the climax of love and mutual understanding which, in Hosea's prayer, will mark the ultimate reconciliation between Ephraim and its God. It marks, then, the glorious finale…of his prophetic utterances."[36] Macintosh thus sees this verse as indicating that Ephraim, now basking in YHWH's "attentive protection…proclaims that now her condition is like that of a luxuriant juniper, a symbol of abiding youth and vigour."[37]

Harper sets out the tension between the two interpretations well. He comments on the difficulties as follows:

> [i]t is difficult to read this of Yahweh, but it is still more difficult to place it in Israel's mouth. In favor of the former is the fact that it is demanded by the following clause of which Yahweh is certainly the subject. Yahweh's shelter and protection of his people are likened to the refreshing shade of the cypress. If the words be referred to Israel, there is the difficulty that Israel is likened in two successive clauses to two different kinds of tree, for the cypress is not a fruit tree. As opposed to this, and in favor of the latter, is the fact that Yahweh is nowhere else likened to a tree. If the figure is used of Israel, the punctuation of MT must be disregarded, and this clause must be taken with ואשורנו = a*nd I look after him like an evergreen cypress.* With all its difficulty, the former is to be preferred.[38]

Line 4

The NRSV translates the fourth line, ממני פריך נמצא, as "your faithfulness comes from me." This may be an attempt to solve a perceived problem with the Hebrew, which literally states "your fruit comes from me" (cf. JPS). As noted above, ברוש is some type of conifer and not generally considered to be a fruit tree. Various efforts to solve this dilemma have been attempted.

Many commentators see fruit (*pry*) as word-play on the name Ephraim (*ʾprym*).[39] According to Macintosh, "Yahweh's exclamation assures the

35. Ibid.
36. Ibid., 577–78.
37. Ibid., 579; cf. Kruger, "Yahweh's Generous Love," 42; Wolff, *Hosea*, 237.
38. Harper, *Amos and Hosea*, 415.
39. Wolff, *Hosea*, 237; Naumann, *Hoseas Erben*, 131; Davies, *Hosea*, 309; King, "Hosea's Message of Hope," 95; Vielhauer, *Das Werden*, 64; Pentiuc, *Long-Suffering Love*, 205; McComiskey, "Hosea," 236; Yee, *Composition and Tradition*, 139; Couturier, "Yahweh et les déesses cananéennes," 250; Gangloff, "Je suis son ʿAnat," 378.

nation that he is the source of her fruit."[40] He further states that "the reference is…to the tenor rather than to the vehicle of the simile. Thus Ephraim's fruit depicts quite generally its vitality and prosperity and not merely its human, animal and agricultural fruit."[41] Andersen and Freedman observe that "the fruit to be offered in worship is, in fact, God's gift. Part of the intention of worship is to acknowledge this fact. This is what Israel had forgotten (2:10)."[42]

McComiskey, in his discussion of 13:15, suggested that "Ephraim's fruitfulness was the result of the ancient promise made first to Abraham and later reiterated to Jacob. It was the promise of numerous offspring that finds emphasis there. Fruitfulness can be found only in Yahweh. It was he who granted them the blessing first granted to their ancient patriarch."[43]

Harper has no question that this part of the verse "is clearly in Yahweh's mouth, and announces, as the last word of the dialogue, that from Yahweh comes all of Israel's prosperity."[44] Davies notes that the emphasis produced by the Hebrew word order falls on "from me," and therefore prefers "it is from me that your fruit comes." He believes that for the first time in this passage God directly addresses Ephraim, hitherto only referred to in the third person.[45] The JPS translation also treats this line as a direct address by God to Ephraim, but it has Ephraim as the speaker in the first three lines.

Wellhausen's Emendation

We now return to Wellhausen's emendation. As noted above, Wellhausen proposed to emend line 2, אני עניתי ואשורנו—"It is I who answer and look after him"—to אני ענתו ואשרתו, "I am his Anat and his Asherah."[46] This emendation gained a new popularity with the recent discovery of archaeological evidence in support of the worship of the goddess Asherah.[47] It must be noted, however, that when Wellhausen made his suggestion, he did not know of a goddess Asherah, but merely

---

40. Macintosh, *Hosea*, 579.
41. Ibid.
42. Andersen and Freedman, *Hosea*, 647.
43. McComiskey, "Hosea," 236.
44. Harper, *Amos and Hosea*, 415.
45. Davies, *Hosea*, 309.
46. Wellhausen, *Die kleinen Propheten*, 134.
47. See J. M. Hadley, *The Cult of Asherah in Ancient Israel and Judah: Evidence for a Hebrew Goddess* (UCOP 57; Cambridge: Cambridge University Press, 2000), passim, and the references there.

the wooden cultic symbol that is also known as an asherah. Nevertheless, Wellhausen does not see a problem with the juxtaposition of Anat, a goddess, with asherah, a cultic symbol. He notes that this should not be surprising, since Hosea calls the images of YHWH, "baals," which are also nothing more than manufactured objects.[48] Furthermore, before the discovery of the Ugaritic material, Asherah was not recognized as a goddess; rather, the term asherah was interpreted to refer to some type of symbol of another deity, often Astarte.[49] The identity of a goddess Anat was without question, although in the Hebrew Bible the name appears only in a few place-names and personal names (e.g. Anathoth, a place name in Jer 1:1 and a personal name in 1 Chr 7:8 and Neh 10:19; Anthothijah in 1 Chr 8:24; Shamgar ben-Anath in Judg 3:31).

Ackroyd considers this evidence, together with the strong sexual imagery of the book of Hosea, to support the claim that YHWH "incorporates the female as well as the male aspects of deity."[50] He also believes that it is "probable" that "the verbal root ʿnh, used frequently for example in Hos. 2, means 'to love' rather than 'to answer'…suggesting that the material here too may be making deliberate allusion to the goddess and to some process of rethinking the relationship between people and deity which incorporates the ideas which belong to the concept of god and consort."[51]

Davies disagrees, noting that the "MT makes good sense as it is, and one may doubt whether Hosea would have indulged in such a flagrant equation of Yahweh with two Canaanite divinities (cf. 2:16–17). At most there is here a dismissive allusion to the sound of their names."[52] Frevel believes that the assonance here with Anat and Asherah is so obvious that a denial of the similarity in pronunciation would be tantamount to ignorance.[53]

Day is one of the most vocal scholars in promoting a word-play on the names of Anat and Asherah here.[54] In partial support of his argument, Day points to eight passages from Hos 13:4–14:9(10) which have parallels to Isa 26:13–27:11. There, he notes that "[i]n view of the probability that the idolatry condemned in Hos 14:9 (Eng. 8) is particularly that of the Asherim, it is striking that the corresponding verse in the

---

48. Wellhausen, *Die kleinen Propheten*, 134.
49. Frevel, *Aschera*, 333.
50. Ackroyd, "Goddesses," 253.
51. Ibid.
52. Davies, *Hosea*, 308.
53. Frevel, *Aschera*, 332.
54. Day, "Asherah in the Hebrew Bible," 404.

Isaianic passage, Isa 27:9, specifically condemns the Asherim and that the abolition of them constitutes the 'full fruit' of the removal of Jacob's sin, just as Hos 14:9 (Eng. 8) makes it clear that Israel's fruit comes from Yahweh rather than the Asherim."[55]

Olyan disagrees with Day's connection with Isa 27, instead suggesting that the reference to asherah in the Isaiah passage is a result of deuteronomistic influence. Furthermore, other deuteronomistic concerns regarding altars and sin and guilt are lacking in Hos 14:8(9), which has only idols, and these do not appear in Isa 27. Olyan thus concludes that "the fact that each passage has different concerns casts doubt on Day's thesis."[56] Olyan further believes that it is unlikely that there is even a suggestion of Anat or Asherah in this verse, let alone an outright mention.[57]

Some scholars seek to connect the verbal allusion to Asherah—who can be symbolized by a tree—and the overt reference here to YHWH as a tree, so identifying the sacred tree as a tree of life.[58] Cornelius sees a "development of the concept: sacred tree → asherah → tree of life → YHWH in the future. Thus YHWH will be their asherah and not the idols…but this is taken even further: He will not only be like the asherah as a symbol of the fertility goddess, He will be like the tree of life in the Garden of Eden in the near future!"[59] Cornelius further takes the second line to say, "I am his goddess and his asherah," where asherah refers to the cult object, and not to the personal name.[60]

Davies admits that "there may be a deliberate allusion to the mythological idea of the tree of life which was widely current in the ancient Near East,"[61] but he points out that the tree of life is not usually depicted as a conifer. Therefore, he believes that a "direct comparison with the

---

55. J. Day, "The Dependence of Isaiah 26:13–27:11 on Hosea 13:4–14:10 and Its Relevance to Some Theories of the Redaction of the 'Isaiah Apocalypse'," in *Writing and Reading the Scroll of Isaiah: Studies of an Interpretive Tradition* (ed. C. C. Broyles and C. A. Evans; VTSup 70; Leiden: Brill, 1997), 357–68 (364).

56. Olyan, *Asherah and the Cult of Yahweh*, 21; and cf. Frevel, *Aschera*, 342–43, who presents four objections to Day's proposal.

57. Olyan, *Asherah and the Cult of Yahweh*, 21.

58. A full examination of the tree of life is beyond the scope of the present study; see Cornelius, "Paradise Motifs," passim; Mays, *Hosea*, 190; Macintosh, *Hosea*, 577; Andersen and Freedman, *Hosea*, 647; Pentiuc, *Long-Suffering Love*, 205; Wolff, *Hosea*, 237; Beeby, *Grace Abounding*, 184, among others.

59. Cornelius, "Paradise Motifs," 63 (cf. p. 47); see also Oestreich, *Metaphors and Similes*, 218–20, 230.

60. Cornelius, "Paradise Motifs," 46.

61. Davies, *Hosea*, 309.

natural species seems most likely. Comparisons with trees are found in love-poetry...but apparently they are not seen as sources of fertility."[62]

Most scholars believe that Hosea is attacking the worship of sacred trees, and therefore goddesses such as Asherah.[63] Keefe mentions the hundreds of female "pillar figurines" found throughout Judah dating from the eighth century B.C.E.,[64] and notes that if a "fertility cult" were the prime foil of Hosea's polemic, these feminine religious forms would have been obvious targets. Yet there is no clear indication in the text that Hosea attacks any of these. This point is generally avoided in the scholarly obsession with Hosea as an opponent of fertility religion. Reverence for fertility as a sacred power was integral to Israel's religion and is not the object of Hosea's attack.[65] Furthermore, the sacred trees are generally identified elsewhere in the Hebrew Bible as terebinths, tamarisks, or oaks.[66] The ברוש is not one of the three species of trees mentioned in Hos 4:13 as a sacred tree. This makes it unlikely, in Oestreich's opinion, that ברוש in Hos 14:8(9) refers to a sacred tree.[67] Oestreich believes that the reason that ברוש "is not mentioned in connection with the sacred trees and groves may be found in the fact that this species (*Juniperus excelsa*) did not grow in Palestine. If the tree simile of Hos 14:9 had been used to point to the sacred groves, it would have to refer to a tree that grew at these sacred places and not to a species that had to be imported from Lebanon."[68] Of course, scholars who believe that ברוש refers to other species of conifers do not have this limitation.

Wacker is not surprised that this verse could refer to a goddess without explicitly naming one:

---

62. Ibid.

63. See the commentaries and the references there; for an alternative interpretation, see K. Berge, "Weisheitliche Hosea-Interpretation? Zur Frage nach Kohärenz und literarischem Horizont von Hosea 14,6–10," in *Wer darf hinaufsteigen zum Berg JHWHs? Beiträge zu Prophetie und Poesie des Alten Testaments: Festschrift für Sigurður Örn Steingrimsson zum 70. Geburtstag* (ed. H. Irsigler and K. Olason; St. Ottilien: EOS, 2002), 3–23, who, instead of interpreting this verse as a polemic against fertility cults, places it in the wisdom tradition.

64. A full discussion of these female figurines is beyond the scope of the present study. See Hadley, *The Cult of Asherah*, 188–205, and the references there.

65. Keefe, *Woman's Body*, 94–95.

66. Cf. Gangloff, "Je suis son 'Anat," 380.

67. Oestreich, *Metaphors and Similes*, 208.

68. Ibid., 209.

> In its original Hebrew, the text of this book [Hosea] is energized to an
> unusual degree by the ambiguities of sound and visual image of the
> written words, and thereby encodes a precise meaning more than disclos-
> ing that meaning. In such a text, unambiguous speech in the sense of direct
> naming of a goddess is not necessarily to be expected. Therefore, text-
> critical restoration of goddess names...should be avoided. It is more
> advantageous to seek traces of the goddess in implications and sound-
> play.[69]

In the case of Hos 14:8(9), Wacker believes that "[w]ith all due caution,
by means of comparison, the symbol of the goddess is identified with the
God of Israel. YHWH assumes characteristics of the tree goddess: her
numinous presence as suggested by the shadow motif, and especially the
nourishing aspect of her fruit."[70] Therefore, this passage "suggests that
the God of Israel can integrate the fascination with the goddess in a
positive way."[71] Although Sellin originally agreed with Wellhausen's
emendation, Loretz notes that in later editions Sellin thought that it is
unlikely that, just in this solemn elevated section, Hosea would declare
the names of deities that he had never mentioned at all elsewhere.[72]

It is clear that this verse has built up a strong opposition, with the use
of מה לי, אני, אני, ממני at the beginning of each line. Frevel notes that with
this, the spoken "I" of YHWH has been emphasized, and thus has brought
YHWH's claim of exclusivity to the fore.[73] But in the text, the *opposition*
is not to tree cults, but to idols. Furthermore, the conifers to which ברוש
refers are unlike the typical "tree of life," so Frevel concludes that a
direct or associative reference to Asherah or any other goddess does not
occur here.[74] In addition, since YHWH is the husband of Israel, in Frevel's
opinion one can hardly support a comparison of YHWH with Anat and
Asherah, as in Wellhausen's emendation. Rather, it is the עצבים that
YHWH rejects, and it is they that represent Israel's lover.[75] However,
there still could be some reminiscence of Asherah especially in Hos

---

69. M.-T. Wacker, "Traces of the Goddess in the Book of Hosea," in *A Feminist
Companion to the Latter Prophets* (ed. A. Brenner; The Feminist Companion to the
Bible 8; Sheffield: Sheffield Academic, 1995), 219–41 (225); and cf. McKinlay,
"Bringing the Unspeakable to Speech," passim.

70. Wacker, "Traces of the Goddess in the Book of Hosea," 236.

71. Ibid., 237.

72. [Dietrich and] Loretz, *Jahwe und seine Ashera*, 174, and see nn. 4–10 for
various other suggestions by scholars concerning the translation of this verse without
a reference to Anat or Asherah.

73. Frevel, *Aschera*, 343.

74. Ibid., 345.

75. Ibid., 348.

14:8(9), since, as the Kuntillet 'Ajrud and Khirbet el-Qom inscriptions indicate,[76] at least up until the mid-eighth century B.C.E. Asherah was paired with YHWH.

Conclusion

It may be that we have here the first attack against the goddess—not strong enough yet to condemn her by name, but only by allusion and the extraordinary co-opting of the symbol of Asherah. Olyan notes that it is surprising that there is no reference to Asherah in Hosea, especially given Hosea's vehement objection to Baal. He thus believes that the opposition to the goddess Asherah as well as the cultic object is "a deuteronomistic innovation. This of course assumes that the deuterono-mistic school was influenced by Hosea, and not vice versa. There is no evidence that the asherah was opposed by anyone in Israel before the reforming kings, who were following a deuteronomistic program."[77] Since the tree represents YHWH, Olyan does not believe this verse should be taken as an anti-Asherah polemic.[78] Frevel asks why Hosea (or anyone later) had only alluded to Asherah, instead of directly attacking the goddess or the cultic image.[79] It may be because, at the time of writing, the worship of Asherah was still too strong to be attacked directly.

It is possible, however, that the writer of this verse wanted to stress that YHWH was able to function as a fertility deity in place of Asherah (or Baal, but Baal lacks the connection with a tree). It may be that the writer intended the ברוש to be YHWH in order to portray YHWH's fertility aspects as even more effective than those of Asherah, as YHWH was a "luxuriant tree, bearing fruit," as opposed to a humanly constructed pole. The anti-asherah polemic need not indicate that the ברוש was Asherah. Additionally, we may also have reason to believe that these verses help to show the gradual evolution of the term asherah from a goddess represented by her cultic image to simply the image itself. One does not need to emend the text in Hos 14:8(9) to be able to see this process occurring.

---

76. A full discussion of these inscriptions is outside the scope of the present study; see Hadley, *The Cult of Asherah*, 84–155, and the references there.

77. Olyan, *Asherah and the Cult of Yahweh*, 22.

78. Ibid., 21.

79. Frevel, *Aschera*, 348–49.

THE TEXT AND INTERPRETATION OF NAHUM 2:2[*]

Edward Ball

עלה מפיץ על־פניך
נצור מצרה צפה־דרך
חזק מתנים אמץ כח מאד:

At first glance, this apparently unproblematic verse seems to offer little
scope for discussion of text and meaning. A rapid perusal of the standard
English translations (where it is Nah 2:1) might appear, initially, only to
confirm the point. The consensus position is well represented by NRSV:

> A shatterer has come up against you.
> Guard the ramparts;
> watch the road;
> gird your loins;
> collect all your strength.

—where "you" is, fairly clearly, the Nineveh named (2:9) and portrayed
in the verses following as under attack, while its defenders are being
called to urgent action against the unidentified assailing force.

Most translations appear to assume this understanding of the latter part
of the verse, while some, indeed, insert the name "Nineveh" as the
explicit addressee in the former part[1] (so GNB, NIV, REB [but not NEB]; JB
has it in the margin), thus removing any remaining element of interpretative ambiguity at this point.[2] Yet alongside NRSV's "shatterer" (so also
Moffatt, RSV[3]), we find such comparable terms as "attacker" (NIV),

---

* It is a pleasure to offer this brief study to my first teacher of Hebrew, with
pleasant and grateful memories of 5.00–6.00 p.m. on Mondays, Wednesdays and
Fridays in the old Cambridge Divinity School.

1. As also in several verses in ch. 1, sometimes with "Assyria" or "Assyrians"
specified as well. GNB additionally introduces further explicit references to Nineveh
in chs. 2 and 3.

2. On the general point here about ambiguity and translation, see the comments
of S. Prickett, *Words and The Word: Language, Poetics and Biblical Interpretation*
(Cambridge: Cambridge University Press, 1986), 4–13.

3. Cf. GNB's paraphrase: "Nineveh, you are under attack! The power that will
shatter you has come."

"aggressor" (REB), "destroyer" (JB), although with such more generalized expressions it is not obvious whether it is MT's מֵפִיץ being so rendered, or some emended form of the word—as is explicitly indicated by NRSV's footnote here.[4] Very strikingly, AV (followed by RV) has "he that dasheth in pieces is come up before thy face," which would seem already to imply some connection with the verb נָפַץ ("shatter"; compare AV at Ps 2:9) rather than with פּוּץ ("scatter")—or is some confusion, or some sense of semantic linkage, between the two roots at work here?[5] Finally, at this juncture, we can note NEB's vivid rendering:

The battering-ram is mounted against your bastions,
the siege is closing in.
Watch the road...

—where it is, however, clear that "battering-ram" and "bastions" appear as a result of emendation.[6] Furthermore, the familiar emendation of מֵפִיץ to the metaphorical מֵפֵץ ("hammer, club"), assumed in NRSV and several of the other modern translations noted above, and taken with the verb עלה, has been—I think, unjustifiably—literalized.

In fact, therefore, the familiar English versions do raise questions about a number of textual details which, though they have often been touched on in commentaries and other studies, may elicit some further interest. In addition, I shall suggest a rather different view of what is going on in the verse as a whole, and more especially in its first part.

I

Quite apart from their other merits, the ancient versions and related commentaries may often still have a valuable heuristic role—even, or especially, where their readings of the text cannot in fact be accepted—in urging the interpreter to consider possibilities which have perhaps too easily been forgotten or foreclosed in modern discussion.

The Septuagint reads (in Ziegler's text[7]):

ἀνέβη ἐμφυσῶν εἰς πρόσωπόν σου ἐξαιρούμενος ἐκ θλίψεως ·
σκόπευσον ὁδόν, κράτησον ὀσφύος, ἄνρισαι τῇ ἰσχύι σπόδρα.

4. "Cn: Heb *scatterer*."
5. Coverdale and the Great Bible have "the scaterer" [*sic*].
6. L. H. Brockington, *The Hebrew Text of the Old Testament: The Readings adopted by the Translators of the New English Bible* (Oxford: Oxford University Press; Cambridge: Cambridge University Press, 1973), 258.
7. J. Ziegler, ed., *Septuaginta: Vetus Testamentum Graecum Auctoritate Academiae Litterarum Gottingensis editum.* Vol. 13, *Duodecim Prophetae* (2d ed.; Göttingen: Vandenhoeck & Ruprecht, 1967), 255–56.

I once discussed this rendering at some length[8] and argued that it should be understood as addressed not to Nineveh but to *Judah* and as offering a message of liberation and renewal. I continue to find this more persuasive than a view which would see here an announcement of punishment addressed to Nineveh.[9] It is, of course, important to note that this is only one aspect of the Old Greek's complex reconstrual of the Hebrew at this point, but I suggested that in the translator's understanding it may have been the starting point for this reconstrual.

Of the patristic commentators on the Greek text, Cyril of Alexandria finds reference to Cyrus "going up" against Nineveh, which at the same time means "breathing on the face of"—that is, bringing release and deliverance for—Judah (the second part of the verse is interpreted of those on their way home from exile).[10] Theodoret of Cyrus sees the text as addressed to God's people;[11] Theodore of Mopsuestia, too, understands it as addressing Judah and speaking of the destroying breath of divine wrath coming on the Assyrians, while in the second part of the verse it is Nineveh which is summoned to prepare itself against attack.[12]

The Targum reads:[13]

דהוו סלקין ומתבדרין על ארעיך

צירין עלך בציר מקימין סכואין על אורחתיך תקיפו קדל חסיני חיללחדא:

Here, though again we have a far from simple-equivalence translation, the phrase "over your land," as rendering the Hebrew's עַל־פָּנָיִךְ, is clearly speaking to Judah—as, indeed, the whole verse is. It is "the wicked" of v. 1 who are spoken of throughout.

---

8. E. Ball, "Interpreting the Septuagint: Nahum 2.2 as a Case-Study," *JSOT* 75 (1997): 59–75.

9. See, e.g., M. Carrez, "Naoum Septante," *RHPR* 70 (1990): 35–48 (38, 44). But M. A. Sweeney, *The Twelve Prophets*, vol. 2 (Berit Olam; Collegeville: Liturgical, 2000), 437, thinks that LXX reads here "a threat against Israel."

10. P. E. Pusey, ed., *Sancti Patris Nostri Cyrilli Archiepiscopi Alexandrini in XII Prophetas*, vol. 2 (Oxford: Clarendon, 1868), 35–39.

11. *PG* 81, cols. 1796–97.

12. H. N. Sprenger, *Theodori Mopsuesteni Commentarius in XII Prophetas: Einleitung und Ausgabe* (Göttinger Orientforschungen, 5/1; Wiesbaden: Harrassowitz, 1977), 2:245–46.

13. A. Sperber, *The Bible in Aramaic: Based on Old Manuscripts and Printed Texts*. Vol. 3, *The Latter Prophets according to Targum Jonathan* (Leiden: Brill, 1962), 455. For translation with notes, see K. J. Cathcart and R. P. Gordon, *The Targum of the Minor Prophets* (The Aramaic Bible 14; Collegeville: Liturgical, 1989), 134–35.

The Peshitta has the rendering:[14]

slq mdbrnᵓ qdmyk wntr mtrᵓ whᵓr ᶜwrhᵓ wᵓhd bhysᵓ wtb hsyn hylh

It is usual to regard *mdbrnᵓ* as a simple inner-Syriac corruption for *mbdrnᵓ*,[15] while the verb forms following this appear to have been interpreted as participles describing the actions of this subject. The whole verse is perhaps understood as God's speech,[16] and is best regarded as addressed to Judah.

We can next note the Vulgate rendering:[17]

Ascendit qui dispergat coram te qui custodit obsidionem contemplare viam conforta lumbos robora virtutem valde

Jerome himself comments that Nahum here turns and speaks to *Nineveh*, though he thinks that Judah is again addressed in the concluding verbs, encouraged by the promise of restoration in the next verse.[18]

It is this view of Nineveh as the addressee in v. 2a—and indeed probably throughout the verse—that, as noted, has been prevalent in later interpretation, so much so that the point scarcely needs documenting. Prevalent, but by no means universally accepted. A lengthy survey is clearly impossible here, but it is worth observing that a range of mediaeval and later commentators see the verse as addressing Judah, though admittedly with considerable variation in the details of their interpretations. For Rupert of Deutz (early twelfth century), the verse speaks *about* Nebuchadnezzar's attack on Nineveh, but is addressed *to* Judah: "in facie tua, O Juda…id est, te praesente vel sciente."[19] A number of the mediaeval Jewish commentators also hear Judah addressed at this point: both Rashi and Kimchi think that Judah is being reminded of

14. A. Gelston, ed., *The Old Testament in Syriac according to the Peshitta Version*. Vol. 3/4, *Dodekapropheton* (Leiden: Brill, 1980), 56.

15. Cf., e.g., A. Gelston, *The Peshitta of the Twelve Prophets* (Oxford: Clarendon, 1988), 99; so already G. H. Bernstein, "Syrische Studien," *ZDMG* 3 (1849): 385–428 (395). But might it be worth considering whether this reading arose under the influence of the Septuagint's identification of a salvific figure at this point? On *mdbrnᵓ* in Christian Syriac, see R. Murray, *Symbols of Church and Kingdom: A Study in Early Syriac Tradition* (Cambridge: Cambridge University Press, 1975), 192.

16. Gelston, *The Peshitta of the Twelve*, 148.

17. R. Weber, ed., *Biblia Sacra iuxta Vulgatam Versionem* (4th ed.; Stuttgart: Deutsche Bibelgesellschaft, 1994), 1406.

18. *S. Hieronymi Presbyteri Opera. Pars I: Opera Exegetica. 6: Commentarii in Prophetas Minores* (CCSL 76A; Turnhout: Brepols, 1970), 542.

19. *PL* 168, col. 552.

the attack by Sennacherib, and, later, Abravanel notes and criticizes their views while yet supporting a "Judah" interpretation;[20] Eliezer of Beaugency (twelfth century) had taken a similar position.[21] A later English writer who consciously takes up this apparently dominant Jewish view is the now almost forgotten Ebenezer Henderson,[22] but by the mid-nineteenth century this was most definitely to swim against the tide.

It is important to emphasize again that the interpretations here may vary considerably in detail and that they are normally bound up with views impossible for modern scholars to accept—for example, the once very widely held belief that Nahum had prophesied during the reign of Hezekiah. Nevertheless, we can at least wonder about the possibility of an understanding of 2:2 which differs from the modern consensus.

II

It is worth noting that a few modern writers have held the view that Judah is addressed in 2:2, though the point is bound up with markedly different understandings of the composition history and the sense of the wider context. W. C. Graham argued on the basis of a particular reconstruction of the historical setting and connections of the section 1:9–2:3 that Nahum was a member of an anti-Assyrian group who here reacts to the opponents of this policy, announcing YHWH's purpose to destroy Assyrian power; and that in 2:2 Judah is assured that the support for Assyria by Pharaoh Necho (the "shatterer"), at that moment passing through Judah ("before thy face"), will come to nothing.[23] Although a connection has often been seen between Nahum and late sixth-century

20. J. D. Sprecher, ed., *R. Abarbanelis Rabbinicus in Nahum Commentarius Latio donatus* (Helmstadt: Hamm, 1703), 19–21. (Ibn Ezra is also cited, as taking the contrary view that Nineveh is addressed.) See also W. Windfuhr, ed., *Der Kommentar des David Qimhi zum Propheten Nahum* (Giessen: Töpelmann, 1927), 8.

21. S. Poznański, ed., *Kommentar zu Ezechiel und den XII Kleinen Propheten* (2 vols.; Warsaw: Eppelberg, 1910), 2:172.

22. E. Henderson, *The Book of the Twelve Minor Prophets, Translated from the Original Hebrew: With a Commentary, Critical, Philological, and Exegetical* (London: Hamilton, Adams & Co., 1845), 279. This had also been considered as a possibility (attributed to "some") by Calvin, though in the end Nineveh was taken as the addressee: J. Calvin, *Commentaries on the Twelve Minor Prophets.* Vol. 3, *Jonah, Micah, Nahum* (trans. J. Owen [1847]; repr., Edinburgh: Banner of Truth Trust, 1986), 452–54.

23. W. C. Graham, "The Interpretation of Nahum 1:9–2:3," *AJSL* 44 (1927/8): 37–48.

anti-Assyrian politics, Graham's is a speculative and awkward reading of the text, and seems to have had little impact; but he does make the point that Judah may be the same (feminine singular) addressee in v. 2 as it already is, unequivocally, in v. 1.

Next, Jörg Jeremias has claimed that Nah 2:2–3 is in origin a unit, spoken not only to, but also *against*, Judah/Jerusalem[24]—this forming part of his larger hypothesis that much of the anti-Nineveh material in Nahum was originally so oriented.[25] He finds the usual linking of v. 1 with v. 3, and correspondingly of v. 2 with vv. 4–11, improbable; rather, v. 3 is to be understood as itself speaking of judgment on Judah ("for YHWH destroys the pride of Jacob..."), and continuing the thought of v. 2, where Judah is threatened with an attacker. Jeremias admits that these verses in their present setting can be read in the familiar way, but this he attributes to their redactional repositioning rather than to Nahum himself. Jeremias's case both here and more generally is argued with great skill and verve, but most have not been convinced by it.[26] Even so, Jeremias makes the important point that, on the usual view of v. 2, there is a certain lack of connection with vv. 4–11, since Nineveh, supposedly, is spoken *to* in the former, but consistently spoken *about* in the latter.[27] But, I will suggest, there may be a better way of explaining this disjunction.

Perhaps even more striking, not least because it offers a reading completely at variance with the standard modern position, is the argument of A. S. van der Woude,[28] who has been followed at this point by B. Becking.[29] The larger proposal is that, since Assyria is still at the height of its power in Nah 1, the book as a whole—taken as an original

---

24. J. Jeremias, *Kultprophetie und Gerichtsverkündigung in der späten Königszeit Israels* (WMANT 35; Neukirchen–Vluyn: Neukirchener, 1970), 25–28.

25. See ibid., 11–55, for this wider hypothesis about Nahum as a whole; for criticism, see, e.g., H. Schulz, *Das Buch Nahum: Eine redaktionskritische Untersuchung* (BZAW 129; Berlin: de Gruyter, 1973), 135–53; on 2:2–3, see pp. 141–43.

26. But see, e.g., W. Dietrich, "Nahum," *TRE* 23 (1994): 737–42 (738).

27. So also L. Perlitt, *Die Propheten Nahum, Habakuk, Zephanja* (ATD 25/1; Göttingen: Vandenhoeck & Ruprecht, 2004), 18.

28. A. S. van der Woude, "The Book of Nahum: A Letter written in Exile," in H. A. Brongers et al., *Instruction and Interpretation: Studies in Hebrew Language, Palestinian Archaeology and Biblical Exegesis* (OTS 20; Leiden: Brill, 1977), 108–26, *Jona, Nahum* (De Prediking van het Oude Testament; Nijkerk: Callenbach, 1978), 97–102.

29. B. Becking, "Is het boek Nahum een literaire eenheid?," *NTT* 32 (1978): 107–24 (114–17), and later studies.

unity—must be dated in the period 660–630 B.C.E., and is best understood "if we assume that Nahum belonged to the exiles of the northern
kingdom and that he revealed the contents of the revelation granted to
him by Jahweh by means of a letter which he sent to certain persons in
Judah."[30] So would not Nahum have something to say about the exiles of
the northern kingdom? According to van der Woude, he does indeed:
2:1–3 is from its origin a coherent authorial unit, not a redactional unity,
in which v. 2 simply continues the promise of v. 1, and עלה מפיץ על
must be translated "the dispersed will go up [i.e. return from exile]
before your eyes [O Judah]." Thus in v. 2aβ–b Judah is called to be
encouraged by this news, since (v. 3) YHWH "will return with the pride
of Jacob" (i.e. the northern exiles). The further details of van der
Woude's remarkable hypothesis need not be considered here, but there
are strong arguments against it, and it is unsurprising that it has not been
widely adopted. To begin with, the broader position is open to serious
criticism: it is clear that the general orientation of the book is to Judah
and its origin there remains by far the most likely position; van der
Woude's broader arguments for a northern-exilic provenance are relatively weak (e.g. the presence of Assyrian loan-words, or the supposed
eyewitness knowledge of Nineveh). It is, further, at least debatable
whether the details of ch. 1 should be as closely correlated with an
immediate external historical situation as van der Woude thinks. In
respect of Nah 2:1–3, the usual interpretation of מפיץ is not so inadequate
as he maintains (see below), while his own preferred understanding of it
as the hiphil participle of פוץ in an intransitive sense appears unlikely:
even if the required collective interpretation of the participle is assumed,
it is not obvious that the other examples adduced[31] supply quite the right
sense in reference to the Israelite exiles as those who have *been* scattered
(by YHWH). Again, the often-noted link with Isa 52:1–2, 7–8, however it
is to be explained, need hardly demand for Nah 2:1–3 a vaguely parallel
(in this case, northern) exilic setting; there are more likely possibilities.
For these and other reasons, van der Woude's position should firmly be
declined. Nevertheless, we may note the argument that על פניך refers to
Judah, in the sense "in your presence, before your eyes."[32]

---

30. Van der Woude, "The Book of Nahum," 113.
31. Exod 5:12; 1 Sam 13:8, and Job 38:24. S. R. Driver would read the qal in all
three places: *Notes on the Hebrew Text and the Topography of the Books of Samuel*
(2d ed.; Oxford: Clarendon, 1913), 100.
32. Van der Woude, "The Book of Nahum," 117.

III

Two items in particular in 2:2a call, then, for further linguistic and textual comment.

First, מֵפִיץ is, as it stands, the masculine singular participle hiphil of פוּץ, hence most naturally translated "a scatterer" (BDB, 807a), unidentified, but clearly to be taken as the subject of עלה. This appears straightforward enough, and some modern writers, with varying general approaches to the book, have found no major difficulty with it.[33] Nevertheless, as noted, there has been a persistent trend[34] to emend the text to מֵפֵץ, as found elsewhere in Jer 51:20 (and the same emendation is commonly made for מֵפִיץ in Prov 25:18, where an *instrument* of war seems likewise necessitated by the context). The emendation is regularly traced back[35] to J. D. Michaelis,[36] though the latter in fact suggested the reading מַפִּיץ—presumably as masculine singular participle hiphil of נפץ (I), "shatter, smash" (BDB, 658b). The same proposal is entertained by some modern scholars,[37] perhaps because it retains the consonants of MT (and furnishes a personal subject for the verb?), though a hiphil of this root is not found elsewhere in Biblical Hebrew.

What is to be said in favour of this emendation? In short, I think there is nothing. The argument regularly put forward, that "the destruction, not the scattering of Nineveh, is the theme of the song"[38] makes a specious

33. See, e.g., W. R. Arnold, "The Composition of Nahum 1–2:3," *ZAW* 21 (1901): 225–65 (252); A. Haldar, *Studies in the Book of Nahum* (UUÅ 1946:7; Uppsala: Lundequistska Bokhandeln, 1947), 40–41; Schulz, *Das Buch Nahum*, 16 n. 53; J. J. M. Roberts, *Nahum, Habakkuk, and Zephaniah: A Commentary* (OTL; Louisville: Westminster John Knox, 1991), 56; K. Spronk, *Nahum* (HCOT; Kampen: Kok Pharos, 1997), 83–84; Sweeney, *The Twelve Prophets*, 437.

34. So persistent (and widespread) that it, too, hardly needs detailed documentation!

35. For example, by W. Nowack, *Die kleinen Propheten übersetzt und erklärt* (2d ed.; HKAT 3/4; Göttingen: Vandenhoeck & Ruprecht, 1903), 259; K. Marti, *Das Dodekapropheton erklärt* (KHCAT 13; Tübingen: J. C. B. Mohr [P. Siebeck], 1904), 316; E. Sellin, *Das Zwölfprophetenbuch übersetzt und erklärt* (3d ed.; KAT 12/1; Leipzig: A. Deichert, 1930), 366; BDB, 807a.

36. J. D. Michaelis, *Orientalische und Exegetische Bibliothek*, vol. 20 (Frankfurt-am-Main: Garbe, 1782), 189.

37. W. Rudolph, *Micha–Nahum–Habakuk–Zephanja* (KAT 13/3; Gütersloh: Gerd Mohn, 1975), 160; H.-J. Fabry, *Nahum übersetzt und ausgelegt* (HTKAT; Freiburg i.B.: Herder, 2006), 159 (though see also p. 168).

38. So Sellin, *Das Zwölfprophetenbuch*, 366; cf., e.g., Nowack, *Die kleinen Propheten*, 259: "why a 'scatterer' is mentioned is incomprehensible"; and more recently, Perlitt, *Nahum*, 19: "4ff. do not describe 'scattering,' but conquest and

distinction. At the same time, it is clear that a personal subject is required for the verb עלה, not a metaphorical "hammer"—the latter makes sense as YHWH's *weapon* at Jer 51:20, but not here.[39] To this fundamental point, we can add one or two others. To begin with, it is worth observing that the closest semantic equivalent to פוץ in Akkadian, *sapāḫu*, though often used with peoples or armies as its object, can also be used with lands or cities.[40] So, for instance, in the king's declaration of innocence in the New Year rites, we read: "I have not destroyed Babylon; I have not commanded its scattering (*sapaḫsu*)."[41] Whether the idea is that of the dispersion of its people, or that of the scattering by destruction of its buildings, need not concern us; the point is that there is nothing very odd in language about a city's being attacked and destroyed by a "scatterer."[42] Next, it is quite often claimed, in connection with the frequent use of older texts in Isa 24–27, that the distinctive vocabulary of Nah 2:3, 10, 11 has been taken up in Isa 24:1, 3,[43] and is used now in the context of a universal, eschatological judgment (thus raising the question whether the Isaiah writer was already reading Nahum in these terms). If so, it is likely that the talk of YHWH's "scattering" (והפיץ) of the world's inhabitants (Isa 24:1) is drawn from the use of מֵפִיץ in Nah 2:2, rather than from (or perhaps in addition to) the ויפץ of Gen 11:8, as is commonly claimed;[44] and this, if so, gives a little further support to the traditional reading in Nahum.

destruction." Van der Woude, "The Book of Nahum," 116, also found reason in this for his different understanding of מֵפִיץ. Rudolph, *Nahum*, 160, simply calls the emendation "more suitable" ("passender").

39. So, e.g., A. van Hoonacker, *Les douze petits prophètes* (EB; Paris: J. Gabalda, 1908), 435; Haldar, *Studies*, 40–41.

40. For examples from various periods, see *CAD*, 15:152 (1[b]), 156 (8[b]).

41. F. Thureau-Dangin, *Rituels Accadiens* (Paris: Leroux, 1921), 144 line 424.

42. Throughout this discussion, of course, the *semantic* linking of "scattering" and "shattering" needs to be borne in mind; this connection between ideas is easy enough to recognize, whether or not there is also an *etymological* link in English (*OED*, *sub* "scatter" [verb], is cautious): "shattering" necessarily involves "scattering." On the etymological connection of נפץ and פוץ, see GK §77d.

43. So, e.g., R. E. Clements, *Isaiah 1–39* (NCB; Grand Rapids: Eerdmans, 1980), 201; R. Scholl, *Die Elenden in Gottes Thronrat: Stilistisch-kompositorische Untersuchungen zu Jesaja 24–27* (BZAW 274; Berlin: de Gruyter, 2000), 230–31; D. C. Polaski, *Authorizing an End: The Isaiah Apocalypse and Intertextuality* (BibInt 50; Leiden: Brill, 2001), 106.

44. For example, by J. Blenkinsopp, *Isaiah 1–39* (AB 19; New York: Doubleday, 2000), 351, though he accepts familiarity with Nahum elsewhere in Isa 24:1–3.

Secondly, the phrase עַל־פָּנָיִךְ calls for some attention. The common view of translators, as noted, and of commentators, is that it is addressed adversatively to Nineveh, exemplifying the familiar usage of עַל with עלה in the sense "go to battle against, attack."[45] An occasional commentator perhaps hints at some awkwardness or difficulty with the text; Buttenwieser suggests that פָּנִים stands here for an intensive pronoun, while Ehrlich thinks of a quite different meaning for עַל פְּנֵי at this point.[46] Furthermore, two emendations to the vocalization of the phrase in Nahum are quite often proposed.

One, followed by NEB and by a number of scholars,[47] would read עַל־פִּנָּיִךְ "against your corners, battlements, bastions," and seems first to have been proposed by F. Perles, who has no more to say in its favour than that it is "much more poetic" than the "colourless" existing text;[48] and though the plural פָּנִים is found elsewhere, in Zech 14:10, the otherwise regular plural of פִּנָּה is פִּנּוֹת. This does not, then, make a very convincing case.[49] The other postulated change to the vocalization is to read עַל־פָּנֶיךָ, on the grounds that the following imperatives, introduced by the infinitive absolute נָצוֹר, are in the masculine singular and the smooth sequence of the verse is clearer if the addressee of עַל־פָּנֶיךָ (perhaps the Assyrian king) is likewise masculine singular.[50] Hitzig long ago argued[51] that this true reading had been replaced by the present feminine singular form under the mistaken impression that the address to Judah in v. 1 was continued here—the same "error" as is found in several of the ancient versions and commentators discussed above. Even on the usual

----

45. So, e.g., BDB, 748b.2c; G. Wehmeier, "עלה *ʿlh* go up," *TLOT* 2:883–96 (887); H. F. Fuhs, "עלה," *TDOT* 11:76–95 (84). Both Wehmeier and Fuhs include Nah 2:2 among their numerous examples.

46. M. Buttenwieser, *The Psalms, Chronologically Treated, with a New Translation* (Chicago: University of Chicago Press, 1938), 230 (cf. BDB, 816a.2a); A. B. Ehrlich, *Randglossen zur Hebräischen Bibel*, vol. 5 (Leipzig: Hinrichs, 1912), 294 ("suddenly, unexpectedly").

47. So, e.g., P. Humbert, "Essai d'analyse de Nahoum 1,2–2,3," *ZAW* 44 (1926): 266–80 (275); Sellin, *Das Zwölfprophetenbuch*, 366; Jeremias, *Kultprophetie*, 27 n. 4.

48. F. Perles, *Analekten zur Textkritik des Alten Testaments* (Munich: Ackermann, 1895), 66 ("viel poetischer…farblose").

49. Cf. Rudolph, *Nahum*, 160 ("kein Grund").

50. So, e.g., H. Ewald, *Die Propheten des Alten Bundes erklärt* (2 vols.; Stuttgart: Krabbe, 1840), 1:355; Nowack, *Die kleinen Propheten*, 259; Sellin, *Das Zwölfprophetenbuch*, 366; more recently, Roberts, *Nahum*, 56–57.

51. F. Hitzig, *Die zwölf kleinen Propheten erklärt* (2d ed.; KEHAT; Leipzig: Weidmannsche Buchhandlung, 1852), 235.

interpretation of the phrase as addressing Nineveh, however, the argument from the following verb forms is by no means secure. Though the
sequence begins with the infinitive absolute (qal) נצור, it is often assumed
that the following forms are masculine singular piel imperatives.[52] Yet all
may just as well be read as infinitives absolute piel: though the form is
not otherwise attested in Biblical Hebrew for the verbs צפה, חזק and אמץ,
infinitives absolute piel in ē are common enough with different verb-
types, and they may be so understood here,[53] in which case the argument
from the abrupt shift from feminine to supposed masculine address can
have no weight. There are the further questions as to whether the
infinitives are then regarded as imperatival in function—perhaps still the
most likely view—or in some other way, and as to whom they are understood as addressed or related. At any rate, there is no convincing ground
for altering the vocalization of על־פניך. I shall now suggest an interpretation of the phrase which, if accepted, would in any event nullify the
case for this emendation.[54]

IV

The consensus position, as we have seen, takes על־פניך with עלה in the
sense "against you (Nineveh)." I now propose a different view. It may be
noted, to begin with, that there is no other instance of עלה על־פני in the
sense assumed.[55] How far על־פני in itself is used in an adversative sense
is questionable:[56] of the three examples given in BDB, 819a.7(a)e, one is
Nah 2:2 itself; in Ps 21:13 the usage appears to be strictly literal; and
Ezek 32:10 may just as well exemplify the usage "before them" (as in

---

52. Apart from many commentators, so, e.g., GK §113bb; P. Joüon and T.
Muraoka, *A Grammar of Biblical Hebrew* (rev. Eng. ed.; Subsidia Biblica 27; Rome:
Pontifical Biblical Institute, 2006), §123u.

53. They are so taken, e.g., by Arnold, "The Composition," 252–53; Marti, *Das
Dodekapropheton*, 316; van Hoonacker, *Les douze petits prophètes*, 435; Ehrlich,
Randglossen, 294; Haldar, *Studies*, 42; Rudolph, *Nahum*, 160; Spronk, *Nahum*, 85.

54. One other proposal of historical interest may be noted in passing: namely,
that על־פניו should be read, as referring to the בליעל of v. 1: so C. F. Houbigant,
Notae Criticae in Universos Veteris Testamenti Libros, vol. 2 (Frankfurt-am-Main:
Varrentrapp & Wenner, 1777), 579. He was followed by W. Dodd, *A Commentary
on the Books of the Old and New Testaments*, vol. 2 (London: Davis, 1780), *Nahum*,
2. It is an improbable suggestion in itself, but Houbigant comments that if the
present text were retained it would have to be taken as addressing Judah.

55. The Vulgate's *coram te* and AV's "before thy face" may be of interest here.

56. Cf. M. Weinfeld, *Deuteronomy 1–11* (AB 5; New York: Doubleday, 1991),
276–77.

NRSV) as "against them." In any case, I suggest that עלה and על־פני should be separated, and that the latter should be taken in the well-attested sense "before you, in your presence, in your sight"[57] (as in van der Woude's interpretation). There is no difficulty in the use of עלה by itself with the meaning "attack."[58] Hence I would translate, "A scatterer has gone up (to attack) before you." There can be no doubt that the scatterer goes up against *Nineveh*, but it is *Judah* who is being invited to see this happening. This understanding preserves the link between vv. 2 and 4, but resolves the tension noted by Jeremias between the second-person address in the former verse and the third-person description in the latter. More importantly, it establishes the continuity of address between vv. 1 and 2, though in a way different from (and simpler than) the positions of many of the pre-modern commentators noted above,[59] and it undercuts the claim that there *must* be a change of addressee between vv. 1 and 2 because of the radical change of content.[60] I suggest that it is more natural to see the relationship of the two verses in this way, not least since in v. 1 an addressee is for the first time in the book unequivo-cally named—arguably differentiating the situation here from the previ-ous shifts between addressees in 1:9–14 (and once Nineveh has finally been named in 2:9, there is no difficulty in seeing a difference between the second feminine singular addressees in 2:2 and 2:14). The "break," then, comes not between 2:1 and 2:2, but between vv. 2aα and 2aβ–b.

How are we to understand the text, therefore? I want to emphasize that what follows is a "final form" approach (to use an admittedly question-begging term), though I do not at all deny the propriety and the necessity of a redaction-critical approach to Nahum, albeit how my reading of 2:2 may have implications for such an approach will not be considered here.[61]

57. See BDB, 816b.7a(a); A. S. van der Woude, "פנים *pānîm* face," *TLOT* 2:995–1014 (1003).

58. See, e.g., Judg 20:28; Isa 21:2; Jer 6:4–5.

59. Among the older commentators, my view would at this point be closest to that of Abravanel, *in Nahum Commentarius*, 21: "Quasi diceret ad regnum Judaicum: *ascendit dissipator in facie tua*, h. e. oculis tuis vides, dissipatorem [Nebuchadnezarem], ire Nineven ad perdendam eam."

60. So, e.g., Rudolph, *Nahum*, 163–64; Fabry, *Nahum*, 167–68.

61. See the interesting discussion of the earlier and the redactional senses of 2:1–3 by B. Renaud, *Michée–Sophonie–Nahum* (SB; Paris: Gabalda, 1987), 293–97. But though he thinks that in "le contexte actuel" Jerusalem is addressed in v. 2, he does not translate the passage correspondingly. My argument would be that על־פניך *never* referred to Nineveh at any stage of the composition.

Judah is being invited to *see* the fall of Nineveh enacted before it. This is the basis for the "good tidings" announced in v. 1; it is how in fact "the wicked...are utterly cut off." What the writer presents is a vivid, dramatic portrayal offered to Judah's imaginative grasp, an envisaging of Nineveh's end. The striking literary features of vv. 4–13 which have so often been noted—the brief, rapidly changing scenes, the clipped descriptions, the sharp changes of referent—stand precisely in the service of this imaginative envisaging of the chaotic scene of destruction. If the verb-forms in the second part of v. 2 are taken, as on the most common view, as addressed (ironically) to Nineveh's defenders, the abrupt shift within the verse coheres well with this picture: Judah's imagination is immediately and dramatically plunged *in medias res*. I should perhaps add that I do not see this in terms of any form of "liturgical drama"; nor do I follow any "liturgical hypothesis" of the book's origin, or see Nahum as a "cultic prophet."[62] Judah is being invited to see God at work in contemporary events—whether they have already happened, or, more likely, are still about to happen—as he was at work in the past (1:11); it is being summoned to an act of faithful imagination.

Two aspects of this should at least be mentioned. First, there is the theological-ethical question of the perspective from which Judah is called to this "seeing." Is it simply to gloat vindictively over Nineveh's fall? Or is it a summons to recognize and trust in (cf. 1:7) the power of YHWH at work in the world to destroy evil and liberate the oppressed? The complex issues involved here cannot be dealt with in the present study,[63] but I simply observe that the address to Judah in 2:2 ties the Nineveh poems more tightly to all that precedes—and contributes to the argument that, whatever its redactional history, the book must be interpreted theologically as an integrated whole. Related to this point, secondly, is the question of the identity of the "scatterer." He has, of course, often enough been identified as a human assailant—known or unknown by the writer, and, for whatever reason, unnamed—but a strong case can also be made for seeing YHWH himself as the attacker,[64] the divine warrior of ch. 1. That leads in turn to a further interpretative

---

62. So with, e.g., Jeremias, *Kultprophetie*, 43–44; Rudolph, *Nahum*, 145; Fabry, *Nahum*, 26, 36–37.

63. On the ethical reading of the book, see especially J. M. O'Brien, *Nahum* (Readings; London: Continuum, 2002), and G. Baumann, *Gottes Gewalt in Wandel: Traditionsgeschichtliche und intertextuelle Studien zu Nahum 1.2–8* (WMANT 108; Neukirchen–Vluyn: Neukirchener, 2005).

64. So, e.g., K. J. Cathcart, "Nahum, Book of," *ABD* 4:998–1000 (1000); Roberts, *Nahum*, 56.

possibility, that the verb עלה is to be read in two ways simultaneously: as announcing the scatterer's victorious attack on the enemy, but also as declaring his royal enthronement (as with עלה in, e.g., Ps 47:6) witnessed by Judah; the latter reading would also tie 2:2 and what follows tightly to 1:2–2:1. The links and comparisons with Isa 40 and 52 that this suggests cannot be pursued here, but on this understanding the scatterer's victory and his enthronement are coincident. The theological significance of that will perhaps need to be worked out elsewhere. Yet the martial language of YHWH as "scatterer" may—with all the interpretative and theological challenges this presents—continue to remind the reader of the utter, self-exerting seriousness with which God purposes to remove evil from his world. It is to be read, too, by the theological interpreter in the context of a canon which speaks also of a God who destroys his enemies by turning them into his friends.

Part IV

THE LANGUAGE AND LITERATURE OF THE WRITINGS

PSALM 102:14 AND *DIDACHE* 10:6 ON GRACE TO COME

William Horbury

In Ps 102:14 the psalmist boldly affirms or asks, "You will arise and have mercy upon (תרחם) Zion: for it is time to pity her (כי עת לחננה), the appointed time has come (כי בא מועד)."[1] For "to pity her" in the present context one might prefer "to show grace towards her" or "to be gracious to her," echoing the assonance of חנן and חן. The grounds for such boldness before God are then stated in the psalm as his servants' tenderness for Zion's ruins (v. 15), and the worldwide reverence awaiting their God (v. 16) when or because he rebuilds the city (כי בנה־יהוה ציון) and is seen in his glory (נראה בכבודו) (v. 17).

Renderings of v. 17 from the Greek and Roman periods mark the orientation of the whole sequence from v. 14 onwards towards an almost realized eschatology.[2] In v. 14 itself this is underlined when Aquila and Symmachus, according to the Syro-Hexaplar version, translate "the promise"—the promised time—"has come."[3] Already in the LXX the

1. The English rendering quoted is from [D. L. Frost, J. A. Emerton and A. A. Macintosh,] *The Psalms: A New Translation for Worship* (London: Collins, 1977), 173. Here and in printed English Bibles the verse numbers are one less than those of printed Hebrew Bibles, followed in the text above.

2. LXX ὅτι οἰκοδομήσει...καὶ ὀφθήσεται; Peshitta "because the Lord is building...and is being seen..." (participles); Jerome (*Psalterium iuxta Hebraeos*) *timebunt gentes...quia aedificavit Dominus Sion, apparuit in gloria sua*; similarly Targum "the nations will fear...because the city of Zion has been built by the Memra of the Lord, his glory has been revealed." This rendering of the Targum and Jerome, with perfect tenses understood as future perfects because of their place in a causal clause, was followed in the comments of Ibn Ezra and the seventeenth-century David Altschuler of Prague, *Metzudath Dawid*, as reprinted in *Miqra'oth Gedoloth, Kethubhim* (Warsaw, 1866; repr., Jerusalem: Schocken, 1947), ad loc. The concord of ancient versions in a future sense was brought out by F. Baethgen, *Die Psalmen* (2d ed.; Göttingen: Vandenhoeck & Ruprecht, 1897), 302.

3. On the basis of Syro-Hexaplar *shudaya* Greek ἐπαγγελία is suggested as the rendering of Aquila and Symmachus here by F. Field, *Origenis Hexaplorum quae supersunt* (2 vols.; Oxford: Clarendon, 1875), 2:257; cf. pp. 707–8 (on the same rendering attributed to Aquila in the Syro-Hexaplar version of Jer 46[26]:17).

imminence of the season and set time for divine mercy and grace was brought out with almost evangelic urgency in the rendering ὅτι ἥκει καιρός. Verse 17 being likewise understood of the near future, these lines culminate in hope for the divine appearance in glory.

They have accordingly helped to shape urgent prayer for the restoration of Jerusalem and the holy place, notably in Ecclesiasticus (36:13–14, asking for mercy on the holy city and the divine glory in the temple) and the Fourteenth of the *Eighteen Benedictions*. An allied but distinct topic is considered here, the contribution of Ps 102:14 in particular to the eschatological understanding of mercy and grace, especially as exemplified in the prayer of *Did.* 10:6, ἐλθέτω χάρις καὶ παρελθέτω ὁ κόσμος οὗτος, "Let grace come, and let this world pass away."

I

In the Greek and early Roman periods the biblical "day of the Lord" and its time took their place in the latter part of a periodized history, and acquired a group of descriptive biblically inspired titles, varying in emphasis between judgment and mercy on lines already suggested by such double-sided passages as Isa 61:2, "year of favour…day of vengeance." P. Volz's collection suggests that "judgmental" titles outnumbered "merciful" ones; he also showed the widespread use in this connection of the ambiguous language of divine "visitation" for good or ill.[4] Both the variation between ominous and propitious titles and the importance of "visitation" were underlined by subsequently discovered Qumran texts.[5] Psalm 102:14, with its emphasis on a coming time and season for mercy and grace, seems of some importance in the antecedents of the relatively select group of titles which emphasize divine mercy.

In this group Volz noted the day of redemption (*1 En.* 51:2), the day of mercy for the righteous (*Pss. Sol.* 14:9), with other similar expressions from the *Psalms of Solomon*, and the days or day of comfort in the Targums and rabbinic literature (יומי נחמתא, *Targ. Hos.* 6:2; יום הנחמה,

4. P. Volz, *Die Eschatologie der jüdischen Gemeinde im neutestamentlichen Zeitalter: Nach den Quellen der rabbinischen, apokalyptischen und apokryphen Literatur* (2d ed. of P. Volz, *Jüdische Eschatologie von Daniel bis Akiba* [1903]; Tübingen: Mohr Siebeck, 1934, repr., Hildesheim: Georg Olms, 1966), 163–65.

5. See, e.g., 1QH vii (formerly xv) 18–20 (the righteous predetermined for "the appointed time of good-will," the wicked consecrated for "the day of slaughter"; cf. Jer 12:3); 1QS iii 14, 26; iv 6, 11, 19, 26 (the "visitation" of the righteous and the wicked).

Mekhilta, Wayyassa 6, on Exod 16:32). The list could be paralleled and extended from New Testament indications of Jewish usage, including the comfort of Israel (Luke 2:25, παράκλησις), the (ultimate) mercy (Matt 5:7; cf. Jude 21, ἔλεος), the day of redemption (Eph 4:30, ἀπολύτρωσις) and perhaps the times of refreshment or revival (Acts 3:20, ἀνάψυξις); and also from later Samaritan expectations of (a time of) good-will or favour (רחותה).[6] Among these titles "day of mercy" and "mercy" particularly recall Ps 102:14, "you will have mercy"—at the appointed time.

Within this group of expressions some part was also played by the biblical phrases "time of favour" (Isa 49:8) and "year of favour" (Isa 61:2), both using רצון, and, in LXX, the adjective δεκτός. This is suggested by the Samaritan usage just noted, by 11Q13 ii 9 on the tenth and ultimate Jubilee as "the year of favour for Melchizedek" to carry out divine deliverance, and by 2 Cor 6:2 on the future "acceptable time" as already present.

In these titles for a day or a time the descriptive noun could stand on its own, as already seen in New Testament and Samaritan references to Comfort, Mercy, and Favour; compare the Rabbinic Hebrew asseveration "May I not see the Comfort."[7] The use of Mercy (in the LXX Pentateuch, ἔλεος can represent not only חסד, but also חן and רחמים) in this absolute way antedates the New Testament, as seen at 2 Macc 2:7 (following the harder reading of Codex Alexandrinus), "until God gathers the ingathering of the people," καὶ ἔλεος γένηται, "and Mercy happens."

In the Psalter, this use seems to be anticipated and encouraged in the prayer not only of Ps 102:14–17, but also in that of Ps 147:1–11, verses forming a separate psalm in the Septuagint. Here emphasis falls on Zion and the ingathering at the start (v. 2) and on mercy at the close: "who wait in hope for his mercy" (המיחלים לחסדו, v. 11).[8] Psalm 33:18–22 is

6. So, for example, in a hymn of Amram Dara (? fourth century): "whoever wishes to see Favour (רחותה), let him be very pure as regards the Sabbath…he shall attain to that Favour"; see Z. Ben-Hayyim, *The Literary and Oral Tradition of Hebrew and Aramaic among the Samaritans*. Vol. 3, Part 2, *The Recitation of Prayers and Hymns* (Jerusalem: Academy of the Hebrew Language, 1967), 76 (Amram Dara, hymn 15, lines 19–20, 24). The prayer "May God prolong your lives till the days of the Taheb, the Tabernacle [restored] and the days of Favour" is quoted from A. E. Cowley, ed., *The Samaritan Liturgy* (2 vols.; Oxford: Clarendon, 1909), 1:363 line 27, in discussion of the time of Favour by J. Macdonald, *The Theology of the Samaritans* (London: SCM, 1964), 359.

7. אראה בנחמה, attributed, for example, to Judah b. Tabbai and Simeon b. Shetah, *t. Sanh.* vi 6; viii 3.

8. For this rendering, see *The Psalms: A New Translation for Worship*, 250.

framed by similar references to hope for mercy. Then emphasis on mercy as the object of hope recurs in Ecclesiasticus (2:7, 9; 23:5; a Hebrew text is not available in these passages) and the Qumran *Hodayoth* ("I have hoped for your goodness and your mercies I await," 1QH xix [formerly xi] 31).

A similar chain of attestation from antecedents in the Psalter onwards to usage in an absolute way as a term for ultimate redemption can be discerned, it may be suggested, for the closely associated noun "grace" (חֵן, חֲנִינָה, χάρις).

II

The association of grace with mercy noticed already in the verbs of Ps 102:14 stands out especially in a series of biblical acclamations which hail the Lord as both merciful and gracious, as at Exod 34:6; Ps 86:5, or (in a seemingly later order) both gracious and merciful, as at Joel 2:13; Ps 111:4; 2 Chr 30:9; Neh 9:17, 31, and in the verbs of Exod 33:19.[9] A conjunction of the two attributes as nouns appears when the Qumran *Hodayoth* anticipate H. F. Lyte's metrical paraphrase of Ps 67, *Deus misereatur*, in the formula "God of mercy, God of grace"—אֵל הָרַחֲמִים וְהַחֲנִינָה (1QH xix [xi] 29).

In these passages the thought of grace and mercy to come can be implicit, as probably in the prayer of Neh 9 and evidently in 1QH xix (xi) (compare line 31, quoted above); but this sense is not drawn out. It appears more clearly when verbs rather than adjectives are used, above all in Exod 33:19 on the divine name and attributes: "I will be gracious to whom I will be gracious, and show mercy to whom I will show mercy." Psalm 102:14 on the time and season for grace and mercy, still with verbs, is almost a commentary on the Pentateuchal promise, bringing out the expectation of a future time which it encourages.

"Mercy" was indeed used absolutely as a term for future redemption, in ways illustrated above. "Grace," however, its regular associate, likewise attained a place in expressions for a good time coming. This is especially clear from the occurrence of the phrase χάρις καὶ ἔλεος in eschatological contexts in the early chapters of the Wisdom of Solomon. Thus Wis 3:9, looking forward to the "time of visitation" (3:7), expects "grace and mercy" (3:9) for the divinely chosen; and Wis 4:15 names "grace and mercy with his chosen" alongside "his visitation with his holy ones."

---

9. For the chronological distinction, see "חָנַן," etc., *ThWAT* 3:23–39.

Turning to Christian usage showing continuity with Jewish developments, it is worth asking whether in the clause "who loved us and gave
us everlasting comfort and good hope ἐν χάριτι" (2 Thess 2:16) the last
words should not be rendered "with grace," in reference not just to
present help but also to the coming time of grace for the chosen. "Grace"
here would then share the future aspect which is presented by "everlasting comfort," as earlier discussion of "comfort" has shown, and also
by "good hope."[10] In another probably first-century Christian text the
noun is clearly used in this sense of grace to come when the "chosen
sojourners of the dispersion" in 1 Peter are exhorted, in words recalling
the injunctions to hope for mercy in Ecclus 2:7, 9: "hope for the grace
brought to you in the revealing of Jesus Christ" (1 Pet 1:1, 13).

"Let grace come" in *Did.* 10:6 can be identified as a prayer for the
grace of the coming kingdom which has just been mentioned (10:5), and
aligned with the invocation "Our Lord, come" which follows (10:6,
Maranatha).[11] It can then be associated with this group of passages,
extending from Wisdom onwards, on future grace at the coming divine
visitation.

III

Didache 10:6 is then in touch with Greek Jewish as well as specifically
Christian usage in giving "grace" the sense of coming divine redemption.[12] As the comparable development of "mercy" might suggest, however, this understanding is not alien to biblical interpretation in Jewish
Semitic-language settings.

---

10. For "good hope" as signifying life after death, see E. Best, *The First and
Second Epistles to the Thessalonians* (Black's New Testament Commentaries;
London: A. & C. Black, 1972), 321. The possibility of taking ἐν comitatively,
followed above, is illustrated by F. F. Bruce, *1 & 2 Thessalonians* (WBC 45; Waco:
Word, 1982), 196, from Eph 4:19; 5:26; 6:24; but he prefers the instrumental
rendering "by."

11. For this interpretation of *Did.* 10:6, see J.-P. Audet, *La Didaché: Instructions des Apôtres* (Paris: Gabalda, 1958), 423, followed by K. Niederwimmer, *Die
Didache* (Göttingen: Vandenhoeck & Ruprecht, 1989), 202 (ET Minneapolis, 1998,
106).

12. 1 Pet 1:13 is the only parallel noted by Niederwimmer, *Die Didache*, 202
(ET p. 106), in his argument for "grace" as eschatological here. H. van de Sandt and
D. Flusser, *The Didache: Its Jewish Sources and Its Place in Early Judaism and
Christianity* (Assen: Van Gorcum; Minneapolis: Fortress, 2002), 301–2, do not
comment on this aspect of the passage.

Thus an eschatological reference was sometimes heard in what was perhaps the most familiar of all passages with חנן, the Aaronic blessing, "the Lord make his face to shine upon you, and be gracious to you" (Num 6:25), paraphrased in reverse in Ps 67:2, "Let God be gracious to us and bless us, and make his face shine upon us." This is suggested by exegesis of the blessing attributed in *Siphre* to the tanna R. Nathan and probably current in the second century, not far from the time of the *Didache*. On this interpretation the light of the divine countenance (Num 6:25) is the light of the Shekinah promised in Isa 60:1, "Arise, shine...," as can be indicated by Ps 67:2, just quoted, and Ps 118:27, "the Lord is God, and he has given us light"; and the peace mentioned soon afterwards in the blessing (Num 6:26) is the peace of the kingdom of the house of David.[13] Here, although "be gracious" (Num 6:25) receives no specific comment, the divine grace is evidently taken to be the gift of the messianic age.[14]

A Hebrew biblical precedent for an understanding of "grace" on the eschatological lines attested in Wisdom, early Christian texts and *Siphre* appears in Ps 102:14, discussed already. It points, within a context of urgent prayer for Zion, to a coming time for divine grace to be shown: "for it is time to show grace towards her, the appointed time has come." A second Psalter-passage on grace, from Ps 84, *Quam dilecta*, another psalm concerning the holy place, can now be associated with Ps 102. Against the background of the prayer of Ps 102:14–17 and other prayer of this kind, Ps 84:12, "the Lord shall give grace (חן) and glory; no good thing will he withhold from those who walk in innocence," can be understood as a promise of grace in future deliverance. "Glory" will now be heard as a hint at the longed-for manifestation of divine glory in the sanctuary, mentioned in prayer like that of Ps 102:17, a thought taken up in the association of Num 6:25 with the appearance of the Shekinah which has just been noted.

---

13. *Siphre* Numbers, 41 and 42, in H. S. Horovitz, ed., *Siphre d'be Rab* (Leipzig: Fock, 1917), 1:44, 46, respectively. The first interpretation recurs anonymously in *Num. Rab.* 11:5, the second with ascription to R. Nathan in *Num. Rab.* 11:7. The probative character of the paraphrase in Ps 67:2 in this connection will arise especially from its concluding "Selah," understood with the Targum as meaning "for ever."

14. The repetition of "be gracious" at the end of Ps 67:2 in the tradition of the Greek Psalter as reflected in Jerome's *Psalterium iuxta LXX*, "Deus misereatur nostri et benedicat nobis: inluminet vultum suum super nos et misereatur nostri," corresponds to a general tendency to repeat suffrages (as with "be gracious" in the Hebrew text of Ps 123:3), but may in Ps 67:2 have been influenced also by understanding of the priestly blessing as an urgent prayer for redemption.

The Septuagintal rendering of Ps 84:12–13 already suggests an understanding of this eschatological kind, with "he shall not deprive those who walk in innocence of good things; Lord of powers, blessed is the man who hopes in thee." Here "good things" (τὰ ἀγαθά) recalls the Deuteronomic expectation of "good things" in national restoration (LXX Deut 28:11; 30:9, ἀγαθά), taken up when Ben Sira advises hope for "good things and everlasting joy and mercy" (Ecclus 2:9), and in the *Psalms of Solomon* on "the good things of Israel in the gathering together of the tribes" and "the good things of the Lord which he will perform" (*Pss. Sol.* 17:50; 18:7). Then the future reference of Ps 84:12–13 is strengthened by the rendering "who hopes" (ὁ ἐλπίζων) in v. 13. Thus, as in Ps 102:14–17, the Septuagintal interpretation brings out and enhances the future aspect of the gift of grace which is already indicated by the Hebrew, especially when it is heard in the context of other Hebrew prayer for Zion, and encourages perception of a reference to coming redemption.[15]

IV

A line can then be traced from the imminent time for grace in Ps 102:14, and the future gift of grace and glory in Ps 84:12–13, both prayer-passages connected with Zion and the sanctuary, through the Septuagintal interpretation of both psalms, to the absolute use of "grace" for coming divine redemption in the Wisdom of Solomon and early Christian texts, notably the *Didache*. Rabbinic literature shows that this line of thought was not alien to Semitic-language interpretation, and the development suggested for "grace" has been seen to match the eschatological development apparent in the understanding of terms for "mercy," from Pss 102 and 147 onwards.

"Let grace come" in the eschatological prayer of *Did.* 10:6 then follows Christian usage seen in 1 Pet 1:13 and perhaps also in 2 Thess 2:16; but that usage has itself appeared as a special exemplification of Jewish usage which is attested in Wisdom and echoed in the midrash, and which develops antecedents found in the Psalter, above all in Ps 102:14, "it is time to show grace." At the same time, discussion has highlighted the significance in the Psalter itself of prayer for grace and mercy at a near time and in Jerusalem.

---

15. On this interpretative tendency in many other Greek Psalter-renderings, see J. Schaper, *Eschatology in the Greek Psalter* (WUNT 2/76; Tübingen: Mohr Siebeck, 1995).

These comments are now offered to Andrew Macintosh in grateful acknowledgment of his friendship and the instruction of his writings over many years, and in happy remembrance of meetings of a committee for translating the Psalter in which he played a leading part.

Wisdom and Psalm 119

Cynthia L. Engle

Introduction

It has long been thought by the majority of biblical scholars that Ps 119 falls squarely into the category of Wisdom Psalms. However, further investigation reveals that, while there are clearly a number of wisdom elements in the psalm, it is inappropriate to apply that label simply and without qualification to this massive composition. Rather, it is more appropriate to identify wisdom elements that appear in the psalm and then determine the degree of wisdom influence present, and how that influence is to be interpreted and understood.

This essay seeks to explore wisdom elements present in Ps 119, first by defining wisdom in the Old Testament in general and, secondly, by summarizing major insights of scholarship regarding wisdom in the Psalter and in Ps 119. Thirdly, there follow identification of additional wisdom elements in Ps 119 and, by contrast, recognition of the absence of those traditional elements that might have been expected. Finally, concluding comments will discuss the implications of wisdom influence upon Ps 119.

Wisdom in General

The wisdom literature of the Old Testament constitutes a distinct category, generally understood to include the books of Proverbs, Job and Ecclesiastes, as well as certain Psalms, though there is much debate regarding *which* psalms. Although the status of wisdom in previous centuries, and even well into the twentieth century, was not especially emphasized, it is now recognized that the influence of wisdom extends also to the Pentateuch (e.g. the Joseph cycle). And certain prophets may well have been trained in wisdom. Despite this growing recognition, clear definitions remain elusive.

Wisdom frequently manifests a distinctly didactic and pragmatic character, expressing approval of moral codes, particularly those relating to daily living. One of its most favoured is the art of living well or skilfully.

The חכם or "wise" person was originally someone who knew how to do well what others could do only indifferently or not at all; he or she was considered a master craftsman at the task of life. The quality of חכמה seems to have been imputed especially to persons who were able to speak the right answer in critical situations, as was Joseph in his ability to interpret Pharaoh's dreams.

Other themes include the order detected in the world, creation, punishment and reward, justice and mercy, the conflict between good and evil, the righteous and the wicked, and life as the supreme good. Also present in the face of the frequent ambiguity of life's events is a stated (though sometimes implicit) confidence in wisdom. Thus, life is best constructed around wisdom and the pursuit of truth as ordering principles.

Wisdom is distilled in certain literary forms such as sayings, admonitions, proverbs, and exhortations, with little appeal to specific laws or commandments. The primary form, however, is the proverb, a single- or double-line sentence dealing specifically with a particular wisdom theme. Other characteristics of wisdom include anthological material, autobiographical narrative (e.g. Ecclesiastes), creation as a fundamental principle and, frequently, the manifestation of wisdom in women. Some scholars note acrostic as a feature, although this is not confined to the wisdom genre.

Although many consider that wisdom in its fullness belongs to the period during and after the Exile, and to the wisdom schools, there is some evidence to indicate that aspects of it may go back to pre-exilic times, and that it reflects a large body of knowledge and experience built up and developed over time from a variety of traditions, both oral and written, possibly having developed in schools and at the royal court. There are various opinions as to how and when wisdom developed, but the actual date of the beginning of wisdom as a literary activity remains uncertain. Parallels from Egypt suggest a literary origin, with an earlier (i.e. pre-exilic) dating likely.

The probability that wisdom developed over time contributes to the difficulty of defining its essence. Crenshaw maintains that wisdom encompasses everything that is not a direct revelation of God, and thus represents unaided human attempts to understand the world. Wisdom, according to von Rad, is general in its approach, but specific in its practical knowledge. Essentially, it is clear that both wisdom elements and influence pervade the Hebrew scriptures, much more so than might be immediately apparent.[1]

---

1.   The preceding is a short summary of introductory material by R. E. Clements, *A Century of Old Testament Study* (rev. ed.; Cambridge: Lutterworth, 1976, 1983),

One major difficulty in defining wisdom is the impression that the genre possesses expanding and contracting, or flexible and fluid, boundaries. While many scholars may agree on the core essentials of wisdom and their presence in a given work, there may still be disagreement regarding the degree to which they are present and the significance of where they are present. Thus, wisdom seems to be an ever-changing, continually shifting landscape. Put another way, the middle ground may be considered *terra firma*, but the outer boundaries, and the criteria for such, remain quite unsettled. Wisdom in the Old Testament, it seems, is not a fixed concept.

Wisdom in the Psalter

As with the category of wisdom in general, there is wide debate regarding the definition of a wisdom psalm. Whybray, for example, states that there is no such category, and he understands that the reason for the lack of consensus among scholars resides in the ambiguity of the terminology used to define words such as wisdom, psalm, cult and school. He warns that it is a mistake to make an absolute distinction between wisdom psalms and other psalms in the Psalter on the grounds of a suspected connection between religious observance and instruction.[2] Whybray believes that some psalms have been assigned a wisdom title on the basis of inadequate criteria, citing the אשרי "blessed" formula as one example of this.[3]

122–43; J. Crenshaw, "The Concept of God in Old Testament Wisdom," in *In Search of Wisdom* (ed. L. G. Perdue, B. B. Scott and W. J. Wiseman; Louisville: Westminster John Knox, 1993), 1–18; idem, *Old Testament Wisdom* (Louisville: Westminster John Knox, 1981; 3d ed. 2010), 11–65; C. Fontaine, "Wisdom in Proverbs," in Perdue, Scott and Wiseman, eds., *In Search of Wisdom*, 99–114; H. Guthrie, *Israel's Sacred Songs* (New York: Seabury, 1966), 171–88; O. S. Rankin, *Israel's Wisdom Literature* (Edinburgh: T. & T. Clark, 1936; rev. ed., 1969), 3–4, 9, 70, 115, 245–47, 250–51; G. von Rad, *Theologie des Alten Testaments* (2 vols.; Munich: Kaiser, 1957), 1:361–65 (ET *Old Testament Theology* [2 vols.; New York: Harper & Row, 1962], 1:364–68).

2. See the following works by R. N. Whybray: "The Wisdom Psalms," in *Wisdom in Ancient Israel* (ed. J. Day, R. P. Gordon and H. G. M. Williamson; Cambridge: Cambridge University Press, 1995), 152, 154; *Reading the Psalms as a Book* (JSOTSup 222; Sheffield: Sheffield Academic, 1996), 4, 36–37; *The Composition of the Book of Proverbs* (JSOTSup 168; Sheffield: Sheffield Academic, 1994), 7, 56–61. In the last-named, Whybray defines חכמה as "life skill" (p. 4; cf. Ps 37:30); it does not appear to be enough to function as a criterion for defining wisdom psalms.

3. Whybray, "Wisdom Psalms," 159, 160.

Scott and Murphy take the view that wisdom psalms are those that
clearly reflect Old Testament wisdom themes.[4]

Brueggemann and Dell expand this definition to include psalms containing themes of creation and order, as also those that reveal various
tensions associated with cosmology and anthropology, such as those
found in Ps 104.[5] Other definitions include Torah psalms, usually understood as Pss 1; 19 and 119 and containing links with the Pentateuch,
as a distinct category either apart from, or included within, the larger
category of wisdom psalms.[6] The vast majority of scholars cite form
criteria, vocabulary, rhetorical and thematic elements, and links with
the corpus of wisdom literature. Again, the difficulty of determining
extent and content is widely rehearsed, and it appears likely that there are
many marginal cases.[7] Perhaps Wilson and Zenger share the most

4. R. B. Y. Scott, *The Way of Wisdom in the Old Testament* (New York:
Macmillan, 1971), 190–200 (Scott classifies as "wisdom" Pss 1; 37; 49 and 112,
but not Ps 119); R. Murphy, "A Consideration of the Classification 'Wisdom
Psalms'," in *Congress Volume: Bonn 1962* (ed. J. A. Emerton; VTSup 9; Leiden:
Brill, 1963), 159–60 (Murphy classifies as "wisdom" Pss 1; 32; 34; 37; 49; 112 and
128, but not Ps 119).

5. W. Brueggemann, *The Message of the Psalms* (Augsburg: Fortress, 1984), 38,
40–42; K. J. Dell, *Get Wisdom, Get Insight* (Macon, Ga.: Smyth & Helwys, 2000),
1–13, 74–76; von Rad mentions these themes in passing (*Theologie*, 1:361–65 [ET
Theology, 1:364–68]); cf. also L. G. Perdue, *Proverbs* (Louisville: Westminster John
Knox, 2000), 1–15; idem, "Cosmology and the Social Order in the Wisdom Tradition," in *The Sage in Israel and the Ancient Near East* (ed. J. G. Gammie and L. G.
Perdue; Winona Lake: Eisenbrauns, 1990), 457–78.

6. L. Allen, *Psalms 101–150* (WBC 21; Nashville: Thomas Nelson, 1983),
139–42; Crenshaw, *Old Testament Wisdom*, 180–85 (Crenshaw does not include
Ps 119); J. Day, *Psalms* (OT Guides; Sheffield: Sheffield Academic, 1990), 56–57;
E. Gerstenberger, *Psalms, Part 2, and Lamentations* (FOTL 15; Grand Rapids:
Eerdmans, 2001), 310–17; J. C. McCann, "The Psalms as Instruction," *Int* 46
(1992): 117–20; C. Westermann, *Ausgewählte Psalmen* (Göttingen: Vandenhoeck &
Ruprecht, 1984), 203–6 (ET *The Living Psalms* [Edinburgh: T. & T. Clark, 1989],
292–94).

7. A. Ceresko, *Introduction to Old Testament Wisdom* (Maryknoll: Orbis, 1999),
161; Gerstenberger, "Psalms," in *Old Testament Form Criticism* (ed. J. H. Hayes;
TUMSR 2; San Antonio: Trinity University Press, 1974), 218–20; A. Hurvitz,
"Wisdom Vocabulary in the Hebrew Psalter: A Contribution to the Study of
'Wisdom Psalms'," *VT* 38 (1988): 41–51; K. J. Kuntz, "The Canonical Wisdom
Psalms of Ancient Israel," in *Rhetorical Criticism: Essays in Honor of James
Muilenburg* (ed. J. J. Jackson; Pittsburgh Theological Monographs 1; Pittsburgh:
Pittsburgh Theological Seminary, 1994), 186–222; J. Ross, "Psalm 73," in *Israelite
Wisdom: Theological and Literary Essays in Honor of Samuel Terrien* (ed. J. G.
Gammie; Missoula: Scholars Press, 1978), 167–68, 170.

comprehensive view: Wilson understands the entire Psalter to be replete with wisdom, containing instruction for the faithful and emphasizing YHWH's kingship, while Zenger believes the Psalter's "canonical *Sitz im Leben* was literary and wisdom-related."[8]

Another area of debate concerns whether wisdom psalms were cultic or non-cultic. Mowinckel, Terrien, Westermann and Whybray consider wisdom psalms to be non-cultic, both in origin and practice. Mowinckel offers criteria for defining wisdom psalms as "non-cultic prayers addressed to God," although he concedes that there always remained some influence from cultic psalms.[9] Dell, Mays and Ross, on the other hand, view wisdom psalms as distinctly linked to the cult, Dell supporting the view that this was early the case. Ross adds that the wisdom schools were associated with the temple, and that research tends to deal with a "false alternative—cultic versus non-cultic, psalmodic versus wisdom," a view that, he claims, arises from a tendency to compartmentalize ancient Israelite religion. He maintains that life must have been experienced in a variety of contexts and places that were not mutually exclusive.[10]

Considerations of space preclude a wider discussion and so the present abbreviated summary must suffice. Given the situation, however, it is safe to assume that what can be said of wisdom literature in general may be applied also to wisdom psalms in particular: characteristic problems include overlapping categories, inadequate criteria and lack of consensus regarding their application, ambiguous terminology, a multitude of definitions, and uncertainty of origin. Clearly, the flexible and fluid boundaries of wisdom in general apply to the sub-category of wisdom psalms as well.[11]

---

8. G. Wilson, "Shaping the Psalter," in *The Shape and Shaping of the Psalter* (ed. J. C. McCann; JSOTSup 159; Sheffield: Sheffield Academic, 1993), 72–82; E. Zenger, *Der Psalter in Judentum und Christentum* (Freiberg: Herder, 1998), 1–57.

9. S. Mowinckel, "Psalms and Wisdom," in *Wisdom in Israel and in the Ancient Near East* (ed. M. Noth and D. W. Thomas; VTSup 3; Leiden: Brill, 1955), 205–24 (Mowinckel also viewed wisdom as a late, literary influence on the Psalms rather than an early cultic one); S. Terrien, "Wisdom in the Psalter," in Perdue, Scott and Wiseman, eds., *In Search of Wisdom*, 51–72 (55); Westermann, *Ausgewählte Psalmen*, 203–6 (ET *The Living Psalms*, 292–94); Whybray, *Reading the Psalms*, 36–51, 60.

10. Dell, *Get Wisdom*, 74–76; J. L. Mays, *Psalms* (Interpretation Commentary Series; Louisville: Westminster John Knox, 1994), 27–29, 381–85; Ross, "Psalm 73," 168, 170.

11. See D. J. Estes, *Handbook on the Wisdom Books and Psalms* (Grand Rapids: Baker Academic, 2005), 190–96, for an excellent brief assessment of the lack of

Wisdom in Psalm 119

In the following section I seek to set out the views of a number of scholars regarding wisdom in Ps 119, a task that presents considerable difficulties. It thus appears necessary to undertake a thorough search in this somewhat amorphous collection of opinions, before attempting an overall evaluation.

Earlier commentators, for example, Delitzsch, Ewald, Kirkpatrick, Briggs and Barnes, detected the presence of more general wisdom elements in Ps 119: the אשרי sayings, concern with the law and its various terms, righteousness, and the metaphors of path and way used in relation to life. The presence of counsellors as teachers indicates a preoccupation with instruction. Delitzsch observed the strengthening and preservation of life, and the word of God as the psalmist's wisdom. Ewald emphasized the constant references to the Pentateuch, the conflict between the righteous and the wicked, and themes of suffering. Kirkpatrick focused more on Torah as the governing principle of life, as well as the psalmist's close relationship to God. Briggs noted the divine origin of instruction, as imparting the only true life. Barnes described the seeking after precepts as an aspect of meditation, the verb דרש here implying the mental and spiritual effort expended in apprehending religious truth.[12]

For the most part, twentieth-century commentators, for example, Kissane and Mowinckel, tend to follow older commentators in noting the standard wisdom features, as also some of the more specific aspects listed above.[13] McCann, Mays and Weeks note associations with Pss 1 and 19.[14] Broyles perceives in the psalm a reflection of the five books of

scholarly consensus. M. Futato, *Interpreting the Psalms* (Grand Rapids: Kregel, 2007), 171, likewise notes the elusiveness of the wisdom category.

12. F. Delitzsch, *Biblischer Commentar über die Psalmen* (Leipzig: Dörffling & Franke, 1867), 677 (ET *Commentary on the Psalms* [3 vols.; Edinburgh: T. & T. Clark, 1876], 3:244); H. Ewald, *Die poetischen Bücher des Alten Bundes—Die Psalmen* (Göttingen: Vandenhoeck & Ruprecht, 1840), 383–84 (ET *Commentary on the Psalms* [2 vols.; London: Williams & Norgate, 1881], 2:268–69); A. F. Kirkpatrick, *The Psalms* (Cambridge: Cambridge University Press, 1902), 700–701; C. A. Briggs, *A Critical and Exegetical Commentary on the Book of Psalms* (2 vols.; ICC; Edinburgh: T. & T. Clark, 1907), 2:422, 430; W. E. Barnes, *The Psalms* (London: Methuen, 1931), 567.

13. E. Kissane, *The Book of Psalms* (2 vols.; Dublin: Browne & Nolan, 1954), 2:224; Mowinckel, "Psalms and Wisdom," 212.

14. McCann, "The Psalms," 117–20 (noting opinions suggesting the possibility that Ps 119 originally concluded the Psalter, forming an *inclusio* with Ps 1); Mays, *Psalms*, 27–29; S. Weeks, *Early Israelite Wisdom* (Oxford: OTM, 1994), 86.

the Pentateuch, and notes the psalm's anthological style, while Terrien detects associations with Proverbs.[15]

The twenty-first-century commentator Limberg highlights the sojourning aspect of the psalm and its didactic elements, and maintains that Torah serves as the pilgrim's guide in the journey of life. Wilcock notes the significance of Torah as order, and also notes prayer associations, but little else that is specifically sapiential. Lane sees wisdom themes in general, and associations with Torah. Goldingay observes associations with Proverbs and YHWH's teaching. Grogan similarly categorizes Pss 1, 19 and 119 as Torah psalms, adding that "the wisdom psalm is the most difficult genre to identify or even to describe accurately, and there is no agreed list. Some even regard it as a pseudo-genre."[16]

Several of the scholars mentioned above have made noteworthy, wisdom-related observations on Ps 119. Though their remarks are not extensive, they nonetheless manifest an awareness of the psalm's heavenward orientation that is not initially apparent. For example, von Rad notes the idea of delight in God's creation, observing that wisdom literature finds God's action "in remote spheres…particularly wonderful"; all creation is "splendid, resounding in praise." With regard to Ps 119, "Israel's most characteristic feature lies in the fact that she accompanied Jahweh's condescension to her, even to the point of a divine *kenosis*, with statements about beauty. Beauty was in the revelation of his will (Ps. cxix *passim*)," and belonged also to Zion.[17] Dahood recognizes the importance of time/space words, usually in the superlative degree.[18] Scott notes 21 words linking Torah piety with wisdom.[19] Kidner celebrates the revelatory aspect of the law contained in the words used; the purpose is to enjoin obedience. He believes that in vv. 98–100 wisdom is God-taught, on a higher plane than human wisdom.[20] Mowinckel's assessment is that love of the Law as a motivation for

15. C. C. Broyles, *Psalms II* (NIBC; Peabody: Hendrickson, 1999), 442–44; Terrien, "Wisdom," in Perdue, Scott and Wiseman, eds., *In Search of Wisdom*, 63–69, 71.

16. J. Limberg, *Psalms* (Louisville: Westminster John Knox, 2000), 405–19; M. Wilcock, *Psalms 73–150* (Downers Grove: InterVarsity, 2001), 193–219; E. Lane, *Psalms 90–150* (Fearn, Scotland: Christian Focus, 2006), 125–39; J. Goldingay, *Psalms* (3 vols.; Grand Rapids: Baker Academic, 2008), 3:367–446; G. W. Grogan, *Psalms* (Grand Rapids: Eerdmans, 2008), 17–18, 195–99.

17. Von Rad, *Theologie*, 1:365 (*Theology*, 1:367).

18. M. Dahood, *Psalms.* Vol. 3, *101–150* (AB, 17A; New York: Doubleday, 1970), 161–93.

19. Scott, *The Way of Wisdom*, 199–200.

20. D. Kidner, *Psalms 73–150* (TOTC; Leicester: InterVarsity, 1975), 417, 421.

prayer is particularly noticeable in this psalm, but not widespread in the rest of the Psalter.[21] Allen, followed by Day, notes hymnic praise throughout and a vow of praise at the end. In his opinion the beth strophe celebrates YHWH as the wisdom teacher *par excellence*, while the lamedh strophe expresses concern with order.[22] Bratcher and Reyburn emphasize joy as the dominant theme of the psalm, but do not elaborate upon this finding, except to say that it takes its origin from obedience to God's law, the source of life, wisdom, comfort and hope.[23] McCann's definition of Torah as instruction from YHWH underscores the comprehensive, summarizing aspect of law.[24]

Brueggemann, recognizing considerable overlap, distinguishes wisdom psalms from Torah psalms by noting that the former tend to be didactic in tone and are best identified by their subject matter, often comprising moral issues. Both are concerned with creation, retribution and general well-being. He classifies Ps 119 as a Torah psalm, noting that the good order of creation is expressed concretely, and understood as God's will and purpose, supporting the very fabric of life. Torah is the way to respond to, and to honour fully, God's well-ordered world. Brueggemann thinks that the intent of Ps 119 is didactic, that it has a dramatic intent, and that the form is commensurate with the message. For him, this is in keeping with the theme of order, thereby conveying utter symmetry and reliability. Torah is an active agent that gives life and is a mode of God's life-giving presence, the indispensable ingredient for enabling continued conversation with God. The keeping of Torah is obedience that initiates the seeking of God's attention and gifts. The psalm is "an articulation of legitimate expectation between partners who have learned to trust each other."[25]

Brueggemann deals thoroughly with the positive aspects of this psalm, but does not take into account other aspects that apparently are associated with lament; here are featured the success of the wicked, the persecution of the psalmist and his pleas for deliverance. In the very fibre of the psalm is an intense appeal for God to intervene, precisely because, for the psalmist, things are very wrong. According to Ps 119 there was no obedient attention by the wicked (within Israel) to the way God had ordered life. The psalm is not didactic at the human-to-human level.

---

21. Mowinckel, "Psalms and Wisdom," 212.
22. Allen, *Psalms 101–150*, 139–42; Day, *Psalms*, 56–57.
23. R. Bratcher and W. Reyburn, *Translator's Handbook on the Book of Psalms* (New York: United Bible Societies, 1991), 997.
24. McCann, "The Psalms," 117–20.
25. Brueggemann, *The Message of the Psalms*, 38, 40–42.

Similarly, given the anthological element, it is possible that the psalmist is using existing material, reworked and reworded, to indicate not only that things are very wrong, but that they have been so for a very long time, possibly throughout the history of Israel. And though Brueggemann states that Torah psalms are not expressly didactic (this quality distinguishing them from wisdom psalms in general), he then maintains that the intent of Ps 119 is in fact didactic. So, does this apparent contradiction indicate overlapping categories, or the ubiquitous fluid boundaries?

Soll observes that two of the most influential authors writing on wisdom psalms (Murphy and Kuntz) have excluded Ps 119 from this category.[26] Soll believes that this conclusion follows from the lack of didactic elements within the psalm (contra Allen, Brueggemann, Terrien and earlier commentators), maintaining that, structurally, the psalm adheres more to the forms of prayer and lament because, after the initial אשרי sayings, it addresses God directly. Soll does not consider the presence of such sayings to be an indication of wisdom literature per se (possibly they represent wisdom *elements* or *influence*, but as to their form they do not warrant the classification).[27] He also notes that, in proverbial sayings, there are general maxims about what makes a life good, particularly in the comparative sayings. However, in Ps 119 these sayings are not generalized, but are introduced by the first-person pronoun and are, therefore, internalized and personalized. He views this dynamic as an affirmation of the piety of the psalmist, a feature particularly associated with prayers and individual lament. From Soll's standpoint, the intent of the psalmist was neither to teach nor to expound Torah. He means that, although the various terms for Torah appear throughout Ps 119, the linking of Torah expressly with wisdom does not occur in the psalm (except perhaps in vv. 98–100). The psalmist's sole study is Torah. Soll suggests that "the 'wisdom' that Torah grants the psalmist is on a completely different plane from the wisdom available to 'teachers' and 'elders'."[28] This would harmonize with the statements that the psalmist makes regarding "understanding" (vv. 27, 34, 66, 98, 100 and 104). Soll attributes the dichotomy between the righteous and wicked more to the complaint of prayer and lament than to wisdom elements. Thus, although some wisdom elements certainly appear in the text, the extent of their influence on Ps 119 is, according to Soll, much less than is generally supposed. Since, in Soll's opinion, the presence of

26. W. Soll, *Psalm 119: Matrix, Form and Setting* (CBQMS 23; Washington, D.C.: Catholic Biblical Association, 1991), 116–17.
27. Ibid., 118–19, 123.
28. Ibid., 121.

wisdom forms and themes has failed to assert itself significantly, he reviews the presence of wisdom vocabulary. However, because he is inclined to the minimal stance advocated by Crenshaw, he limits himself to terms that are characteristic of a strictly defined wisdom corpus within the Hebrew Bible. Accordingly, he eliminates much vocabulary that is commonly associated with the biblical wisdom writings: חכם, ישר, צדק, עולה לב, ירא, דרך and ריב. On the other hand, Soll includes as wisdom vocabulary words such as עצה, דעת, פתיים, בין, זכה, and טעם, and, though noting affiliations with Deuteronomy, he is nonetheless convinced that Deuteronomy is not classified distinctly as wisdom literature. He concludes, with von Rad, Hermisson and others, that the instruction from YHWH for which the psalmist prayed is far superior to that communicated by human teachers, including those of his own community, thus reducing significantly the human element usually associated with wisdom. Further, although the presence of wisdom terminology is demonstrable, and even significant, it is secondary to the influence of lament in the psalm. Soll clearly states that the psalmist "appears conversant with technical wisdom terminology and…makes use of some of it." He recognizes that, although comparison with wisdom literature indicates something about the psalmist's cultural setting, it says nothing of why the psalm was written.[29]

Soll makes a telling point in his assertion that wisdom literature often manifests a didactic character, but that it does so in a distinctly pragmatic way, this particularly when related to daily living. Psalm 119, by contrast, is notable for its non-specific tone. It does not relate so much to the events of daily life but rather to life itself. Events are not mentioned. Additionally, in didactic literature a superior addresses an inferior. Nowhere in Ps 119 does this happen. Nowhere does God address the psalmist, nor does the psalmist address another human. The psalmist addresses God directly, or tells God about others (e.g. the blameless, enemies). Accordingly, either the second-person singular address (to God) or the third-person plural (describing others or their situations) is employed. The first-person form is used, but frequently as an object that further describes the circumstances (e.g. they are doing this "to me"); sometimes it is the subject (e.g. "I am a stranger," "My soul cleaves to the dust"), which is characteristic of lament. Though non-specific, the psalm is extremely personal.

Whybray does not deal directly with Ps 119 other than to note a few very obvious features: meditation on Torah; its placement immediately preceding the Songs of Ascent; the use of ירה (hiphil) with God as

29. Ibid., 123–25.

subject, originally predicated of wisdom teachers; the presence of למד
and בין; and, in order to dissent from it, Westermann's opinion that
Ps 119 may have concluded the Psalter. He classifies Pss 1 and 119 as
pure Torah psalms, suggesting that Ps 119 is a late addition to the
Psalter, added to provide instructional and devotional reading matter for
the individual. Overall, his discussion is helpful, but the cursory handling
of Ps 119 is striking, since some of the more marginal wisdom psalms—
Pss 8; 14; 53; 90 and 139—are given significant consideration. In
Whybray's treatment, as in that of many others, Ps 119 is often mentioned in the context of the study of other psalms with which it may
share some features.[30]

Summary

Opinions regarding wisdom literature in general, and wisdom psalms
specifically, tend to be inconsistent, in that they frequently ignore or
dismiss Ps 119, or note only superficial elements in it. The significance
of such opinions within the broader context of wisdom literature or the
study of the psalm itself is discussed little, if at all. Treatments of specific
wisdom elements in Ps 119 are somewhat more cohesive than studies of
the psalm as a whole, but they are gleanings at best, a dead end at worst.
There is a general consensus that the psalm falls broadly into the
category of wisdom literature, and specifically as a Torah psalm. There is
also general agreement regarding a number of its constituent wisdom
elements and motifs. Their presence is noted, but there is little discussion
of their significance, particularly in connection with other aspects of the
psalm, which may or may not be characterized as wisdom. Again, while
affinities with Pss 1 and 19 are noted, no firm conclusions are reached in
relation to their content. The more comprehensive treatments tend to
focus on one or two themes to the exclusion of other elements of the
psalm. Brueggemann is a primary example of this.

   Overall, the most thoughtful wisdom-related discussions have come
from Soll, Terrien and Brueggemann. Terrien classifies Ps 119 as a
wisdom/Torah psalm; Soll does not. Brueggemann emphasizes the
connection between creation and Torah, and the right relationship to
Torah as an expression of right relationship to creation. This is a highly

---

30. Whybray, *Reading the Psalms*, 36–87, and "Wisdom Psalms," 154, 157.
BDB lists occurrences of ירה (hiphil) in Pss 25:8, 12; 32:8; 45:5; 64:5, 8; 86:11,
making a total of seven besides Pss 27:11 and 119:33, 102. God as subject of ירה
occurs in Pss 25:8, 12; 27:11 (imperative); 32:8; 64:8; 86:11; 119:33, 102.

useful distinction whereby Torah psalms may be distinguished from wisdom psalms in general, and it provides a specific criterion for classification. Brueggemann astutely observes that Torah is the indispensable beginning of obedience to God; his affirmation of Torah's agency is vital to any understanding of Ps 119.

Additional Wisdom Elements

Additional aspects of Ps 119 may fall broadly into the wisdom category. First, there are elements of confession as expressions of faith that display an autobiographical style in their descriptions of the psalmist's circumstances as well as his actions and state (vv. 10–11, 19, 23, 26, 55, 62–63, 101–2, 121). In fact, at least once in each strophe there appears to be a verse of this type. "Autobiographical" is understood as referring to personal engagement with, and response to, that which constitutes wisdom, its teachings and instruction; the psalmist has both internalized wisdom and performed wise actions. The psalmist also prays that YHWH "execute judgment" (v. 84). Here are understandings of wisdom from which proceed wholesome actions (cf. Ecclus 51.13–30). This aspect is distinct from the autobiographical aspects of lament, which state the psalmist's personal situation, his feelings about it, and the actions of his enemies. Here there is usually no record of specific actions undertaken by the psalmist other than what may be implied by the vow of praise related towards the end of the psalm.

While there are few, if any, didactic elements at the human level, there is enormous emphasis upon YHWH's teaching and the response of understanding. This is clear from such verbs as ירה, למד, שכל and שׂיח, and the nouns דעת and טעם. This teaching/understanding does not appear to occur at the human-to-human level of interaction, but is asked, even demanded, directly of YHWH, as if he alone is capable of it (cf. Soll and Kidner above). It is inextricably bound up with Torah, as it is defined almost always by one of the legal terms. Forms of למד occur frequently with חקים, possibly indicating a perceived deficiency on the part of the psalmist regarding this aspect of the law. "My counsellors," אנשי עצתי, are mentioned, but with no further elucidation; Torah remains the supreme counsellor. References to elders and teachers are non-specific, occurring typically in a neutral context.

There is a pervasive sense of the universal and the infinite, particularly as applied to YHWH, his law and the psalmist's love for it, and all these are related to creation. Time/space words appear frequently (cf. the juxtaposition of קדם and לעולם in v. 152). The law is associated with the heavenly realm, and the earth is described as "established" because of it (vv. 89–91, 96).[31] The term נפלאות may be a sapiential expression of the excellence of divine instruction (v. 18).

A standard wisdom feature, the contrast between the righteous and the wicked, is more developed here than in most wisdom texts. This contrast is very sharply drawn between "I" (the psalmist) and "they" (his enemies/ the wicked). There is no gentle advice about theoretical situations, but urgent warnings concerning a present or imminent reality, a matter of life and death, founded directly upon the psalmist's past experiences. As opposed to the usual generalities of the psalm, this one aspect stands out as more personally and extensively developed, and may well (with Soll) be a product of lament, rather than wisdom. Although not strictly synonyms, there are several related designations for the psalmist's enemies: "those who persecute," "princes," "rulers," "wicked," "cursed," "those going astray," and possibly the "elders, aged" (v. 100), though the tone of this strophe (mem) is decidedly positive compared with that of the preceding strophe.

There is one saying with טוב that is clearly comparative (v. 72, the climax of the teth strophe), but there are a number of constructions with comparative מן "more than" (vv. 98–100 [half the mem strophe], 103 and 127: "more than my teachers," "more than my enemies"). These constitute some of the few times that the psalmist describes human-to-human interaction.

Wisdom Elements Not Present

Although Ps 119 is often classified as a wisdom psalm, it is useful to identify standard wisdom features *not* present in the psalm. These are as significant as the features that are present. There are no proverbs, riddles, stories, fables or allegories, analogies, or numerical sayings, although the numeral 8 is an essential schematic feature. There is no dialogue (as in Job), whether between one human and another, or between author and reader. There is no didactic element or teaching from father to son. There is no exhortation of others (cf. Ps 37); all speech is directed to YHWH, including meditations on the wonder of creation (cf. especially vv. 89–96). There are no lists, except for the 8+ legal terms that appear at intervals, and no personification of wisdom as a female figure. Nothing and no one is named except YHWH himself—no people, places, things,

---

31. A number of words denoting "firmness, establishment," per the roots כון, עמד, דור, יצב, עולם, קום, אמן, שמר, occur; see, e.g., the lamedh strophe.

animals or physical features ("dust," "pit," "heaven" and "earth" are references of a general kind).[32]

There is little if anything in the psalm that can be construed as moral teaching. The reflections on the meaning of life are restricted to the contrast between the innocence of the psalmist and the persecution by his enemies. They are specifically located in this time and this space, in what is immediately present; they are not related in a universal and timeless sense or manner. This contrast is reminiscent of that (in the dialogue especially) between Job and his friends, although here no names are given. As with Job, there are the sufferings of the psalmist and the demands for justice from YHWH, but, unlike Job, there are no divine speeches in Ps 119. The psalmist is not explicitly answered, though the vow of prayer and praise at the end, in the taw strophe, may suggest that some sort of answer was given.

There is no direct mention of cult, school or court. Unlike Qohelet, there is no ambiguity in the psalmist's relationship with YHWH, and little in the way of self-justification other than the recurring phrase לא אשכח, "I do not forget." There is no mention of death (though the psalmist's life is clearly in danger) or of familial relations (e.g. "my son"). There is no explicit mention of wisdom understood as skill, especially in the living of daily life. It is clear that some wisdom elements are missing, features that would be of primary interest at the human-to-human level. Does their absence imply that human-to-human dynamics are no longer as central as once they were? Or that human-to-God dynamics are severely diminished?

Conclusions

It is clear that Ps 119 eludes standard definitions, this even in a field as elusive as wisdom. It is also clear that research, in all aspects of wisdom study, has not identified a satisfactory method for defining wisdom psalms. Hurvitz, Day and Perdue offer useful criteria based on content, linguistic features and stylistic considerations. Whybray produces comprehensive treatments of several wisdom psalms, but offers little on Ps 119. Thus, while many scholars classify Ps 119 as an example of wisdom literature, there has been little explanation of the reasons for this judgment.

---

32. See C. V. Camp, *Wisdom and the Feminine in Proverbs* (Bible and Literature 11; Sheffield: Almond, 1985), 190–91, 196–97, 201.

This study concludes that vocabulary, form and content are the primary indicators for a wisdom classification. Yet the mere presence of these indicators is not enough to establish a definite classification of this sort. It appears, rather, to be a matter of how these terms are used, or of their influence within a particular work. Significantly, Weinfeld's study of wisdom terms in Deuteronomy may prove to be more telling, given the psalm's clear affinities with that book.[33]

Weeks's comment that Proverbs encourages certain ideals or patterns of behaviour, and assumes existing knowledge of them on the part of the readers, is significant.[34] Something similar applies in respect of Ps 119. Although the psalmist goes to great lengths to name the law and its related terms, these are summary, comprehensive terms, never specifically elucidated other than by their attendant verbs (e.g. "keep," "love," "delight in," "do not forget"). Other elements are repeated and specifically emphasized in Ps 119: the contrasting of the psalmist with the wicked, his requests couched in urgent tones (e.g. "teach," "preserve life"), terms for establishment and firmness, and various reminders of imminent danger contrasted with the psalmist's personal focus (e.g. "I delight in/I do not forget/I meditate"). While the situation at hand is clearly specific in the mind of the psalmist, the descriptive terms are deliberately general and comprehensive and, if not ambiguous, then perhaps intentionally left undeveloped.

The central questions remain: first, should Ps 119 be classified as a wisdom psalm, a Torah psalm, or neither? Secondly, if it is not a wisdom psalm or a Torah psalm, then how should it be categorized? And thirdly, to what extent do wisdom elements shape the psalm? Hymnic elements are present, but Ps 119 is not a hymn. The entire psalm acknowledges YHWH as the lawmaker, lawgiver, judge and counsellor. The didactic elements are not explicit, but implicit. Laws that should have been taught or learned appear not to have been. Hence the demand that YHWH himself teach (למד, piel) extraordinary knowledge, in such a way that the psalmist may learn and understand and be lifted higher. While the acrostic and the אשרי sayings have some association with wisdom literature, it is impossible to argue that their presence warrants a classification strictly in such terms.

---

33. M. Weinfeld, *Deuteronomy and the Deuteronomic School* (Oxford: Clarendon, 1972), 244–46, 255–74; in Deut 4:5–8 the laws of Torah are identified with wisdom.

34. Weeks, *Early Israelite Wisdom*, 86.

Prayer is a powerful motif throughout the psalm, as is lament. Although the psalm is variously understood as prayer, lament, or an expression of piety, these alone do not constitute satisfactory labels. There is much more to the psalm. The comparative sayings also provide a personal expression of matters usually associated with wisdom literature, though the מִן + טוֹב combination is notably absent here. The ideas and vocabulary of the psalm clearly indicate wisdom influence, but the lack of didactic elements, the presence of lament, and the direct second-person address to YHWH, as well as the distinct form of prayer, render the wisdom label most unlikely. There is too much else at work. The distinctive presence of some wisdom elements coupled with the absence of others points to the conclusion that, while wisdom is a definite feature of the psalm, such factors preclude simple wisdom classification. Perhaps the best solution, then, is to accord the psalm the specific description, a "Torah-prayer"—one of extraordinary intensity and scope. In this way the uniqueness of the great Ps 119 and its considerable affinities with wisdom literature are both recognized.

THE HILLS ARE ALIVE!
THE PERSONIFICATION OF NATURE IN THE PSALTER*

Hilary Marlow

1. *Introduction*

"The hills are alive with the sound of music," sings Julie Andrews, and, for some of us at least, the mind's eye is transported to a flower-filled alpine meadow, where children sing and play, and where, over the nearby mountain, lies the hope of a better future. Yet no one believes that the hills are really "alive" in the same way as a human being or a mountain goat or even a tree. Rather, the song-writer's personification of nature is a figure of speech, testifying to the vibrancy of the children's music-making echoing around the mountains and to the latter's significance in the story that follows. This study is concerned with the personification of nature, including mountains and hills, that is found in the Hebrew Bible, and especially the Psalter, in a variety of contexts. However, as we shall see, it is rather more difficult to determine to what extent and in what sense the biblical authors regarded these natural phenomena as "alive."

Even a quick glance at the poetic and prophetic material of the Hebrew Bible demonstrates that language personifying the natural world is found in a variety of forms and texts. Instances of personification range from the prophets' ambiguous description of the earth "mourning" on account of human transgression or YHWH's judgment (e.g. Isa 24:4; Jer 4:28; Hos 4:3),[1] to Deutero-Isaiah's call for the mountains to sing and the trees to clap their hands (Isa 55:12). They include two unequivocal examples of talking animals, the serpent of Gen 3 and Balaam's ass in Num 22, as well as Jotham's parable in which trees are given the power

* I am grateful to Dr. Diane Hakala and Dr. Deborah Rooke for their comments on an earlier draft of this study, and to Dr. Daniel Weiss for assistance with Rabbinic Hebrew.

1. See K. M. Hayes, *'The Earth Mourns': Prophetic Metaphor and Oral Aesthetic* (SBLABib 8; Atlanta: Society of Biblical Literature, 2002).

of intellect and speech (Judg 9). It will not be possible in this essay to do justice to this wide range of material. Instead, the present aims are three-fold: first, to offer a conceptual overview of the literary phenomenon of personification and how it has been understood by selected Bible commentators; secondly, to consider the claim by Michael Stone that the personification of nature differs significantly in post-biblical literature compared with the Hebrew Bible; and thirdly, to examine a number of texts from the Psalter that personify nature, in order to consider how personification functions in the text and why it is used in such an extensive manner.

2. *Personification in Literary and Biblical Analysis*

Defining "Personification"
The Oxford Dictionary of English defines personification as "the attri-bution of a personal nature or human characteristics to something non-human, or the representation of an abstract quality in human form."[2] A number of ancient treatises on rhetoric contain definitions of personi-fication (Greek *prosopopeia* or Latin *conformatio*),[3] an early example with particular clarity being the anonymous Latin work *Rhetorica ad Herennium*, dating from the late first century C.E. and formerly attributed to Cicero. This states that

> Personification consists in representing an absent person as present, or in making a mute thing or one lacking form articulate, and attributing to it a definite form and a language or a certain behaviour appropriate to its character... Personification may be applied to a variety of things, mute and inanimate.[4]

This short but dense passage encapsulates, according to James Paxson, "most of the connotations and subordinate varieties of personification to which rhetoricians after the Latin Golden Age attend."[5] Two features of the *Rhetorica ad Herennium* definition are of particular interest as far as this study is concerned: the inclusion of language or articulation (*eloquens*) as an aspect of personification, and the suggestion that the

2. C. Soanes and A. Stevenson, eds., *The Oxford Dictionary of English* (Oxford: Oxford University Press, 2003). Accessed via Oxford Reference Online (www.oxfordreference.com).
3. J. Paxson, *The Poetics of Personification* (Cambridge: Cambridge University Press, 1994), 8–34.
4. Cicero, *Rhetorica Ad Herennium* (trans. H. Caplan; LCL 403; Cambridge, Mass.: Harvard University Press, 1968), IV, 66.
5. Paxson, *Poetics of Personification*, 14.

speech or behaviour should be appropriate to the "character" (*ad dignitatem adcommodata*) of that personified. When it comes to the biblical material, in numerous instances it is the faculty of speech that is attributed to various natural elements; moreover, the connection between a subject and the manner of its personification has significance, as we shall see.

Paxson notes that it is only in the late Hellenistic and Roman periods, with their interest in rhetoric, that such clear definitions of personification are produced. It is perhaps less certain whether earlier periods in the ancient world regarded personification as a rhetorical device rather than, say, as the ascription of actual personhood (or divinity) to a nonhuman subject. However, Claudia Camp suggests that the literary trope of personification "is present in some of the earliest records of the human intellectual enterprise," although she adds by way of qualification: "This presence does not...always involve conscious use of it."[6] Her perspective is amplified by literary critic Bertrand Bronson, who maintains: "The personifying impulse, in whatever varying degrees of elaboration, is a radical tendency of the human psyche, embedded in the very roots of languages, basic to every impulse towards dramatic representation."[7]

Biblical Commentators and Personification

Jewish and Christian commentators across the centuries have explored the use of metaphorical language in biblical texts, without giving much attention to personification itself.[8] One interesting feature of such studies is the extent to which ideas concerning the purpose of biblical metaphor in early commentators resurface in the work of modern scholars many centuries later. A notable example is the Venerable Bede's study of rhetoric, *De schematibus et tropis*, in which he posits a schematic account of the trope "metaphor" as transfer,[9] and notes that the purpose of such a transfer is "either from necessity or for the sake of ornamentation" (*necessitatis aut ornatus gratia*), the latter reflecting the fact that

6. C. V. Camp, *Wisdom and the Feminine in the Book of Proverbs* (Bible and Literature 11; Sheffield: Sheffield Academic, 1985), 213.

7. B. Bronson, "Personification Reconsidered," *English Literary History* 14 (1947): 163–77 (166).

8. Exceptions include brief discussions in G. B. Caird, *The Language and Imagery of the Bible* (London: Duckworth, 1980), 136–37, and in A. Preminger and E. L. Greenstein, *The Hebrew Bible in Literary Criticism* (New York: Ungar, 1986), 160–63.

9. Bede, *Libri II De Arte Metrica et De Schematibus et Tropis. The Art of Poetry and Rhetoric: The Latin Text with an English Translation, Introduction and Notes* (trans. C. B. Kendall; Saarbrücken: AQ-Verlag, 1991), 168–69.

"the language of the Scriptures is sometimes found to be arranged, for beauty's sake, differently from the way common usage would dictate."[10] This distinction between the purpose of different kinds of metaphors is developed in recent treatments of biblical metaphor, most notably by Peter Macky, who distinguishes between metaphors that use well-known symbols to illuminate a subject that is mysterious and not easily understood ("prototypical metaphors"), and "ornamental metaphors" in which both subject and symbol are well known. The purpose of the latter, he suggests, "seems to be aesthetic, to catch the reader's attention, [and] provide a memorable image."[11] Like Bede, Macky makes no specific reference to personification, but the categories and distinctions introduced by these two scholars may be instructive in exploring texts later in this study.

A number of mediaeval Jewish commentators engage in extensive and detailed discussion of metaphor in their work, and at least one of these, Abraham ibn Ezra, gives specific attention to personification. It is perhaps not surprising, given these commentators' theological interest in maintaining the integrity and uniqueness of YHWH, that they seem primarily concerned with anthropomorphic language used of God, rather than with the personification of nature. Indeed, Maimonides devotes the first 49 chapters of his *Guide of the Perplexed* to this subject,[12] and David Kimchi takes great care to explain that God does not literally possess hands, or face or eyes, but that such phrases in Scripture are "all by way of *mashal* in order to help people understand."[13] For his part, Abraham ibn Ezra makes a clear distinction between the personification of non-human entities and anthropomorphic descriptions of God, and locates his discussion of these two tropes within a wider theory of language:

> There is no speaking [being] in the lower world except for man alone; also [the] listener is human, whom the speaker wishes to make understand what is in his heart. And [since] a rational being cannot create language except [from] that which is known and present (נמצא), all languages are based on the model of the human image.[14]

---

10. Ibid., 169.

11. P. W. Macky, *The Centrality of Metaphors to Biblical Thought: A Method for Interpreting the Bible* (Lewiston: Edwin Mellen, 1990), 65.

12. Moses Maimonides, *The Guide of the Perplexed*, with an Introductory Essay by L. Strauss (2 vols.; trans. S. Pines; Chicago: University of Chicago Press, 1963).

13. David Kimchi's *Commentary on Jeremiah*, cited in M. Cohen, *Three Approaches to Biblical Metaphor: From Abraham Ibn Ezra and Maimonides to David Kimchi* (Leiden: Brill, 2003), 206.

14. In his Exodus commentary, cited in ibid., 86.

He explains that human vocabulary is, of necessity, limited to that which is based on human experience, and that the "limitations of language" mean that inanimate objects must be spoken of in human terms:

> If [one] would like to speak about [beings] beneath human beings, he must "elevate" their status, and speak of them in human terms (lit. make them like the image of humans) in order for the listener to understand.[15]

Ibn Ezra's approach has much in common with the theory of metaphor developed in the 1980s by Lakoff and Johnson. They note that personification metaphors "allow us to make sense of the world in human terms— terms that we can understand on the basis of our own motivations, goals, actions and characteristics. Viewing something…in human terms has an explanatory power of the only sort that makes sense to most people."[16] Lakoff and Johnson suggest that the use of such metaphorical language is almost unconscious: "[it] is not poetic, fanciful or rhetorical; it is literal."[17] Similarly, for Ibn Ezra, according to Mordechai Cohen, personification, like anthropomorphism, "is a *necessary linguistic convention*… not an optional literary device employed for poetic or other purposes."[18] Interestingly, Ibn Ezra seems to go beyond this pragmatic understanding of personification in his commentary on Ps 19, in which he explains the conundrum of v. 3(4)[19]—"There is no speech, or language, nor are their voices heard"—in this way: "Scripture notes that a human being's wisdom can comprehend the truth that the heavens declare…by employing the vision of the corporeal eye and the perception of the eye of the inner soul."[20] For Ibn Ezra in this instance the use of personification serves to stress that both rational faculties and inner awareness are necessary to understand God's glory fully, perhaps hinting that there is an element of "hidden mystery" behind such language.[21]

---

15. Ibid., 86.

16. G. Lakoff and M. Johnson, *Metaphors We Live By* (Chicago: University of Chicago Press, 1980), 34.

17. Ibid., 5.

18. Cohen, *Three Approaches*, 92 (italics original).

19. Hebrew versification, where differing from the English text, is given in parentheses.

20. H. N. Strickman, *Abraham Ibn Ezra's Commentary on the First Book of Psalms: Chapter* [sic] *1–41* (Boston: Academic Studies, 2009), 145.

21. Ibn Ezra's approach is echoed by Rashi, who describes personification in his commentary on Ps 98:8 as speaking "in a language that the ear understands" (M. I. Gruber, *Rashi's Commentary on Psalms* [Leiden: Brill, 2004], 601).

Rhetorical Criticism
The substitution model for analysing metaphor adopted by Bede, and
implicit in Ibn Ezra's work,[22] can be found, with myriad variations, in
biblical commentaries across the centuries, and has only recently come
under scrutiny. One of the positive outcomes of this questioning of
traditional understandings of biblical language is rhetorical criticism,
defined by Patrick and Schult as "the means by which a text establishes
and manages its relationship to its audience in order to achieve a
particular effect."[23] Since James Muilenburg's seminal address to the
Society of Biblical Literature in 1968, there is renewed interest in the
interaction between speaker and audience, and in the dynamic potential
of a discourse both to act upon and to affect its hearers.[24] The means of
communication becomes as important as the content. Metaphor, rather
than being static, has a dynamic, performative function, and is capable of
being reinterpreted and reapplied in different contexts.[25] Understanding
personification in the light of this view of metaphor requires a subjective
act of judgment on the part of the hearer to transform the speaker's
words and create new conceptual frameworks. But such acts of judgment
can serve to constrain the impact of a text as well as to expand it, as we
shall see in the rationalistic explanations of the personification of nature
offered by some modern biblical scholars.

Summary
To summarize this section of our study: the phenomenon of personification in the Hebrew Bible is explained by scholars in a number of
ways. For some biblical commentators, ancient and modern, personification reflects the self-conscious use of a literary trope, whether for
aesthetic purposes or to reveal a hidden mystery by expressing it in
familiar language. For others, the use of personification metaphors is a
virtually unconscious act in order to fill linguistic gaps in terms that
make sense to human ears.[26] Finally, rhetorical approaches may suggest a
more dynamic, performative function for metaphor (and therefore for
personification) in the interplay between speaker and hearer. Following

22. Cohen, *Three Approaches*, 255–58.
23. D. Patrick and A. Schult, *Rhetoric and Biblical Interpretation* (JSOTSup 82;
Sheffield: Almond, 1990), 12.
24. Muilenburg's address was subsequently published as "Form Criticism and
Beyond," *JBL* 88 (1969): 1–18.
25. See K. Nielsen, *There is Hope for a Tree: The Tree as Metaphor in Isaiah*
(JSOTSup 65; Sheffield: JSOT, 1989).
26. Also known as catachresis; see J. M. Soskice, *Metaphor and Religious
Language* (Oxford: Clarendon, 1985), 61.

the discussion of selected psalms in Section 4 we shall reconsider these potential explanations, although it may be that the biblical authors will defy any attempts to categorize their use of language.

3. *Personification in Post-Biblical Literature*

Before looking at the selected psalms, there is one further issue to consider, namely, whether a distinction can be made between biblical and post-biblical literature as far as the personification of nature is concerned. This is the contention of Michael Stone in an essay on attitudes to nature in Second Temple Judaism.[27] Stone begins by noting that, in the literature of the Second Temple period, the workings of the natural world are regarded as paradigmatic of divine order and providence. In several places in *4 Ezra* the regularity of the natural order is conveyed by means of a number of images and parables of nature, in which "the comparison with the natural phenomenon serves to stress the fixed order of the world."[28] Stone cites other examples which, he maintains, suggest that the powers of nature are viewed as independent personalities and that "nature is the very best example of that which is regular, harmonious and orderly."[29] Thus, Ecclus 16:28 speaks of the created works of YHWH that "do not crowd one another and never disobey his word," and in *1 En.* 5:2 we read, "all his works serve him and do not change, but as God has decreed everything is done."

Stone maintains that this post-biblical perspective differs considerably from the Hebrew Bible where, although the natural world is appealed to and in some degree personified as a literary device, the various natural forces are not accorded separate or individual personalities, nor do they seem to have their own will or consciousness. The clear attribution of personality and will to natural elements in post-biblical literature is, he suggests, another example of the move from a radically demythologized view of time and space in pre-exilic Israelite religion to its partial re-mythologization in post-biblical literature:

> The idea of deities or demi-gods connected to natural elements surely has its roots in polytheistic world views. Such attitudes were vigorously combated in the First Temple period, precisely it seems, because of their

27. M. E. Stone, "The Parabolic Use of Natural Order in Judaism of the Second Temple Period," in *Gilgul: Essays on Transformation, Revolution and Permanence in the History of Religions. Dedicated to R. J. Zwi Werblowsky* (ed. S. Shaked, D. Shulman and G. G. Stroumsa; Leiden: Brill, 1987), 298–308 (307).
28. Ibid., 305.
29. Ibid.

polytheistic connotations. They resurge again in the Second Temple period...[they] never return, however, to a properly pagan form.[30]

Whether Stone is right to make such a clear distinction between biblical and post-biblical literature is debatable on a number of counts. First, he makes only passing reference to the Hebrew Bible and therefore clearly underestimates the number and range of texts that personify nature. Secondly, although he is undoubtedly correct that some of the biblical authors were concerned to counter polytheistic religion by demythologizing their material, the textual evidence is by no means clear-cut. As we shall see, several of the psalms seem little concerned to avoid ascribing speech and other faculties usually reserved for gods and human beings to the natural world. Thirdly, in the biblical material, nature is frequently appealed to as a source of order and regularity in the world, contrary to Stone's claim that this characteristic is unique to post-biblical literature. Finally, Stone makes an arbitrary and somewhat unsubstantiated distinction between personification as a literary device in the Psalter, and "the true attribution of...personality" to natural elements in the Second Temple literature.[31] This raises all kinds of questions about personification—what it is and what it does—to which we shall return.

4. *Personification in the Psalter*

In this section of the study we shall examine in more detail some biblical texts in which the natural world is personified to a greater or lesser extent. The decision to focus on the Psalter reflects the fact that its poetic form makes it a rich resource for examples of such language, with approximately 15 psalms containing material that might fall into the category of "personification of nature,"[32] while examples abound in other poetic and prophetic material as well.[33] Although, in some psalms, personification is merely alluded to or spoken of in passing, others offer an extended and fascinating insight into the author's use of language and theological perspective on the world, and it is these that will command

30. Ibid., 307; see also Michael Stone, "Three Transformations in Judaism: Scripture, History, and Redemption," *Numen* 32 (1985): 218–35.

31. Stone, "The Parabolic Use," 300.

32. I have identified the following: Pss 19, 50, 65, 66, 69, 76, 96, 97, 98, 100, 104, 121, 145, 148, 150. This includes psalms calling for praise from "all the earth," which may reasonably include the whole of creation. Equally as interesting, but outside the scope of the present study are those texts which use similes of animate creatures to describe inanimate elements (e.g. Pss 29:6; 114:4, 6).

33. A notable example is Isa 55:12.

most of our attention. The Psalms are notoriously difficult to date, and no attempt will be made to do so in what follows. The discussion is based on the assumption that the majority of the psalms formed part of the worshipping life of the post-exilic Yehud community, and that a number of them originated, at least in part, in the First Temple period. Unless otherwise specified, and as a tribute to Andrew Macintosh's knowledge and love of Biblical Hebrew, the English translation used will be that of the Liturgical Psalter, to which he was a major contributor.[34]

Personification and Polytheism

Our first consideration is Stone's inference that the few occurrences of personification in the Hebrew Bible may simply be a relic of ancient polytheistic belief in the divinity of natural phenomena, something not completely eradicated by biblical authors. Two texts in the Psalter may particularly support this contention, namely Pss 68:15–16(16–17) and 121:6, and we shall examine them in turn. Although it is rather fragmentary in nature, Ps 68 has as its overall theme the supremacy of YHWH—over his enemies (v. 1), over the natural elements (v. 8) and over the mountains (vv. 15–16[16–17]), the latter addressing the mountains in person. As an answer to the problem of the location of Mount Bashan in v. 15(16), there is much to commend John Emerton's suggestion that the verse be translated as a question:

> Is Mount Bashan a mountain of God,
> Many-peaked mountain, Mount Bashan?[35]

This sets up a contrast with the mountain of God in v. 16(17), and also parallels nicely the question addressed to the other mountains in the first part of that verse:

> O mountains of many peaks, why look so enviously
> at the mountain where God is pleased to dwell,
> where the Lord will remain for ever?

This striking rhetorical question undoubtedly has as its backdrop the notion, found in both Ugaritic and Mesopotamian mythology, of mountains as the dwelling places of gods.[36] What is less clear is whether the

34. S. P. Brock et al., *The Psalms: A New Translation for Worship* (London: Collins, 1977).

35. J. A. Emerton, "The 'Mountain of God' in Psalm 68:16," in *History and Traditions of Early Israel* (ed. A. Lemaire and B. Otzen; VTSup 50; Leiden: Brill, 1993), 24–37.

36. Similar ideas occur elsewhere in the Hebrew Bible, culminating in the Zion traditions of the exilic period (e.g. Ps 48:1–2[2–3]; Isa 2:2–4). See R. J. Clifford, *The*

personalized address indicates that the mountains themselves are regarded as deities or not. As in Canaanite mythology, it seems here too that the distinction between a god and his dwelling places remains blurred.[37] Yet the psalmist is not concerned with a need to remove allusions to polytheistic beliefs; rather, the personification of the mountains serves to contrast YHWH and his mountain with the other mountains/gods, and to affirm his supremacy over them.

The second text that might reflect a polytheistic background in its use of personification is Ps 121. This psalm offers a clear affirmation of trust in YHWH as protector and guardian of Israel, providing help that cannot be found by appealing to the hills (v. 1). The safeguarding "from all evil" that YHWH offers is made specific in v. 6: "the sun shall not strike you by day nor shall the moon by night." Although the picture conjured up by the sun "striking" (נכה, hiphil) may refer merely to the physical dangers of noonday heat (cf. Isa 49:10; Jonah 4:8), its pairing here with the moon suggests an echo of prevalent ancient Near Eastern beliefs in solar and lunar deities and their ability to cause harm, over which YHWH triumphs as the psalmist's all-powerful protector (cf. Isa 24:23).[38] In this psalm, then, as in Ps 68, although there may be hints of deification behind the personification of nature, the emphasis is on the supremacy of YHWH over cosmic phenomena, whether natural or divine.

Personification of the Cosmos: Psalm 19
The connection between the personification of nature and polytheistic beliefs, or at the very least the adaptation of polytheistic worship of nature, can be found in certain other psalms that speak of celestial bodies worshipping YHWH.[39] Some scholars argue that psalms such as Pss 19

Cosmic Mountain in Canaan and the Old Testament (Cambridge, Mass.: Harvard University Press, 1972).

37. Ibid., 58–64.

38. L. P. Maré, "Some Remarks on Yahweh's Protection against Mythological Powers in Psalm 121," in *Psalms and Mythology* (ed. D. J. Human; LHBOTS 462; New York: T&T Clark International, 2007), 178–80. Worship of the sun and moon is expressly forbidden in a number of Yahwistic texts (e.g. Deut 17:3; 2 Kgs 23:5; cf. Job 31:26). This prohibition contrasts with other texts that appear to ascribe solar qualities to YHWH (e.g. Ps 84:11[12]); see M. S. Smith, "The Near Eastern Background of Solar Language for Yahweh," *JBL* 109 (1990): 29–39 (30).

39. For example, Dahood suggests that Ps 19:1–6 is a Yahwistic adaptation of a Canaanite hymn to the sun; see M. J. Dahood, *Psalms 1–50: Introduction, Translation and Notes* (AB 16; New York: Doubleday, 1965), 121. See also H.-J. Kraus, *Psalms 1–59: A Commentary* (Minneapolis: Augsburg, 1988 [German orig. 1978]), 270. Another obvious psalm to include in the category of material adapted

and 65, with their description of solar bodies and the cycles of day and night praising YHWH, function to de-deify nature and emphasize that these cosmic elements are subject to YHWH, not deities alongside him.[40] But this seems strange given that these psalms attribute to the heavenly realms the power of speech (Pss 19:1–2; 65:8), a key aspect of personi-fication in *Rhetorica ad Herennium*.[41] If Stone's thesis were correct, a much clearer tactic for thoroughly removing any hint of the divine from these natural elements would be to depersonalize them. Even more intriguing, in the case of Ps 19, is the psalmist's awareness of the poten-tial problems created by such terminology. Although he self-consciously attributes the capacity for speech to the heavens (v. 1[2]), he also recognizes that this is perhaps an anomaly (v. 3[4]), and in the end offers no real answer to his own question; he merely affirms the part played by the cosmos in communicating to the furthest reaches of the world (v. 4[5]). One further point to note in this psalm is its concern for the maintenance of God-ordained order in the world, evident both in the regularity of the cosmos as the sun tracks its daily path (vv. 5–6[6–7]), and in human society, as Torah is honoured and obeyed (vv. 7–11[8–12]). The personification of nature presented here testifies to the cosmic order that both precedes and is to be mirrored by human moral rectitude, suggesting that such ideas are not confined to post-biblical texts such as Ecclus 16 and 17, as maintained by Stone.[42]

Let All Creation Praise: Psalm 148
Of particular interest are psalms that invoke the natural world in praise of YHWH alongside human beings, some of which contain very specific examples of personification. The end of the Psalter with its resounding conclusion "Let everything that has breath praise the Lord!" (Ps 150:6) represents probably the best known call to praise YHWH. The scope of this invocation is expanded in Ps 148, which more or less follows the sequence of creation in Gen 1, and includes inanimate as well as animate created matter in its scope. The listing of natural phenomena here and

from Canaanite hymnody is Ps 29, but this contains no explicit personification of nature.

40. P. C. Craigie, *Psalms 1–50: Introduction, Translation and Notes* (WBC 19; Waco: Word, 1983), 181; W. E. Barnes, *The Psalms with Introduction and Notes.* Vol. 1, *Psalms i–xli* (London: Methuen, 1931), 91.

41. Later in Ps 65, as in other psalms of praise, hills and valleys are invited to sing for joy (vv. 12–13); a similar feature is found in Isaiah (e.g. 35:1–2; 44:23; 49:13).

42. Stone, "The Parabolic Use," 301–2.

elsewhere in the Old Testament may, as von Rad suggests, have its origins in Egyptian onomastica,[43] but the function of this psalm is not to offer a catalogue of species. Rather, geological structures, natural elements, and various species of flora and fauna are woven together in a comprehensive survey of the created order, one that emphasizes the created status of both the heavens (vv. 1–6) and the earth and its contents (vv. 7–12), and which places praise of YHWH and his glory (v. 13) at the heart of creation's purpose and role. The psalmist is not concerned with explaining *how* inanimate elements such as fire (v. 8) and geological features such as mountains (v. 9) fulfil this mandate; his emphasis is rather that they, together with human beings, are called to praise YHWH. In this psalm, the personification of the natural world seems to perform the function of inclusion, incorporating the whole world, human and non-human, animate and inanimate, in the unified declaration הללו־יה, "Praise the Lord!"

Let the Rivers Clap their Hands: Psalms 96 and 98
Can the same be said of other invitations to praise that personify nature? We turn now to two texts that seem to attribute very specific human capacities to the natural world in response to YHWH, namely Pss 96 and 98. These kingship psalms, with their extended and detailed appeals to worship addressed to all creation, are by far the most interesting of this study.

Psalm 96 opens with a call to praise YHWH, one that immediately introduces a universal remit: "Sing to the Lord, all the earth" (v. 1b) and "Declare his glory among the nations" (v. 3a). The first part of the psalm undoubtedly refers to human populations addressed in the command: "Render to the Lord the honour due to his name, bring offerings and come into his courts" (v. 8). However, the possibility that the whole creation may be involved is hinted at by the use of "all the earth" in vv. 3 and 9.[44] The psalm reaches its climax in v. 10, with the pronouncement "The Lord is king" (יהוה מלך), affirming his role as judge over all peoples, and emphasizing the stability and permanence of the created

43. G. von Rad, "Hiob xxxviii und die altägyptische Weisheit," in *Wisdom in Israel and in the Ancient Near East* (ed. M. Noth and D. W. Thomas; Leiden: Brill, 1955), 293–301.

44. Other examples in the Psalter where כל־הארץ seems to indicate the whole created order include Pss 57:5(6), 11(12); 108:5(6). The use of חיל/חול "to whirl or dance" in 96:6 echoes the theophanic description in Ps 97:4, in which the appearing of YHWH affects the whole cosmos (see also Pss 29:9; 114:7). The theophanies of Ps 18:7(8) and Judg 5:4 use different vocabulary to convey similar ideas. Space prohibits discussion of these more negative portrayals of nature.

world under YHWH'S reign: "He has made the world so firm that it can never be moved."

It is in response to this climactic pronouncement of YHWH's sovereignty and the resulting stabilization of the earth that the natural world is invited to join the nations in celebrating his kingship and his anticipated coming as judge over all the earth:

> Let the heavens rejoice and let the earth be glad;
> let the sea roar, and all that fills it.
> Let the fields rejoice, and everything in them,
> then shall all the trees of the wood
> shout for joy before the Lord;
> For he comes, he comes to judge the earth;
> he shall judge the world with righteousness,
> and the peoples with his truth. (vv. 11–13)

The psalmist seems to connect YHWH's coming to establish order and justice among the nations with creation's capacity to worship. It is left deliberately ambiguous whether praise by the non-human creation is a *sign* of what YHWH will accomplish in human society as judge and king, or whether creation's voice can be heard as a *result* of this order and stability in the world. What follows is a very specific list of natural elements involved in this praise: the sea roars, fields rejoice and trees shout for joy (vv. 11–12). The personification in these verses is explained by commentators in a variety of ways, from the literal to the metaphorical. Those who are concerned with rational explanations take the ascription of speech to trees to indicate the production of some kind of sound, whether leaves rustling or branches scraping or even birds singing in the treetops.[45] Others view the extravagant and exaggerated language as symbolic representation of the importance of YHWH's coming.[46] None of these explanations is entirely satisfactory, and it is perhaps preferable to acknowledge the sense of wonder, even mystery, that such verses engender. What seems most significant is the close relationship between natural phenomena and YHWH, and the comprehensive extent of the proclamation of praise, which includes the whole created order and not just human society.

Psalm 98 differs only slightly from Ps 96 in that, in addition to the roaring of the sea, the rivers are exhorted to clap their hands and the

---

45. W. E. Barnes, *The Psalms with Introduction and Notes.* Vol. 2, *Psalms xlii–cl* (London: Methuen, 1931), 463.

46. E.g. M. Tate, who notes the symbolic importance of trees and tree metaphors in temple contexts (*Psalms 51–100* [WBC 20; Dallas: Word, 1990], 515).

mountains to sing their praise (vv. 7–8).[47] In contrast to contemporary society where hand-clapping as a form of applause almost always signifies approbation, it is a rather more unusual and ambiguous activity in the Hebrew Bible.[48] However, here in Ps 98 the context of joyful praise gives the phrase an uncharacteristically positive meaning. As is the case with Ps 96, some commentators try to explain the phenomenon in literalistic terms, as the sound of waves crashing on the shore or the turbulence created by two rivers converging.[49] Interestingly, Ibn Ezra offers two very different interpretations. His explanation of Ps 96:12 is naturalistic: the earth giving forth its produce and the field its fruit. Likewise the sea roaring in v. 11 signifies the clouds of spray rising up from it.[50] This contrasts with his anthropocentric interpretation of Ps 98:8 as human beings praising God: "The sons of men from the ships of the sea and the rivers, and on the mountains, will give a joyous cry."[51] This lack of consistency highlights the difficulties he faced in trying to interpret these texts, and suggests that, although he crafted his own definition of personification, this was by no means sufficient for explaining the phenomenon in the texts themselves.

47. See also Isa 55:12, where mountains and hills sing and the trees clap their hands. For discussion of the relationship between Deutero-Isaiah and Pss 96 and 98 (and other kingship psalms), see H.-J. Kraus, *Psalms 60–150: A Commentary* (trans. H. C. Oswald; Minneapolis: Augsburg, 1989 [German orig. 1978]), 263–64, and M. Buttenwieser, *The Psalms: Chronologically Treated with a New Translation* (New York: Ktav, 1969), 326–32. The relationship between these texts may be complicated by the repetition of part of Ps 96 (and Ps 105) in 1 Chr 16. As with all questions of intertextuality, the level and direction of dependence is open to debate.

48.   Several different verbs are used with כף or יד to denote hand-clapping, but it is only rarely a positive activity, e.g., in 2 Kgs 11:12 (נכה) and Ps 47:1(2) (תקע). Elsewhere the expression "clap hands" has negative connotations denoting derision and mockery (e.g. Ezek 6:11 [נכה]; 25:6 [מחא]; Nah 3:19 [תקע]; Job 27:23; 34:37; Lam 2:15 [ספק]).

49.   A. Cohen, *The Psalms: Hebrew Text and English Translation with an Introduction and Commentary* (London: Soncino, 1958), 321; F. Delitzsch, *Biblical Commentary on the Psalms* (3 vols.; London: Hodder & Stoughton, 1889), 3:63.

50.   R. Abraham ibn Ezra, מקראות גדולות, vol. 10 (New York: Pardes, 1951).

51.   Rashi also treats these two texts differently, interpreting the trees of the forests in Ps 96:12 allegorically as "all the rulers of the Gentiles" (Gruber, *Rashi's Commentary*, 597), but emphasizing that the rivers clapping in Ps 98:8 "is rather a metaphor for happiness and joy" (p. 601).

5. *Conclusion*

It has proved relatively easy to demonstrate that, *pace* Michael Stone, personification of nature occurs frequently in the Hebrew Bible and seems unlikely to be an overlooked relic of polytheistic religious beliefs. The psalmists do not seem overly concerned to select language that "radically demythologizes" nature, and the attribution of human faculties, in particular speech, to non-human entities does not seem to disturb them. However, their focus is on YHWH as creator, sustainer and deliverer; the whole creation, human and non-human, animate and inanimate, is called upon to respond in praise and worship. In this respect, then, these psalms "de-divinize" the natural world. This suggests, contrary to Stone, that the personification of natural elements is distinct from deifying them.

It has also been shown that the biblical material anticipates post-biblical literature in connecting the orderly and harmonious working of the world with the behaviour of natural elements. The personification of the natural elements seems an important part of their function of affirming YHWH's supremacy and highlights their unique place in the created world over which he rules. However, despite the attempts by scholars to define personification and the variety of interpretations offered for the texts we have considered, more precise explanations of the phenomenon remain elusive. Since the subject matter—the natural world—is seemingly well known, should we think with Macky (and Bede) of "ornamental" language designed to grab attention and be memorable? These psalms certainly have that effect. Or does the personification fall into Macky's category of "prototypical" metaphor, symbolizing a hidden mystery concerning the workings of the world and God's relation to it? Perhaps, as Lakoff and Johnson (and Ibn Ezra) maintain, such language is necessary and literal—a way of explaining the world in human terms. Yet the personification we have encountered offers an explanation of reality that is profoundly ambiguous, and one that defies rational explanation. The psalmists' willingness to embrace this ambiguity suggests their awareness that relationship between creator and creation has profound theological implications and is rather more mysterious than our modern rationalistic minds would allow.

BIBLICAL TEXTS IN NEW CONTEXTS:
THE BOOK OF JOB IN THE ENGLISH CHORAL TRADITION

Katharine J. Dell

I am pleased to write this essay for the honorand of this volume, Andrew Macintosh.[1] Approaching the subject of musical renditions of Job was in part inspired by the thought that he has had the rare privilege, by virtue of being for many years Dean of St. John's College, Cambridge, of hearing the world famous St. John's choir almost every day. Whether they have ever performed the music I will be discussing here, given its relative obscurity, is another matter…

The book of Job has long been an inspiration to musicians,[2] and the very full bibliography in David Clines's commentary on Job[3] lists 145 compositions by composers of all nationalities and from all periods of history. Looking at this list, it is noteworthy that, in relation to the passages of Job that are actually used, virtually all are from the dialogue section (chs. 3–31) and within that the majority of passages are words

---

1. I would also like to mention that I have a personal connection with Andrew in that he was taught at Ridley Hall Theological College in Cambridge by my father, Robert Dell. My father's speciality, though, was church history, not Biblical Hebrew!

2. Furthermore, the character of Job was, from mediaeval times, associated with music, based on a tradition in the *Testament of Job* that Job threw worms from his body to pay the musicians who played to him to cheer him up and that the worms turned into gold rings. There is a considerable literature on Job as a patron of music, e.g. W. Brennecke, "Hiob als Musikheiliger," *Musik und Kirche* 24 (1954): 257–61; K. Meyer, 'St. Job as a Patron of Music," *The Art Bulletin* 36 (1954): 21–31; H. Seidel, "Hiob, der Patron der Musiker," in *Alttestamentlicher Glaube und Biblische Theologie: Festschrift für H. D. Preuss zum 65. Geburtstag* (ed. J. Hausmann and H.-J. Zobel; Stuttgart: Kohlhammer, 1992). On the *Testament of Job* tradition see L. L. Bessermann, *The Legend of Job in the Middle Ages* (Cambridge, Mass.: Harvard University Press, 1979).

3. D. J. A. Clines, *Job 38–42* (WBC 18B; Nashville: Thomas Nelson, 2011), 403–10.

spoken by Job himself.[4] Apart from these, there is one piece featuring words by each of Eliphaz (Maurice Greene's anthem using Job 22:21–30; see discussion below), Bildad (Johann Sebastian Bach's use of Job 8:9 ["Unser Leben ist ein Schatten"] in a motet) and Zophar (Juan Vasquez, a Spanish composer, using Job 20:18–22 for one of a number of motets based on Job), a number based on words of Elihu ("Responde mihi") in Job 33:5 (Juan Esquival de Barahona, Estevao de Brito, Sebastien Brossard, Josquin Des Prez, Juan Vasquez), one anthem based on the wisdom poem in Job 28, notably v. 12 (William Boyce—see below) and one piece based on the words of God from the whirlwind (Job 38:12, by the American composer, Randall Thompson). Also featured in the pieces of a number of composers are the two passages attributed to Job in the Prologue, Job 1:21 and 2:10. Indeed, Job 1:21 is one of three passages that belong to the funeral sentences in the Anglican church liturgy, together with Job 14:1–2 and Job 19:25–27, and so all three are widely used in that context.

I am interested, in the present study, in the way that passages from Job are used in musical contexts, specifically here in the English choral tradition. Some compositions are wholly based on Job texts. Others use phrases from Job within larger works. There is often a "Christianizing" agenda in the use of selected texts, often translated in such a way as to fit in with other major Christian texts or key theological motifs. There is already quite a considerable literature on the use of Job in the famous German composers,[5] such as Bach and Brahms,[6] and so, in the interests

---

4. Job 7:16–21 is particularly popular and this choice is interesting as it is one of the passages where the technique of parody is clearly used; see K. J. Dell, *The Book of Job as Sceptical Literature* (BZAW 197; Berlin: de Gruyter, 1991), Chapter 3.

5. See the very full discussion in M. Heymel, "Hiob und die Musik: Zur Bedeutung der Hiobgestalt für eine musikalische Seelsorge," in *Das Alte Testament und die Kunst: Beiträge des Symposiums "Das Alte Testament und die Kultur der Moderne" anlässlich des 100. Geburtstags Gerhard von Rads (1901–1971), Heidelberg, 18.–21. Oktober 2001* (ed. J. Barton, J. C. Exum and M. Oeming; ATM 15; Münster: Strube, 1999), 129–63. Heymel mentions the orchestral work by the English composer Ralph Vaughan Williams, *Job: A Masque for Dancing*, but he does not consider English choral music that uses Job texts as I shall do here.

6. See C. Cebulj, "Warum? Ijob zwischen Händel und Brahms," *Katechetische Blätter* 130 (2005): 427–45, on Bach and Brahms. The author interestingly suggests that Brahms was deliberately parodying the *Trauermusik* of the time in a piece based on Job 3:20–33. The subversion is clear in the way no christological text is used, and "the heart" replaces Christ as the central motif, although even that is missing from the key New Testament text that is used (Jas 5:11). The cultural hero, Bach, is deliberately recalled at the end of the piece rather than any reference being made to Christ, which gives the whole a rather secular feel. It seems that the book of Job invites parody at all levels, not only at that of the original text, but by interpreters also.

of limitation, I have decided to focus on the less well known body of choral music in the English-speaking world.[7]

The Burial of the Dead

Verses from the book of Job feature prominently in the Anglican liturgy for the Burial of the Dead—indeed, there are more verses from Job than from any other single biblical book. Job 19:25–27, 1:21 and 14:1–2 appear in that order. The opening sentences of the burial service contain John 11:25–26 followed by Job 19:25–27 and then by a conflation of 1 Tim 6:7 and Job 1:21. These first two passages formed part of the Catholic offices of the dead,[8] being an Antiphon and a Respond from Matins and Lauds, hence well known in monastic daily devotions too. The latter conjunction is original to Cranmer and is interesting in the way that it combines the reflections that we came into the world with nothing and that we can take nothing away with us, a sentiment that precedes the verse that is cited but not used—"Naked came I out of my mother's womb and naked shall I return thither" (Job 1:20).[9] Instead, a similar sentiment is chosen from a New Testament text and then joined with this sentiment from the prologue of Job before his main diatribe begins. One wonders about the motivation for this choice; perhaps a need was felt to keep some kind of balance between Old and New Testament citation. After these verses a psalm is usually sung. Interestingly, Ps 39, which is often aligned with Job as a wisdom psalm, is one choice; Ps 90, a lament but also with wisdom elements in the middle section (vv. 3–12), is the other. The lesson is then taken from 1 Cor 15:20–58 and it is not until the graveside itself that the first sentiment is from Job 14:1–2, "Man that is born of a woman hath but a short time to live, and is full of misery. He cometh up, and is cut down, like a flower; he fleeth as it were a shadow, and never continueth in one stay." The use of this verse at this point is known from the Sarum "Dirige." This is immediately followed by some

---

7. I had the intention of including the quite extensive oratorio tradition of using Job (notably, William Russell, Edmund Chipp, C. Hubert H. Parry, David Jenkins, Peter Maxwell Davies), rather a later development than the choral works treated here, but that proved too major a discussion to include in this essay and will be published elsewhere. The first part of this work on Russell, Chipp and Parry will be published under the provisional title "The Book of Job in Nineteenth-Century British Oratorio."

8. On the Roman Catholic liturgy of the dead, see J. Dowdall, "The Liturgy of the Dead," *The Furrow* 8/10 (1957): 617–30.

9. I am using the King James Version of the Bible for quotations throughout this essay because that is the text most used by the composers whom I will be considering, and because it is used in the 1662 *Book of Common Prayer*.

sentences known as the "Media Vita," thought to have been composed by Luther but taken by Cranmer from Hermann's "simple and Religious Consultation" and Coverdale's "Goostly Psalmes."[10] Philippians 3:21 completes the committal section with the hope of resurrection, followed by Rev 14:13, which is the last of the scriptural passages cited. The collect is based on John 11:25–26, with which the service started.

The service, the beginning of which I have outlined here, is that of the 1662 prayer book. What is often forgotten is that the prayer book was first written, in 1549, by Thomas Cranmer and there are some significant differences between this early version and its later standard counterpart.[11] It is interesting that the "Edwardian" 1549 version contained a eucharistic celebration and petitions for the deceased, both of which had been cut out not only by 1662 but before that in an interim prayer book of 1552[12] and in that of 1559, promulgated by Queen Elizabeth I on her succession. It is often thought that the more purgatorial theology of the Catholic liturgy was given a new emphasis by Cranmer in the direction of the certain hope of resurrection. There was also a leaning in a more Protestant direction overall.

The opening sentences are the same in both versions, although there are small changes of wording, which are of interest to a biblical scholar. The 1662 version of John 11:26 reads "whosoever liveth and believeth in me, shall never die," following the KJV, while the 1549 contains "whosoever liveth, and believeth in me, shall not die for ever" (arguably following the Greek εις τον αιωνα, "unto the age," more closely). Sheppy[13] argues that the 1549 version is a more explicit reference to the "second death" of Rev 2:11 and Matt 10:28 which was subtly amended by the 1662 liturgists, although he notes that one cannot really know the thinking behind such changes. Turning to Job 19, the 1662 version includes the reference to worms eating the body, as KJV, which had not featured in the 1549 edition. The 1549 wording is "I know that my redeemer liveth, and that I shall rise out of the earth in the last day, and shall be covered again with my skin, and shall see God in my flesh; yea, and I myself shall behold him, not with other but with the same eyes." Another key difference is that "I shall rise out of the earth in the last day," a clear reference to the individual resurrection of the deceased

---

10. See G. Rowell, *The Liturgy of Christian Burial: An Introductory Survey of the Historical Development of Christian Burial Rites* (London: SPCK, 1977), 79–80, for its history.

11. See discussion in ibid., Chapter 5, and in P. Sheppy, *Death, Liturgy and Ritual: A Commentary on Liturgical Texts*, vol. 2 (Aldershot: Ashgate, 2004).

12. See Rowell, *The Liturgy*, Chapter 5.

13. Sheppy, *Death, Liturgy and Ritual*, 28–29.

person, is replaced in the 1662 version by "he shall stand at the latter day upon the earth," clearly referring to "my Redeemer." The 1549 follows the Vulgate here, whilst the 1662 version reveals the work of English translators and is the same translation as found in the KJV. It is thought that a possible Puritan influence at the time favoured the idea of the resurrection of all on the last day over the idea of individual resurrection. Another slight variant is in the citation of Job 1:21, where the 1549 version has "The Lord giveth and the Lord taketh away. Even as it pleaseth the Lord, so cometh things to pass; blessed be the name of the Lord," thus adding the middle sentence "Even as it pleaseth the Lord, so cometh things to pass," following the Septuagint rather than the shorter version of 1662 (which follows the KJV and MT).

In a Christian context the Redeemer is assumed to be Christ, although we know that in the original context of Job the identity of the גאלי is a much more complex issue.[14] The translation "after my skin" for ואחר עורי (v. 26a) points towards an afterlife, "after my skin worms destroy this body" (KJV), as does the rendition of "outside/without my flesh" for ומבשרי (v. 26b, so NRSV), though other alternatives do not (the 1549 suggests a "re-covering" with skin at the last day).[15] "In my flesh" for ומבשרי (KJV), however, suggests some continued bodily presence. This is another well discussed translation problem in the book of Job. It is interesting that the *Book of Common Prayer* (*BCP*) citation of Job 19:27 ends mid-verse, so that the rest of the verse, "though my reins be consumed within me" (KJV), does not feature. The conflation of 1 Tim 6:7 and Job 1:21 is the work also of the 1662 *BCP*; 1549 puts them together but not in the same paragraph. The wording used for Job 14:1–2 is not from the KJV but is a paraphrase, possibly from the Sarum "Dirige."[16]

---

14. It is debated, for example, what exactly Job is calling for here. Is he asking for an intermediary to adjudicate between him and God or is the "redeemer" another way of referring to God himself?

15. Another rendition of this verse is well known from Handel's *Messiah* (Handel might just qualify as an English composer since he lived in England for much of his life). Here the translation "though worms destroy this body, yet in my flesh shall I see God" (KJV with omission of "after my skin") suggests the rotting of the physical body but still maintains a fleshly dimension in the subsequent "view" of God. This verse, coming at the beginning of Part 3 of the work, is placed in the context of a celebration of resurrection. It is thought that the texts were chosen by the librettist, Charles Jennens, to underline the stubbornness of the Jews in not realizing the messianic dimension of their own scriptures.

16. The Sarum rite was a Latin liturgy developed in Salisbury in the thirteenth century and widely used in England.

When we come on to the composers that were to set these words to music, the different versions of the prayer book must have made the task more complex. There were a number of composers from this period of the formation of the prayer book who took it upon themselves to write music to accompany parts of the burial service. So we find all the scriptural passages set to music as well as other parts of the service such as the "Media Vita." Thomas Tomkins (1572–1602) wrote his Burial Sentences set to the 1549 service. In the original he chooses not to write out every word, but assumes that the words are known.[17] The opening words from John 11 form the first three stanzas, followed by Job 19 in the next five. He uses the version "I shall rise" but then uses an etcetera sign for the rest of v. 25, beginning with words again at "yea and I myself shall behold him, not with other, but with the same eyes." This is followed by the verse from 1 Timothy and then by the Job sentiment with only chosen words written out: "The Lord giveth etc....so cometh things to pass etc...blessed." The text from Revelation, "I heard a voice from heaven," follows to round off the piece under the liturgical note "After the interment." Tomkins does a four-part setting for mean, countertenor, tenor and bass, and uses the key of F minor.[18]

Thomas Morley (1557–1602), composing at the same time, would also have been familiar only with pre-1662 versions, although his editors have revised the score to fit the 1662 model. He uses the key of G minor in a four-part anthem with the same sequence of texts. Composers subsequent to these two who wrote settings for parts of the burial service include William Croft (1678–1727) and William Boyce (1711–79) and both are based on the 1662 service. Croft writes in G minor in slow and solemn mode, again a four-part piece. A setting of Job 14:1–2 is also included in the key of C minor followed by the "Media Vita." Croft also wrote a setting for the text from Revelation in G minor. In the edited version in my possession, Purcell's "Thou knowest Lord" has been inserted amongst the Croft material, presumably for completeness. Boyce chooses to write in four parts also, but in the key of E minor. The funeral sentences are there followed by Job 14:1–2 and the "Media Vita" in exactly the same by now well known formation of texts. Novello made

17. This is not so in the version of the piece in the *Musica deo Sacra*, 4 (Early English Church Music 27; London: Stainer & Bell, 1982), 119–31, edited by Bernard Rose, where the words are written out in full under the music.

18. I am aware that church composers of this period often used modes rather than keys in the modern sense. However, we have all these pieces in edited versions that do feature key signatures and it is these that I am following when I mention the particular key of a piece.

a comment in his 1855 edition of the Anthems of William Boyce on Boyce's rendition of the burial service as follows: "Of this extremely rare Service, the only known Copy is the one preserved in Page's 'Harmonia Sacra,' published after the death of Dr. Boyce. From its dignified simplicity and pathetic solemnity of style, it deserves to be much more generally known and more frequently brought forward." Clearly, it was rarely used or known, even in the nineteenth century!

Anthems based on sentences from the burial service went on to inspire.[19] Purcell's famous setting of "Man that is born of a Woman," four parts in C minor, composed 1680–82 is a case in point. He also wrote music to the words of the "Media Vita"—"In the midst of life…" and "Thou knowest Lord…"[20] Similarly there is the anthem of Samuel Sebastian Wesley (1810–1876) on the Job 14 text, also in C minor and in four parts for SATB.[21] These pieces are uniformly slow, solemn and ponderous as befits the occasion of a funeral; they are all in minor keys with considerable use of semibreves.

Paraphrases of Job Texts in the Songs of Purcell

Henry Purcell (1659–95) found inspiration in the book of Job for settings of various of his songs. We have already considered his "Man that is born of a woman" in the context of the burial service, but, interestingly, he wrote another piece based on the same text, beginning at the sentiment "of few days and full of trouble" (Job 14:1b KJV). In this song and in the other pieces based on Job there is a heavy paraphrasing of the text to make it rhyme in verse (cf. hymn forms of psalms). The text of "Ah! Few and full of sorrow" is classified as a song for four parts, with the provision that the second part can be either alto or tenor (and in E minor). It was composed c. 1680. It reads as follows (omitting repeats), and I am placing below it the passages from Job on which the paraphrase is based.

19. C. L. Seow in a paper on interpreting Job 14 with attention to different musical renditions draws attention to a piece by the English madrigalist John Willbye (1574–1638) based on 14:1–2, a text widely known through the funeral service, but set to music outside that context too. See C. L. Seow, "Hope in Two Keys: Musical Impact and the Poetics of Job 14," in *Congress Volume: Ljubljana 2007* (ed. A. Lemaire; VTSup 133; Leiden: Brill, 2010), 495–510. I am grateful to Dr. Seow for drawing my attention to his work.

20. Purcell's completed Funeral Sentences were composed for the funeral of Queen Mary in 1695, including a reworking of his earlier "Man that is Born of a Woman."

21. Not all these settings of the burial service are for SATB, for example that of Hugh Blair (1862–1932) who wrote his for treble voices only.

Ah! Few and full of sorrow are the days of man from woman sprung.

He like an empty shadow glides away, and all his life is but a winter's day.

Wilt thou thine eye before a vapour bend or with so weak an opposite contend?

Who can a pure and crystal current bring from such a muddy and polluted spring?

Oh, oh, since his days are number'd, since thou hast prescrib'd him bounds that are not to be passed.

A little with his punishment dispense. Till he have serv'd his time and part from hence.

Oh oh, that thou woulds't conceal me in the grave, immure with marble in that secret cave.

Until the tempest of thy wrath be past; a time prefix and think of me at last!

I will expect until my change in death and answer at thy call.

Job 14

[1] Man that is born of a woman is of few days, and full of trouble.

[2] He cometh forth like a flower, and is cut down: he fleeth also as a shadow, and continueth not.

[3] And dost thou open thine eyes upon such an one, and bringest me into judgment with thee?

[4] Who can bring a clean thing out of an unclean? not one.

[5] Seeing his days are determined, the number of his months are with thee, thou hast appointed his bounds that he cannot pass;

[6] Turn from him, that he may rest, till he shall accomplish, as an hireling, his day.

[13] O that thou wouldest hide me in the grave, that thou wouldest keep me secret, until thy wrath be past, that thou wouldest appoint me a set time, and remember me!

[14] If a man die, shall he live again? all the days of my appointed time will I wait, till my change come.

This is a very free paraphrase of the Job text. The text is said to be by George Sandys. The sentiment of flowering and then being cut down in Job 14:2 is omitted in favour of the second part of the verse comparing death to the passing of a shadow, which is represented in the sentiment that "all his life is but a winter's day." The lack of flowers in winter perhaps suggested this image to the paraphrast. The sentiment of shadow or vapour in this case is then cleverly continued in the song, a feature not in the original Job text, although the sense of the Job original still comes across. The paraphrase also brings in the idea of springs and water, a feature not in the original; it is as if the paraphrast is wishing to make the images more concrete. The idea of punishment is also explicitly mentioned, an idea suggested in the Job text but not expressed. The sense, however, remains much the same, which is the genius of a paraphrase. We then jump a few verses of Job to the sentiment of wishing to be hidden in the grave until God's anger has passed. Again the paraphrase inserts the concrete image of marble in a cave, containing an overtone of the idea of a tomb. The final line gives a hint of an afterlife, arguably contained in the original, but more explicit in the paraphrase.

Another work of Purcell is the song for solo voice, "Let the night perish: Job's Curse," based on Job 3. It is interesting that it has the subtitle of "Job's Curse," acknowledging its source of inspiration. This was composed in 1688 in the key of C minor and the text is a paraphrase by Jeremy Taylor.

> Let the night perish. Cursed be the morn wherein 'twas said: there is a man child born!
> Let not the Lord regard that day, but shroud its fatal glory in some sullen cloud.
> May the dark shades of an eternal night exclude the least kind beam of dawning light;
> Let unborn babes, as in the womb they lie, if it be mentioned, give a groan and die;
> No sounds of joy therein shall charm the ear,
> No sun, no moon, no twilight stars appear
> But a thick veil of gloomy darkness wear.
> Why did I not, when first my mother's womb discharg'd me thence,
> Drop down into my tomb?
> Then I had been as quiet, and mine eyes had slept and seen no sorrow;
> There, there the wise and subtle counsellor, the potentate,
> Who for themselves built palaces of state
> Lie hush'd in silence; there's no midnight cry caus'd by oppression and the tyranny of wicked rulers; there, there the weary cease from labour, there the pris'ner sleeps in peace;
> The rich, the poor, the monarch and the slave
> Rest undisturbed and no distinction have within the silent chambers of the grave.

Job 3

[3] Let the day perish wherein I was born, and the night in which it was said, There is a man child conceived.

[4] Let that day be darkness; let not God regard it from above, neither let the light shine upon it.

[5] Let darkness and the shadow of death stain it; let a cloud dwell upon it; let the blackness of the day terrify it.

[7] Lo, let that night be solitary, let no joyful voice come therein.

[9] Let the stars of the twilight thereof be dark; let it look for light, but have none; neither let it see the dawning of the day:

[11] Why died I not from the womb? why did I not give up the ghost when I came out of the belly?

¹³ For now should I have lain still and been quiet, I should have slept: then had I been at rest,

¹⁴ With kings and counsellers of the earth, which built desolate places for themselves;

¹⁷ There the wicked cease from troubling; and there the weary be at rest.

¹⁸ There the prisoners rest together; they hear not the voice of the oppressor.

¹⁹ The small and great are there; and the servant is free from his master.

In this paraphrase there is more omission of verses from Job (vv. 6, 8, 10, 12, 15, 16). Of particular note is the emphasis on the night in the first line of the song (day and night are mentioned in Job itself) but then the mention of day in the next line. Then there is the surprising addition in the paraphrase of the image of unborn babies preferring to die rather than to hear of that day/night. This is not in the original text but it has overtones of Job 3:16 that is omitted later on: "Or as an hidden untimely birth I had not been, as infants which never saw light."

The final song from Purcell's pen, based on a paraphrase of Job is "O I'm sick of life," composed c. 1680 for men's voices, tenor 1, tenor 2 and bass in the key of C minor. This is a paraphrase of Job, the text again by George Sandys. It is based around Job 10.

O, I'm sick, I'm sick, O, I'm sick of life!
Nor will control my passion, but in bitterness of soul thus tear the air:
What should thy wrath incense to punish him who knows not his offence?
Ah! Dost thou in oppression take delight?
Wilt thou thy servant fold in shades of night and smile on wicked counsels?
Dost thou see with eyes of flesh?
Is truth concealed from thee?
What, are thy days as frail as ours?
Or can thy years determine like the age of man that thou shouldst my delinquencies enquire
And with variety of tortures tire?
Cannot my known integrity remove thy cruel plagues?
Wilt thou remorseless prove?
Ah! Wilt thou thine own workmanship confound?
Shall the same hand that did create now wound?
Remember, remember, I am built of clay and must resolve to my originary dust.
O, since I have so short a time to live, a little ease to these my torments give
Before, before I go where all in silence mourn
From whose dark shores no travelers return.
A land where death, confusion, endless night and horror reign, where darkness is their light.

Job 10

[1] My soul is weary of my life; I will leave my complaint upon myself; I will speak in the bitterness of my soul.

[2] I will say unto God, Do not condemn me; shew me wherefore thou contendest with me.

[3] Is it good unto thee that thou shouldest oppress, that thou shouldest despise the work of thine hands, and shine upon the counsel of the wicked?

[4] Hast thou eyes of flesh? or seest thou as man seeth?

[5] Are thy days as the days of man? are thy years as man's days,

[6] That thou inquirest after mine iniquity, and searchest after my sin?

[7] Thou knowest that I am not wicked; and there is none that can deliver out of thine hand.

[8] Thine hands have made me and fashioned me together round about; yet thou dost destroy me.

[9] Remember, I beseech thee, that thou hast made me as the clay; and wilt thou bring me into dust again?

[20] Are not my days few? cease then, and let me alone, that I may take comfort a little,

[21] Before I go whence I shall not return, even to the land of darkness and the shadow of death;

[22] A land of darkness, as darkness itself; and of the shadow of death, without any order, and where the light is as darkness.

This paraphrase is closer to the original. The first section of Job 10 is used, up to v. 9, and then the text jumps to vv. 20–22. One gets the impression here that the paraphrast is familiar with the wider context of Job and so he makes v. 2 more explicitly refer to Job's familiar plea that he does not know why he has caused offence to God, that is, what his sin is. He uses the imagery of the "shades of night" which does not appear in this passage, but which does elsewhere and is a very familiar image from Job. The paraphrast changes the sense of the "days" in v. 5—the text is asking whether God's days are the same as those of humans, but in the song man's days are seen as frail and the question is whether God's are the same, and the paraphrast links the thought of days and years to God's right to question humanity about its iniquities. Job's resignation in v. 7 is, in the paraphrase, made into more of a plea to God to change the situation and is more in the mood of a lament psalm. Questions replace Job's gloomy certainties. But then, by contrast when Job asks the question, "wilt thou bring me into dust again?" (i.e. will you let me die?), the paraphrase removes the question to convey the idea of the certainty of death.

Purcell was not the only English composer to use this method of paraphrasing the text of Job to create a piece based on the book. William Byrd (1542–1623), a century before, used a paraphrase of Job 10:20–22, although he wrote in Latin. This is a motet for six voices (SATTBB) in G minor. The sentiment remains much the same in the paraphrase, although the words are quite far removed from the text itself. We read in the KJV:

> Are not my days few? cease then, and let me alone, that I may take comfort a little, before I go whence I shall not return, even to the land of darkness and the shadow of death; A land of darkness, as darkness itself; and of the shadow of death, without any order, and where the light is as darkness.

Of course, this piece is primarily in Latin, but the English translation provided is as follows:

> Throughout the long days in which I sojourn here I wait the hour of going hence when I shall be no more seen. Send me away therefore that I may mourn awhile, with tears of sorrow ere that I go hence that I return not to pine here in misery where prevails naught of order but everlasting chaos encircles us.

It is interesting that details of "the land of darkness" are omitted and that the idea is transferred to Job's misery leading to a state of chaos. The lament is thus internalized and made more personal in the paraphrase. Thus the work of the paraphrasts was to convey the main sentiments of the biblical text and stay close enough to selected verses of the original for that original to be recognizable. However, their first priority was to put the text into rhyming verse which would then be more easily set to music.

The Use of Texts from Job but not from the Mouth of Job

All the examples used so far are based on the words of Job himself, which is scarcely surprising in a biblical book that is dominated by his laments. However, in this section I am interested in texts that are not from the mouth of Job but are from another friend or another section of the book.

Maurice Greene (1696–1755) based an anthem for alto solo on a paraphrase of Job 22:21–30, "Acquaint thyself," based on the words of Eliphaz in the third round of speeches. The first section of the anthem is slow—Largo—and paraphrases Job 22:21a and 22b: "Acquaint now thyself with him, and be at peace...and lay up his words in thine heart." The anthem runs: "Acquaint thyself with God, and be at peace with him. And lay up his words in thine heart." Then the mood changes to *vivace*, paraphrasing Job 22:23a, 25a, with two words from vv. 26 and 27a: "If thou return to the Almighty, thou shalt be built up, thou shalt put away iniquity... Yea, the Almighty shall be thy defence...thy delight... Thou shalt make thy prayer unto him, and he shall hear thee." The paraphrase reads: "If thou return to the Almighty put away iniquity from thee. Then shall he be thy defence and thy delight. Thou shalt make thy prayer unto him and he will hear thee, and he will hear thee." It is interesting that reference to material rewards, as in the KJV, is omitted in the paraphrase, as is paying vows. The final chorus, still *vivace*, is based on Job 22:29b: "There is lifting up; and he shall save the humble person," although the reference to the deliverance of the righteous might have been suggested by v. 19, "The righteous see it, and are glad," or by a verse from elsewhere. The paraphrase reads: "The Lord will deliver the righteous. He will save the humble man." The key is major for a change, and two-thirds of the anthem is fairly upbeat. It is ironic that this is a speech of one of the friends—a line ultimately rejected by the book (by God himself in 42:7)—that is presented here as a model for believers to follow.

William Boyce (1711–1779) wrote the anthem, "O where shall wisdom be found?," based on Job 28:12–15, 18 and 20–28. The text is faithful to the KJV. It is one of the few pieces I have found with an upbeat melody, which is not surprising for a hymn of praise (often seen as a separate hymn to wisdom in Job scholarship). It is for two treble voices, alto, tenor and bass in the key of C minor. There are interesting unison climaxes at vv. 23 and 28, both the key places where God is mentioned. The final verse is repeated a number of times at the end indicating that it is indeed the climax of the whole piece and the most important sentiment. This is probably true of many interpretations of the poem as a whole; it is the only verse that links the fear of God with wisdom and hence links the human quest with the divine gift of wisdom. The scholarship has sometimes regarded this verse as a later addition. That clearly would not be the view expressed in a musical context.

Conclusion

This brief survey has shown that there is a select but rich tradition of basing liturgical music, songs, anthems and motets on the book of Job. Quite often a paraphrase is used, notably in songs where adherence to the text is not so important as producing rhythmic verse. The words of Job in his state of lament are the most frequently used, as are his musings on life and death. However, we have seen a few examples of other texts from Job being used. The biblical text goes on living in ever new contexts: for composers and their paraphrasts Job provided a vital inspiration for the music itself. Often sung and performed in a Christian context, the words would be carefully chosen to align with that broader theological arena. This was particularly true in the liturgy for the burial of the dead. And as for the choir of St. John's: I find that they have at least recorded Purcell's "Man that is born of a woman."[22] It is my hope that this short essay may inspire some digging out of some of these more obscure Job pieces so that they might once more see the light of day and bring the biblical text (or something resembling it) to a new audience, as happens with each fresh performance.

22. Part of "Purcell, The Complete Funeral Music," *Purcell: Ceremonial Music*: The Choir of St. John's College, Cambridge; George Guest (conductor); Stephen Cleobury (organist); Argo ZRG724, 1972.

AN OVERLOOKED SUGGESTION AT PROVERBS 1:10

H. G. M. Williamson

Recent years have seen the publication of a number of fine commentaries on the book of Proverbs. They all give some attention to the problems of the Hebrew text, though the amount of detail inevitably varies according to the conventions of the series for which they were written.[1]

It is a striking fact that they all explain the anomalous last word of Prov 1:10 in more or less the same way:

בני אם־יפתוך חטאים אל־תבא

That is to say, they construe it as deriving from the verb אבה. This verb normally means "to be willing," but in the present context it would have to be given the extended meaning of "consent": "My child, if sinners entice you, do not consent" (NRSV). Support for the extended meaning may be found at 1 Kgs 20:8:

ויאמרו אליו כל־הזקנים וכל־העם אל־תשמע ולוא תאבה

> Then all the elders and all the people said to him, "Do not listen or consent."[2]

---

1. See, for instance (in chronological order since 1970), W. McKane, *Proverbs: A New Approach* (OTL; London: SCM, 1970); O. Plöger, *Sprüche Salamos (Proverbia)* (BKAT 17; Neukirchen–Vluyn: Neukirchener, 1984); R. N. Whybray, *Proverbs* (NCB; London: Marshall Pickering; Grand Rapids: Eerdmans, 1994); R. E. Murphy, *Proverbs* (WBC 22; Nashville: Thomas Nelson, 1998); R. J. Clifford, *Proverbs: A Commentary* (OTL; Louisville: Westminster John Knox, 1999); M. V. Fox, *Proverbs 1–9: A New Translation with Introduction and Commentary* (AB 18A; New York: Doubleday, 2000); A. Lelièvre and A. Maillot, *Commentaire des Proverbes*. Vol. 3, *chs. 1–9* (Lectio Divina, Commentaires 8; Paris: Cerf, 2000); B. K. Waltke, *The Book of Proverbs Chapters 1–15* (NICOT; Grand Rapids: Eerdmans, 2004); T. Longman, *Proverbs* (Baker Commentary on the Old Testament Wisdom and Psalms; Grand Rapids: Baker Academic, 2006).
2. Cf. B. Johnson, "אבה," *ThWAT* 1:23–27 = *TDOT* 1:24–26.

While this gives good sense, it overlooks the peculiar spelling of תבא,
a peculiarity only heightened by the presence of the anticipated form in
1 Kgs 20:8, namely תאבה. It is true that the expected aleph is sometimes
dropped in this position. According to GK §68h, this is not infrequent
with the verb אסף. With other verbs it is very rare, however, and even
then several of the examples listed there are probably due to scribal error
or should be differently construed. Moreover, it never happens elsewhere
in Biblical Hebrew with אבה, though the related spelling תובא at Ecclus
6:33[3] is noteworthy and suggests that spelling may have been less
rigorous later on, no doubt in part due to Aramaic influence. In Aramaic,
to which appeal has also been made in connection with our verse, the
dropping of the initial aleph is certainly attested as early as Imperial
Aramaic, and it becomes commoner later on.[4] Moreover, the dropping of
the final he, with consequential vocalization with ṣērê rather than segōl,
has also to be explained as due to Aramaic influence, according to GK
§75hh (see too BL §59g), but it is striking that this accounts better for the
vocalization than for the loss of the he,[5] which is certainly rare, if attested
at all, in the early period; even later, it is unusual.[6] These examples,
however, do not give exact parallels in terms of the spelling, with both
being anomalies from a Hebrew point of view, and in any case it is
difficult to know why this word in Proverbs should suddenly adopt an
unusual Aramaic form[7] at this point when a standard Hebrew form of
spelling was readily available.

In short, there are two significant anomalies in the spelling of this
word. Each can just about be explained, though without great conviction.

3. See P. C. Beentjes, *The Book of Ben Sira in Hebrew: A Text Edition of all
Extant Hebrew Manuscripts and a Synopsis of all Parallel Hebrew Ben Sira Texts*
(VTSup 68; Leiden: Brill, 1997), 29.

4. See, for instance, T. Muraoka and B. Porten, *A Grammar of Egyptian Aramaic*
(HOS 1/32; Leiden: Brill, 1998), 124; K. Beyer, *Die aramäischen Texten vom Toten
Meer* (Göttingen: Vandenhoeck & Ruprecht, 1984), 481; *Ergänzungsband* (1994),
296. We may note also such spellings in Biblical Aramaic as למֵמַר (Ezra 5:11). See
further M. L. Folmer, *The Aramaic Language in the Achaemenid Period: A Study in
Linguistic Variation* (OLA 68; Leuven: Peeters, 1995), 102–23.

5. The reference by Lelièvre and Maillot to the addition of an aleph at Isa 28:12
(אבוא) is quite beside the point; cf. GK §23i.

6. No examples seem to be listed by Muraoka and Porten, *A Grammar*, 134–35
and 137–38, but for Qumran see Beyer, *Die aramäischen Texte*, 493, and vol. 2
(2004), 337. F. E. König, *Historisch-kritisches Lehrgebäude der hebräischen
Sprache* (2 vols.; Leipzig: Hinrichs, 1881), 1:576, follows Kimchi in stating that א is
a variant for ה. But that is an observation, not an explanation.

7. Muraoka and Porten, *A Grammar*, 124, comment that in Egyptian Aramaic
syncope of the glottal stop in Pe–Aleph verbs "is exception, not the rule."

That the two should be combined to produce the Masoretic form will for
some scholars, at any rate, strain credulity beyond the breaking point.
The fact that some mediaeval manuscripts read the expected form תאבה
strengthens this conclusion, though textually the reading is clearly
secondary. The occasionally attested vocalization תָּבֹא is equally understandable as an easier reading and for that very reason equally uncon-
vincing. The observation that some of the ancient versions read the
unpointed text this way again serves only to highlight how unlikely the
present form of the text really is.

There is an additional oddity in this verse to which a number of commentators also draw attention, namely the issue of line length. The
analysis of biblical poetry is an inexact science at best, and it is rarely
sufficient evidence on its own to cast doubt on the integrity of a particular text. Nevertheless, some things are more probable than others, and if
there is reason to suspect that something has gone wrong in the course of
textual transmission and the proposed solution to that difficulty happens
also to result in a more regular line of poetry, then that has always
seemed to me to add some support to any case under consideration. In
the present instance, בני אם־יפתוך חטאים is a reasonable first half of a line
when it is compared to the wider context, but אל־תבא is then obviously
too short to balance it. *BHS* therefore proposes reading the following
אם־יאמרו at the start of v. 11 as part of the same line, but that is clearly
unacceptable in terms of sense division. Various other devices have been
proposed to get round this perceived difficulty, such as the moving of
לכה אתנו from the following line to stand after חטאים in our line. That is
entirely conjectural, however, and so should not be entertained if a better
solution can be proposed; furthermore, from the point of view of sense it
effectively only lengthens the first half of the verse, with which it would
clearly belong, so still leaving אל־תבא isolated. It is therefore far from
being a self-authenticating solution.

The present form of the text of Prov 1:10 thus leaves us with a delicate
text-critical question. By appeal to linguistic abnormalities that might
just about be defended (for instance, a scribe might have unconsciously
assimilated his spelling to an unusual form of the Aramaic of his day)
together with an acceptance that even in what is a passage of regular line
lengths exceptions can occur, some will prefer to remain with the transmitted form of the text. Others, however, will be more comfortable with
some form of conjectural emendation, provided it clears up all the problems and can be explained as due to an intelligible error in transmission.
An intriguing suggestion of this kind has been advanced for the present
verse, but, as already noted, it does not appear to have reached the

attention of the modern commentators.[8] Its pedigree is, however, one that my own experience of Andrew Macintosh's teaching of other Hebrew Bible texts suggests that he would at least enjoy considering.

Just over 100 years ago this different approach to the problem was advanced by D. H. Müller.[9] It was repeated with a slightly fuller discussion by G. R. Driver in an article in 1960.[10] The reason this approach has dropped from view may have been that Müller's publication was somewhat obscure and Driver's discussion was included in the course of an article which referred to a great many other passages, so that in neither case was it flagged up by a title or similar device that might have led to it becoming part of the common parlance of our discipline. I first became aware of it in lectures by my own teacher, Driver's pupil J. A. Emerton. In my opinion, the solution deserves to be considered carefully, and it is the purpose of this short study to attempt to ground it by a fuller analysis and so to put it back on the scholarly agenda.[11]

In brief, the essence of their proposal is that אל־תבא is an abbreviation for אל־תלך בדרך אתם, "do not walk in the way with them," taking the first letter of each word following the initial אל (hence effectively אל־ת'ב'א'). This is not as remote a possibility as might at first appear. Verse 10 is a short conditional sentence, and it is followed in vv. 11–15

---

8. I note also that there is no reference to the suggestion in the recently published *BHQ* volume: J. de Waard, *Proverbs* (BHQ 17; Stuttgart: Deutsche Bibelgesellschaft, 2008), 3 and 31* (where there are valuable comments on variant vocalizations).

9. D. H. Müller, *Komposition und Strophenbau: Alte und neue Beiträge* (Jahresbericht der Israelitisch-Theologischen Lehranstalt in Wien 14; Vienna: Verlag der Israel.-Theol. Lehranstalt, 1907), 70–71. His suggestion is mentioned with approval by N. H. Tur-Sinai, *The Book of Job: A New Commentary* (rev. ed.; Jerusalem: Kiryat-Sefer, 1967), 201 n. 1.

10. G. R. Driver, "Abbreviations in the Massoretic Text," *Textus* 1 (1960): 112–31 (128–29). Driver makes a brief reference to Müller's work in a footnote at the end of his discussion, so there is no doubt that he derived his proposal from there rather than thinking it up independently. A copy of Müller's work was in Driver's personal library, the older part of which (so probably including Müller's work) he inherited from his father. See the bookplate in the copy in the Oriental Institute Library, Oxford (classmark HD533M).

11. It is mentioned briefly, though apparently not adopted, by B. Gemser in the second edition of his commentary *Sprüche Salomos* (HAT 16; Tübingen: J. C. B. Mohr [Paul Siebeck], 1963), 20, a commentary which explicitly relied on Driver for many textual and philological comments; see the Preface to the second edition as well as the Appendix. It was also mentioned in the apparatus of *BHK*, whence it is cited, though again not with approval, by T. L. Forti, *Animal Imagery in the Book of Proverbs* (VTSup 118; Leiden: Brill, 2008), 26.

by a more extended conditional sentence, again starting with אם, but reaching its apodosis only in v. 15 with, following a resumptive בני, precisely the same phrase, אל־תלך בדרך אתם. In other words, the proposed abbreviation in v. 10 stands in an identical syntactic position to that of the full form of the phrase in v. 15. Although there is no directly textual evidence to support this proposal, it is one of those suggestions that is so brilliantly attractive that it scarcely requires external evidence to be judged convincing.

That is not to say, however, that it does not leave several loose ends that need to be tied up. Driver's explanation relates the proposal to the wider issue of line balance. In his own words, the abbreviation was

> wrongly imported from below, where it is in place; it had presumably been accidentally omitted in copying the archetype and was added in abridged form in the margin, whence it was subsequently and erroneously transferred to its present place in the M.T.

He then goes on to follow Beer who, with appeal to the Septuagint and with reference to Jer 27:9, 14 and Isa 35:4, conjecturally restored אליך לאמר following יאמרו in v. 11 to give:

> My son, if sinners entice thee
>   If they speak <unto thee, saying>
>   Come with us....

This, he maintains, restores the rhythmical balance of the clauses.

As we shall see, there is no doubt that if אל־תבא is omitted we can achieve a more satisfying line length. Driver's proposal of how it came mistakenly to be included here is, however, improbable. To rehearse his proposal in order, the words אל־תלך בדרך אתם were accidentally omitted from v. 15. That is obviously possible. Noting the error, the same scribe or a later one added the abbreviated form in the margin as a correction. In that case, it was most likely the original scribe who did so, as it is not clear otherwise how a later scribe would have known what words had been omitted. From there, the abbreviation was mistakenly added back at v. 10. This fails to explain, however, how it comes about that the correct text now stands in v. 15. Did the later copyist understand the abbreviation correctly and so restore the text of v. 15, which *ex hypothesi* was defective? But if so, why did he restore it in full in v. 15 but only in the abbreviated form in v. 10? It would have been more logical to do this the other way round, with the abbreviated form following the full one. In any case, however, if, as seems to be assumed, he correctly restored v. 15, how did it come about that it was "subsequently and erroneously transferred to its present place in the M.T."? There are too many unlikely steps involved in this scenario to command conviction.

Müller himself had a different suggestion. He thought more simply that a reader made an abbreviated note in the margin of v. 10 drawing attention to the apodosis in v. 15 and that this was simply but mistakenly incorporated later on. Although Müller does not explicitly say so, I presume he thought that his "reader" was concerned by the length of the double protasis in vv. 10–14 and so gave a marginal indication of the words of the apodosis following the brief first protasis in v. 10.

This seems to me a more plausible explanation than Driver's. The only alternative would be to suppose that the full form once stood in v. 10 and that it got abbreviated for some unknown reason. It would make a perfectly acceptable balance as the second half of a line following 10a, so that superficially this might be considered attractive. The trouble then is that the identical apodosis would be repeated, which seems improbable, so that on balance Müller's suggested explanation is to be preferred.

What effect might this have on line balance? Both Müller and Driver want to expand slightly the length of v. 11a on the basis of the LXX in order to make it into an acceptable second half to go with 10a.[12] Müller adds just אליך (hence, אם יאמרו אליך), while Driver goes one step further by also adding לאמר.[13] The loss of לך (which could have been spelt לכה in the pre-Masoretic period) or אליך by haplography with the immediately following לכה is intelligible,[14] so that of these two proposals I again prefer Müller. I am not so sure, however, that any lengthening is necessary. The LXX certainly joins the first words of v. 11 with v. 10, but the facts that יאמרו is translated unusually by παρακαλέσωσί and that in any case the LXX construes the whole line as an admonition rather than as a conditional clause suggest that the rendering may be somewhat free at this point, so that to put weight on its continuation σε λέγοντες may be a case of relying on what is only an idiomatic rendering of MT.

---

12. For the most recent analysis of the LXX of Proverbs, including verse-by-verse discussion of the whole of this chapter and demonstrating that the translator undertook a "free rendering of his parent text," see J. Cook, *The Septuagint of Proverbs: Jewish and/or Hellenistic Proverbs? Concerning the Hellenistic Colouring of LXX Proverbs* (VTSup 69; Leiden: Brill, 1997). The citation is from p. 316.

13. That, at least, seems to be the implication of his discussion and translation. In fact, he never supplies a fully restored text.

14. Nevertheless, we should not lose sight of the alternative possibility that in (the *Vorlage* of?) the LXX and Peshiṭta לכה (לך) was repeated by dittography; cf. C. H. Toy, *A Critical and Exegetical Commentary on the Book of Proverbs* (ICC; Edinburgh: T. & T. Clark, 1899), 19.

Besides, do we miss anything at this point? I do not believe so. The following two words, לכה אתנו, can equally easily be taken with this clause to give three stresses to match the three of 10a, and the rest of v. 11 may then be construed as a line in its own right as 2 + 3, which is acceptable. I conclude that with the simple deletion of the anomalous אל־תבא and without the need for any further emendation, we can, in fact, overcome the problem of line balance that we discussed earlier.

Two further questions might be asked about the plausibility of this conjecture. First and simplest, is there any parallel for what might be called a double protasis, that is, אם + אם without a waw on the second occurrence? The answer is that there is. Without going further afield than a closely comparable context in Proverbs, we have Prov 2:1–5, בני אם...כי אם...אם...א.[15]

More challenging is the question whether abbreviations were used in the biblical period. Almost inevitably this is not a question that can be answered with complete certainty, but the case in favour seems strong, even though, in my opinion, G. R. Driver exaggerated it very considerably.[16] In the first place, we know that later, in Rabbinical Hebrew, the practice became common.[17] Secondly, the evidence from coins in particular shows that the use of abbreviations was not foreign in the Levant in a time close to that which we may postulate is relevant to our present concern.[18] Third, although Tov is adamant that there are no abbreviations of partial or complete words in the Qumran manuscripts, he finds abundant evidence for the use of letters as abbreviated forms of numbers there (as they frequently were elsewhere, of course).[19] Finally, however, there is a small number of passages where the translation in the versions suggests that they took a group of letters in their Hebrew *Vorlage* to be an abbreviation. Whether they were correct to do so needs to be debated in each case. Sometimes, they were almost certainly

15. The syntactical question is not affected by the discussion among a small minority of scholars whether parts or the whole of vv. 2–9 are later additions; for the former, see Toy, *Proverbs*, 31–40, and for the latter, Whybray, *Proverbs*, 49–51.

16. To his article cited in n. 10 above, he later added another: "Once Again Abbreviations," *Textus* 4 (1964): 76–94. Many of the suggestions he makes in these two articles seem highly improbable to me, but that need not prevent us from agreeing with one or two cases, which is sufficient for the present purpose.

17. See the massive compilation in A. Stern, *Handbuch der Hebräischen Abbreviaturen* (Sighetul-Marmatiei: Kaufman, 1926).

18. For just one collection with many examples, see Y. Meshorer and S. Qedar, *The Coinage of Samaria in the Fourth Century BCE* (Jerusalem: Numismatic Fine Arts International, 1991).

19. E. Tov, *Scribal Practices and Approaches Reflected in the Texts Found in the Judean Desert* (STDJ 54; Leiden: Brill, 2004), 235.

mistaken. But the point is that this still serves as evidence that the device was sufficiently familiar to them to be something that they would consider. And since the evidence includes the LXX, that would seem to bring us to a point in time quite as early as the postulated origin of the abbreviation in Prov 1:10. I cite four examples from Driver's work by way of example.

In Prov 6:3 the word אפוא in עשה זאת אפוא (NRSV "so do this") is peculiar, though not impossible. The LXX renders ποίει υἱέ ἃ ἐγώ σοι ἐντέλλομαι, "My son, do what I command you," on which Cook comments "[i]t is not immediately clear how he came to this reading,"[20] while *BHQ* seems to think that the translator omitted to translate the Hebrew word אפוא altogether. In fact the answer seems clear enough: the translator took it as an abbreviation (א'פ'א) for אשר פקדתי אליך, which has a parallel at Zeph 3:7 (אשר־פקדתי עליה).[21]

Similarly, it may be wondered why the LXX rendered איך in Jer 3:19 as γένοιτο κύριε ὅτι. This probably came about under some sort of influence from 11:5, where אמן יהוה is also rendered γένοιτο κύριε; it is attractive to suppose that איך was here treated as an abbreviation for אמן יהוה כי. It is certainly not correct in terms of the text of Jeremiah, but it again testifies to the likelihood that the use of abbreviations was sufficiently familiar to the translator for the misunderstanding to arise in the first place.[22]

The second half of Ezek 18:10 is an obscure verse at best, and most commentators emend in one way or another: ועשה אח מאחד מאלה. The LXX appears to have no equivalent for the last word, but starts v. 11 very differently from MT: ἐν τῇ ὁδῷ τοῦ πατρὸς αὐτοῦ τοῦ δικαίου οὐκ ἐπορεύθη ("in the way of his righteous father he has not walked"). No explanation for this other than rationalizing paraphrase has been proposed, so that Driver's suggestion that it represents the reading of באלה (for מאלה) as an abbreviation for בארח אביו לא הלך is attractive.[23]

At Esth 9:25, MT בבאה is taken as "how he [Haman] came" by the LXX (which is scarcely possible), and as "when it [Haman's plan] came" by many modern commentators. The Vulgate, Peshitta and Targum, however, render as though the full text were בבוא אסתר המלכה, a conjecture enthusiastically endorsed by Moore.[24]

20. Cook, *The Septuagint of Proverbs*, 158.
21. See Driver, "Abbreviations," 128.
22. See ibid., 129, though he surprisingly misses the link with Jer 11:5 in stating that this formula of affirmation is not found elsewhere.
23. Driver, "Abbreviations," 124.
24. C. A. Moore, *Esther: Introduction, Translation, and Notes* (AB 7B; New York: Doubleday, 1971), 94.

I conclude on the basis of this evidence that it is by no means unreasonable to expect that abbreviations may have found their way into the text of the Hebrew Bible, and that this hypothesis provides the most satisfying solution to the puzzle of Prov 1:10. The suggestion at least deserves more discussion than it has received to date.

I am delighted to have the opportunity of contributing to this volume in honour of Andrew Macintosh. I learned much from his teaching of Hebrew texts in graduate student days and I have continued to profit from his wisdom, enthusiasm and friendship over many years since.

NEBUCHADNEZZAR'S DREAM IN DANIEL 2

Erica C. D. Hunter

The aggadot or "midrashic" stories of Daniel (chs. 1–6) have been described as court tales originating "in the eastern Jewish Diaspora during the Hellenistic period."[1] Composed in the third person, to narrate the experiences of the hero Daniel living in Babylon, following Nebuchadnezzar's deportation of the Jews, the tales are written in a robust and lively style. The inclusion of several major dream sequences connects the aggadot with the apocalyptic portion of Daniel (chs. 7–12) since the dreams revealed by Daniel transcend the historical horizons of the Exile and serve to focus on the time when history would culminate in a final kingdom of God in Palestine. The aggadot were composed partly in Hebrew (Dan 1:1–2:3) and partly in Aramaic from the Persian or early Hellenistic periods (2:4–7:28) for an audience that was located in Palestine during the second century B.C.E. Historical anomalies, particularly the references to Nebuchadnezzar and Belshazzar, led Harold Ginsberg to opine that they "betray too great an ignorance of Babylonian and Persian history to be pre-Hellenistic."[2] Some facts are undoubtedly confused,[3] but, as Alan Millard has pointed out, the aggadot also contain a high proportion of accurate detail.[4]

---

1. A. R. Millard, "Daniel 1–6 and History," *EvQ* (1977): 67–73 (68), quoting G. Fohrer, *Introduction to the Old Testament* (trans. D. Green; London: SPCK, 1970), 474.

2. H. L. Ginsberg, "The Book of Daniel," in *The Cambridge History of Judaism*. Vol. 2, *The Hellenistic Age* (ed. W. D. Davies and L. Finkelstein; Cambridge: Cambridge University Press, 1989), 510–11.

3. For discussion of the historical problems, see D. J. Wiseman, *Some Historical Problems in the Book of Daniel* (London: Tyndale, 1965), 9–18; M. Henze, *The Madness of King Nebuchadnezzar* (Leiden: Brill, 1999), 53–57.

4. Millard, "Daniel 1–6," 71.

The most immediate indication of the Babylonian setting comes from the Akkadian and Persian loan-words described by Franz Rosenthal as "ancient cultural loans."[5] In his study of these technical terms that relate principally to aspects of court-life and its personnel, Rosenthal made only passing reference to the various divinatory orders of the Mesopotamian court. This essay discusses these terms before proceeding to examine the dream interpretation episode of ch. 2. In doing so, it points out the dynamics of the aggadot in which practices of the Babylonian court were recalled but whose "double-entendre" enabled both Jew and Gentile to interpret the episodes according to their differing perspectives, thus lending support to Harold Rowley's opinion that the author of Daniel "made use of traditions older than his day, but moulded them to suit his purpose."[6]

The Wise Men at Court

Various categories of diviners were summoned to interpret the dreams of Nebuchadnezzar (Dan 1; 2; 4) and also were requested by Belshazzar to interpret the writing on the wall (ch. 5). Their presence epitomized the mantic practices of the Babylonian court, in contrast to Egypt where wisdom was realized by the prudent teachings from father to son, or by master to pupil. The Babylonian court maintained numerous divinatory orders that, using various rituals, aimed to ascertain the will of the gods and thereby thwart bad omens. They also interpreted dreams. References to various categories of wise men, in differing combinations, appear at various points throughout the aggadot, there being apparently no prescribed order for their citation.[7] In this vein, James Montgomery stated: "the several classes of diviners are listed with no technical or exact sense."[8]

5. F. Rosenthal, *A Grammar of Biblical Aramaic* (6th ed.; Wiesbaden: Harrassowitz, 1995), 61.

6. H. H. Rowley, *The Servant of the Lord and Other Essays on the Old Testament* (Oxford: Basil Blackwell, 1965), 276 n. 1.

7. J. A. Montgomery, *A Critical and Exegetical Commentary on Daniel* (ICC; Edinburgh: T. & T. Clark, 1927), 143, where he also tabulates the orders of citation. His opinion is echoed in R. H. Charles, *A Critical and Exegetical Commentary on the Book of Daniel* (Oxford: Clarendon, 1929), 28.

8. See Charles, *Critical and Exegetical Commentary*, 28, for tabulation of the listings.

Of all the divinatory orders, the *āšipu*, "conjurer, enchanter," was probably the best known and most commonly cited, occurring in all the references to wise men in both the Hebrew and Aramaic sections of Daniel.[9] The Aramaic term was a straight transliteration of the Akkadian designation, *āšipu*, "exorcist," that appears in Middle Assyrian and Middle Babylonian texts.[10] The direct borrowing of the Aramaic from the Akkadian reflects the proximity and parallel usage of the two languages in Mesopotamia during the first millennium B.C.E., not just in the restricted circles of the royal courts but in all aspects of life, including trade and commercial activities.[11] The Hebrew term was derived from the Aramaic.[12] As well as performing exorcisms, the *āšipu* conducted apotropaic rituals, including the purification of houses and temples.[13] Especially qualified to interpret signs from the gods, and in their capacity as exorcists, the *āšipu* served as consultant for uncertain or difficult decisions, including the prediction of the course of a disease (which was interpreted as demonic possession) from signs observed on the patient's body. In response they offered incantations as well as remedies indicated by the diagnosis.[14]

Discussing Dan 2:2, *Midrash Tanḥuma* (*Miqqets*, Gen 10) qualified the term *āšipu* as "*Ashshafim*, these are those who press (lay stress) upon the planetary constellation."[15] This specification, to "press down the planets," was still reiterated in Jewish Babylonian Aramaic incantation bowls whose dating can be placed as late as the seventh century C.E.

9. BDB, 80, for אַשָּׁפִים, Dan 1:20; 2:2; and p. 1083 for אָשֵׁף, Dan 2:10, אָשְׁפִין, Dan 2:27; 5:11, אָשְׁפַיָּא, Dan 4:4; 5:7, 15.

10. See entry *āšipu* in *CAD*, 1/II:431–35.

11. H. V. Hilprecht and A. T. Clay, *Business Documents of Murashû Sons of Nippur Dated in the Reign of Artaxerxes I (464–424 B.C.)* (Philadelphia: University of Pennsylvania, Department of Archaeology and Palaeontology, 1898); A. T. Clay, *Business Documents of Murashû Sons of Nippur Dated in the Reign of Darius II* (Philadelphia: University Museum, University of Pennsylvania Press, 1912).

12. Montgomery, *Commentary on Daniel*, 153.

13. *CAD*, 1/II:432–33.

14. A. L. Oppenheim, *Ancient Mesopotamia: Portrait of a Dead Civilization* (Chicago: University of Chicago Press, 1977), 304.

15. S. Buber, *Midrasch Tanchuma: ein agadischer Commentar zum Pentateuch von Rabbi Tanchuma ben Rabbi Abba* (Wilna: Wittwe & Gebrüder Romm, 1885), 190: אמר ר׳ סימון...ולאשפים מהו ולאשפים אלו שדוחקים את המזל ואין הלשון הזה אלא לשון דוחק. J. Townsend, *Midrash Tanḥuma: Translated into English with Introduction, Indices and Brief Notes (S. Buber Recension).* Vol. 1, *Genesis* (Hoboken: Ktav, 1989), 254, translates: "R. Simon said: ...THE ENCHANTERS. What are the enchanters (ᵓShPYM)? These are ones who push fortune. So this word is nothing but a word of duress."

The repeated call to "press down" (expressed by √HPK) that commenced a popular genre of incantation texts, whose written formulae were probably also uttered orally, was always directed towards the earth, heavens, stars and planets, thus highlighting the incantation's astrological orientation.[16] An Aramaic incantation bowl from Nippur uses √AŠP in conjunction with the casting of spells: אישפנא לכון באישפנא דימא אישפאו דלויתן תנינא, "I will lay a spell on you, the spell of the Sea and of the monster Leviathan."[17] Syriac and Mandaic cognates articulate similar semantics, viz., Syriac ܐܫܦ, "stroke, soothe, charm," nominal ܐܫܦܐ, "charm, incantation,"[18] Mandaic √AŠP "to use magical arts, exorcize, read incantations."[19]

In various Old Testament books, notably Genesis, Kings, Isaiah, Jeremiah, Ezekiel and Habbakuk, as well as Dan 5:30 and 9:1, the appellation Chaldaean was synonymous with the general practice of astronomy/astrology.[20] The more restricted meaning denoting a professional divinatory order occurs only in Dan 2:5, 10; 4:4; 5:7, 11. With the gentilic yod + ṣērê in Aramaic indicating an ethnic group or race, many commentators have considered כשדאי, "Chaldaeans," as a racial term and that its use for a special class of learned men was anachronistic.[21] Alan Millard has, however, noted "the complete absence of the word as an ethnic term from the royal inscriptions of Nebuchadnezzar, his father and his successors," also pointing out the lack of evidence for Chaldaean as a professional name in Babylonian texts.[22] Commenting on the emergence of the two meanings of Chaldaean, he proposed that the specific connotation developed from the generic application seen in Neo-Assyrian records from the ninth and eighth centuries B.C.E. where the epithet was

---

16. See E. C. D. Hunter, "Manipulating Incantation Texts: Excursions in Refrain A," *Iraq* 64 (2002), 259–73, for discussion of this refrain that was used widely in Mesopotamia.

17. J. A. Montgomery, *Aramaic Incantation Texts from Nippur* (Philadelphia: University Museum, University of Pennsylvania Press, 1913), 121, citing Text 2:3–4.

18. J. Payne Smith, *A Compendious Syriac Dictionary* (Oxford: Clarendon, 1903), 31, and R. Payne Smith, *Thesaurus Syriacus* (Oxford: Clarendon, 1868–1901), 409.

19. E. Drower and R. Macuch, *A Mandaic Dictionary* (Oxford: Clarendon, 1963), 41, citing Drower collection 44:644. When Hibil Ziua, one of the 'Uthre or light beings, journeyed in his capacity as a Saviour to the underworld, before the creation of Tibil, in order to prevent the forces of darkness attacking the light, he exclaimed *kd miša...'šup*, "like Moses...I employ magical arts."

20. P. R. Davies, *Daniel* (Sheffield: JSOT, 1985), 38. See BDB, 1098, *sub* כַּשְׂדִּי.

21. Millard, "Daniel 1–6," 69, and n. 10, citing N. Porteous, *Daniel: A Commentary* (OTL; London: SCM, 1965), 28.

22. Ibid., 70.

an overall name for a group of tribes. He also pointed out its restricted usage in Herodotus' *Histories*, where the Chaldaeans are named as priests of Bel.[23] In both Syriac and Mandaic, the term was synonymous with astronomy/astrology, viz., ܟܠܕܝܘܬܐ, "Chaldaean knowledge, that is, astrology/astronomy," ܟܠܕܝܐ, "Chaldaean, astronomer, astrologer," with denominative verb (pali, aphel), "to consult the stars, consult an oracle";[24] Mandaic *kaldaia*, "Chaldaean, astrologer, soothsayer, magician."[25]

גָּזְרִין in Dan 2:27; 5:11 and גָּזְרַיָּא in Dan 4:4(7); 5:7, "the determiners (of fate)," have often been described as astrologers and soothsayers.[26] Cognates in Syriac, targumic Aramaic and Mandaic might suggest that the term denoted priests who read organ entrails, that is, practised extispicy. In targumic Aramaic, the range of meanings of √GZR, from "cut off, guard, enact a prohibition, decree, ordain" to "cut, split, circumcise, decree, prohibit," encompasses both the physical and legal.[27] Similarly, Mandaic GZR means "cut (off), hew, circumcise, cut the throat, condemn, give judgment,"[28] whereas in Syriac the connotation is purely physical: "cut or hew stone, tear, circumcise."[29]

חַרְטֻמִּים (Dan 1:20; 2:2) and its Aramaic counterpart חַרְטֹם (2:10), חַרְטֻמִּין (2:27; 5:11), חַרְטֻמַיָּא (4:4, 6), meaning "magician(s)," was a term of Egyptian origin,[30] derived from ḥrtp, which has been interpreted as a priest who was an interpreter of dreams.[31] The term was already attested in Standard Babylonian texts in reference to craftsmen and professional persons who were taken to Mesopotamia as prisoners-of-war in Esarhaddon's Egyptian campaigns during the seventh century B.C.E.[32] Oppenheim

23. Ibid., 69–70, referring to Herodotus, *Histories* 1.181 on p. 69.

24. Payne Smith, *Syriac Dictionary*, 215; Payne Smith, *Thesaurus*, 1745.

25. Drower and Macuch, *Dictionary*, 197, noting that the term occurs in *Ginza Rba Yamina* (20:10; 279:14–15; 301:20, 24) and the Mandaic *The Book of John* 95:4; 97:13, for which see *Das Johannesbuch der Mandäer* (ed. M. Lidzbarski; Giessen: Töpelmann, 1915).

26. Charles, *Critical and Exegetical Commentary*, 28. See also entry in BDB, 1086.

27. M. Jastrow, *A Dictionary of the Targumim, the Talmud Babli and Yerushalmi, and the Midrashic Literature* (2 vols.; New York: Luzac, 1903), 1:231.

28. Drower and Macuch, *Dictionary*, 87.

29. Payne Smith, *Syriac Dictionary*, 67; Payne Smith, *Thesaurus*, 699–700.

30. See BDB, 355 and 1093, for the respective Hebrew and Aramaic terms.

31. A. L. Oppenheim, *Interpretation of Dreams in the Ancient Near East* (Philadelphia: American Philosophical Society, 1956), 238, referring to A. Gardiner, *Ancient Egyptian Onomastica* (2 vols.; London: Oxford University Press, 1947), 1:56.

32. See *CAD*, 6:116, *sub ḥarṭibi*.

notes that Egyptian interpreters of dreams were consulted at the Assyrian court before or during the period of Assurbanipal, since oneiromancy was considered to be the highest achievement in Egyptian divination technique.[33] The Egyptian loan word passed into Akkadian and into the Old Testament as well as into talmudic Aramaic where חרטם, "magician, charmer," appears in *Exodus Rabbah* (*Shemot* 10) and also in *Num. Rab.* 18: כל חרטומי העולם, "all the magicians of the world."[34] Necromantic overtones emerge in *Midr. Tanḥ.* 11 (*Miqqets*, Gen 10) where חרטומין are identified: "[t]hese are the ones who consult the bones (ṬYMY) of the dead."[35]

Interpreting Daniel 2

The dream narrative outlined in Dan 2 has many elements in common with the Babylonian divination technique represented by *pašāru/pišru* that was specifically designed to remove a dream either by the help of the gods or through magic practices.[36] It encompassed three stages:[37]

1. reporting a dream to another person;
2. interpreting an enigmatic dream by that person;
3. dispelling or removing the evil consequences of that dream by magic means.

When he summoned his magicians, exorcists, sorcerers and Chaldaeans, telling them collectively, "my mind has been troubled to know what my dream was" (Dan 2:3), Nebuchadnezzar was requesting *pišru*. The Chaldaeans "speaking in Aramaic," that is, the language of Mesopotamia, responded saying, "Tell us what you dreamt and we will tell you the interpretation." In response to their request, Nebuchadnezzar retorted: "If you do not tell me both the dream and the interpretation, you shall be torn in pieces [dismembered] and your houses shall be made into dung-hills" (2:5). On the contrary, if both the dream and the interpretation were articulated, Nebuchadnezzar promised, "you will be richly rewarded and loaded with honours" (2:6). At this point, the diviners repeated their

33. Oppenheim, *Interpretation of Dreams*, 238, referring to British Museum tablet 851 where the term appears in a concatenation of priestly experts: "conjuration priests, diviners, exorcists and augurs."

34. Jastrow, *Dictionary of the Targumim*, 51.

35. Townsend, *Midrash Tanḥuma*, 254. For the text, see Buber, *Midrasch Tanchuma*, 190.

36. See *CAD*, 12:236–44, for the entry *pašāru* and its extensive range of meanings (esp. p. 242).

37. Oppenheim, *Interpretation of Dreams*, 219.

request that the monarch divulge his dream, but were met with accusations of attempting to "buy time" (2:8–9). Since the diviners did not know the details of Nebuchadnezzar's dream they could not proceed with its interpretation and realize the ultimate aim of *pišru*—the dispelling of any evil consequences of the dream.

Unable to realize the initial stage of *pišru*, the diviners made the excuse that "there is no one but the gods…who can give you the answer" (2:12). Nebuchadnezzar decreed their execution but, during the night (the traditional time for dreaming), "the secret was revealed" to Daniel in a vision (2:19) following his decision to "ask the God of heaven in his mercy" (2:18). This is an important point in the narrative, not only affirming Daniel's association with the Gentile practitioners, but also simultaneously highlighting the fact that Daniel did not resort to the normative divinatory rituals even though he had been instructed in the "literature and language of the Chaldaeans" (1:4). Daniel then asked Arioch to arrange an audience with Nebuchadnezzar to interpret the dream, which he proceeded to do (2:31–45), causing the monarch to prostrate himself and worship Daniel saying, "Your god is indeed God of Gods and Lord over kings, a revealer of secrets, since you have been able to reveal this secret" (2:47). When Daniel stated, "the dream is sure and its interpretation is to be trusted" (2:45), he effectively announced that he had solved the vexing dream, thus removing any threat from Nebuchadnezzar who bestowed great wealth and honours on Daniel, as he had promised.[38]

Daniel's already considerable reputation as a *šāʾilu*, "diviner or dream interpreter," capable of "interpreting visions and dreams of every kind" (1:18) was enhanced by the "loosening" of Nebuchadnezzar's dream and any evil connotations.[39] As Oppenheim noted, once the message of a dream was understood it did not pollute the dreaming person.[40] On the contrary, when a dream remained enigmatic, that is, uninterpreted, its danger lingered. The Babylonian Talmud likened an uninterpreted dream to an unopened, that is, unread, letter (*Ber.* 55a).[41] Clever interpretations

---

38. Jewish commentators experienced great difficulty over this relationship between Nebuchadnezzar and Daniel, in which the Babylonian monarch was shown in a favourable light. See Henze, *Madness of King Nebuchadnezzar*, 101–42, for discussion of Nebuchadnezzar's characterization in early rabbinic literature.

39. *CAD*, 17/1:111–12. Oppenheim, *Interpretation of Dreams*, 223, points out the range of functions performed by the *šāʾilu* priest; these were not restricted to dream interpretation but also encompassed necromancy.

40. Oppenheim, *Interpretation of Dreams*, 219.

41. J. Neusner, *The Talmud of Babylonia: An Academic Commentary*. Vol. 1, *Bavli Tractate Berakhot* (Atlanta: Scholars Press, 1996), 369, 371.

of dreams were greatly admired and suitably rewarded, especially when
the dreamer had forgotten the contents. The fact that Nebuchadnezzar
did not relate the details of his dream in response to his diviners' two
requests might indicate that he had forgotten it or could not remember
all details, rather than that he was trying to trick or upstage his diviners—an interpretation that Robert Payne Smith already suggested in
1886.[42] Commenting on Dan 2:1, *Midrash Tanḥuma* (*Miqqets*, Gen 10)
quotes Rabbi Hiyya's opinion that Nebuchadnezzar dreamed only one
dream, but the plural "dreams" was used because he had forgotten the
dream.[43]

Concluding Comments

Payne Smith wrote that Daniel was "deeply versed in their [i.e. Baby-
lonian] system of divination, both by means of the stars and by the
traditional roles for the interpretation of dreams…he would also learn
their venerable liturgies and hymns."[44] Alone of all the diviners at the
Babylonian court, Daniel was able to release Nebuchadnezzar's dream
and realize its *pišru* through his unique skills that demonstrated his piety
and sagacity as a god-inspired interpreter to his colleagues, to his monarch and to later Jewish readers. Since interpretations were made not
primarily to establish the actual content of the dream, but simply to rid
the person of the impact of the enigma, it was this latter need, rather than
one of "bad character," that may have dictated Nebuchadnezzar's dire
threats to his diviners of dismemberment and destruction of their house-
holds, if they could not perform the task—in contrast to the rewarding of
honours should they be successful.

The court of Nebuchadnezzar provided the setting for the *aggadot*, but
over the centuries many details became confused and facts corrupted.
Yet Babylonian divinatory practices continued long after the fall of
Babylon and would have been familiar to the Jewish communities settled
in Mesopotamia well into the first millennium C.E. The Babylonian
Talmud's prescription of a prayer to turn forgotten dreams into favourable prognostics: "Lord of the world I belong to you, and my dreams
belong to you. I dreamed a dream and I do not know what it is…and just
as you turned the wicked Balaam's curse into a blessing, so turn all of

42. R. Payne Smith, *Daniel: An Exposition of the Historical Portion of the
Writings of the Prophet Daniel* (London: Nisbet, 1886), 54.

43. Townsend, *Midrash Tanḥuma*, 253–54; Buber, *Midrasch Tanchuma*, 190,
for text.

44. Payne Smith, *Daniel*, 6.

my dreams into good for me" (*Ber.* 55b), recalls *pašāru/pišru*.[45] In this context, the embedding of Dan 2 within Babylonian mantic praxis may have occasioned the switch from Hebrew to Aramaic at Dan 2:4, since it might have been considered more appropriate to employ secular rather than sacred language in connection with Gentile divinatory rituals.

---

45. Neusner, *Talmud of Babylonia*, 372.

THE TEXT OF DANIEL 3:16*

B. A. Mastin

The MT of Dan 3:16 reads: ענו שדרך מישך ועבד נגו ואמרין למלכא
נבוכדנצר לא־חשחין אנחנה על־דנה פתגם להתבותך. Because the Masoretes
put *athnach* at למלכא and so separated it from the following word
נבוכדנצר, it is necessary to translate the beginning of the verse,
"Shadrach, Meshach and Abed-nego answered and said to the king, 'O
Nebuchadnezzar'." Montgomery, however, correctly observes that "[t]he
discourteous vocative of the Mass[oretic] pointing was not only
impossible in etiquette but also in the spirit of the writer."[1] The difficulty
can be resolved in three ways. Hitzig thinks the *athnach* should be
moved from למלכא to נבוכדנצר, so that the clause would mean, "[they]
answered and said to king Nebuchadnezzar."[2] Alternatively, Torrey
believes that "in the original text of this verse the words מלכא and
נבוכדנצר were transposed," giving "[they] answered and said to Nebuchadnezzar, 'O king'."[3] A third solution is provided by Kamphausen and
Bludau, who both restore מלכא after נבוכדנצר on the authority of the
LXX, which reads τῷ βασιλεῖ Ναβουχοδονοσὸρ (–εσὸρ 967) βασιλεῦ.[4]
Kamphausen compares v. 9, transfers the *athnach* to נבוכדנצר and
comments that the LXX "rightly begins the address…with מלכא, which

---

* J. Ziegler, ed., *Susanna, Daniel, Bel et Draco* (Septuaginta: Vetus Testamentum Graecum Auctoritate Societatis Litterarum Gottingensis editum 16/2; Göttingen:
Vandenhoeck & Ruprecht, 1954; 2d ed., ed. J. Ziegler, O. Munnich and D. Fraenkel,
1999), is cited as follows: Ziegler 1954 = the first edition; Ziegler and Munnich =
those portions of the second edition for which both scholars are responsible; Ziegler
1999 or Munnich = those portions of the second edition for which only one scholar
is responsible.

1. J. A. Montgomery, *A Critical and Exegetical Commentary on the Book of
Daniel* (ICC; Edinburgh: T. & T. Clark, 1927), 208.

2. F. Hitzig, *Das Buch Daniel* (KHAT 10; Leipzig: Weidmann, 1850), 50.

3. C. C. Torrey, "Notes on the Aramaic Part of Daniel," *Transactions of the
Connecticut Academy of Arts and Sciences* 15 (1909): 241–82 (262).

4. Cf. Munnich, 266.

through a transcriptional error has dropped out" of the MT.[5] Bludau, who compares both v. 9 and Dan 6:7, keeps נבוכדנצר as a vocative and so obtains "[they] said to the king, 'Nebuchadnezzar, O king'."[6] The emendation to the text of Ps 42:6–7 which is adduced as a parallel by Kamphausen has fallen out of favour,[7] but it is easy to see how a second מלכא could have been omitted by accident at Dan 3:16.

I

Some assistance is offered by the ancient versions.

Ziegler, like Swete[8] and Rahlfs,[9] treats τῷ βασιλεῖ Ναβουχοδονοσόρ in both the LXX and Theodotion as a unit and begins the confessors' speech with Βασιλεῦ and Οὐ χρείαν respectively.[10] The other printed editions that I have consulted, which include the *editio princeps* of the LXX manuscript 88, together with the accompanying edition of Theodotion,[11] the edition of Holmes and Parsons[12] and (for Theodotion) the Complutensian Polyglot,[13] understand the texts in the same way. This judgment is supported, as far as the LXX is concerned, by the punctuation in the only known manuscript of the Syro-Hexapla which contains the book of Daniel. It is dated by Ceriani to the eighth century A.D.[14] In the

5. A. Kamphausen, *The Book of Daniel* (SBOT 18; Leipzig: J. C. Hinrichs, 1896), 4, 22.

6. A. Bludau, *Die alexandrinische Übersetzung des Buches Daniel und ihr Verhältniss zum massorethischen Text* (Biblische Studien 2/2, 3; Freiburg im Breisgau: Herder, 1897), 49 n. 2.

7. Cf., e.g., F. Buhl in *BHK*, ad loc., H. Bardtke in *BHS*, ad loc., and H.-J. Kraus, *Psalmen*, I (BKAT 15/1; Neukirchen–Vluyn: Neukirchener, 1958–60), 317 n. m.

8. H. B. Swete, *The Old Testament in Greek according to the Septuagint* (3 vols.; Cambridge: Cambridge University Press, 1887–94), 3:514–15.

9. A. Rahlfs, *Septuaginta, id est Vetus Testamentum Graece iuxta LXX interpretes* (2 vols.; Stuttgart: Privilegierte Württembergische Bibelanstalt, 1935), 2:884.

10. Ziegler 1954, 117, retained in Ziegler and Munnich, 266–67.

11. [Simon de Magistris], Δανιὴλ κατὰ τοὺς ἑβδομήκοντα ἐκ τῶν τετραπλῶν Ὠριγένους; *Daniel secundum Septuaginta ex tetraplis Origenis* (Rome: Typis Propagandae Fidei, 1772), 14, 145; but cf. p. 232, where Ναβουχοδονοσόρ is treated as a vocative in the LXX.

12. R. Holmes and J. Parsons, *Vetus Testamentum Graecum cum variis lectionibus* (5 vols.; Oxford: Clarendon, 1798–1827), vol. 4, ad loc. (no pagination).

13. Complutensian Polyglot (6 vols.; Alcalá: University of Alcalá [printed in 1514–17, probably published 1522]), vol. 4, ad loc. (no pagination).

14. A. M. Ceriani, ed., *Codex Syro-Hexaplaris Ambrosianus photolithographice editus* (Monumenta Sacra et Profana 7; Milan: Bibliotheca Ambrosiana, 1874), folio 145 recto (text) and p. 140 (date).

absence of a case-ending it cannot be shown that Ναβουχοδονοσόρ is not vocative, but there is widespread agreement, confirmed by the Syro-Hexapla in the case of the LXX, that it is dative. I have been unable to discover the basis for Montgomery's statement that "βασιλεῦ is *sub asterisco*."[15]

Some authorities for the Vetus Latina, however, understand the passage in a different way. Codex Wirceburgensis, which is the only known manuscript of this version to contain Dan 3:16, reads *regi Nabuchodonosor*,[16] which is the equivalent of Theodotion's τῷ βασιλεῖ Ναβουχοδονοσόρ. But both Burkitt[17] and Ziegler[18] rightly note that Cyprian's four quotations of the confessors' speech in Dan 3:16–18, which are almost entirely based on a theodotionic text, include some features taken from the LXX. One of these is the placing of *rex* after *Nabuchodonosor*. Cyprian cites the whole of Dan 3:16 in *Ad Quirinum* III.10. Though Hartel punctuates *et dixerunt regi Nabuchodonosor: rex*,[19] it is preferable to follow Weber, who has the confessors address the king as *Nabuchodonosor rex*.[20] The citations in *Ad Fortunatum* XI[21] and *Epistulae* VI.3; LVIII.5[22] are introduced by material which does not come from this verse, though there is no reason to doubt that *Nabuchodonosor rex* does. Thus in Cyprian's text of the Vetus Latina these words were presumably regarded as a phrase spoken by the confessors. They are not preceded by *regi* in *Ad Fortunatum* XI and *Epistula*

---

15. Montgomery, *Commentary on the Book of Daniel*, 208.

16. E. Ranke, ed., *Par Palimpsestorum Wirceburgensium* (Vienna: G. Braumüller, 1871), 129.

17. F. C. Burkitt, *The Old Latin and the Itala* (Texts and Studies 4/3; Cambridge: Cambridge University Press, 1896), 25–26, 28. His judgment that *regi* is "distinctively from Theodotion" but that *rex* is not "distinctively from the LXX" is wrong, because τῷ βασιλεῖ is common to both the LXX and Theodotion, whereas *rex* is not paralleled in Theodotion.

18. Ziegler 1954, 25, retained in Ziegler and Munnich, 98.

19. G. Hartel, ed., *S. Thasci Caecili Cypriani Opera Omnia* (3 parts; CSEL 3/1–3; Vienna: C. Geroldi filius, 1868–71), 1:121.

20. R. Weber and M. Bévenot, eds., *Sancti Cypriani Episcopi Opera* (CCSL 3; Turnhout: Brepols, 1972), 1:98. Weber records the variant reading *et dixerunt ad Nabuchodonosor regem* for *et dixerunt regi Nabuchodonosor rex* in manuscript E and the omission of *regi* in F and of *rex* in T and U.

21. Hartel, *Cypriani Opera Omnia*, 1:337; Weber and Bévenot, *Sancti Cypriani Episcopi Opera*, 204.

22. Hartel, *Cypriani Opera Omnia*, 2:483, 660; G. F. Diercks, ed., *Sancti Cypriani Episcopi Epistularium* (*Sancti Cypriani Episcopi Opera* 3/1; CCSL 3B; Turnhout: Brepols, 1994), 35; idem, *Sancti Cypriani Episcopi Epistularium* (*Sancti Cypriani Episcopi Opera* 3/2; CCSL 3C; Turnhout: Brepols, 1996), 326.

LVIII.5, and, although a few manuscripts punctuate *aiunt regi Nabuchodonosor: rex* in *Epistula* VI.3,[23] it is more satisfactory to interpret this passage and the quotation in *Ad Quirinum* III.10 in the light of the other two examples, where the evidence is clearer. Moreover, in Jerome's commentary on Daniel, in which the earlier part of v. 16 is not cited, the confessors' speech begins *Nabuchodonosor rex*. Jerome explains that *in hebraeo non habet regem*, but he considers the possibility that someone whom he characterizes as *contentiosus* might insist on reading it.[24] Thus he is aware of a manuscript or manuscripts which add the word "king" to the verse, and, though he disapproves, he thinks that Nebuchadnezzar would then be addressed as "King Nebuchadnezzar." Without this addition Nebuchadnezzar would have been addressed by his name, and so in A.D. 407, when this commentary was completed,[25] the tradition represented in the MT was presumably already known to Jerome, who was in touch with Jewish biblical scholarship.[26]

According to a reading in the margin of the Syro-Hexapla, αὐτῷ should be inserted before τῷ βασιλεῖ. The construction with a proleptic suffix which represents this, *lh lmlkʾ*, is good Syriac,[27] and the Syriac lectionary 9l6 uses it at Dan 3:16, with a small change in the wording.[28] It is also found in Biblical Aramaic (cf. Dan 5:12, 30). Hamm claims that the intention was to replace τῷ βασιλεῖ, and not to include both expressions. Since there are several occasions on which the translator of LXX Daniel supplies a pronoun where the MT has a noun, he believes that the primitive text of the LXX may have read αὐτῷ Ναβουχοδονε(-νο-)σὸρ βασιλεῦ. He maintains that it is impossible to tell what the underlying

23. Diercks, *Epistularium* (*Opera* 3/1), 35.

24. *S. Hieronymi Presbyteri Opera*, 1/5 (CCSL 75A; Turnhout: Brepols, 1964), 800–801. *Rex* is read after *Nabuchodonosor* by manuscripts F, R and, apparently, A, but is omitted by G and M.

25. J. N. D. Kelly, *Jerome: His Life, Writings, and Controversies* (London: Duckworth, 1975), 236–37, 298.

26. J. Braverman, *Jerome's Commentary on Daniel: A Study of Comparative Jewish and Christian Interpretations of the Hebrew Bible* (CBQMS 7; Washington, D.C.: The Catholic Biblical Association of America, 1978); H. F. D. Sparks, "Jerome as Biblical Scholar," in *The Cambridge History of the Bible*. Vol. 1, *From the Beginnings to Jerome* (ed. P. R. Ackroyd and C. F. Evans; Cambridge: Cambridge University Press, 1970), 539.

27. T. Muraoka, *Classical Syriac: A Basic Grammar with a Chrestomathy* (Porta Linguarum Orientalium NS 19; Wiesbaden: Harrassowitz, 1997), 88.

28. *The Old Testament in Syriac according to the Peshitta Version*, 3/4. Section 2. *Daniel and Bel and the Dragon* (Leiden: E. J. Brill, 1980), 9.

Aramaic is likely to have been.[29] If he is right, the LXX once interpreted
the verse, "they said to him, 'King Nebuchadnezzar'." Munnich, however, who does not discuss Hamm's theory, thinks that, as with other
anonymous marginal readings in the Syro-Hexapla, it is not easy to
determine the bearing of αὐτῷ on the text. He considers that it is
probably a correction made in error, and, unless I have misunderstood
him, his reason is that it is not needed as well as τῷ βασιλεῖ.[30] In that
case, Ναβουχοδονοσόρ could have been taken either with τῷ βασιλεῖ or
with βασιλεῦ. But there may have been a Greek reading αὐτῷ τῷ
βασιλεῖ, and, if so, this might have been a literal rendering of the
Aramaic phrase לה למלכא. Equally, neither of the explanations offered
by Hamm and Munnich can be excluded. Too much uncertainty remains
for Hamm's conjecture to be a safe guide to the original reading of the
LXX.

Leaving aside Dan 3:16, in the LXX of Daniel kings are called
βασιλεῦ without the addition of a name or of any other title on 17 of the
23 occasions on which they are addressed (2:7, 11,[31] 28, 29, 31, 37; 3:10,
17; 4:16, 17, 19; 5:23; 6:12,[32] 22[*bis*], and, *sub asterisco*, 3:18, 91). This
is also how the king is addressed in Bel 11, 15–17, 19, 26, 27, though he
is called κύριε at v. 7 in 967,[33] and in any case the king is not named in
the LXX version of these stories. Parallels to Ναβουχοδονοσὸρ βασιλεῦ
are far fewer. A king is addressed twice as κύριε βασιλεῦ (2:4;[34] 3:9)
and once as Δαρεῖε βασιλεῦ (6:12), while a voice from heaven first says
Ναβουχοδονοσὸρ βασιλεῦ (4:28), then Ναβουχοδονοσὸρ βασιλεῦ
Βαβυλῶνος (4:30), and finally simply Ναβουχοδονοσόρ (4:30c) after
Nebuchadnezzar's kingdom has been taken away from him. Thus it
would be consistent with the normal usage of LXX Daniel for Nebuchadnezzar to have been addressed as βασιλεῦ in Dan 3:16, and it is
possible that this word was added because it seemed the appropriate way
to begin a speech to the king.

29. W. Hamm, *Der Septuaginta-Text des Buches Daniel Kap. 3–4 nach dem
Kölner Teil des Papyrus 967* (PTA 21; Bonn: Rudolf Habelt, 1977), 207, 209; idem,
*Der Septuaginta-Text des Buches Daniel Kap. 1–2 nach dem Kölner Teil des
Papyrus 967* (PTA 10; Bonn: Rudolf Habelt, 1969), 143.
    30. Munnich, 28.
    31. But cf. Munnich, 246.
    32. Cf. A. Geissen, *Der Septuaginta-Text des Buches Daniel Kap. 5–12,
zusammen mit Susanna, Bel et Draco sowie Esther Kap. 1,1a–2,15 nach dem Kölner
Teil des Papyrus 967* (PTA 5; Bonn: Rudolf Habelt, 1968), 41, 172–73.
    33. Ibid., 268–69.
    34. But cf. Munnich, 242.

Another possibility is that the translator used a *Vorlage* which included מלכא. At LXX Dan 2:28 βασιλεῦ does not correspond to anything either in the MT or in any other version, but it would correspond to מלכא if this should be restored at 4QDanᵃ 3 i 12.³⁵ In eight other places LXX Daniel has a reading which is shared with a Qumran scroll but with no other authority (2:20 = 4QDanᵃ 3 i 1; 2:40 = 4QDanᵃ 3 ii 5 9; 3:91 = 4QDanᵈ 2 ii 5; 5:7 = 4QDanᵃ 9 17; 8:3 = 4QDanᵇ 17 6; cf. 4QDanᵃ 14 14; 8:4 = 4QDanᵃ 14 16; 10:5 = 4QDanᶜ I 1; 10:16 = 6QpapDan 4 4).³⁶ There may be further instances at 2:23 = 4QDanᵃ 3 i 5; 10:6 = 4QDanᶜ I 4.³⁷ While LXX Daniel was not translated from a *Vorlage* which is identical with the text found in any of the Qumran scrolls, these readings may well go back to a Semitic original which differed from the tradition that is represented in the later MT. βασιλεῦ at 3:16 may be another example of this.

In 410, which is a witness to Theodotion, λέγοντες, which immediately precedes τῷ βασιλεῖ in most authorities for this version, is placed after it. This makes "Nebuchadnezzar" (without the title "king") the first word of the confessors' reply. But there appears to be no other Greek manuscript of Daniel which has this reading, and it is best understood as an inner-Greek corruption caused by the accidental transposition of λέγοντες and τῷ βασιλεῖ. Although this word order is also attested in Hippolytus, *In Danielem* 2.22.1, where it is found in one Greek manuscript,³⁸ τῷ βασιλεῖ is omitted on the other two occasions on which Hippolytus cites this passage,³⁹ and the name "Nebuchadnezzar" does not occur in any of the three quotations. It is impossible to tell whether the discourtesy of the later Masoretic punctuation is already present in Theodotion.

---

35. E. Ulrich, in E. Ulrich et al., *Qumran Cave 4. XI: Psalms to Chronicles* (DJD 16; Oxford: Clarendon, 2000), 244–46.

36. Ulrich, *Qumran Cave 4. XI*, 244–45, 247–48, 249–50, 252–53, 266–67, 272–73, 281–82; M. Baillet, in M. Baillet et al., *Les 'Petites Grottes' de Qumrân: Textes* (DJD 3; Oxford: Clarendon, 1962), 115.

37. Ulrich, *Qumran Cave 4. XI*, 244, 246, 272–73. 4QDanᵃ 3 i 5 is, however, apparently restored differently by M. Abegg, P. Flint and E. Ulrich, *The Dead Sea Scrolls Bible* (Edinburgh: T. & T. Clark, 1999), 487.

38. C. Diobouniotis, "Hippolyts Danielcommentar in Handschrift No. 573 [so the title-page; the title of the article has, wrongly, 'Nr. 373' (p. 45)] des Meteoronklosters," *TU* 38 (1911): 45–58 (50–51); G. N. Bonwetsch and M. Richard, eds., *Kommentar zu Daniel* (2d ed.; *Hippolyt Werke* 1/1; GCS NF 7; Berlin: Akademie, 2000), 100.

39. *In Danielem* 2.17.2; 2.23.2.

It was noted above that in Jerome's commentary on Daniel the reading at 3:16 which he defends has *Nabuchodonosor* as the first word of the confessors' speech. Jerome gives this speech in a Vulgate text. According to Cassiodorus, the arrangement of the entire Vulgate *per cola et commata* goes back to Jerome himself.[40] This claim is, however, implicitly questioned by Parkes, who believes that Jerome did no more than set out the text of Isaiah and Ezekiel in this way.[41] In either case, the manuscripts which have *dixerunt regi/Nabuchodonosor non oportet* may be presumed to represent his rendering more faithfully than the manuscripts and printed editions which have *dixerunt regi Nabuchodonosor/ non oportet*.[42] The different word division may be due to scribal inadvertence, or to the correction of what seemed to be a mistake. It must remain an open question whether it involves a deliberate repudiation of Jerome's understanding of the verse.

The seventh-century manuscript 7a1, which is printed in an emended form as the basic text of Daniel in the Leiden Peshiṭta, reads *lnbwkdnṣr mlkʾ* and an accent separates this phrase from the confessors' speech.[43] If I have understood him correctly, Hamm thinks that, when the name נבוכדנצר is not accompanied by a royal title in the MT, it is normally rendered *nbwkdnṣr mlkʾ* by the Peshiṭta. He believes that this accounts for the word order at Dan 3:16.[44] In that case, נבוכדנצר would have been translated, but not מלכא. By contrast, Hitzig says that the Peshiṭta recognizes that מלכא and נבוכדנצר are in apposition, though he supposes that the change in word order is unnecessary.[45]

Leaving aside Dan 3:16, the Peshiṭta retains the order (any) king's name + *mlkʾ* on the sixteen occasions on which it occurs in the MT of

40. *Institutiones* 1. Preface 9; 1.12.4; 15.12 (R. A. B. Mynors, ed., *Cassiodori Senatoris Institutiones* [Oxford: Clarendon, 1937], 8, 37–38, 48).

41. M. B. Parkes, *Pause and Effect: An Introduction to the History of Punctuation in the West* (Aldershot: Scolar, 1992), 15–16. Cf. Jerome's prefaces to his translations of Isaiah and Ezekiel (R. Weber, ed., *Biblia Sacra iuxta Vulgatam Versionem* [2 vols.; 2d ed.; Stuttgart: Württembergische Bibelanstalt, 1975], 2:1096, 1266).

42. *Biblia Sacra iuxta Latinam Vulgatam Versionem* (18 vols.; Rome: Typis Polyglottis Vaticanis [vols.1–16], Libreria Editrice Vaticana [vols. 17–18], 1926–95), 16:62. The first hand of one manuscript reads *Nabuchodonosor regi*, and two manuscripts add *rex* after *Nabuchodonosor*.

43. A. M. Ceriani, ed., *Translatio Syra Pescitto Veteris Testamenti ex Codice Ambrosiano sec. fere VI photolithographice edita* (2 vols.; Milan: A. della Croce, 1876–83), vol. 2, folio 207 verso.

44. Hamm, *Daniel Kap. 1–2*, 125; idem, *Daniel Kap. 3–4*, 195, 209.

45. Hitzig, *Das Buch Daniel*, 50.

Daniel (1:21; 3:1, 2[*bis*], 3, 5, 7, 9, 24, 31; 4:25, 28; 5:1; 6:7, 26; 8:1), and this order is also found eight times when the MT has only the name נבוכדנצר (1:18; 3:3 [second example], 13, 14, 19, 26, 28; 4:30), and once where neither word has a parallel in the MT (4:26), though when this is the case at 3:25 *mlk*ʾ is added by itself. At 9:25 *mšyḥ*ʾ *mlk*ʾ corresponds to the MT's משיח נגיד; the words are transposed in 9l6.[46] The Leiden Peshiṭta records no other variant that has a bearing on the argument of this or the following paragraph. It is significant that the order king's name + *mlk*ʾ is used for the opposite order in the MT in three out of six instances (2:46; 4:15; 6:10, but not 2:28; 5:9, 11), and that the order *mlk*ʾ + king's name is never employed where the MT has the order נבוכדנצר מלכא. In addition to the three occasions on which the order *mlk*ʾ + king's name is retained, it occurs once where the MT has only a king's name (5:29), and *mlk*ʾ ʾstygws at Bel 1 corresponds to ὁ βασιλεὺς ʾΑστυάγης in Theodotion. Thus there is a clear preference for the order king's name + *mlk*ʾ (29 examples) as against the order *mlk*ʾ + king's name (5 examples). Since this is a feature of the translator's style, Hitzig misses the point when he calls the change in word order at Dan 3:16 unnecessary.

It might be expected that Nebuchadnezzar's name would be treated in the same way as the names of other kings, but, when their names stand by themselves in the MT, the Peshiṭta either does not add *mlk*ʾ (5:2, 22; 6:2, 29) or uses the order *mlk*ʾ + king's name (5:29). Thus this material does not corroborate Hamm's position. Moreover, Hamm notes that the Peshiṭta does not add *mlk*ʾ to the name *nbwkdnṣr* at 4:1; 5:18. Five further examples (2:1[*bis*]; 4:31, 34; 5:2) should be taken into account. These seven instances balance the eight places in the Peshiṭta of Daniel where נבוכדנצר is rendered *nbwkdnṣr mlk*ʾ. In addition, if Hamm is right, מלכא has been omitted by the Peshiṭta and the preposition lamedh has been prefixed instead to the phrase which renders נבוכדנצר. This would be surprising, since in other respects the Peshiṭta provides a literal translation of Dan 3:16, apart from one extra word (*mlt*ʾ), which Taylor thinks may be an explanatory gloss.[47] Furthermore, it is significant that the order *nbwkdnṣr mlk*ʾ is preferred in the Peshiṭta of Daniel, and that, leaving aside Dan 3:16, the order מלכא נבוכדנצר in the MT is reversed three times in line with this. Thus Hamm's theory is unsatisfactory, and it is likely that the Peshiṭta's *lnbwkdnṣr mlk*ʾ renders למלכא נבוכדנצר. The translator(s) would then have thought that מלכא and נבוכדנצר were in apposition, as Hitzig claims, and that the confessors' reply began

---

46. *Daniel and Bel and the Dragon* (the Leiden Peshiṭta), 36.
47. R. A. Taylor, *The Peshiṭta of Daniel* (MPI 7; Leiden: Brill, 1994), 100.

לא־חשׁין. The punctuation in the seventh-century manuscript 7a1 is consistent with this.

The consonantal text of the MT is supported by Theodotion, the Vulgate and, in all probability, the Peshiṭta. Since the word order in the Peshiṭta is a feature of the translator's style, Montgomery is wrong to imply that it may confirm the transposition of מלכא and נבוכדנצר favoured by Torrey.[48] It is also doubtful whether a second מלכא should be restored in the MT on the authority of the LXX. As was noted above, there are some eight or ten places where LXX Daniel has a reading which is also found in one, or on occasion perhaps two, of the copies of Daniel from Qumran, but nowhere else. The earliest of these, 4QDanᶜ, is dated palaeographically towards the end of the second century B.C.,[49] and Collins, for example, thinks that LXX Daniel should probably be assigned to "the late second century" B.C.[50] These manuscripts from Qumran share a family relationship with the MT, but they also show the variety which existed before the MT was standardized. If, as may well be the case, the LXX included βασιλεῦ at 3:16 because מלכא was in its *Vorlage*, this would be of interest for the history of the pre-Masoretic text, but it cannot be assumed that it necessarily has any bearing on the Masoretic tradition.

It was noted above that Kamphausen and Bludau restore מלכא with the LXX in accordance with normal court etiquette, and this is the strongest argument for the emendation, though it is not conclusive. On occasion in the LXX there are comparable additions in speeches to Nebuchadnezzar, and Richter believes that βασιλεῦ was inserted as the first word of the confessors' reply as part of a strategy to soften a response which could have sounded impudent.[51] Nebuchadnezzar is addressed twice as κύριε βασιλεῦ (2:4;[52] 3:9) when the MT has מלכא, and at 2:28 βασιλεῦ εἰς τὸν αἰῶνα ζήσῃ is supplied when there is nothing corresponding to it in the MT. Moreover, at 2:7, 11 the LXX has the vocative βασιλεῦ where מלכא in the MT is the subject of a jussive or a participle. βασιλεῦ may have been added at 3:16 because this seemed the appropriate opening for a speech to a king. Such an opening is, however, omitted four times in the MT, when the Chaldaeans (2:10), Arioch (2:25) and Daniel (2:27) speak

48. Montgomery, *Commentary on the Book of Daniel*, 208.

49. Ulrich, *Qumran Cave 4. XI*, 270.

50. J. J. Collins, *Daniel: A Commentary on the Book of Daniel* (Hermeneia; Minneapolis: Fortress, 1993), 9.

51. H.-F. Richter, *Daniel 2–7: Ein Apparat zum aramäischen Text* (SSB 8; Aachen: Shaker, 2007), 51.

52. But see n. 34 above.

to Nebuchadnezzar in a chapter in which no rudeness is intended, and also, perhaps less surprisingly, when Daniel harangues Belshazzar (5:17). A similar directness at the beginning of the speech in Dan 3:16–18, in the course of which Nebuchadnezzar is addressed correctly as מלכא (vv. 17, 18), ought not to be excluded *a priori*.[53] Further, though the preceding למלכא could have influenced the loss of מלכא from the MT, it could equally well have led to its addition in the *Vorlage* of the LXX. In view of these considerations, there is no sufficient reason for emending the MT on the basis of a reading from a period when there was fluidity in the text of the Hebrew Bible.

In Dan 3 there is greater hostility towards Nebuchadnezzar in the LXX than in the MT. This is seen most sharply, but not exclusively, in the Additions.[54] Even so, the discourtesy of the later Masoretic punctuation is absent. It is also absent in the Peshitta. It is impossible to be sure where narrative ends and speech begins in LXX Dan 3:16, since the normal usage of LXX Daniel and the punctuation in the Syro-Hexapla support the printed editions of the LXX in placing the break after Ναβουχοδονοσόρ, while representatives of the Vetus Latina, as quoted in writings from North Africa in the middle of the third century A.D. and from Bethlehem at the start of the fifth century A.D., have *Nabuchodonosor rex* as the opening words of the speech. It would therefore be unwise to accept uncritically the way in which the text is set out in modern editions of the LXX, and it may be presumed that caution should also be exercised in using the printed editions of Theodotion. It is impossible to tell whether either version took Ναβουχοδονοσόρ to be vocative or dative. Jerome, however, may well have known already the Jewish tradition represented later in the MT, and it is likely that the Vulgate originally had the confessors address the king by his name alone. It is unclear whether the different understanding in many manuscripts and the printed editions of the Vulgate is due to scribal inadvertence or deliberate revision of the text.

II

Jerome maintains that the Aramaic text has the confessors say "O Nebuchadnezzar," and not "O King Nebuchadnezzar," "lest they should

53. But cf. K. Koch, *Daniel*. Vol. 1, *Dan 1–4* (BKAT 22/1; Neukirchen–Vluyn: Neukirchener, 1986–2005), 283.

54. T. J. Meadowcroft, *Aramaic Daniel and Greek Daniel: A Literary Comparison* (JSOTSup 198; Sheffield: Sheffield Academic, 1995), 136, 150–51, 156–60, 243.

seem to flatter an impious man or to term 'king' someone who was forcing them to unlawful acts."[55] Similarly Rashi, who is followed by Slotki,[56] comments, "Why is his [sc. Nebuchadnezzar's] name mentioned unless that is what they said to him? If our duty is to accept your decree to pay taxes and agricultural tax and capitation tax, then you are a king over us. If our duty is to renounce the Holy One, blessed be He, then Nebuchadnezzar is a mere lowly human, and thou art despised of the people." Moreover, Metsudat David states, "they addressed Nebuchadnezzar by name, and not by the title 'king,' meaning by this, 'you will not be king over us and you will not rule over us'," and explains that they continue by telling him, "We are not reacting to this terror by replying to you with appeasing or pleadings."[57] Recent defences of the Masoretic punctuation also recognize that the confessors were discourteous. Lacocque claims that this is appropriate in stories of this kind,[58] and Wesselius believes that the discourtesy follows naturally from the way in which the confessors' reply echoes the structure of Nebuchadnezzar's accusation.[59] In addition, Haag thinks that the king is called "Nebuchadnezzar" to emphasize the confessional character of vv. 16–18.[60] All three scholars have in mind the experiences of martyrs.

Hitzig,[61] however, as was noted above, maintains that the Masoretic punctuation is erroneous. He supposes that it has the confessors address Nebuchadnezzar as a lowly member of society ("wie einen Plebejer"), though it would be more exact to say that they speak to him as if he were an equal. Yet in the course of their speech he is twice addressed as "king" (vv. 17, 18), and Hitzig rightly identifies an inconsistency in the MT. Moreover, with the exception of Dan 5, Jews in these stories do not

---

55. Latin text in *S. Hieronymi Presbyteri Opera*, 1/5, 800–801.

56. J. J. Slotki, *Daniel Ezra and Nehemiah* (Soncino Books of the Bible; London: Soncino, 1951), 25.

57. Texts in מקראות גדולות (12 vols.; Warsaw: J. Levensohn, 1860–66), vol. 12, ad loc. I am grateful to Dr. Andrew Macintosh for providing the translations of these passages.

58. A. Lacocque, *Le Livre de Daniel* (CAT 15b; Neuchâtel: Delachaux & Niestlé, 1976), 58.

59. J. W. Wesselius, "Language and Style in Biblical Aramaic: Observations on the Unity of Daniel II–VI," *VT* 38 (1988): 194–209 (204–8); idem, "The Literary Nature of the Book of Daniel and the Linguistic Character of its Aramaic," *Aramaic Studies* 3 (2005): 241–83 (261–62; cf. 268 [Dan 3 and 6 are "martyrs' stories"]).

60. E. Haag, "Die drei Männer im Feuer nach Dan 3, 1–30," *TTZ* 96 (1987): 21–50 (26), reprinted in J. W. van Henten, ed., *Die Entstehung der Jüdischen Martyrologie* (SPB 38; Leiden: Brill, 1989), 20–50 (25).

61. Hitzig, *Das Buch Daniel*, 50.

show disrespect to their foreign rulers. Both the immediate and the wider context indicate that rudeness is out of place on the confessors' lips. Hitzig considers that originally מלכא and נבוכדנצר were in apposition, and that מלכא was put first for emphasis, to stress that the confessors were talking in this way to a king. Later, because the construction seemed strange, the words were separated. Presumably Hitzig wishes to explain the unusual order מלכא נבוכדנצר, since the normal Aramaic order, which is found fourteen times in Daniel, is נבוכדנצר מלכא (Dan 3:1, 2[*bis*], 3, 5, 7, 9, 24, 31; 4:25, 28; 5:1; 6:7, 26). Montgomery tentatively agrees that מלכא may sometimes have been placed first for emphasis.[62] Even so, neither scholar attempts to demonstrate that this is conveyed by any of the other six examples in the Aramaic of Daniel (2:28, 46; 4:15; 5:9, 11; 6:10). I hope to show elsewhere that the order מלכא נבוכדנצר is best understood as a Hebraism, and that there appears to be no special reason for its use in Daniel. Since, however, the order נבוכדנצר מלכא occurs nine times in Dan 3, Lacocque's claim that the Masoretes would have been sensitive to the unexpected change in the word order is plausible.[63] Moreover, according to the Peshitta the confessors' reply once began abruptly with לא־חשחין. In addition, between Dan 3:13 and 3:28, with the exception of v. 24, and apart from v. 16, Nebuchadnezzar is always referred to by his name alone (vv. 13, 14, 19, 26, 28). There is a further instance at Dan 3:25 in 4QDan[d] 2 ii 4.[64] Such stylistic features may have influenced the Masoretic punctuation of Dan 3:16, but would hardly have been enough to suggest the extreme discourtesy of the MT.

Attention should also be paid to van Henten's observation that "a number of martyr texts show a common pattern of narrative elements, which often occur in the same sequence." These texts include the descriptions of the martyrdoms of Eleazar and of the seven brothers and their mother in 2 Macc 6:18–31; 7 "if the context of these stories is taken into account." Except for the substitution of a miraculous rescue for the execution of the confessors, this narrative pattern is shared by Dan 3,[65] and Collins rightly sees this story as "a forerunner of the martyr legend."[66] Moreover, it is not surprising that there should be a note of defiance in the confessors' speech as they confront a hostile and arrogant

62. Montgomery, *Commentary on the Book of Daniel*, 208.

63. Lacocque, *Le Livre de Daniel*, 58 n. 2.

64. Ulrich, *Qumran Cave 4. XI*, 281.

65. J. W. van Henten, *The Maccabean Martyrs as Saviours of the Jewish People: A Study of 2 and 4 Maccabees* (JSJSup 57; Leiden: Brill, 1997), 8–9.

66. Collins, *Daniel*, 192, with further discussion on pp. 46, 186–87, 272.

king and reject his demands (v. 18). It is likely that, as Humphreys claims, some while after the stories of Dan 1–6 were composed, joining them to the visions of Dan 7–12 "served to heighten the element of conflict within these tales between the Jew and his environment," and that in addition "the events in the period of the Maccabees and the policy of Antiochus IV Epiphanes" influenced the way in which they were read.[67] Such factors may well have contributed to a reinterpretation of Dan 3:16.

In the course of the confessors' speech Nebuchadnezzar is twice called מלכא (vv. 17, 18). It is difficult to see why the confessors would use this respectful form of address if they were being discourteous. Moreover, no discourtesy is shown to Nebuchadnezzar in the Peshiṭta's rendering of Dan 3:16, which almost certainly supports the consonantal text of the MT and takes לא־חשחין as the first words of the confessors' reply. Taylor recognizes that the Peshiṭta of Daniel cannot be dated precisely, but prefers a date in the second century A.D.[68] In A.D. 407, however, as was noted above, Jerome knew an interpretation which is found later in the final form of the MT. It is likely that rudeness which is unparalleled elsewhere in the stories of Dan 1–6 was brought into the text between these dates by changing the punctuation and making נבוכדנצר, and not לא־חשחין, the first word spoken by the confessors.[69] It is of interest that, though a particular form of the consonantal text of the Hebrew Bible had become canonical, its interpretation was presumably modified in the accompanying oral tradition. A new understanding of the verse may well have been encouraged by the factors which were discussed above, but no doubt the experience of persecution lies behind it. The emendation proposed by Torrey is unsatisfactory because it fails to take account of the stability of the consonantal text both before and after the confessors are represented as discourteous.

Although Hitzig's treatment of Dan 3:16 shows greater insight, it is preferable to think, not of a corrupt text which requires emendation, but of the reconstruction of the history of the text. Because it is reasonable to suppose that the punctuation of the MT was intended to interpret it in a particular way, it is hardly possible to restore a more correct original version. Instead, three stages in the development of the text can be

---

67. W. L. Humphreys, "A Life-Style for Diaspora: A Study of the Tales of Esther and Daniel," *JBL* 92 (1973): 211–23 (222).

68. Taylor, *The Peshiṭta of Daniel*, 321–22.

69. A similar conclusion was reached independently by E. Reuss (*Die politische und polemische Litteratur der Hebräer* [Das Alte Testament 7; Braunschweig: C. A. Schwetschke & Son, 1894], 165 n. 4).

identified. During the first of these, the text of the Hebrew Bible was in a fluid state. Very little relevant information has survived from this period. All that is known is that the LXX's βασιλεῦ may reflect a reading מלכא, and that Theodotion was translated from a text identical to the consonantal text of the MT. How it was interpreted is unclear. In the second stage, after this type of text had become canonical, the confessors' speech began without any formal salutation; Dan 2:10, 25, 27; 5:17 may be compared. Finally the text was repunctuated to make the confessors impertinent.

On this occasion conjectural emendation of the MT is not appropriate, and a more descriptive approach is needed. Applying this strategy more generally to the text of the Hebrew Bible raises some interesting historical and theological questions, but they cannot be discussed here.

It is a great pleasure to dedicate this essay to Andrew Macintosh, who has been a friend for over fifty years.

Part V

THEMES AND RESONANCES OF BIBLICAL LANGUAGE
AND LITERATURE

SOME COMMENTS ON THE CONNOTATIONS
OF THE STEM נער IN EARLY RABBINIC TEXTS

Stefan C. Reif

How very appropriate that Andrew Macintosh and I, both of whose professional lives have been devoted to academic pursuits, should first have made contact some forty years ago in the pages of a scholarly periodical and, consequently, have seen our names together enter the dictionaries of Biblical Hebrew.[1] In 1969, Andrew was promoted from chaplain to the combined posts of Tutor and Assistant Dean at St. John's College in the University of Cambridge. It was clear to him that in such a role he was expected to research and publish, and the passion he had developed for Biblical Hebrew, under the tutelage of David Winton Thomas, Regius Professor of Hebrew in the Faculty of Oriental Studies (as it then was), and Henry Hart, Reader in Hebrew and Intertestamental Studies in the Faculty of Divinity, was such that what was almost his first venture into print was on a linguistic topic in the Hebrew Bible.[2] Analysing carefully the occurrences in the Hebrew Bible of the root נער, he convincingly demonstrated the inadequacy of the English translation "rebuke" and concluded that the root basically denotes passionate anger and its physical expression ("snorting fury"). When used with God as subject, Andrew pointed out, נער conveys the further sense of the effective working out of his anger. So far so good. But then Andrew went on to make another claim. He suggested that the translation of נער with words signifying moral rebuke "may be held to be a reflection of the intense moral and legal nature of post-exilic Judaism and affords evidence that, at least from the third century B.C. onwards, the Jews understood the word נער primarily in these terms."[3]

---

1. See, e.g., A. Caquot's article on the root נער in *TDOT*, 3, 49–53.
2. A. A. Macintosh, "A Consideration of Hebrew נער," *VT* 19 (1969): 471–79.
3. Ibid., 478.

That was a red rag to a bullish young Jewish scholar by the name of Stefan Reif, then teaching in the Department of Hebrew and Semitic Languages at the University of Glasgow. On the sharp lookout as I somewhat zealously was for anything published that was insufficiently appreciative or inaccurately descriptive of post-biblical Jewish learning, and ambitiously anxious as I had become to make progress with my scholarly publications, I examined the topic closely to see whether indeed Jewish scholars of later generations understood the root נער primarily in terms of moral rebuke. Unsurprisingly, of course, given the vast range of post-biblical Judaica, I found adequate evidence that the mediaeval Jewish commentators on the Hebrew Bible had located within the root various other facets of meaning and had therefore to some degree anticipated the findings that Andrew had presented in his article.[4] When my short response drawing attention to such evidence appeared in print, I had a most gracious letter from Andrew, welcoming its appearance, defending his overall treatment but acknowledging that by using the phrase "from the third century B.C. onwards" he had laid himself open to the "just criticism" that I had advanced. More significantly, he reported that while he was conscious that the views of mediaeval Jewish exegetes were at times rejected by modern scholarship, he now saw the need to consult them.[5]

In fact, Andrew has since then done a great deal more than consult them. He has consistently subjected them to close examination, both in Arabic and in Hebrew, and has taken great pleasure in fathoming their sometimes obscure exegetical depths. Since my arrival in Cambridge in 1973, he has often invited me to discuss these sources with him, and I believe that they have, as a result, become clearer and more accessible to both of us. Andrew's important scholarly work has regularly made reference to the lexicographical skills and exegetical insights demonstrated by such scholars as Jonah ibn Janaḥ and Abraham ibn Ezra, and I believe that his admiration for their deep understanding of the Hebrew language has grown over the years.[6] In a recent message to me, he generously noted that my short response to his article had been "a formative moment in my particular pilgrimage for it jolted me (a gentile parson!) into understanding that your Rabbis *must* be consulted on all such topics."[7] It

---

4. S. C. Reif, "A Note on נער," *VT* 21 (1971): 241–44.
5. Typewritten letter from Macintosh to Reif, 13 April, 1971.
6. See, e.g., his *Isaiah xxi: A Palimpsest* (Cambridge: Cambridge University Press, 1980), and *A Critical and Exegetical Commentary on Hosea* (ICC; Edinburgh: T. & T. Clark, 1997).
7. Electronic mail, Macintosh to Reif, 29 July, 2010.

has been my privilege not only to have co-operated with him in his research into such mediaeval texts but also to have benefited from his kind patronage at St. John's, to have joined and to have enjoyed the fellowship there with his active support, and to have developed a warm friendship with him that has brought me added joy in happy times and personal comfort in sadder circumstances.

Having been invited to contribute to this much deserved tribute to a meticulous scholar, an inspiring teacher and a fine individual, I glanced back at what he and I wrote four decades ago, and focused a more mature eye on the topic. What was still needed was a close examination of the talmudic–midrashic sources that straddled the period from the early Christian centuries until the classical Jewish Bible commentators of the high middle ages. Does such literature contribute anything to our knowledge of how the Hebrew root נער was employed and does it take us any further than the conclusions reached by Andrew and myself, as each of us took his first faltering steps as a scholar in print, כאשר ימשש העור באפלה (Deut 28:29)? I have tried to identify the different nuances associated with the root in the midrashim and to place these under separate headings. There is inevitably a degree of overlap and I am not convinced that every single instance may be so categorically and tightly defined. But that is the inevitable nature of lexicographical research. I believe that there are enough instances in each case, and that I have in general cited a large enough proportion of existing passages, to give an accurate overall impression and to permit some tentative conclusions.[8]

1. *Moral Rebuke or Reprimand*

Midrashic texts regularly testify to such a sense of the root in late talmudic and early mediaeval times. The *Tanḥuma-Yelammedenu* midrashim—which exist in two versions, namely, the common printed edition and the manuscript-based Buber edition—probably originated in the land of Israel in the late talmudic period and underwent a process of redaction in Babylon in the subsequent two centuries. In his treatment of the opening two words of the book of Exodus, the aggadist stresses the importance of disciplining one's children. By way of an exegesis of Pss 2:1 and 3:2, he forges a link between the lack of such parental

8. For the dating of midrashic compilations, I have used G. Stemberger, *Introduction to the Talmud and Midrash* (trans. M. Bockmuehl; 2d ed.; Edinburgh: T. & T. Clark, 1996). For identifying sources that include the root נער, I have gratefully utilized the Bar-Ilan University's Responsa Project and the Ma'agarim Project of the Hebrew Language Academy in Jerusalem.

activity, and its consequences, and two verses describing the war of Gog and Magog at the end of time. While in the earlier eschatological verse, as the rabbinic preacher sees it, it is only the nations that are stirred up against Israel, the latter verse has David bewailing the deep enmity of his own children towards him. All this because he had failed to provide them with appropriate parental guidance. With regard to Adonijah, the Hebrew expression is ולא גער בו, and this could well be rendered as "he failed to issue the necessary moral rebuke due from a father to a child." The midrashic text further notes that, although Adonijah engaged in disreputable behaviour, his father did not call him to task over this (ולא רידהו אביו), providing further evidence of the point being made.[9] The text is paralleled in the later midrash *Shemot Rabbah* without significant variation.[10]

Eli, the priest at the Shiloh sanctuary, judge in Israel, and the mentor of the prophet Samuel, also denied adequate discipline to his children, in this case of course the source being the biblical verse itself. According to *Midrash Shemuel* (edited in the mediaeval period but containing much earlier material), the meaning of the expression ולא כהה בהם in 1 Sam 3:13 is that לא גער בהון, that is to say, he offered no moral rebuke.[11] The family context and the rebuke delivered to a child by a parent is again the theme in a midrash about King Solomon that apparently belongs to a late collection of tales that stress his piety rather than his shortcomings. When wandering the world as a beggar, he is given menial tasks in the kitchen of the king of Ammon whose daughter Naamah falls in love with him. Her mother chides her for this (ואמה גערה בה), suggesting more appropriate alliances, but the daughter has her way and not only do they live happily ever after but Naamah is also accorded a high religious status by the talmudic–midrashic literature.[12]

This general and expected sense of "moral rebuke" for the root גער is found in many other midrashic contexts, in collections from different periods, with particular reference to the activities of various biblical

---

9. *Midrash Tanḥuma* (2 vols. in 1; Warsaw: J. Munk, 1879), 62a–62b.

10. *Shemot Rabbah* (*Midrash Rabbah*; 3 vols. in 2; Vilna: Widow and Brothers Romm, 1878), 2a. For the English edition, see *Midrash Rabbah: Exodus* (trans. S. M. Lehrman; 3d ed.; London: Soncino, 1961), 3.

11. *Midrash Shemuel* (ed. S. Buber; Cracow: J. Fischer, 1893), 10.1, 76. The use of the Aramaic word בהון appears to indicate that the aggadist may here be citing a targumic version of the verse. A. Sperber, *The Bible in Aramaic*. Vol. 2, *The Former Prophets According to Targum Jonathan* (Leiden: E. J. Brill, 1959), 101, records the variant נזף for כהה in Codex Reuchlinianus but makes no mention of a variant גער that would be parallel to the midrashic rendering here cited.

12. *Ozar Midrashim* (ed. J. D. Eisenstein; 2 vols.; New York: Eisenstein, 1915), 2:530.

characters. According to *Pirqe de-Rabbi Eliezer* (eighth–ninth centuries?), Zimri, son of Salu (Num 25:1–15), did not follow the example of his ancestor Simeon who, with his brother Levi, made an aggressive stand against the sexual immorality of the Shechemites vis-à-vis their sister Dinah (Gen 31), but chose not to condemn the Israelites' whoring with the Midianite women (ולא נער בבחורי ישראל). What is more, he himself indulged in such behaviour and was consequently dispatched by the more zealous Phinehas.[13] The verse in Qoh 7:5 that refers to נערת חכם is explained by the *Qohelet Rabbah* and *Yalquṭ Shim'oni* as alluding to the admonitions delivered by Moses to Israel, by *Pesiqta Rabbati* as God's unsuccessful warnings to Israel, and by *Leqaḥ Ṭov* as the moral advice given by Solomon himself in the book of Qohelet.[14]

A remarkable exegesis relating to the same verse in Qohelet is found in *Qohelet Rabbah* and *Midrash Zuṭa* and contrasts the phrases נערת חכם and שיר כסילים.[15] The former is taken as a reference to those (דרשנים) who offer moral or halakhic guidance (נערה) by way of addresses in the synagogue while the latter is explained as an allusion to those who expand on the biblical text by way of a targumic method (מתורגמנין). This could refer to those who deliver loudly to the people what the teacher has quietly communicated to them, or to those who translate and expand the biblical verses in Aramaic. Given that the word שיר is being interpreted,

13. *Pirqei de-Rabbi Eliezer* (ed. C. M. Horowitz; Jerusalem: Makor, 1972), 43a; ed. M. Higger in *Ḥoreb* 10 (1948): 235. For the English edition, see G. Friedlander, *Pirkê de Rabbi Eliezer (The Chapters of Rabbi Eliezer the Great) According to the Text of the Manuscript Belonging to Abraham Epstein of Vienna* (London: Kegan Paul, Trench, Trubner, 1916), 369.

14. *Qohelet Rabbah* (*Midrash Rabbah*; 3 vols. in 2; Vilna: Widow & Brothers Romm, 1878), 19a; for the English edition, see *Midrash Rabbah: Ecclesiastes* (trans. A. Cohen; 3d ed.; London: Soncino, 1961), 179; *Yalquṭ Shim'oni* (ed. Y. Shiloni; Jerusalem: Rav Kook, 1973–2010, final volumes still awaited), no. 973; *Pesiqta Rabbati* (ed. M. Friedmann; Vienna: J. Kaiser, 1880), 132b; *Pesiqta Rabbati: A Synoptic Edition of Pesiqta Rabbati Based Upon All Extant Manuscripts and the Editio Princeps* (ed. R. Ulmer; South Florida Studies in the History of Judaism, 155; 2 vols.; Atlanta: Scholars Press, 1997–99), 2:667; for an English edition, see *Pesikta Rabbati: Discourses for Feasts, Fasts, and Special Sabbaths* (trans. W. G. Braude; Yale Judaica Series, 18; 2 vols.; New Haven: Yale University Press, 1968), 2:543; *Lekach-Tob* (ed. S. Buber; Vilna: Widow & Brothers Romm, 1894), on Deuteronomy, 1a.

15. *Qohelet Rabbah*, 19a; English edition, 179; *Midrash Suta* (ed. S. Buber; Berlin: Itzkowski, 1894), 109; *Kohelet Zuta* (ed. S. Buber; Vilna: Widow & Brothers Romm, 1925), 134. But compare the significant textual variation in G. Feinberg, ed., *Tobia ben Elieser's Commentar zu Koheleth (Lekach Tob) samt Einleitung und Commentar* (Berlin: Itzkowski, 1904), 32.

however, it seems likely that the criticism here is of the *payyeṭanim* who expanded on the biblical verses by way of their poems, often providing linguistic and literary entertainment rather than moral guidance.[16]

These examples—and various others—indicate that midrashic Hebrew of the talmudic and early mediaeval period continued to use the root for descriptions of "moral rebuke" but usually with a favourable, exemplary and welcome sense.

2. *Authoritative Aspect*

A common feature of some talmudic and midrashic texts is the use of the root to describe a serious censure, at times involving unceremonious or even dishonourable dismissal. In such instances the Hebrew is a little more complex and takes the form of a sentence such as גער בו והוציאו בנזיפה. This is not easily rendered in English but conveys something like "he censured him severely and discharged him" or, more popularly, "he ticked him off and sent him packing." Some examples will undoubtedly clarify the overall sense intended. When, as detailed in the tannaitic midrash *Siphre* and in the post-talmudic tractate *Avot de-Rabbi Nathan*, the angel of death approached Moses and demanded that he give up his soul, Moses claimed superiority of rank and dismissed the angel. It was God himself who then arranged for Moses a special place in the celestial world and who consigned his soul to that fate.[17] The same four-word idiom occurs in the well-known story of the would-be proselyte who approached Shammai with some difficult and provocative questions about the rabbinic notion of Torah and some demands about his future status as a Jew. While Shammai dismissed him angrily, Hillel treated him with greater patience, engaged him in religious dialogue and won him over to Judaism. The tale is told in Hebrew in numerous texts, including the Babylonian Talmud and *Avot de-Rabbi Nathan*, but occurs

16. Opposition to *piyyuṭim* is a well-recognized phenomenon in rabbinic literature from as early as the middle of the geonic period in the eighth century; see J. J. Petuchowski, *Theology and Poetry: Studies in the Medieval Piyyut* (Littman Library of Jewish Civilization; London: Routledge & Kegal Paul, 1978), 16–19.

17. *Sifre on Deuteronomy* (ed. L. Finkelstein; New York: Jewish Theological Seminary of America, re-publication of the Berlin edition of 1939, repr., 1969), 326–27; for the English edition, see R. Hammer, *Sifre: A Tannaitic Commentary on the Book of Deuteronomy* (Yale Judaica Series 24; New Haven: Yale University Press, 1986), 296–97; *Avoth de-Rabbi Nathan: Solomon Schechter Edition* (ed. M. Kister; New York: Jewish Theological Seminary of America, 1997), Recension A, 25a–25b; for the English edition, see J. Goldin, *The Fathers According to Rabbi Nathan* (Yale Judaica Series 10; New Haven: Yale University Press, 1955), 65–66. See also *Yalquṭ Shim'oni* (ed. Shiloni), no. 940.

in a different form in *Qohelet Rabbah*, where the two rabbinic characters are Rav and Samuel, the inquirer is a Persian and the language is Aramaic. More correctly, the language of the pericope is Aramaic with the exception of our phrase וגער בו והוציאו בנזיפה![18]

Rabbi Eliezer ben Hyrcanus was a leading second-century scholar and teacher of Rabbi Akiva. Banished by his colleagues from their society for refusing to abide by majority decision, Eliezer seems to have led a lonely life, and his teachings were deliberately ignored. The talmudic story has it that, when he lay dying, he was visited by Akiva and other rabbis who sat at a distance, unsure of whether they ought to come closer. It was Friday afternoon and Eliezer's son, Hyrcanus, in keeping with a rabbinic ruling about not wearing *tefillin* on the sabbath, attempted to remove his father's set because of the approaching dusk, but was summarily dismissed by Eliezer (גער בו והוציאו בנזיפה).

Hyrcanus's comment that his father had lost his senses elicited from the old man the remark that he was the sane one in the family. "How can you abandon a Pentateuchal law, the neglect of which is punishable by death, because of a rabbinic prohibition?" The visiting rabbis drew closer to hear more, but maintained the distance of "four amot" because of the ban.[19] Our expression occurs again in the tale of another unexpectedly favourable assessment of a character normally subject to severe criticism. The question is asked in *Seder Eliyahu Rabbah* (from the geonic period?) why some credit accrues to the arch-idolater Jeroboam II (ben Joash) and the reply is given that he refused to countenance the scandalous remarks made about the prophet Amos by the priest Amaziah but sent him on his way "with a flea in his ear" (גער בו והוציאו בנזיפה).[20] In addition, when *Avot de-Rabbi Nathan* criticizes those who refuse hospitality to a poor beggar it utilizes our expression to describe how the door is slammed in his face (וגוערין בו והוציאו בנזיפה).[21]

Another way of describing such a serious censure involves the use of the alternative phrase גער בו גערה גדולה...נזף בו. *Avot de-Rabbi Nathan* explains how Satan challenged God in the matter of the genuineness of Job's piety. Once this had been proved, God censured Satan severely and

---

18. *b. Shab.* 31a; *Avoth de-Rabbi Nathan*, 31a–31b; English edition, 80–82; *Qohelet Rabbah*, 19b; English edition, 187.

19. *b. Sanh.* 68a.

20. *Seder Eliahu Rabba and Seder Eliahu Zuta* (ed. M. Friedmann; 2d ed.; Jerusalem: Bamberger & Wahrman, 1960), 88 and 184, citing 2 Kgs 14:23–29 and Amos 7:10–17. See also *Yalqut Shim'oni* (ed. Shiloni), no. 232.

21. *Avoth de-Rabbi Nathan*, 17b; English edition, 48.

banished him from the celestial sphere (והשליכו מן השמים).[22] In a number
of other midrashim, the word נער is used more simply but it is in each
case obvious from the context that a severe reprimand is intended. When
Moses ascends to heaven at God's invitation in order to take delivery of
the divine Torah, various angels meet him and object strongly to his
presence among them. Each one challenges him in an offensive manner
(נער בו במשה), asking him "What are you, Amram's mortal son, doing
here among such holy company?"[23] In some instances there are interesting variations in the different treatments of the theme of God and his
confrontations with the angels.[24] In other cases a more aggressive act
on the part of God appears to be presupposed and they are therefore
included in section 7 below.[25]

In all these passages there is a clash between two characters, with the
more powerful of the two censuring the other for some unacceptable
behaviour and dismissing, or attempting to dismiss, him from the
environment under his control.

3. Rejection

A weaker sense of the root נער connoting "dismissal," more akin to
"rejection" than to "rebuke" or "reprimand," is to be found in a talmudic
baraita reporting a question by a woman who had experienced sexual
intercourse at the age of three. She asked whether she was permitted to a
priest in marriage, presumably aware that such an act might define her as
a זונה, who is forbidden to a priest (Lev 21:7). Rabbi Akiva replied in the
affirmative, presumably on the grounds that this, at such an age, had not
been a voluntary act. She then put her case in a different light by way of
a simile. Her case is like that of an infant whose finger is dipped into
honey. The child angrily pushes it away twice but on the third occasion
sucks it with pleasure. Akiva appreciated her point and revised his ruling,
albeit inviting objections from his students. The word describing the
infant's initial rejection of the honey is נוער.[26]

Here the root is being used to denote no more than a gentle refusal.
There are no moral implications, no degree of censure, no question of
authority and no hint of anger.

22. *Avoth de-Rabbi Nathan*, addendum 2, to Recension A, 82b.
23. *Pesiqta Rabbati* (ed. Friedmann), 96b; ed. Ulmer, 1:422–23; English edition,
1:405–6; *Ozar* (ed. Eisenstein), 2:306.
24. *Pesiqta Rabbati* (ed. Friedmann), 203a; *Tanhuma* (ed. Warsaw), 124a–24b.
25. See n. 43.
26. *b. Nid.* 45a.

4. *Reprimand*

Another use of the root נער belongs to a similar semantic context but with a somewhat weaker application, perhaps best rendered "reprimand" rather than "moral rebuke." It is found in a midrashic parable that occurs in a large number of compilations, as early as *Pesiqta de-Rabbi Kahana* in the talmudic period and *Tanḥuma* and *Pitron Torah* in the geonic, and as late as *Yalquṭ Shim'oni*, perhaps in the thirteenth century.[27] In promoting the tithing of one's produce (Deut 14:22), the aggadist tells of a householder who built up large stores of wine and oil but paid no tithes. Divine punishment was meted out to him in what reads as a somewhat amusing fashion. His mind was taken over by a mischievous sprite that induced him to take a stick and set about smashing all the jars that he himself had stored. When one of his domestic staff took issue with him (נער בו בן ביתו), the householder beat him on the head for his pains and complained: "Instead of helping me, you lecture me (תחות מסייעת יתי את גער בי)." Quick to learn, his servant followed his master's example and smashed twice as many jars.

The Babylonian Talmud makes use of the verb when reporting Rabbi Joshua's response to one of the miracles said to have occurred in apparent support of the individual views of R. Eliezer ben Hyrcanus against the majority views of his colleagues. R. Eliezer calls on the walls of the rabbinical school to demonstrate that his view is correct and they do so by threatening to collapse. At which point, R. Joshua chides them (נער בהם רבי יהושע) for interfering in a matter that concerns only the halakhic experts.[28] In a liturgical context, the Palestinian Talmud reports that when a precentor bowed too low when reciting his prayers, one of the talmudic teachers (whose identity is uncertain) removed him. A different version of the story is then offered according to which he was not removed but was subject to נערה.[29] If this constitutes less of a

---

27. *Pesikta de Rav Kahana* (ed. B. Mandelbaum; 2 vols.; New York: Jewish Theological Seminary of America, 1962), 1:164; for English edition, see *Pesikta de-Rab Kahana* (trans. W. G. Braude and I. J. Kapstein; 2d ed.; Philadelphia: Jewish Publication Society of America, 1978), 189; *Midrash Tanḥuma* (ed. S. Buber; 2 vols.; Vilna: Widow & Brothers Romm, 1885), 2, on Deuteronomy, 12a; for English edition, see *Midrash Tanḥuma* (trans. J. T. Townsend; 3 vols.; Hoboken: Ktav, 1989–2003), 3:312; *Tanḥuma* (ed. Warsaw), 108b; *Sefer Pitron Torah* (ed. E. E. Urbach; Jerusalem: Magnes, 1978), 259–60; *Yalquṭ Shim'oni* (ed. Shiloni), nos. 892 and 932.

28. *b. B. Mes.* 59b.

29. *y. Ber.* 1.5(4) (3d); for an English translation, see *The Talmud of Jerusalem*. Vol. 1, *Berakhoth* (trans. M. Schwab; London: Williams & Norgate, 1886), 24–25,

stricture than removal, it must bear a fairly mild sense, perhaps akin to
"rebuke" or, more likely, "reprimand."

These examples, then, testify to a reprimand that is no more than what
we would colloquially call a "ticking off."

5. *Dissolution*

An awareness that the root גער may in midrashic literature carry a sense
that goes significantly beyond that of reprimand, moral rebuke and
authoritative censure is found in the twelfth-century midrash *Sekhel Ṭov*.
The author, Menaḥem ben Shelomo, comments on the phrase ויגער בו
אביו (Gen 37:10) that describes Jacob's response to Joseph's reports of
the dreams he had experienced. The aggadist explains that there are two
meanings of the root גער. The first describes the frank reprimand that is
given to a junior, to a child or to a pupil by way of censure, and examples occur in this Genesis verse as well as in Qoh 7:5 and Jer 29:27. The
second refers to a call for dissolution (גערת מאמר השמר), as in Pss 68:31,
9:6 and 80:17.[30] In this respect, the compiler of *Sekhel Ṭov* is more of a
linguist and has more in common with the mediaeval rational exegetes
such as Ibn Ezra and Kimchi[31] than with other midrashim of assorted
dates, such as *Bereshit Rabbah*, *Midrash Aggadah* and *Yalquṭ Shim'oni*,
that comment on the same Genesis verse. They simply cite the first of the
two meanings and make a link between the reprimand recorded here and
that noted in Jer 29:27.[32] The idea of גערה as dissolution is taken further
in a talmudic passage that explains the substantive גערה as one of the
various descriptions of death. Death in a day is a swift death; in two days
a delayed death; in three, the result of גערה; in four, the result of נזיפה;

and *The Jerusalem Talmud: First Order: Zera'im: Berakhot* (trans. H. W. Guggen-
heimer; Berlin: de Gruyter, 2000), 138.

30. *Sechel Tob* (ed. S. Buber; 2 vols.; Berlin: Mekize Nirdamim, 1900), 1:216. It
is contextually clear that this phrase is intended to mean "dissolution" but less
obvious how this is to be explained from the final word, unless it has the sense of
"threat" or "warning." The text should perhaps be emended to השמד and, given that
this could mean "apostasy" to a censor (rather than the intended "destruction"), it is
not difficult to imagine why it was changed. I am grateful to my friend and colleague
Dr. Avi Shivtiel for helping me to clarify this.

31. See Reif, "Note," 242–43.

32. *Bereschit Rabba* (ed. J. Theodor and Ch. Albeck; 3 vols.; 2d ed.; Jerusalem:
Wahrmann, 1965), 2:1014; for the English edition, see *Midrash Rabbah: Genesis*
(trans. H. Freedman; 3d ed.; London: Soncino, 1961), 777–78; *Midrash Aggadah:
Agadischer Commentar zum Pentateuch* (ed. S. Buber; Vienna: A. Fanto, 1894), 89;
Yalquṭ Shim'oni (ed. Shiloni), no. 141.

and in five, a normal death. Interesting for our purposes here is the notion that נערה is the kind of curse that results in injury or death.[33]

6. *Fatal Curse*

This latter sense, which extends to controlling, overpowering, execrating and eliminating, is also recorded in numerous midrashim. The giant Og, king of Bashan, is a popular figure in midrashic literature which enjoys expanding on the huge dimensions already presupposed for him in the Pentateuch. In one post-talmudic tractate, he is identified with Abraham's loyal servant, Eliezer, and it is said that Abraham so execrated him (נער בו) that one of his teeth fell out. Not passing up a chance to benefit from such a mishap, Abraham promptly used the tooth to build himself an ivory bed where he always subsequently slept, or, according to another view, an ivory chair in which he regularly sat.[34] Two midrashic passages cited by Eisenstein refer to a scream so terrifying (נערה גדולה) that the one against whom this is directed instantly takes flight.[35]

An extensive and assorted list of aggadic passages, early and late, use the root נער to describe the destruction of Israel's enemies at the end of time. Utilizing one of numerous phrases in Ps 68 that are virtually impossible to translate and therefore a great gift to the rabbinic homilist, the exegesis recorded in one talmudic and three midrashic passages centres on the words נער חית קנה in v. 31. It sees there a reference to the ultimate destruction (נער) of the people who are associated with the reed and it sometimes spells this out as Edom/Esau/Rome, possibly meaning Christianity.[36] Already in Dan 7, the various empires from which the Jews suffered were designated as beasts, so that it is not altogether surprising to find the word חיה similarly used by the aggadist. The under-lying reasons for associating the word קנה with Rome relate, variously, to that city's alleged origin in a reed planted in the sea by the angel Gabriel when Solomon married Pharaoh's daughter, to the quill it used to sign its anti-Jewish decrees, and to its living among the reeds (an unclear allu-

33. *b. M. Qat.* 28a.
34. *Massekhet Soferim* (ed. M. Higger; New York: Debe Rabbanan, 1937), addendum 1, section 2, 366–67.
35. *Ozar* (ed. Eisenstein), 1:73 and 2:382.
36. *b. Pes.* 118b; *Shemot Rabbah* 63b; English edition, 434; *Midrash Tehillim: Schocher Tob* (ed. S. Buber: Vilna: Widow & Brothers Romm, 1891), 160b; English edition, *The Midrash on Psalms* (trans. W. G. Braude; Yale Judaica Series 13; 2 vols.; Yale University Press, 1959), 1:548; *Aggadat Bereshit* (ed. S. Buber; Vilna: Widow & Brothers Romm, 1925), 50a and 57b.

sion). There may also be some connection here with the root קנה and its meaning of taking possession and, possibly, with the wood of the cross.

The theme of God's ultimate destruction of Israel's enemies, who are constantly devising evil against her, and the use of the word נער to describe this, are common to a number of other midrashim from various dates and provenances, but in this case by way of their interpretation of Ps 9:6 where the root נער occurs in parallel with the root אבד (גערת גוים אבדת רשע). In five midrashic texts, the wicked individuals and nations are identified as Esau/Edom and Amalek/Haman, and these midrashim carefully note that Jacob/Israel is excluded from this ultimate elimination from the scene.[37] In other pieces of aggada, the Hebrew of Ps 119:21 (גערת זדים ארורים השגים ממצותיך) is understood as a reference to the ultimate and serious punishment of those who transgress some of the most essential requirements for civilized behaviour. Their misdemeanours include idolatry, adultery, incest, murder and slander and these are often the result of drunkenness.[38] The root that we are discussing obviously carries in these passages a fearful and destructive sense.

7. Powerful Control

We already encountered how Satan and the angels were severely censured. There are other midrashic tales that use the root נער to describe an act of control or the exercise of power. They usually relate to what may be remnants of ancient Israelite myths about creation, celestial beings, fire and water, and the major figures and events in early Israelite history. It is not an unusual phenomenon for midrashic literature to preserve ancient Israelite myths that tended to be curtailed or totally suppressed when the battle with idolatry was still such an ongoing one in the biblical period.[39]

---

37. *Pesikta de Rav Kahana* (ed. Mandelbaum), 43. *Pesiqta Rabbati* (ed. Friedmann), 48b–51a; ed. Ulmer, 1:179; trans. Braude, 1:225–31; *Midrash Tanhuma* (ed. Buber), on Deuteronomy, 2:20a; English edition, 3:342; *Midrash Tehillim* (ed. Buber, 42a); English edition, 1:137; *Yalquṭ Shim'oni* (ed. Shiloni), no. 938.

38. *Bemidbar Rabbah* (*Midrash Rabbah*; 3 vols. in 2; Vilna: Widow & Brothers Romm, 1878), 2:35b; for the English edition, see *Midrash Rabbah: Numbers* (trans. J. J. Slotki; 3d ed.; London: Soncino, 1961), 348; *Midrash Tanhuma* (ed. Warsaw), 2:13b; *Pitron Torah* (ed. Urbach), 30.

39. On various aspects of the midrashic genre, see M. Hirshman, *A Rivalry of Genius: Jewish and Christian Biblical Interpretation* (trans. B. Stein; Albany: State University of New York Press, 1996); I. Jacobs, *The Midrashic Process: Tradition and Interpretation in Rabbinic Judaism* (Cambridge: Cambridge University Press, 1995); idem, *The Impact of Midrash* (JSSSup 19; Oxford: Oxford University Press,

During the creation, according to two midrashim, the angel of darkness objected to God's plan to create light. God therefore exercised his power over him and over all the other angels (גער בהם) and, according to some versions, threatened them with destruction (אני גוער בך ומאבדך מן העולם), so that they scattered.[40] In other collections, it is explained that the primaeval waters had the intention of spreading wherever they wished but God prevented this. He exercised control over them (גער בהם or גער בים), set their limits and restricted them to certain areas.[41] *Tanḥuma* (Warsaw edition) cites Ps 104:7 and provides an explanation of how the root גער is being understood in this context by paraphrasing it with the use of the root בעט meaning "kick" or, less literally, "militate against."[42]

One aggadic tale, repeated in various collections, describes God's powerful intervention when an attempt was made to prevent the *'aqedah*. When Abraham and Isaac were in danger of drowning in the river that Satan placed in their path as they proceeded to Mount Moriah, God took control of the waters and dried them up, or, in another version, overpowered Satan.[43] Similarly, another attempt to prevent a historical miracle was thwarted by God. When the Israelites wished to cross the Red Sea during their escape from Egypt, the waters tried to resist but God overpowered them and they parted.[44] The Israelites complained so much in the desert that God began to consume them with fire (Num 11:2). The biblical verse reports that Moses prayed to God, but a midrash makes the remarkable claim that Moses overpowered the divine fire

2006); R. Kasher, "The Interpretation of Scripture in Rabbinic Literature," in *Mikra: Text, Translation, Reading and Interpretation of the Hebrew Bible in Ancient Judaism and Early Christianity* (ed. M. J. Mulder; Assen: Van Gorcum; Philadelphia: Fortress, 1988), 547–94; G. G. Porton, *Understanding Rabbinic Midrash: Texts and Commentary* (Hoboken: Ktav, 1985).

40. *Midraš Berešit Rabbati ex libro Mosis Haddaršan collectus* (ed. Ch. Albeck; Jerusalem: Mekize Nirdamim, 1940), 10; and *Pesiqta Rabbati* (ed. Friedmann), 95a and 203a; ed. Ulmer, 1:414; English edition (ed. Braude), 1:400.

41. *b. Ḥag.* 12a; *Bereschit Rabba* (ed. Theodor and Albeck), 1:31–35; English edition, 34–36; *Shemot Rabbah*, 30a–30b; English edition, 190–91; *Tanḥuma* (ed. Warsaw), 32a–32b; *Batei Midrashot* (ed. S. A. Wertheimer and A. Wertheimer; 2 vols.; 2d ed.; Jerusalem: Mosad ha-Rav Kuk, 1953), 1:25; 2:422; *Yalquṭ Shim'oni* (ed. Shiloni), nos. 560 and 913; *Ozar* (ed. Eisenstein), 2:314.

42. *Tanḥuma* (ed. Warsaw), 32b.

43. *Tanḥuma* (ed. Warsaw), 30b; *Midrash Aggadah* (ed. Buber), 51; *Yalquṭ Shim'oni* (ed. Shiloni), no. 99; *Berešit Rabbati* (ed. Albeck), 89; *Ozar* (ed. Eisenstein), 1:147.

44. *Midrash Tehillim* (ed. Buber), 238a; English edition (trans. Braude), 2:221; *Yalquṭ Shim'oni* (ed. Shiloni), no. 873.

(משה גער באש).[45] *Qohelet Rabbah* expands on the wickedness of Titus who not only destroyed the Jerusalem Temple but also performed acts of violence, blasphemy and fornication in its precincts. Experiencing a storm at sea during his return to Rome, he then claimed that Israel's God had power only in the sea. God immediately decided to take his revenge by other means and imposed calm on the sea (מיד גער הקב"ה לים). He later dispatched the Roman general by means of one of nature's tiniest creatures, the mosquito.[46] What these latter midrashim have in common is their compilers' conviction that the miraculous, as against the natural, was enthusiastically employed by God, or permitted by him through Moses, in the overwhelming divine desire to support the promotion, survival and vindication of Israel. Forms of the root גער constituted appropriate expressions to describe how power was miraculously employed to that purpose.

Conclusions

Clearly, גער was widely used over a long period to signify moral rebuke, but there are also numerous examples through the whole midrashic era of its occurrence with a sharper connotation, as when it conveys the sense of a serious censure by someone with a degree of authority over an inferior. In this latter sense, the narrative often employs a stereotyped, literary expression. There are also weaker meanings for the verb and these range from the talmudic to the late midrashic periods, that is, until the high middle ages. Such meanings include the kinds of refusal or reprimand that are more akin to questions or appeals and that imply no more than a negative preference or a gentle chiding. But, as in the Hebrew Bible, there is a usage that hints at a much stronger act than that of moral rebuke. There the result is damage, death or dissolution and these are brought about by way of an oath or curse loudly uttered by the perpetrator. The tales about such acts may have early origins in Hebrew mythology, since the topic is often the divine control over the powers of nature. There are, however, also cases where the deserving victims may be the enemies of Israel at various points in her history or where the perpetrator is Moses. Once again, it is well-nigh impossible to associate the linguistic usage with one particular period since it is documented in various midrashim dating from different times. On the other hand, it is

45.   J. Mann, *The Bible as Read and Preached in the Old Synagogue* (2 vols.; 2d ed., with prolegomenon by B. Z. Wacholder; New York: Ktav, 1971), 1:80 (Hebrew section); *Yalquṭ Shim'oni* (ed. Shiloni), no. 406.
46.   *Qohelet Rabbah*, 15a; English edition, 140.

well recognized that the midrashic genre is such that the date of the tale or the idea may be singularly at odds with the date of the compilation, and one's expectations in this respect cannot be high. Having also briefly glanced at some of the *piyyuṭim* in which the root נער occurs, it seems to me that much of what has been said above about the midrashic texts applies also to the poetic ones which, after all, date from the same period and often use similar themes. But there may be additional nuances that can be detected among the *piyyuṭim* and it might therefore be worthwhile for researchers to examine this in detail at some future date.

In sum, Andrew was correct in identifying moral rebuke and passionate anger as two sides of the same linguistic coin in the case of the root נער, and I was justified in pointing out that these two meanings had been discussed by the mediaeval Jewish exegetes. Neither of us was then fully aware of the wider nuances that were to be found in the rabbinic texts and that have been located in the passages cited above. It is good not only to be able to pay tribute to Andrew in this essay but also to be in a position to compliment him on the valuable linguistic assessment he made at such an early stage of his academic career. I hope that we may be blessed with many more years of active academic co-operation and close friendship.

Wine Production in Ancient Israel and the Meaning of שְׁמָרִים in the Hebrew Bible*

William D. Barker

In some commentaries and modern English translations of the Hebrew Bible, there are questions about the meaning of שמרים in Isa 25:6 and its supposed underlying root, שמר I.[1] Most scholars assume that שמרים refers to a type of wine, but there is disagreement about its nature and quality. This is apparently due to some confusion about the presence and function within this wine of sediments from the wine production process: some allege that this wine "rested on its lees" (i.e. remained on the sediment that was initially necessary for fermentation), while others argue that שמרים refers to a wine which has been well strained (i.e. no sediment remains in it). This is problematic because such variations in the wine production process result in notable differences in the quality of wine produced—although it might explain why there is also disagreement among scholars about whether שמרים refers to a wine of a low or high quality.[2] In spite of all this, studies continue to acknowledge the important uses and symbolic functions of wine in ancient Israel, while

---

*   It is a joy and a privilege to present this study in honour of the Revd Dr. Andrew Macintosh, who has a contagious passion for the Hebrew language, and has contributed to our understanding of Classical Hebrew through his scholarship in the classroom and on the printed page.

1.   *HALAT* 4:1464–65.

2.   For examples of the various descriptions of the wine, its dregs, and the debate about its quality (or lack thereof), see W. L. Holladay, *Jeremiah* (2 vols.; Hermeneia; Minneapolis: Fortress, 1989), 2:357–58; O. Kaiser, *Der Prophet Jesaja: Kapitel 13–39* (Göttingen: Vandenhoeck & Ruprecht, 1976), 161–62; J. A. Motyer, "Zephaniah," in *The Minor Prophets* (ed. T. E. McComiskey; 3 vols.: Grand Rapids: Baker, 1998), 3:912; and E. J. Young, *The Book of Isaiah* (3 vols.; Grand Rapids: Eerdmans, 1969), 2:193; also cf. the comment of Ginsberg on Isa 25:6 that "the meaning of the Heb[rew] is uncertain," in H. L. Ginsberg, ed., *The Book of Isaiah: A New Translation* (Philadelphia: Jewish Publication Society, 1973), 87 n. *c*.

overlooking any inquiry into the meaning of שמרים.[3] In the hope of obtaining greater clarity about this term with respect to wine production, sedimentation and quality, I shall briefly explore the wine production process in ancient Israel, and then examine the meaning of שמרים in each of its occurrences in the Hebrew Bible.

1. *Wine Production in Ancient Israel and the Meaning of* שמרים

Ancient wine production probably involved several stages. First, grapes were trampled or pressed and the juice was removed from most of the pulp. Then the juice was left to ferment in a large tank, typically housed in rock-hewn chambers, in an attempt to control the temperature and humidity. This was the first of two fermentation periods, and this first period typically lasted from eight to ten days. During this time, the natural yeast cells within the "must" of the juice began the chemical reactions necessary for fermentation to occur.[4] At the close of the first fermentation period, the wine was strained to separate the liquid from the large particulate matter in the must. Then the juice was left to begin its second fermentation period, this one typically lasting from twenty to thirty days. During this time the juice sat upon its "dregs" or "lees," a residue that settled at the bottom of the fermentation tank during the maturation from juice to wine. The juice needed to sit long enough to ferment into wine; however, if left upon its dregs for too long, the wine would become acidic. After the twenty- to thirty-day period ended, the

---

3. For example, some fairly recent studies that admirably highlight either the types or the uses of wine in ancient Israel, but which unfortunately overlook the issues related to שמרים, include M. Broshi, *Bread, Wine, Walls and Scrolls* (JSPSup 36; Sheffield: Sheffield Academic, 2001), 144–72; S. J. Fleming, S. H. Katz and P. McGovern, eds., *The Origins and Ancient History of Wine* (Amsterdam: Gordon & Breach, 1996); and P. McGovern, *Ancient Wine: The Search for the Origins of Viniculture* (Princeton: Princeton University Press, 2003).

4. Any pulp that slipped through the initial straining process with the juice, the skin of the grapes, the grape seeds, and the grape pips is referred to as "must." For more on the chemical processes involved in fermentation, especially those involving the must and the lees, see A. D. Webb, ed., *The Chemistry of Winemaking* (Advances in Chemistry 137; Oxford: Oxford University Press, 1974), and B. Zoecklein, K. C. Fugelsang and B. H. Gump, *Wine Analysis and Production* (2d ed.; New York: Springer, 2005); cf. M. A. Murray, "Viticulture and Wine Production," in *Ancient Egyptian Materials and Technology* (ed. P. T. Nicholson and I. Shaw; Cambridge: Cambridge University Press, 2000), 577–608, for the similarities to wine production in ancient Egypt.

wine was strained from off its lees. The next step in the process was to transfer the wine from the straining tank to holding containers. It was during this step that additional fermentation (i.e. "ageing") of the wine occurred, adding to its quality. If a significant quantity of lees still remained in the wine, then the wine could be left to sit for days or weeks to allow the sediment to collect. The wine would be strained (or, "decanted") again. This process could be repeated several times as long as the wine was continually strained from off its lees to ensure that the lees would not contribute too much acidity to the wine. If only a small quantity of liquid remained, the lees themselves could be pressed to strain off the wine. However, with each successive pressing, the wine would be of a lesser quality because of increased acidity and a lower probability of clarity in the liquid. Finally, the wine was poured into wineskins or large, sealed wine containers. The wine was again stored in cool, dry, rock-hewn chambers, which functioned as wine cellars of fairly consistent temperature.

Having now outlined the basic wine production process in ancient Israel, it is important to consider the function of the lees in the process, given the various views of commentators and translators concerning the meaning of שמרים in the Hebrew Bible. Often scholars have misunderstood the function of the lees within the wine production process, assuming that wine sitting upon its dregs for a lengthy period of time would produce a high-quality, aged wine. However, this is not necessarily the case. As we have noted, wine left upon its dregs for a significant quantity of time would actually produce a bitter, acidic wine. Thus, one conventional understanding of wine production—namely, that wine is best when aged at any point in its production process—is incorrect. Rather, the increase in the quality of a wine due to ageing (and the resultant additional fermentation) must occur after the removal of the majority of its sediment (i.e. its dregs or lees). There are only two exceptions to this. The first exception is when there is a significant quantity of lees present in the fermenting wine, and the wine is left to sit upon its lees for a predetermined time before being strained. This procedure involves a delicate balance between allowing the wine time to strengthen upon its lees and straining it before the lees ruin the wine. Secondly, some types of wine can be produced by a process that leaves the lees in the wine with the intention of producing a strong, bitter wine. This involves pouring the wine into wineskins after having strained the must, but without straining the lees.[5]

5. Michael Galvin (Vineyard Owner, Paradise Road Vineyard, Santa Barbara CA); interview by author, Cambridge, UK, 17 October 2003.

An understanding of the function of the lees in the wine production process, and of their significance for the quality of wine produced, helps illuminate occurrences of שמרים in the Hebrew Bible. Some of the misunderstandings of the biblical term may actually have arisen under the influence of the expression יין שמרים as used in rabbinic literature. In the rabbinic corpus, יין שמרים refers to the low-quality wine created by pressing the dregs a second time, after the initial straining of the wine.[6] This wine was considered such a poor item for consumption as to be unfit for use in the temple.[7] Given the high acidity levels noted above, one can understand why this would be considered too poor a quality for cultic use.

In the light of this, the rabbinic low-quality distillation does not appear to be the wine mentioned in the Hebrew Bible. As we shall see, שמרים in the Hebrew Bible appears to refer to the dregs of the lees themselves, or to a high-quality, well-strained wine. Although the terminology could scarcely be more similar (i.e. MT שמרים and rabbinic יין שמרים), the contexts governing the biblical references will not allow for the two terms to denote the same thing. Furthermore, the archaeological data concerning wine production in ancient Israel allow for multiple uses of the lees resulting in varying qualities of wine. It is easy to see how terminology associated with these lees could also have different denotations. In sum, שמרים probably had a different meaning in the biblical period, thus creating confusion for those commentators influenced by rabbinical usage.

2. שמרים *in the Hebrew Bible*

a. *Psalm 75:9*
Psalm 75:9 speaks of a cup of judgment that YHWH will force the wicked of the earth to drink. It is a helpful verse for the purposes of our inquiry,

---

6. R. Frankel, *Wine and Oil Production in Antiquity in Israel and Other Mediterranean Countries* (JSOT/ASOR Monograph Series 10; Sheffield: Sheffield Academic, 1999), 43, 202; cf. N. MacDonald, *What Did the Ancient Israelites Eat? Diet in Biblical Times* (Grand Rapids: Eerdmans, 2008), 22–23. Manufacturing wine in this fashion was not limited to Israel. By looking at descriptions of wine produced in a similar manner in the ancient world, we may deduce information about the quality and use of this type of wine. One such description is given to us by Pliny, who wrote that these wines were known in the Greek world as *deuterias* and among the Romans as *vinum faecatum*—a sub-variety of "after-wines." Further, Pliny believed that these beverages were of such a low grade that they did not deserve to be classified as wines. See Frankel, *Wine and Oil Production*, 3:202, and Pliny, *Natural History* 14.12.86.

7. *b. Pes.* 42a; *b. B. Bat.* 97a–b; *t. Men.* 9:10.

because it describes in detail the cup of wine and its contents. Given that
שמר I is present in a cup of יין in this psalm, it does not appear that שמריה
here refers only to drinking the cup down to the last liquid drop. Rather,
שמריה seems to be a direct reference to the actual, sedimentary dregs that
were sometimes left in certain types of wine. Thus, drinking אך־שמריה
indicates consuming every ounce of the liquid, including, and especially,
those final mouthfuls that contained the sedimentation. Such an interpretation fits the context well because dregs which remained in wine were
typically so bitter that most individuals would have refused to drink
them. Thus, in Ps 75 YHWH will have כל רשעי־ארץ metaphorically drink
even the שמרים, in order to emphasize the severity and bitterness of the
punishment that he will bring upon them. In this case, the שמרים are the
sedimentary lees of the wine.

b. *Zephaniah 1:12*
In the case of Zeph 1:12, שמר I is not used in direct connection with
wine. Rather, the phrase על־שמריהם (lit. "upon their dregs") is used in
reference to the sedimentary dregs of wine. The expression conveys the
idea that even as wine becomes an acidic, poor-quality drink when it is
not decanted from off the top of its dregs for a lengthy phase of time, so
certain individuals have been unmoved by YHWH for protracted periods
of time. With both the wine and the humans, the stagnant situation is
unacceptable. This idiomatic use of שמר I finds its background, then, in
the dregs upon which fermenting wine would sit.

The fact that the שמרים should usually be filtered suggests that the
term, in Ps 75 and Zeph 1, refers to the lees themselves, rather than the
wine. Although the semantic domain of שמרים has a wider scope than
this one denotation, its use in these two citations implies the sedimentation, or the "dregs," of the wine.

c. *Jeremiah 48:11–12*
Jeremiah 48:11–12 may be the MT's best source of information concerning dregs and the wine-straining process. These verses confirm the
interpretation of the archaeological data about the wine production
process and the שמרים in two significant ways. First, they describe the
straining process that separates wine from lees. Secondly, they inform
the reader of the quality of wine when it is left to ferment for a considerable period of time before being separated from its dregs. Consequently,
in this case, שמר I could refer to wine that had been left sitting upon its
dregs for a lengthy span. If left unstrained and unmoved, this wine would
become acrid. However, if strained, the wine would improve its taste,
aroma and value.

As I have observed, wine left upon its lees for too long would incur an unwelcome acidity, resulting in poor taste. Likewise, wine that remained unfiltered would also become astringent, as it would contain the dregs, which are themselves bitter.[8] This wine, commonly known as lees-wine was, and still is occasionally, used for consumption despite its bitter taste and the retention of its dregs. Such a pungent and acrid lees-wine appears to be the type of unstrained wine described in Jer 48:11 that YHWH will destroy because of its character (v. 12).

d. *Isaiah 25:6*

In Isa 25:6, the שמרים apparently undergo a straining process, as is indicated by מזקקים. The fact that the שמרים have undergone filtering suggests that the wine is dregs-free. Thus, the unfiltered, bitter lees-wine found in Jer 48:11 is, ostensibly, a contrast to the well-strained wine of the Isa 25 banquet. This means that the wine of Isa 25:6 is meant to represent a divine *vinum excellens*, and to serve as a contrast to the dreg-filled wine of YHWH's judgment that the wicked are required to drink to the last metaphorical drop (Ps 75:9; cf. Isa 51:17; Ezek 23:24).[9] Unfortunately, many translations of Isa 25:6 only refer to "refined" wine, obscuring the absence of the dregs in the banquet (e.g. KJV, RSV, NIV, NAB, NAU). By translating the Hebrew term for wine in Isa 25:6 as "excellent, dregs-free wine," both the quality of the wine and the absence of dregs are apparent to the reader. An example of this in modern English translation would be the "wine strained clear" offered by the NRSV (cf. Delcor's translation into French: "de vins vieux, clarifiés"[10]). This is such an important translation issue because it communicates the high quality of the wine at the banquet of Isa 25:6, as well as the symbolism of the absence of God's judgment.

Such an understanding of the שמרים in Isa 25:6 as part of the "feast of wine" stands in stark contrast to the absence of wine in the larger context of Isa 24. Whereas the punishment of YHWH in Isa 24 brings about mourning and an absence of wine, the feast of YHWH in Isa 25 brings with it superior wines and rich, succulent foods. This represents an inversion of typical Near Eastern banquets with regard to selective distribution. The presence of the fatty meats symbolizes the presence of

---

8. Galvin (see n. 6).

9. On the "*vinum excellens*," see *HALAT* 4:1465, and F. Zorrell, *Lexicon hebraicum et aramaicum Veteris Testamenti* (Rome: Pontifical Biblical Institute, 1947–54), §866b.

10. M. Delcor, *Études Bibliques et Orientales de Religions Comparées* (Leiden: Brill, 1979), 122.

YHWH's blessing, even as the well-aged, dregs-free wine symbolizes the absence of YHWH's judgment. This is in continuity with the message of Isa 25:6–8, which declares the establishment of a new cosmic order: no longer are both the blessing and the curse a choice for Israel (e.g. Deut 11:26; Josh 8:34); rather, the presence of blessing and the absence of curse represent a divine gift.

3. *Concluding Thoughts*

As we have seen from the archaeological data on wine production in ancient Israel, and from the necessary components of the chemistry of wine production (e.g. the function of the must, the lees, the yeast, the decanting process), the biblical references to שמרים can have one of two different denotations. In the first instance, שמרים does not refer to wine, but rather to the dregs themselves. In the second instance, שמרים refers to wine that sat upon its dregs long enough to have become a quality, aged product, but which was strained from its dregs to prevent the onset of bitterness and eliminate the presence of bitter dregs during consumption.

This clarification of the ancient wine production process and the terms associated with שמר I in the Hebrew Bible can then be further categorized on the basis of usage. When the terms are used to refer to the dregs of the wine production process (as in Ps 75:9; Zeph 1:12; Jer 48:11–12), they represent bitterness and the presence of God's judgment. However, when שמרים is used, not as a reference to the dregs of the wine production process, but as a specific type of wine as in Isa 25:6, then the term is not appropriately translated either as "a wine that rested upon its lees" or as "a well-refined wine." Rather, the best translation of שמרים in this verse is "a well-strained wine" of the highest quality. This wine, then, represents a clear, dregs-free wine, and it symbolizes the absence of God's judgment at the eschatological banquet of Isa 25:6–8.

THE CHERISHED CHILD:
IMAGES OF PARENTAL LOVE IN THE HEBREW BIBLE

Rachel M. Lentin

This essay examines six biblical images, and suggests how the multiple levels upon which they operate may be conveyed in translation.[1]

1. *Caring for Ephraim: Developing Analytical Tools*

a. *The Meanings of "Metaphor"*

Confusingly, "metaphor" is used specifically, for one particular trope, but also generally, for figurative language, setting it in opposition to "literal language." Consider Isa 66:10–13:

10 שמחו את־ירושלם וגילו בה כל־אהביה
שישו אתה משוש כל־המתאבלים עליה

11 למען תינקו ושבעתם משד תנחמיה
למען תמצו והתענגתם מזיז כבודה

12 כי־כה אמר יהוה
הנני נטה־אליה כנהר שלום
וכנחל שוטף כבוד גוים
וינקתם על־צד תנשאו ועל־ברכים תשעשעו

13 כאיש אשר אמו תנחמנו כן אנכי אנחמכם ובירושלם תנחמו

Verse 10 seems to belong to the "metaphor," but is also literal, while v. 11 might itself be termed a metaphor, or else be said to contain two metaphors, or one metaphor repeated in two forms. Verse 12 contains two similes in addition to a metaphor, and v. 13 combines a simile with a statement that reads literally, but seems to sum up the entire passage.

---

1. See also R. Lentin, *Seeing Double: Strategies for Understanding Imagery, with Reference to the Wine-Related Images of the Hebrew Bible* (Leiden: Brill, forthcoming).

Consequently, I shall limit "metaphor" to its specific sense, and use "figurative language" or "imagery" (or, more precisely, "tropic imagery") as general terms.[2] Isaiah 66:10–13 may then be more coherently described as a passage of tropic imagery, with metaphors in vv. 11–12 and similes in vv. 12–13. All these tropic images have "two components" commonly known as "tenor" and "vehicle"; for instance, v. 11 conveys the prophet's perception of a tenor (how Jerusalem will sustain its inhabitants) through words which suggest a vehicle (a mother comforting her baby).[3]

b. *Tropic Themes*
Isaiah 66:10–13 may be considered part of a broader "metaphor" in vv. 7–9, describing Jerusalem and its inhabitants as a mother and her children.[4] Since this "metaphor" also occurs in 49:20–23; 51:17–20 and 60:4–5, one might argue that it is *re*-used here, but this downplays the originality of each passage, and the effects created by the interaction of its particular vocabulary.[5] Instead, I shall term the underlying thought, "regarded as an abstraction from the…statements in which it [occurs]" and "available for repeated use, adaptation, and modification by a variety of speakers or thinkers on any number of specific occasions," a "tropic theme."[6]

c. *Vocabularies and Janus-words*
Roger M. White proposes that "[t]he metaphorical sentence is a sentence constructed in such a way as to permit two different readings," leading us "to see the situation described by the one reading as if it were the situation described by the other"; such a sentence "may be regarded as the

---

2. See B. Dupriez, *A Dictionary of Literary Devices* (trans. and adapted by A. W. Halsall; New York: Harvester Wheatsheaf, 1991), 221–22, 276. "Tropic" (or "indirect") imagery uses tropes (e.g. simile, allegory and symbol, besides metaphor), while "direct" (or "non-tropic") imagery appeals directly to experience of the object described.

3. I. A. Richards, *The Philosophy of Rhetoric* (New York: Oxford University Press, 1936), 96; J. M. Soskice, *Metaphor and Religious Language* (Oxford: Clarendon, 1985), 15.

4. Isaiah 66:10–13 more specifically describes "Jerusalem nurturing the faithful as a mother nurtures a baby or a toddler" (J. D. W. Watts, *Isaiah 34–66* [rev. ed.; WBC 25; Waco: Word, 2005], 939).

5. See R. M. White, *The Structure of Metaphor: The Way the Language of Metaphor Works* (Oxford: Blackwell, 1996), 4, 282 n. 32.

6. M. Black, "More About Metaphor," in *Metaphor and Thought* (ed. A. Ortony; Cambridge: Cambridge University Press, 1979), 19–43 (25); Black's term is "metaphor-theme."

result of conflating two other implied sentences," and "will be a jumble of words taken from two different vocabularies."[7]

The first step in understanding tropic imagery is to identify these vocabularies. Adapting White's methods, I shall mark the "tenor-vocabulary" and "vehicle-vocabulary" in a "construal."[8] Here the tenor-vocabulary (concerning Jerusalem's relationship with her inhabitants) appears in bold, and the primary vehicle-vocabulary (concerning a mother's relationship with her child) is underlined, with an auxiliary vehicle-vocabulary (of flowing water) in italics:

10   **Rejoice with Jerusalem, <u>be happy for her</u>, <u>all those who love her</u>,
     <u>join in her joy</u>, <u>all those who set themselves in mourning for her</u>,**
11   <u>that[9] you will feed[10]</u> **and be filled with the comfort of her** <u>breast,</u>
     <u>that you will drink deep</u>, **and delight in the riches of her** <u>milk—</u>
12   **for thus says the Lord,**
     "<u>Behold</u>, <u>I am sending her peace</u> *like a river,*
     and the riches of nations *like a stream in flood"*
     <u>—and so you will feed; you will be held close, and
         cherished on her lap.</u>
     <u>Like one whose mother</u> **comforts** <u>him</u>, **so** <u>**will I comfort you**</u>; **you
         will be comforted in** **Jerusalem.**

Construal highlights "janus-words" (expressions which simultaneously belong to multiple vocabularies),[11] and shows that vv. 10 and 13b do indeed read literally—but on two levels; tropic imagery works by combining layers of literal language, undermining any simple distinction between figurative and literal.

d. *In Praise of Simile*
Far from being a sub-form of metaphor,[12] simile has particular emphases which suit certain usages. Structurally, it is identified by a linking word, for instance, "as" or "like" in English or כְּ in Biblical Hebrew. This acts

---

7.   White, *Structure*, 116, 204.
8.   White's terms are "primary vocabulary" and "secondary vocabulary"; he marks different vocabularies with different kinds of underlining (ibid., 16–20).
9.   Those who translate לְמַעַן with "that" (for "in order that") should acknowledge that it will be read as "because" in this context; J. N. Oswalt uses "because" explicitly (*The Book of Isaiah, Chapters 40–66* [Grand Rapids: Eerdmans, 1998], 678).
10. In English, babies are generally said to "feed" rather than "suck" (the typical translation for יָנַק) or "nurse" (J. Blenkinsopp, *Isaiah 56–66* [AB 19b; New York: Doubleday, 2003], 302; NIV; NRSV).
11. White terms such usage "bifurcation" (*Structure*, 22–24).
12. Black, "More About Metaphor," 31.

as an explicit trigger for figurative reading, directing readers to understand the vehicle-vocabulary at a second level and prompting an evocative question, such as "What *is* 'a stream in flood' like?" (Isa 66:12).

Since similes imply that the likeness described is not an identity, they may be used to keep tenor and vehicle distinct, particularly when the tenor is divine, as in Isa 66:13, where the Lord is "likened to a mother lovingly comforting her children";[13] John Oswalt notes the "careful distancing of God from the nursing motif."[14] More pragmatically, the similes of 66:12 prevent confusion of the river-related auxiliary vehicle with the maternal primary vehicle.

In most similes, the vehicle-vocabulary tends to be self-contained, as in v. 12. It may, however, also be linked to the tenor-vocabulary through repeated janus-words, such as the verb נחם ("comfort," v. 13); in such similes, the vehicle will exemplify the janus-words, but unless translators render these janus-words with expressions that fit both vocabularies the usage seems rather banal.

e. *Proportional Metaphors*

Aristotle describes a type of metaphor that works by analogy, whereby "the second relates to the first just as the fourth relates to the third," so that "a cup relates to Dionysus just as a shield relates to Ares; therefore the cup may be called 'the shield of Dionysus' and the shield 'the cup of Ares'."[15] Such "proportional metaphors"[16] combine tenor- and vehicle-vocabularies in genitive structures, which may convey many relationships; consequently they are inherently ambiguous, and particularly apt for use in tropic imagery.

In Isa 66:11, the proportional metaphors involve double genitives. For instance, משד תנחמיה (lit. "from the breast of comfort of her") could either be translated "from her breast of comfort"[17] or "from the breast

---

13. A. S. Herbert, *The Book of the Prophet Isaiah, Chapters 40–66* (Cambridge: Cambridge University Press, 1975), 194.

14. Oswalt finds this "distancing" through understanding the vehicle as "a mother who embraces her grown son" (*Isaiah, Chapters 40–66*, 678).

15. Aristotle, *De Arte Poetica Liber* (ed. R. Kassel; 2d ed.; Oxford Classical Texts; Oxford: Oxford University Press, 1966), 34 [1457b ll. 16–22 (§ 21)] (my translation).

16. White, *Structure*, 39.

17. Following this pattern are: "her consoling breast[s]," C. Westermann, *Isaiah 40–66: A Commentary* (trans. D. M. H. Stalker; London: SCM, 1969), 418; Blenkinsopp, *Isaiah 56–66*, 302; JB; RSV; NRSV; "her comforting breast[s]," Oswalt, *Isaiah, Chapters 40–66*, 672; NIV.

of her comfort,"[18] but it may be that both are intended.[19] תנחמיה is a janus-word, but some translations undermine its role in the vehicle-vocabulary by using words related to "console," which function more easily in the tenor-vocabulary.[20] This disguises the link with v. 13 (where the verb נחם occurs three times), and downplays the concept of "comfort" in the passage as a whole.

The second proportional metaphor of Isa 66:11, מזיז כבודה (lit. "from the זיז of glory of her"), is difficult because זיז is rare. The structural parallel with משד תנחמיה suggests it is vehicle-vocabulary, with כבודה operating as a janus-word.[21] זיז is used elsewhere as a general collective noun in the phrase זיז שדי, describing "beasts of the field."[22] While there is no obvious synchronic connection between the two usages, it is possible that they were once linked etymologically, with the sense "milk" for Isa 66:11,[23] related to the sense "beasts" on the understanding that these animals produced milk. This sense creates a link to the "flowing" similes of the next verse, which is emphasized by the repetition of כבוד.[24] Indeed, the purpose of these similes is to elaborate on מזיז כבודה—peace, and the riches of the nations, will flow through Jerusalem to her inhabitants "like a river" or "a stream in flood," that is, in great abundance. Likewise, the much questioned וינקתם ("and you will

18. See "the breast[s] of her consolations," R. N. Whybray, *Isaiah 40–66* (NCB; London: Oliphants, 1975), 285; Watts, *Isaiah 34–66*, 934; AV.

19. "Her" restricts the ambiguity in English, as it can apply to only one noun; so some translators change the structure, for instance, "from the breasts that give comfort" (Herbert, *Isaiah, Chapters 40–66*, 193); "[with] your comfort from [her] breast" (E. Achtemeier, *The Community and Message of Isaiah 56–66: A Theological Commentary* [Minneapolis: Augsburg, 1982], 138); "you may suck comfort from her" (REB). Furthermore, rather than "of comfort," English expects an adjective such as "comforting" (see n. 17 above), which is a less effective janus-word. I preserve the ambiguity by transposing the nouns.

20. Westermann, *Isaiah 40–66*, 418; Blenkinsopp, *Isaiah 56–66*, 302; Watts, *Isaiah 34–66*, 934; AV; RSV; JB; NRSV.

21. Transposing the nouns and translating כבוד as "riches" preserves its ambiguity.

22. Pss 50:11; 80:14 (in the latter with רעה, "graze," implying ruminants). *DCH* 3:101b and *HALOT* 1:268a suggest insects; BDB has "moving things (i.e. beasts)" (265a).

23. Herbert, *Isaiah, Chapters 40–66*, 193; Whybray, *Isaiah 40–66*, 285 (or "nipple"); REB. Others suggest "abundance" (see n. 27 below); "bosom" (Oswalt, *Isaiah, Chapters 40–66*, 672; Blenkinsopp, *Isaiah 56–66*, 302; NRSV); "teat" (*DCH* 3:101b); "breast[s]" (*HALOT* 1:268a–b; JB).

24. Achtemeier, *Community*, 138, 145; P. A. Smith, *Rhetoric and Redaction in Trito-Isaiah: The Structure, Growth and Authorship of Isaiah 56–66* (VTSup 62; Leiden: Brill, 1995), 165; Watts, *Isaiah 34–66*, 934, 939; AV.

suck," v. 12)[25] links back via מזיז to תינקו...תנחמיה (v. 11),[26] and the thought develops with the reiteration of the theme of comfort in v. 13. If מזיז כבודה is translated at a single level, either that of the tenor-vocabulary ("from the abundance of her glory")[27] or that of the vehicle-vocabulary ("her plentiful milk"),[28] this subtle progression is obscured.

f. *Multiple Vehicle-vocabularies in Hosea 11:1–4 and Jeremiah 31:18–20*

Hosea 11:1–4 describes God's relationship with Israel as that between a parent and child:

1 כי נער ישראל ואהבהו וממצרים קראתי לבני

2 קראו להם כן הלכו מפניהם
  לבעלים יזבחו ולפסלים יקטרון

3 ואנכי תרגלתי לאפרים קחם על־זרועתיו
  ולא ידעו כי רפאתים

4 בחבלי אדם אמשכם בעבתות אהבה
  ואהיה להם כמרימי על על לחיהם
  ואט אליו אוכיל

1　When Israel was a child, **I loved him**, **and I called** my son from Egypt.

2　As for them,[29] those to whom they called,[30] they turned from— to the baals they sacrifice, to the idols they burn offerings.

25.　LXX has τὰ παιδία, leading *BHS* (and others) to emend to וינקתה "and her sucklings" (collective). Others follow MT: Herbert, *Isaiah, Chapters 40–66*, 193; Achtemeier, *Community*, 138; Smith, *Rhetoric*, 165; Oswalt, *Isaiah, Chapters 40–66*, 673 n. 37; Watts, *Isaiah 34–66*, 935; AV; RSV; NIV; NRSV.

26.　For the verbal link, see J. A. Alexander, *The Later Prophecies of Isaiah* (New York: Wiley & Putnam, 1847), 483; Smith, *Rhetoric*, 165.

27.　Westermann, *Isaiah 40–66*, 418; Achtemeier, *Community*, 138; Watts, *Isaiah 34–66*, 934; BDB, 265b; AV; RSV.

28.　Herbert, *Isaiah, Chapters 40–66*, 193; REB. See also "from her rich supply of milk," Whybray, *Isaiah 40–66*, 285; "full breast," *HALOT*, 1:268a-b.

29.　The progression from God's action to Israel's response is made explicit because, while the switch from singular to plural is unproblematic in Hebrew, in English it creates confusion, heightened by the additional indirect object, להם, also third person plural. A. A. Macintosh interprets this as the *dativus commodi*, corresponding to the subject, translating "[t]hey have made their own call"; either way, the focus is Israel's behaviour, and קראו need not be emended to the first person (*A Critical and Exegetical Commentary on Hosea* [ICC; Edinburgh: T. & T. Clark, 1997], 439, 441).

30.　The object ("those to whom they called") is probably Egypt (ibid., 439–40). I preserve the word order, reading לבעלים as an ambiguous "hinge" between כן הלכו מפניהם in v. 2a and יזבחו. Although the sense "they turned from them to the baals" is immediately overridden by יזבחו, it suggests a reason for Israel's faithlessness.

3   **It was I who taught** Ephraim **to walk,**[31] **who embraced them,**[32]
     but they did not know that I protected them.[33]
     With ties of affection *I led them*, with ropes **of love,**
4   **and became for them** *like those who raise the yoke on their jaws,*
     in order to offer him *food.*

The italics indicate an auxiliary vehicle-vocabulary concerning a farmer's treatment of his animals. This begins with the janus-word אמשכם, "I led them" (v. 4a), which operates in all three vocabularies, and is followed by בעבתות, "with ropes," which is parallel to בחבלי ("with ties") but belongs only to the auxiliary vehicle-vocabulary. The verse continues with a simile, combining a discrete block of auxiliary vehicle-vocabulary with the janus-words ואט אליו אוכיל, although the singular suffix of אליו directs us back to Israel in v. 1, rather than to the plural Israelites of vv. 2–4 or the animals to which they are compared in v. 4.[34]

By contrast, REB extends the main tropic theme through v. 4b:

3   **It was I who taught** Ephraim **to walk,**
     I who took them **in my arms;**
     but they did not know that [4] **I secured them** with reins
     and led them with bonds **of love,**
     that I lifted them like a little child to my cheek,
     that I bent down **to feed them.**[35]

Although widening the implications of the primary vehicle creates a charming picture, what the image relates about the tenor is vaguer, because it has lost the focus given by two overlapping vehicle-vocabularies. Moreover, בחבלי אדם (lit. "with bonds of humanity") is a proportional metaphor which operates in both tenor- and primary vehicle-vocabularies by virtue of the word אדם, but by translating "reins," the animal-related

31. Contra ibid., 441–43. Following the common tropic theme "life as a journey," תרגלתי describes both divine guidance of Israel's journey to nationhood and parental guidance of a child's first steps. Consequently, "It was I who taught Ephraim to walk" becomes a general statement including the action of v. 1, with God's "embrace" of Israel as a parallel action; children who can walk still wish to be picked up!

32. Adding "who" shows how even English may slip coherently between first and third person; "embraced" conveys the janus-word זרועתיו ("his arms"/"his strength").

33. Macintosh, *Hosea*, 443–45.

34. Macintosh also understands the suffix in the context of a double-level reading, but places the contrast between the plural Israelites and the singular "beast of the metaphor" (ibid., 448).

35. See also GNB, JB, NRSV.

sense is placed where it did not exist in Hebrew and is promptly over-written by a fortuitous modern link with toddlers. This in turn trivializes what is expressed about God's relationship with Israel.[36]

Finally, while the Hebrew simile inserts a block of animal-related vehicle-vocabulary into a passage with a child-related vehicle, REB's simile, with yet more child-related vehicle-vocabulary, seems strangely redundant. Its over-simplification is probably a reaction to the seemingly abrupt shift from child to animal, but the emphasis should rest on the farmer's care for his animals. This easily lends itself to a parent's care for a child, and to God's care for his people. Jeremiah 31:18–20 develops the combination:

18   שמוע שמעתי אפרים מתנודד
 יסרתני ואוסר כעגל לא למד
השיבני ואשובה כי אתה יהוה אלהי

19   כי־אחרי שובי נחמתי
ואחרי הודעי ספקתי על־ירך
בשתי וגם־נכלמתי כי נשאתי חרפת נעורי

20   הבן יקיר לי אפרים אם ילד שעשעים
כי־מדי דברי בו זכר אזכרנו עוד
על־כן המו מעי לו רחם ארחמנו נאם־יהוה

18   **Clearly, clearly, I heard** Ephraim **falter,**
    "You gave me rebuke, and I took the rebuke, *like a calf which has*
        not been trained;
    bring me back, O let me come back, for you are the Lord my
        God.

19   **For after I turned back, I repented;**
    after I understood, I struck my thigh;
    I was ashamed—dishonoured—for I bore the disgrace of my
        youth."

20   **Is not** Ephraim **my precious** son, **a cherished** child?
    For no matter how often I speak against him, dearly, dearly do I
        remember him still.
    And so my heart sighs for him, and tenderly, tenderly will my
        compassion for him grow.
    Word of the Lord.

Ephraim describes himself as an untrained calf (v. 18b), but in v. 20 God replies in terms which emphasize his love—Ephraim is not merely a beast needing discipline, but a "cherished child."[37]

36. W. Rudolph, *Hosea* (Gütersloh: G. Mohn, 1966), 210.

37. The "womb vocabulary" of רחם ארחמנו is emphatic; God encompasses *both* parents' roles (see W. McKane, *A Critical and Exegetical Commentary on*

g. *Poetic Patterns*

Translation should acknowledge poetic effects, as well as conveying sense and structure. Besides the linked forms of יסר (v. 18) and שוב (vv. 18–19), Jer 31:18–20 uses infinitives absolute (vv. 18 and 20 [×2]), but many translators convey only their sense (an emphatic force), possibly because English lacks this device.[38] An appropriate alternative is simple repetition, which, although less sophisticated, has both poetic and emphatic effect. Similarly, poetic metre may seem superfluous, but translators should avoid fractured rhythms which undermine the sense.[39]

2. *Translating on Many Levels: An Exploration of Job 38:8–11*

In their determination to capture one level of sense, translators may miss others, but these may be recovered if the mechanics of tropic imagery are examined in "slow motion."

a. *Skeleton Sentences and Dummy Names*

The trigger for reading a metaphor on two levels is subtler than that for a simile, arising from an awareness that some words seem out of context and fit together to form a vehicle-vocabulary. White mimics this process by forming a vehicle-type "skeleton sentence" from the vehicle-vocabulary, with words belonging purely to the tenor-vocabulary represented by "dummy names" (e.g. "*Z*" or "*Y*"),[40] for instance, for Job 38:8–11:

8 ויסך בדלתים ים בגיחו מרחם יצא
9 בשומי ענן לבשו וערפל חתלתו
10 ואשבר עליו חקי ואשים בריח ודלתים
11 ואמר עד־פה תבוא ולא תסיף ופא־ישית בגאון גליך

Jeremiah. Vol. 2, *Commentary on Jeremiah XXVI–LII* [ICC; Edinburgh: T. & T. Clark, 1996], 802; J. R. Lundbom, *Jeremiah 21–36: A New Translation with Introduction and Commentary* [AB 21B; New York: Doubleday, 2004], 447).

38. For instance, "surely" (G. L. Keown, P. J. Scalise, and T. G. Smothers, *Jeremiah 26–52* [WBC 27; Dallas: Word, 1995], 117); "certainly" (B. Becking, *Between Fear and Freedom: Essays on the Interpretation of Jeremiah 30–31* [OTS 51; Leiden: Brill, 2004], 207); "indeed," "assuredly" (Lundbom, *Jeremiah 21–36*, 440, 444). See also AV; NIV; NRSV.

39. Compare JB or REB for Jer 31:18–19 with AV; instinctive use of metre makes AV so much more memorable than its modern counterparts.

40. White's expression for skeleton sentences is "open sentences" (*Structure*, 77).

8   <u>Who hedged in the</u> *(Z)* <u>with doors,</u> <u>when he</u> *(Y)*ed <u>from the womb</u>
     <u>and came out,</u>
9   <u>when I set</u> *(X)* <u>its garment and</u> *(W)* <u>its swaddling band,</u>
10   <u>and I</u> *(V)*ed <u>upon it my boundary, and I set bars and doors,</u>
11   <u>and said,</u> "<u>to here may you go,</u> <u>but no farther;</u> <u>here will be fixed in</u>
     (U) <u>your</u> *(T)*s"?

The reader then focuses on the tenor-vocabulary, producing a *tenor*-type
skeleton sentence. Dummy names now represent words belonging purely
to the vehicle-vocabulary:

8   **Who hedged in the sea with** *(A)***s, when it burst from the** *(B)* **and**
     came out,
9   **when I set cloud its** *(C)* **and heavy cloud its** *(D)*,
10   **and I broke upon it my boundary, and I set** *(E)***s and** *(F)***s,**
11   **and said, "to here may you go, but no farther; here will be fixed**
     in exultation your waves"?

b. *Tenor- and Vehicle-type Sentences*

Besides ensuring that translations reproduce the demarcation of a text's
multiple levels, skeleton sentences can be adapted to check for sense and
fluency, by using real words as dummy names, in "tenor-type sentences"
and "vehicle-type sentences."[41]

8   **Who hedged in the sea with** [barriers]**, when it burst from** [the
     earth] **and came out,**
9   **when I set cloud its** [cover] **and heavy cloud its** [wrapping]**,**
10   **and I broke upon it my boundary, and I set** [limits] **and** [barriers]**,**
11   **and said, "to here may you go, but no farther; here will be fixed**
     in exultation your waves"?

8   <u>Who hedged in the</u> [baby] <u>with doors,</u> <u>when he</u> [broke] <u>from the</u>
     <u>womb and came out,</u>
9   <u>when I set</u> [a robe] <u>his garment and</u> [a blanket] <u>his swaddling band,</u>
10   <u>and I</u> [placed] <u>upon him my boundary, and I set bars and doors,</u>
11   <u>and said,</u> "<u>to here may you go,</u> <u>but no farther;</u> <u>here will be fixed in</u>
     [excitement] <u>your</u> [games]"?

Both "type sentences" should read far more coherently, preserving the
janus-words. I shall now re-shape the tenor-type ("t-t") and vehicle-type
("v-t") sentences of Job 38:8–11 verse by verse.

---

41.   White terms these "primary sentences" and "secondary sentences" (*Structure*,
78).

(1) *Verse 8*. Initially, וַיָּסֶךְ, "[he] hedged about," seems unnatural in both vocabularies, but, as a janus-word (broadly equivalent to "enclosed"), its sense is obstructive in the tenor-vocabulary and protective in the vehicle-vocabulary, embodying "God's hedging in and limitation of the waters in the setting of protection with clouds as clothes and swaddling bands."[42]

Wayne Horowitz relates Job 38:8–11 to the "bolt" of the sea mentioned in Babylonian flood stories.[43] If this motif was well-known, then בדלתים, "with doors," and בריח ודלתים, "bar(s) and doors," in v. 10 may be janus-words, linking "cosmic" doors enclosing the sea with the more prosaic doors kept closed around a baby. Alternatively (as above), they may simply be vehicle-vocabulary, the construal most likely for modern readers, unaware of Mesopotamian parallels.

AV uses a simile in v. 8b ("when it brake forth, as if it had issued out of the womb"), distancing tenor from vehicle. Modern translations typically translate "when it burst forth from the womb,"[44] echoing AV's construal because "burst forth" fits the tenor-vocabulary of raging waters, but not the vehicle-vocabulary of birth. By contrast, in Classical Hebrew the verb גיח seems to operate in both vocabularies,[45] so translation of בגיחו requires a janus-word, such as "break,"[46] or risks an "inverted reading" which distorts the image by presenting the vehicle in terms of the tenor rather than *vice versa*, implying the power of a baby's birth rather than the intimacy of God's creation of the sea.

t-t   **Who enclosed the sea with doors, when it broke from [the earth] and came out,**

v-t   Who enclosed [the baby] with doors, when he broke from the womb and came out,

---

42. E. van Wolde, "Towards an 'Integrated Approach' in Biblical Studies, Illustrated with a Dialogue between Job 28 and Job 38," in *Congress Volume: Leiden 2004* (ed. A. Lemaire; Leiden: Brill, 2006), 357–80 (366). BDB (692a) and *DCH* (6:130a) imply obstructive senses; *HALOT* (2:754a) proposes סכך, with qal protective and hiphil obstructive. Compare שוך ("hedge up"), obstructive in Hos 2:8, but protective in Job 1:10 (BDB, 962a; *HALOT* 3:1312b; *CDCH*, 434a-b).

43. W. Horowitz, *Mesopotamian Cosmic Geography* (Winona Lake: Eisenbrauns, 1998), 326–27.

44. RSV; NIV; see also "burst out" (NRSV); "burst in flood" (REB); "burst from" (GNB).

45. BDB's "burst forth" does not reflect its recognition that גיח is also used of birth in Mic 4:10, and possibly Ps 22:10 (161b); see also *DCH* with "burst out" (2:344a-b). *HALOT* also has "burst forth," but omits Ps 22:10 altogether, and translates Mic 4:10 as "scream (?)" (1:189a-b).

46. "Break" reflects Hebrew idioms for birth (see BDB, 991a; *HALOT* 4:1404b; *CDCH*, 447b), and is used idiomatically both of waves and of "waters of childbirth" (see *DCH* 2:344a-b).

(2) *Verse 9.* Some translations omit בשומי ("when I set"), and treat the second noun of each phrase as verbs; the pattern of interaction remains.[47]

> t-t　**when I** [covered] **it in mist and** [wrapped] **it in cloud,**
> v-t　when I dressed him in [clothes] and swaddled him in [a blanket],

(3) *Verse 10.* NRSV translates ואשבר with the janus-word "prescribed," but even this seems unnatural for a baby. By contrast with vv. 8–9, where the vocabularies are closely entwined and implications about the baby transferred to the sea, ואשבר appears to be emphatic tenor-vocabulary,[48] underlining the contrast with the vehicle.

> t-t　**and forced my boundaries upon it and bolted the doors,**
> v-t　and [imposed] my rules over him and bolted the doors,[49]

(4) *Verse 11.* I follow REB's translation of בגאון ("in exaltation") as "surging," evoking the height of the waves and hinting at pride. Since בגאון גליך does not function as vehicle-vocabulary, each translator may insert whichever dummy names seem most appropriate, revealing which vehicle they have selected, and therefore which implications may be guiding their perceptions of the tenor.

> t-t　**and said, "Here may you go, but no farther; here will your**
> 　　　　**surging waves remain"?**
> v-t　and said, "Here may you go, but no farther; here will your [growing
> 　　　　games] remain"?

(5) *Restoration.* The revised translation functions fluently and accurately on two levels:

> 8　**Who enclosed the sea with** doors, **when it broke from** the womb
> 　　**and came out,**
> 9　**when I dressed it in** mist **and** swaddled **it in** cloud,
> 10　**and forced my boundaries upon it and** bolted the doors,
> 11　**and said, "Here may you go, but no farther; here will your**
> 　　**surging waves remain"?**

---

47. GNB, REB; JB treats the first phrase this way, NIV the second.

48. *HALOT* (4:1403a–b) suggests a technical usage, "to break into, to make a mark in the ground," supporting construal with the tenor-vocabulary. Construal of ואשבר as vehicle-vocabulary (see n. 46 above) obscures the clause.

49. For בריח ודלתים, see on v. 8; I omit ואשים and change בריח into a verb, as in v. 9.

c. *Replicating Poetic Effect*

Construal is also helpful when assessing the poetic qualities of a translation against those of the original Hebrew:

> 8   **Who pent up the sea behind** closed doors
>   **when it leapt tumultuous out** of the womb,
> 9   **when I wrapped it** in a robe **of mist**
>   **and made black clouds its** swaddling bands;
> 10 **when I marked the bounds it was not to cross**
>   **and made it fast** with a bolted gate?
> 11 **Come thus far, I said, and no farther:**
>   **here your proud waves shall break.** (JB)

This is certainly vivid, but lacks unity; while בדלתים (v. 8) is translated with "doors," ודלתים (v. 10) becomes a "gate." An effective proportional metaphor is added to v. 9a, but this loses the structural parallel with v. 9b. Furthermore, the translation of בגיחו (v. 8) as "when it leapt tumultuous" is even less natural for a baby's birth than "when it burst forth." Finally, "break" (v. 11) evokes the waves striking the shoreline while also implying the futility of attacking divinely appointed boundaries—but all this is absent in the Hebrew.

In summary, by highlighting levels of sense and poetic effects, the exegetical tools described above allow a surprisingly precise translation of tropic imagery.

3. *Embracing Ambiguity: The "Weaned Child" in Isaiah 28:9 and Psalm 131:2*

The "ability to be suggestive of multiple meanings" is crucial in generating "the rich significance" of a tropic image.[50] Ambiguity is, however, extremely difficult to translate because it uses structures and puns which may be peculiar to a particular language. Moreover, by its very nature, it may provoke "a genuine uncertainty about [the image's] precise import"[51] which translators, by *their* very nature, are unwilling to leave unresolved.

50. J. C. Exum, "Of Broken Pots, Fluttering Birds and Visions in the Night: Extended Simile and Poetic Technique in Isaiah," *CBQ* 43 (1981): 331–52 (333); White, *Structure*, 41.

51. White, *Structure*, 96.

a. *Ambiguity with Intent*

Tropic imagery requires translators to be alert for puns, despite their wariness of the root fallacy, which discourages any linking of senses which could derive from the same etymological root. Particularly elusive are subversive puns, where the tenor-vocabulary is undermined by janus-words with a contrasting sense in the vehicle-vocabulary. For example, Isa 28:9 uses גמולי ("well-fed infants"[52]) and עתיקי ("removed"), but the context implies that these expressions have alternative senses in the tenor-vocabulary, respectively "contented"[53] and "advanced":[54]

> 9 את־מי יורה דעה ואת־מי יבין שמועה
> גמולי מחלב עתיקי משדים

9 **To whom does he teach knowledge, to whom will he explain the message?**
   To those who are content—but only from milk? **To those who have progressed**—but only from the breast?

These puns are unsurprising in the context of Isa 28:1–8, with its wealth of double-level meaning,[55] but they require translators to understand the subtleties of not only the Hebrew expressions but also their English equivalents. For instance, the word-play is lost if גמולי is simply translated as "weaned infants," because the English verb "to be weaned from" fits the semantic field of deprivation, but the Hebrew verb גמל belongs to that of completion, allowing the link between infants filled with milk and those who are satisfied with life.[56] The message is strongly negative; those who should hear the message are less worthy of it than those least able to understand it.

---

52. Or "weaned infants," but see below.

53. W. A. VanGemeren, "Psalm 131:2–*kegamul*: The Problems of Meaning and Metaphor," *Hebrew Studies* 23 (1982): 51–57 (52).

54. Like "removed," the sense "advanced" can be related to עתק (BDB, 801a–b; *DCH* 6:640a–41b).

55. J. C. Exum, "'Whom will he teach knowledge?': A Literary Approach to Isaiah 28," in *Art and Meaning: Rhetoric in Biblical Literature* (ed. D. J. A. Clines, D. M. Gunn and A. J. Hauser; JSOTSup 19; Sheffield: JSOT, 1982), 108–39 (112, 119).

56. For the latter, see H. Wildberger: "Isaiah's opponents are thus attacked at the very point where they believe themselves most deserving of honor; they carry out the duties of their office, having acquired the necessary knowledge" (*Isaiah 28–39: A Continental Commentary* [trans. T. H. Trapp; Minneapolis: Fortress, 2002], 22).

b. *Accidental Ambiguity*

Translation may also create new ambiguities; consider Ps 131:1–2:

1 שיר המעלות לדוד

יהוה לא־גבה לבי ולא־רמו עיני

ולא־הלכתי בגדלות ובנפלאות ממני

2 אם־לא שויתי ודוממתי נפשי

כגמל עלי אמו כגמל עלי נפשי

> 1 **A song of the ascents, for David;**
>   **O Lord, my heart is not upheld too high, my eyes are not raised up too far,**
>   **I do not deal with things too great, too wonderful for me.**
> 2 **Have I not subdued my soul and made it still,**
>   <u>**Resting contented**</u>[57] <u>as a well-fed baby with his mother?</u> <u>Likewise</u> <u>**contented rests**</u> **my soul with me.**

Many translations neglect the contrast with the "lofty" pretensions of v. 1[58] by allowing the vehicle of the baby to dominate the verbs of v. 2a, imposing a new level of sense:

> <u>**But I have calmed and quieted**</u> **my soul.**[59]

In fact, there is no evidence that שוה (piel: "make smooth, agreeable") and דמם (polel: "make still, silent") were used of babies (as "calm" and "quiet" are in English), and both seem to lack emotion.[60]

Secondly, while some translate גמל as "a weaned child,"[61] I follow those who claim that it is not weaned at all.[62] גמל actually describes any

---

57. As in Isa 29:9, גמל may imply both an infant full of milk and "one who is contented." I use "a well-fed baby" in the first clause, preserving the repetition with "rest contented."

58. M. Dahood, *Psalms III: 101–150* (AB 17A; New York: Doubleday, 1970), 239.

59. NRSV; likewise VanGemeren, "Psalm 131:2," 56; AV; RSV; NRSV; REB.

60. See, respectively, BDB, 1000b; *HALOT* 4:1437b–38a; *CDCH*, 453a; and BDB, 198b–99a; *HALOT* 1:226a-b; *DCH* 2:450b–51a). Referring to Isa 28:25 and 38:13, P. A. H. de Boer translates, "I have made myself without resistance or movement" ("Psalm CXXXI 2," *VT* 16 [1966]: 287–92 [292]); Dahood has "I have kept my soul level and tranquil" (*Psalms III*, 238).

61. L. C. Allen, *Psalms 101–150* (rev. ed.; WBC 21; Nashville: Thomas Nelson, 2002), 258–61; BDB, 168a; *TDOT* 3:26–27; *HALOT* 1:197a; *DCH* 2:363b–64a; AV; JB; NIV; NRSV; REB.

62. W. R. Taylor in *The Interpreter's Bible* (ed. G. A. Buttrick; 12 vols.; New York: Abingdon-Cokesbury, 1951–57), 4:683–84; C. J. Labuschagne, "The Metaphor of the So-Called 'Weaned Child' in Psalm cxxxi," *VT* 57 (2007): 114–18

child that has had its fill of milk, both permanently (as a weaned child) or temporarily (as a well-fed baby), but it does not follow that the sense is ambiguous in Ps 131,[63] because similes tend to have an emphatic role, especially when the vehicle-vocabulary is restricted and repeated, as here. Such a simile requires a vehicle which is an obvious exemplar for a particular action or concept. The context supplied by v. 1 implies that, whatever a גמל is, it exemplifies humble satisfaction, but a weaned child "is not *ipso facto* a tranquil child."[64] Even those who prefer this translation have to explain why such a child is contented,[65] which in itself weakens their case.

c. *Ambiguity as the Agent of Relevance*

Dan Sperber and Deirdre Wilson observe that "[a] good creative metaphor is precisely one in which a variety of contextual effects can be… understood as weakly implicated by the speaker," thereby enabling the crucial "search for optimal relevance."[66] Each reader selects whichever implications about the vehicle seem most appropriate to them and are relevant to the tenor, forming implicatures (or "indirect implications") to shape perception of the tenor; for example, in Ps 131:2 the soul is small and helpless, but deeply loved.[67] Similarly, if the vehicle is unidentified, readers may select whichever vehicle seems most relevant to them and the tenor.

Translators must therefore put aside their own interpretations and maintain ambiguities which allow readers to use their own perceptions of a vehicle. Claus Labuschagne's exegesis of Deut 33:12 is informed by awareness of how non-Western babies are carried on their mothers' backs between feeds. Consequently, he understands the Lord's protection of Benjamin in such terms, inferring that the גמל of Ps 131:2 is "a 'breast-feeding infant' that has just been nursed and quieted" and now rests on his mother's back:

(114, 117); possibly C. A. Briggs and E. G. Briggs, *The Book of Psalms* (2 vols.; ICC; Edinburgh: T. & T. Clark, 1907), 2:466–67; Rashi (see M. I. Gruber, *Rashi's Commentary on Psalms* [Leiden: Brill, 2004], 717); RSV.

63. Contra VanGemeren, "Psalm 131:2," 52–53; GNB.

64. Taylor, *Interpreter's Bible*, 4:684. See de Boer ("Psalm CXXXI 2," 291–92) for another atypical exemplar.

65. For instance, he is content with other food, or loves his mother for her own sake, or has loved her longer; see VanGemeren, "Psalm 131:2," 54–56.

66. D. Sperber and D. Wilson, *Relevance: Communication and Cognition* (2d ed.; Oxford: Blackwell, 1995), 236–37.

67. For alternative implications about a גמול (vulnerability and trust), see Isa 11:6–8.

> 2 **On the contrary, I have remained calm and <u>quieted</u> my soul**;
> <u>like an infant on its mother's back, like an infant on my back</u>,
> **so is my soul**.[68]

His reasoning is persuasive, but this translation may actually undermine the image for most Western readers; any location specified must be one where they would automatically expect a well-fed baby to rest.[69]

Another over-defined vehicle occurs in Leslie Allen's commentary: "[l]ike toddlers who soon run out of their own limited resources and gladly submit to being carried, we find God to be one on whom we can depend."[70] This is itself a powerful tropic image, which successfully develops the readers' perception of the tenor, the humble soul, but his vehicle is rather different from that of the Hebrew original.[71]

Such elaboration perfectly fulfils the role of a commentary, but let us end this investigation into the *translation* of tropic imagery on a note of humility, in keeping with Ps 131. Translators should indeed ensure that their "eyes are not raised up too far," setting aside their own creative impulses in favour of conveying the insights of the original and forming a firm foundation for the exegetical flourishes of others.

4. *Conclusion*

White's declaration that "[e]xamples are the beginning, middle and end of a significant study of metaphor"[72] should be reassuring to biblical scholars, with their eyes fixed firmly on the text. I hope to have provided a range of tools to assist in our endeavours.

I offer this essay as a token of my great admiration and affection, and in honour of the love that Andrew Macintosh and his wife Mary have shown the many children they have fostered.[73]

---

68. Labuschagne, "Metaphor," 115–18; formatting adapted.

69. Therefore, although the Hebrew gives no precise location, one may use the English idioms "at its mother's breast" (RSV) or "in its mother's arms" (JB, GNB). The former also implies why the baby is satisfied, as is not apparent from "lies quietly" (GNB) alone.

70. Allen, *Psalms 101–150*, 258–59, 261, interpreting גמל as "a weaned child" and עלי (×2) as "upon."

71. Changing the vehicle loses certain implicatures; for instance, that the soul is content.

72. White, *Structure*, 3.

73. My thanks to my husband Richard Wood, and George, James and Bethany, our own three cherished children, for allowing me time to work, and to Zoe, Megan and Toby Coward for their care of Bethany.

BEGINNING, ENDING AND ABUNDANCE:
GENESIS 1:1 AND THE GOSPEL OF JOHN*

David F. Ford

I was taught Hebrew by Andrew Macintosh at the very beginning of my theological studies and early in his teaching career in St. John's College, Cambridge. Many years later I returned to a post in Cambridge and remarked to him one day how sad I was not to have kept up my Hebrew. The result has been a Hebrew reading group with diverse member-ship (the latest recruits are Irish, Japanese and Mongolian) that has been a sheer delight—no homework, no examinations, and above all the leisurely, unpressurized savouring of some text from the Hebrew scrip-tures. At the heart of the sessions are adventures with words—mainly Hebrew, of course, but regularly drawing on Arabic parallels, on the various English and other modern translations, sometimes on the Latin of the Vulgate, and most frequently on the Greek of the Septuagint. I begin now from *en archēi*, the Septuagint translation of the first phrase of the Hebrew Bible, *bᵉrēšît*, as used by the author of the Fourth Gospel.

The key point to be made is simple but, as so often in this Gospel, has many ramifications. It concerns a possible relationship between the opening verse of Genesis and the beginning and ending(s) of the Gospel of John. John 1:1 quotes the first two words of the Septuagint[1] and then diverges from it. Where the Septuagint has *en archēi epoiēsen ho theos* ("In the beginning God created/made...") John has *en archēi ēn ho logos* ("In the beginning was the Word..."). The rest of John's Prologue can be seen as a midrash[2] on Gen 1:1, in which God's Word is in some sense

    *   I am grateful to my final-year class on "The Theological Interpretation of the Gospel of John" in 2011 for their discussion of an earlier version of this chapter, and to Simeon Zahl and Frances Clemson for their comments and editorial assistance.
    1.   It is generally agreed that this is a quotation from the Septuagint.
    2.   By "midrash" I mean an interpretation that does not claim to be the plain sense of the text in its original context but attempts to interpret it in relation to new circumstances and issues. Cf. C. A. Evans, "Jewish Exegesis," in *Dictionary for Theological Interpretation of the Bible* (ed. K. Vanhoozer et al.; Grand Rapids: Baker Academic; London: SPCK, 2005), 381.

identified with God and with Jesus Christ. The rest of the Gospel tells the story of Jesus, concluding in chs. 20 and 21. Most scholars see ch. 20 as the original conclusion, with ch. 21 as an appendix offering a further conclusion. For present purposes the most significant verses are 20:30 and 21:25:

> Now Jesus did (*epoiēsen ho Iēsous*) many other signs in the presence of his disciples, which are not written in this book. (20:30)

> But there are also many other things that Jesus did (*epoiēsen ho Iēsous*); if every one of them were written down, I suppose that the world itself could not contain the books that would be written. (21:25)

My suggestion is that John has finally come to the culmination of his midrash on Gen 1:1 and taken up where he left off. Having diverged after *en archēi* he resumes with *epoiēsen*; but, in line with the main point of the midrash, the agency of God in Genesis (*epoiēsen ho theos*) is now identified with the agency of Jesus (*epoiēsen ho Iēsous*).

I have not been able to find any commentators who notice this resonance with Gen 1:1 in both endings of the Gospel of John. All the translations take the verb *epoiēsen* in its obvious sense as what Jesus "did," but the word *epoiēsen* is also used by the Septuagint in Genesis for "created." The reading of John is enriched by noting this further meaning, even if the author did not intend it. It is, of course, impossible to tell whether or not he did intend it, but it would be in line with the increasing respect for John (as I will call the author[s] of this Gospel) as a literary craftsman and a master of intertextuality.[3] According to this reading, the strong opening reference to Gen 1:1, cutting off after the first two words and leaving the *epoiēsen ho theos* in suspense, is completed and resolved at the end, making what is perhaps the central theological point of the Gospel: God's self-revelation and agency in and through Jesus.

---

3. See, e.g., R. A. Culpepper, *The Gospel and Letters of John* (Nashville: Abingdon, 1998); F. J. Moloney, *The Gospel of John* (Sacra Pagina 4; Collegeville: Liturgical, 1998); M. W. G. Stibbe, *John* (Sheffield: Sheffield Academic, 1993); J. Frey et al., eds., *Imagery in the Gospel of John: Terms, Forms, Themes and Theology of Johannine Figurative Language* (Tübingen: Mohr Siebeck, 2006); S. Hylen, *Allusion and Meaning in John 6* (Berlin: de Gruyter, 2005); D. Lee, *Flesh and Glory: Symbolism, Gender and Theology in the Gospel of John* (New York: Crossroad, 2002); J. Nissen and S. Pedersen, eds., *New Readings in John: Literary and Theological Perspectives* (London: T&T Clark International, 2004); F. F. Segovia, ed., *What Is John?* (Literary and Social Readings of the Fourth Gospel 2; Atlanta: Scholars Press, 1998).

In what follows I will make a case for the felicity of this reading of John 1:1; 20:30 and 21:25 and also reflect on its theological significance today.

1. *John 20:30–31 as an Appropriate Ending*

The strongest argument for the suggested reading is its appropriateness when John 20 is understood as the ending of the Gospel written both in order to recall the opening of the Gospel and to conclude in line with the rest of the Gospel and especially with 20:1–29.

There are various resonances between John 1 and John 20, such as the themes of seeing and believing, taking away sin, giving the Holy Spirit, and Jesus as Rabbi (teacher), but the most important for our argument is the direct statement of the divinity of Jesus. The Prologue's affirmations ("the Word was God," "God the only Son") are given their most explicit confirmation in Thomas's confession: "My Lord and my God" (20:28). This makes it especially appropriate for 20:30 to reinforce this echo of the prologue by also recalling Gen 1:1, but with Jesus as the subject of the doing/creating. (There may be another echo of Gen 1 in the use of *sēmeia* [Gen 1:14; John 20:30].) Many commentators have argued for John 20 as a fitting conclusion to the Gospel, accumulating numerous points in favour of this contention; my interpretation of *epoiēsen* in 20:30 adds a further point.

Yet it is not just its connection with the beginning of the Gospel that makes *epoiēsen* appropriate at this point. The verb has been used throughout the Gospel, and several instances are worth noting in relation to my suggestion.

In 2:11 *epoiēsen* is juxtaposed with *archēn* in relation to the first of the signs that Jesus did, turning water into wine. This recalls the Prologue, as does the mention of glory and believing in the same verse, and it does so in association with an action (*poiein*) that recalls an act of creation, bringing something new into existence—it is later described as his making (*epoiēse*) the water wine (4:46). In 2:18–19 the doing (*poiein*) of a sign, the cleansing of the Temple, is linked to Jesus' resurrection. Other instances regularly link *poiein* with signs and miracles, and in 4:54 and 5:11, 15, 16 the doing (*poiein*) of a healing on the Sabbath is directly connected by Jesus with the ongoing creative activity of both his Father and himself: "My Father is still working, and I also am working" (5:17). The Jews perceive this as making (*poiōn*) himself equal to God. This leads into a discourse by Jesus, mostly about himself in relation to his Father (vv. 19–47), in which the verb *poiein* is used eight times. In addition, a compound of the verb, *zōopoiein* ("to give life, make alive"), is used in a key statement: "Indeed, just as the Father raises the dead and gives them life, so also the Son gives life to whomever he wishes" (5:21). Once more, the "make/create" range of meaning of *poiein* is emphasized.

John 8:28–29 again takes up the theme of the congruence of the Son's and the Father's *poiein* and leads into discussion of the *poiein* of the Jews, Abraham and the devil (8:31–58), culminating with a radical statement by Jesus indicating his own divinity: "Very truly, I tell you, before Abraham was, I am" (8:58). The theme recurs in 10:22–39, this time expressed as "the works that I do in my Father's name" (10:25), leading into another discussion of blasphemy in which Jesus' claim to be doing the works of his Father is pressed even further to the conclusion that "the Father is in me and I am in the Father" (10:38).

Immediately after the raising of Lazarus from death the language of *poiein* is used together with that of believing (11:45; cf. 20:30–31), and then comes the key phrase *epoiēsen Iēsous* with reference to Jesus having raised Lazarus (11:46). This is the climactic sign done by Jesus and it can hardly be an accident that the language is repeated in the summary statement about the purpose of the Gospel in 20:30–31.

In the Farewell Discourses (chs. 13–17) significant uses of *poiein* include instructing the disciples that after Jesus' death they should do as he has done ("you should also do as I have done to you," 13:15), and reaffirming the coincidence of what Jesus and the Father do (14:10; cf. 14:31), before making the astonishing promise that "the one who believes in me will also do the works that I do and, in fact, will do greater works than these, because I am going to the Father. I will do whatever you ask in my name, so that the Father may be glorified in the Son. If in my name you ask me for anything I will do it" (14:12–14). The "life in his name" that believers are to have (20:31) is here connected with the ongoing *poiein* of Jesus, coinciding with the *poiein* of believers. The coinherence of agency is then intensified in the parable of the vine, using the language of abiding, bearing fruit, keeping commandments and love (15:1–17). As Jesus prays his final prayer in John 17, he sees his death as the glorious fulfilment of his *poiein*: "I glorified you on earth by finishing the work that you gave me to do" (17:4).

So it is clear that by the time John uses the phrase *epoiēsen ho Iēsous* in 20:30 it has gathered a weight and range of meaning that corresponds to *epoiēsen ho theos*. The Prologue's identification of Jesus with the Word of God through which creation came into being has been affirmed in many ways, notably through the language of *poiein*. So it is fitting that the summary final statement of the Gospel should take up the Prologue's midrash on Gen 1:1 and complete it by replacing *epoiēsen ho theos* with *epoiēsen ho Iēsous*.

2. _John 21:25 as an Appropriate Ending to the Epilogue_

The reuse of _epoiēsen ho Iēsous_ in 21:25 is significant whatever theory one has about John 21. If the author of John 21 is the same as the author of John 20 the repetition of the phrase shows that it was important to him or her. If John 21 is by a different hand and written independently of John 20 then the recurrence of the phrase may be an even stronger indication that it was important, since both sources agree in using it. If an editor has combined the two into the Gospel's present form and has either left the phrase in both chapters or added it to one or both, its presence in the final redaction of both chapters again shows its importance. This importance might, of course, be different from what I suggest, but I hope I have already made a plausible case for the resonance of 20:30 with Gen 1:1. Is it possible to strengthen that case by examining ch. 21 in a similar way?

The ending in 21:24–25 has several differences from 20:30–31. Of special relevance to the possibility of further resonance with Gen 1:1 are two points.

One is the difference between "many other signs" in 20:30 and "many other things" in 21:25. The latter is more embracing and could be read as being in line with the Prologue's "all things came into being through him" (1:3).

A stronger (and complementary) point is the cosmic scope of 21:25: "If every one of them were written down, I suppose that the world (_kosmon_) itself could not contain the books that would be written." This is often seen as hyperbole in line with other ancient parallels.[4] Keener comments: "Although John's Christology (cf. 1:1–3) may diminish the element of hyperbole here, the text probably speaks of Jesus' incarnate signs (cf. 20:30), not works in creation (1:3)."[5] He offers no argument in favour of his "probably," and I would suggest that the balance of probability shifts towards including works in creation when one notes the resonance with Gen 1:1 and the meaning that the verb _poiein_ has gathered

---

4. My favourite is that quoted by Raymond E. Brown, _The Gospel According to John (xiii–xxi)_ (New York: Doubleday, 1970), 1130: "In the minor Talmudic tractate _Sopherim_ 16:8, Rabbi J. ben Zakkai (c. A.D. 80) is reported to have said: 'If all the heavens were sheets of paper, and all the trees were pens for writing, and all the seas were ink, that would not suffice to write down the wisdom I have received from my teachers; and yet I have taken no more from the wisdom of the sages than a fly does when it dips into the sea and takes away a tiny drop'."

5. C. S. Keener, _The Gospel of John: A Commentary_ (2 vols.; Peabody, Mass.: Hendrickson, 2003), 2:1241.

in the course of the previous twenty chapters. Indeed, the very reference Keener gives to "signs" in 20:30 suggests an opposite conclusion: the more general "other things" in 21:25 can extend beyond the incarnate signs, just as *epoiēsen* can stretch beyond historical "doing" to include "making" in the sense of creating; and the reference to "the world itself" makes this more plausible.

Second, the occurrences of "testifying" and "his testimony is true" in 21:24 reinforce the connection with the Prologue, where the typical Johannine themes of testimony and truth are first introduced. If one extends the opening of the Gospel further to include the rest of John 1 and takes 21:24–25 in the context of the whole of John 21 then there are further parallels, notably on discipleship and following. Both chapters are concerned with who Jesus is; the characters in common include Peter, Nathanael and unnamed disciples; and following Jesus, including the command (or invitation) "Follow me," is prominent (1:37, 38, 40, 43; 21:19, 22).

Overall, as Brown argues in his persuasive case for calling John 21 an epilogue rather than an appendix or a supplement, "having an epilogue at the end of the Gospel gives balance to the presence of a prologue at the beginning."[6] If this is so, then it should not be surprising if the key scriptural text on which the Prologue is based, Gen 1:1, is taken up again in the Epilogue's final verse in *epoiēsen ho Iēsous*, broadening the reference of the same phrase at the end of the main Gospel in 20:30.

3. *Broader Considerations:*
Intertextuality; Levels of Meaning; Daring in the Spirit

The suggestion that the midrash on Gen 1:1 is completed in the two endings of John can be strengthened by noting three further general features of the Gospel.

a. *Intertextuality*
John 1:1 is just one example of the interplay between the Gospel and John's scriptures. There is far less direct quotation of the Old Testament in John than in the other Gospels, but, as Barrett and others show, it would be a serious mistake to conclude that John is less steeped in the Old Testament than they are.[7] On the contrary, his Gospel may be even

---

6. Brown, *The Gospel According to John*, 1079.

7. See C. K. Barrett, "The Old Testament in the Fourth Gospel," *JTS* 48 (1947): 155–69, and *The Gospel According to St. John: An Introduction with Commentary and Notes on the Greek Text* (2d ed.; London: SPCK, 1978), 27–30.

more pervasively and subtly shaped by the Old Testament. There is much reference, explicit and implicit, to Moses and the Exodus;[8] Deutero-Isaiah is profoundly influential;[9] and there are many echoes of Ezekiel, Zechariah, the Psalms, the Wisdom literature and other biblical books.

For our purposes it is important that the same is true of Genesis. Hoskyns shows how formative for John the first three chapters of Genesis are, even though they are never directly cited.[10] My suggestion might be seen as an extension of Hoskyns' study. It is also in line with the general characteristics of John's intertextuality with regard to the Old Testament, such as subtlety, allusiveness, imaginativeness,[11] originality and daring. Further, Barrett makes the point regarding certain texts from Deuteronomy, Leviticus and 1 Samuel, that "the Old Testament themes, never formally buttressed by the quotation of texts, are Christologically worked out."[12] This is what I suggest has happened in relation to Gen 1:1 in both John's Prologue and the endings.

b. *Levels of Meaning*

My suggestion requires that the same word, *epoiēsen*, be taken in more than one sense, or in an extended sense, as meaning both "did" and "made" or "created," allowing for the agency of Jesus to correspond to the divine agency. This would not be at all surprising in the context of John's Gospel. John often uses words or expressions that can be taken more than one way; indeed it is a distinctive mark of his style. In John 3, for example, *anōthen* is used to mean both "again" and "from above," and *pneuma* is used to mean "wind" and "spirit."

Words having two meanings are often hard to distinguish from words with rich meaning in which facets merge into one another, and this is perhaps more the case with *poiein*. For example, *menein* ("to remain, stay, dwell, endure, continue") can refer literally to where Jesus is staying (1:38, 39) but also to the Holy Spirit remaining on him (1:32, 33), and later to "food that endures for eternal life" (6:27), to continuing in

---

8. Cf. J. J. Enz, "The Book of Exodus as a Literary Type for the Gospel of John," *JBL* 76 (1957): 208–15; R. H. Smith, "Exodus Typology in the Fourth Gospel," *JBL* 81 (1962): 329–42.

9. Cf. D. R. Griffiths, "Deutero-Isaiah and the Fourth Gospel," *ExpTim* 65 (1953–54): 355–60.

10. Cf. E. C. Hoskyns, "Genesis i–iii and St. John's Gospel," *JTS* 21 (1920): 210–18.

11. For a perceptive study of John's allusive and imaginative use of the Old Testament, see K. Nielsen, "Old Testament Imagery in John," in Nissen and Pedersen, eds., *New Readings in John*, 66–82.

12. Barrett, *The Gospel According to St. John*, 30.

Jesus' word (8:31), to the Messiah remaining forever (12:34), to the Father indwelling the Son (14:10) and, in a flood of uses, to the mutual indwelling of Jesus and his disciples (15:4, 5, 6, 7, 9, 10, 11, 16).

This is perhaps the closest parallel to *poiein*. Both words combine ordinary uses with unusual theological ones, and their range develops as John repeatedly employs them in different ways, while yet never allowing the more ordinary to lose touch with the more theological. Indeed, John's use of these two verbs and their cognates might be seen as a linguistic pointer to the incarnation, in which God becomes flesh and his glory is seen in the ordinariness of doing and dwelling.

c. *Daring in the Spirit*
Right from the start of his Gospel, in his midrash on Gen 1:1, John shows his capacity for daring theological innovation. It is as if he has taken to heart the teaching of Jesus in the Farewell Discourses, that the Holy Spirit will guide into all the truth (16:13), and he is pressing forward confidently into that "all." The Prologue sets the Gospel within a horizon of God and the whole cosmos, clearly ascribing the creation of "all things" to the mediation of Jesus. John 20 is the fulfilment of the Prologue's incarnational thrust: "My Lord and my God!" (John 20:28); and John 21 concludes with the creative agency of Jesus set within a cosmic horizon. How fitting that they should be united by the midrash on Gen 1:1!

The form that this theological daring takes is worth noting: interpretation of scripture. Both endings write about writing and books, and one of the most striking things John does is to claim implicitly that his own writing is on a par with Genesis and the rest of the Old Testament. The Spirit's guidance into all the truth leads to a book that can stand alongside the Jewish scriptures. Yet that is not all: the same Spirit is given to the readers of John. What might that mean?

That is a question leading directly into the theological task today.

4. *The Open Ending of John: Implications for Today*

What sort of twenty-first-century theology might be inspired by the above interpretation of the beginning and endings of the Gospel of John? It might be summed up as a biblical theology that does not simply repeat the Bible but interprets it creatively, seeking to be guided by the Spirit "into all the truth" (16:13).

Jesus' teaching in his Farewell Discourses in the Gospel of John can be seen as encouraging innovation that is in line with his example and actions but which moves beyond them. His followers "will do greater

works" than he has done (14:12); the Holy Spirit will teach them "everything" while also reminding them of what Jesus has said (14:26); overall,
because of the gift of the Holy Spirit, the Paraclete, Jesus says that "it is
to your advantage that I go away" (16:7). Having set up his own writing
to have authority alongside the Old Testament, John's interpretation of
the Old Testament might be taken as a guide to how to interpret John
himself. He wrote his book "so that you may come to believe [or, in
another reading, 'continue to believe'] that Jesus is the Messiah, the Son
of God, and that through believing you may have life in his name"
(20:31). That life includes reading the Old Testament, John's Gospel and
other writings about Jesus. John has himself given a model of such
reading guided by the Spirit: intertextual, truth-seeking, subtle, allusive,
imaginative, original and daring.[13] He also makes clear that this reading
is to happen in a community of love, prayer, service and witness.

Doing theology shaped by reading in the Spirit as John read is
therefore not at all the same as doing theology that repeats what John
said. John expects his readers to continue to be guided into all the truth,
part of which is reading the Bible in new ways, faithful to Jesus who
always has more to reveal. In relation to the Old Testament, John was
steeped in it and constantly echoes it. In relation to testimony to Jesus,
scholars endlessly debate the relation of the Fourth Gospel to the other
three. Did he know one or more of them, or only some of their sources?
Whatever the facts, it is clear that he made his sources his own, and any
repetition is in the interests of his own distinctive presentation. In relation to the culture of his own time, he wove together many of its Jewish
and Hellenistic strands, symbolized by his opening verse's use of *logos*,
a key word in the Septuagint which also carried wide resonances in the
cultures with which John was familiar. He also recognized the power of
the book as a medium that endlessly generates further communication.

His response to all this is not to promote a fundamentalist fixation on
one form of words, on one book, or on one book with an authoritative
commentary. Rather, he encourages deep immersion in the Old Testament, in testimonies to Jesus and in the contemporary world, accompanied by imaginative yet responsible improvisation to the glory of God.
The prayer of Jesus in John 17 at the climax of the Farewell Discourses

---

13. A consequence of this view is that, in order to be true in John's sense, a
suggestion such as the one being made in the present study does not have to be able
to demonstrate that John intended to complete his opening midrash on Gen 1:1 in
one or both of the Gospel's endings. It is enough to show that it is in line with his
Gospel in its way of interpreting scripture and other sources, and that it is theologically fruitful.

offers a vision of his disciples participating in the mutual glorification of Father and Son, an intensity of divine communication in love that also embraces future believers. It is also itself probably an improvisation on John's sources, a testimony in the Spirit to the relationship between Father and Son suggested by John 1:18: "God the only Son, who is close to the Father's heart." John's theology is one of ongoing, overflowing glory into which he wants to draw his readers. This superabundance is headlined in the Prologue ("the light of all people," "the glory as of a father's only son, full of grace and truth," "from his fullness we have all received, grace upon grace"), and frequently recurs through the Gospel, perhaps best summed up in what is said about Jesus in relation to eternal life and the Spirit: "he gives the Spirit without measure…whoever believes in the Son has eternal life" (3:34, 36). Such light, glory, grace, truth, life and Spirit are impossible to confine or definitively package, and John does not try to do so. Instead he thinks and writes from within them, in a relationship of mutual indwelling with Jesus Christ, constantly stretching to do fuller justice to them and inviting others to do the same.

This is therefore a theology that is always unfinished, whose horizon as set out in the Prologue is nothing less than God and all creation. It is an invitation to continual theological creativity.[14] The ending of the Epilogue envisages so many books testifying to the creativity (*poiein*) of Jesus that the world could not contain them. There is no hint of criticism of this possibility, rather it is a theological musing ("I suppose," 21:25) in the face of overwhelming abundance. This is an ending which denies closure. It suggests my own musing about the theological relationship of John 21 to the rest of the Gospel.

5. *Epilogue: The Theology of Abundance in John 21*

John 21, however it came about, reads like an overflow of John 1–20. Not only that, it enacts a theology of abundance—literally, verbally and intertextually.

The catch of fish caught at Jesus' direction is abundant: "they were not able to haul it in because there were so many fish" (21:6; cf. "net full of fish," 21:8; "Simon Peter went aboard and hauled the net ashore, full of large fish, a hundred and fifty-three of them," 21:11; also note the intertextuality with Synoptic accounts of being fishers of people, Mark 1:16–20 and parallels). The repeated word *helkuein* ("haul") is used elsewhere

---

14. For a discussion of what theological creativity in the twenty-first century might be like, see D. F. Ford, *The Future of Christian Theology* (Oxford: Wiley-Blackwell, 2011), 12–22.

in John (cf. the extended uses of *poiein* and *menein* above) for being drawn to Jesus: "No one can come to me unless drawn by the Father who sent me" (6:44, also in a context of feeding); "'And I, when I am lifted up from the earth, will draw all people to myself.' He said this to indicate the kind of death he was to die" (12:32–33; note the abundant "all"). In both cases the key focus is on Jesus: "It is the Lord!" (21:7). So, as often in John, there is a strong connection between the person of Jesus and abundant life (cf. the Prologue; water into wine, 2:1–11; God's love for the world, 3:16; water of eternal life, 4:13–14; bread, 6:48–51; the good shepherd and Jesus coming that people may "have life, and have it abundantly," 10:10; raising the dead, 11:25–26; a grain of wheat multiplying, 12:24; vine bearing fruit, 15:1–5; breathing the Spirit, 20:22). It is a theme deeply connected with the abundance of creation, as in the days of creation in Gen 1: the first (light and darkness), the second (water), the third (vegetation, seeds, fruit-bearing), the fourth (light and darkness again), the fifth (fish), the sixth (animals and humans) and the seventh (Sabbath) are all drawn upon by John to represent the abundance Jesus brings. In John 21 the connections are with the first and fourth (night and daybreak, 21:3, 4), second, third (bread, 21:13), fifth, sixth (sheep, 21:15–19; disciples passim) and perhaps the seventh (the disciple whom Jesus loved reclining next to him, 21:20). This recapitulation of the elements of creation sits well with John 21 balancing the Prologue.

The exchange between Jesus and Peter (21:15–19) is about abundance of love: "Simon, son of John, do you love me more than these?" (21:15). The threefold repetition with variation intensifies the theme of love, and the intertextual resonances abound—notably with Old Testament shepherd and sheep imagery, with ch. 1, with Jesus as the good shepherd (ch. 10) and with the many references to love in the Old and New Testaments. John's theme of the greatest love being seen in laying down one's life for one's friends is recalled by the prophecy of Peter's death, and the narrator comments that this would "glorify God," tying it into what is arguably the most comprehensive term for God's distinctive divine abundance: glory.

John 21 concludes with the image of an abundance of books generated by the creative activity of Jesus. Since all things were created through the Word, no conversations, discourses, arts, humanities, sciences, cultures, communications media or religious expressions can be unconnected with him. Therefore theological thinking needs to try to cope with the abundance of meaning, knowledge, truth and wisdom symbolized by the world's books.

But what about John 21:20–23 on "the disciple whom Jesus loved"? This nuances the theme of abundance. It criticizes a claim to know the future, and in the process relativizes a dominant and controversial topic among the first Christians: the return of Jesus. The abundance of vivid prophecy and expectation surrounding this topic (cf. Mark 13 and parallels) is notably lacking in John. The recognition, almost in passing, of the reality of the return of Jesus—"if it is my will that he should remain until I come, what is that to you? Follow me!" (John 21:22; cf. 21:23)—refocuses attention away from dramatically abundant apocalyptic expectation and on to the ordinary drama of following Jesus as part of life in the church. Following in love is the core message of John 21, and abundant life in Jesus is to be found there, without the distraction of claims to know precisely what is going to happen. This is still abundance, but centred in the interpersonal drama of daily life and service in the community of disciples.

This overflow of an already superabundant Gospel has the effect of drawing readers into a world of ordinary work (fishing), daily life ("Come and have breakfast," 21:12) and church life (feeding lambs and sheep, rumours about the beloved disciple) without losing touch with the cost of discipleship. It is the extraordinary ordinariness of those who have been given "power to become children of God" (John 1:12) and have seen the glory of the Word made fragile, mortal flesh. But the horizon of that Word is also vital: God and "all things" that were created through the Word. If my suggestion rings true, the Prologue's opening affirmation of creation through Jesus Christ is still present in the Epilogue's concluding reference to his agency, just as the Epilogue's immersion in ordinary ongoing life is in line with the Prologue's summary statement that the Word "lived among us" (1:14).

6. *Supplement: On Biblical Scholarship and Theology*

In conclusion I offer some remarks that might be taken as the overflow of the previous section's overflow. It is a reflection on some of those books imagined in 21:25.

Andrew Macintosh has mostly written scholarly Old Testament books and articles. I have mostly written theological works, though in some I have also tried to integrate "guild" biblical scholarship and theology.[15] The foregoing has been a further attempt to marry the two, partly inspired by what happens around the table with Andrew in our Hebrew

---

15. Especially in F. M. Young and D. F. Ford, *Meaning and Truth in 2 Corinthians* (London: SPCK, 1987; repr., Eugene, Ore.: Wipf & Stock, 2008).

reading group. There we pay close attention to scholarly concerns, including philology, but also pursue other questions, including theological
ones. We call them our red herrings, but perhaps they should be seen as
more like the abundance of fish in John 21.

What determines the range of questions that are addressed to the
Gospel of John? Who says that asking about the meaning of *poiein* is
appropriate but that pursuing the implications of the answer for current
life and thought is not? There are settings where that judgment is made,
either explicitly or implicitly. It is not just a matter of different academic
specialisms, but some faculties or departments see the latter question as
inappropriate in the setting of a university. This is not the place to argue
the case,[16] but I would contend that this institutionalizes distinctions that
either are arbitrary or are in line with presuppositions likely to distort the
study of John's Gospel, a Gospel which claims to be relevant and true
beyond the time of its writing, and indeed to all times and to the God
who relates to all.

Given the present divisions regarding religion, it is perhaps inevitable
that some settings will make it impossible or at least very difficult to ask
about the truth and current implications of John's Gospel, just as other
settings will make it impossible or difficult to raise radically critical
questions about it. But if a society such as ours, which is simultaneously
and complexly both multi-religious and secular (and often has great
diversity within particular religious and secular traditions or world-
views), is to be able to inquire into the truth and relevance of a text such
as the Gospel of John, it needs to have settings where diverse approaches
can be followed and brought into conversation with one another.

Andrew Macintosh's working life has not only been dedicated to
biblical scholarship and to being an Anglican priest; he has also put a
huge amount of time and energy into his Cambridge college, St. John's,
and into the Cambridge University Faculty of Divinity. These are places
where those of many faiths and none are engaged in learning and
research. The undergraduate course in the Faculty of Divinity is appropriately called "Theology and Religious Studies," and its ethos allows for
those who wish to pursue questions of truth, practice and contemporary
relevance in relation to the Gospel of John and much else. No one is
required to do so, or to take any particular theological position, but a
setting has been developed where there is inquiry into the questions

---

16. For my arguments concerning the way the field of theology and religious
studies is organized, see *Shaping Theology: Engagements in a Religious and Secular
World* (Oxford: Blackwell, 2007), 115–42, and *The Future of Christian Theology*,
148–67.

raised by and within particular religions as well as between them and about them. Not the least of Andrew Macintosh's achievements is his contribution to the flourishing of a college and faculty where his enthusiasm for philology and his commitment to Jesus Christ can be brought into conversation with the concerns of those in other disciplines, including contemporary theology, and with those of other faiths and none. Hence the importance of his Hebrew reading group, and of those red herrings, which might turn out to be a way into the abundance in which God wants all to share.

INDICES

INDEX OF REFERENCES

Index of References

INDEX OF AUTHORS